Notes from the Field:

Strategies toward Cultural Transformation

BELDEN PAULSON

D1361770

Thistlefield Books

Notes from the Field: Strategies toward Cultural Transformation by Belden Paulson
Copyright © 2014 by Belden Paulson

All photos, unless otherwise noted, are from the personal collection of the author.

Cover diagram (*also see pages 255–56*): As English writer C.P. Snow noted, the number of connections grows exponentially when the number of people increases arithmetically. If the connections are all straight lines, as in the diagram, the complexity is considerable. However, in our world of more than seven billion people, where every individual and every culture has a unique "DNA," today's great challenge is to utilize this rich diversity to create connections that will build a more prosperous and peaceful world. Adapted from the April 1986 *Bulletin of the Atomic Scientists* by Michael Yanoff.

First Printing 2014
Printed in the United States of America

ISBN-13: 978-0-9816906-4-3
Library of Congress Control Number: 2013947443

Editor: Carolyn Kott Washburne
Design and Production: Kate Hawley, Kate Hawley by Design
Proof reader: Paula Haubrich

Thistlefield Books

Published by Thistlefield Books
W7122 County Road U
Plymouth, Wisconsin 53073
(920) 528-8488
www.thistlefieldbooks.com

Notes from the Field is available through Amazon.
Odyssey of a Practical Visionary is available through Thistlefield Books.
The Searchers: Conflict and Communism in an Italian Town (out of print) is available used
 through Amazon.

Dedication

The title of this book, Notes from the Field . . . says it all. The collection of my writings is based on real-world activities and projects with which I have been involved personally since college days, well over half a century ago.

As the world has changed, from the communist crises in Cold War days to new international threats, to perils facing the planet with climate change and new needs to be met, different problems continue to cry out for relevant problem-solving solutions.

Thus this book ranges over a broad landscape with the plethora of conditions challenging us as we go about our lives and struggle to better our communities, country, and world. Some efforts are successful, some may not work out, and some require even longer time frames to measure results.

In any event, hundreds of people have participated with me in the programs described here. These writings are no more than a sampling. When I think of all the key people needed for each initiative to happen, the list is very long.

Now I can do no more than dedicate my modest endeavors to each of you for your role, your help, and sometimes your essential inspiration.

Acknowledgments

Since this book uses abstracts of articles, papers, and documents that I have written over decades (plus a few relevant materials written by others), one absolutely essential job was to find someone to consult with me on the materials selected and prepare them for my editor and book designer/producer. Who else could even begin take on this responsibility than—you guessed it—my wife Lisa.

As with so many of my writings, including my memoir of several years ago, Lisa is the critical actor. Whenever I tell her that, given her busy life, I'll recruit someone else for this arduous activity, her response is always the same: "Who else knows your mind, is sensitive to the twists and turns of your life, your positives and shortcomings. Even though I'm up to my ears with my own writing projects, I know it's important to collaborate with you in this enterprise." So once again, thank you, Lisa.

Two other key players working with me on this project have been my editor, Carolyn Kott Washburne, who has scrutinized my material. Even though most of it was published or made available elsewhere, it required her usual expert editorial attention. Kate Hawley is another genius who grabs hold of whatever I give her and finds ways to transform raw text and graphics into a stylish product that captures my intent. To these two special people, another big THANK YOU.

Behind the scenes, there are the usual other actors whose contributions, if indirect, have played or play incredibly important roles in what I do: my late parents, who imbedded in me the idealism to struggle to build a better world no matter what the obstacles; my sister Polly who always believes in me no matter how far out the idea or project; and our two sons, Eric and Steve, and their families, who participate with me in one way or another in much of what happens.

I definitely must also acknowledge the publications and other sources that we have used, from which we abstracted materials that I either wrote or used. This book is not a commercial publication; it is written mainly for educational and archival purposes.

And, of course, as noted in the Dedication, I acknowledge the broad array of colleagues who were active participants in the projects described covered in this book.

Table of Contents

Preface

I'VE WITNESSED A LOT OVER THE YEARS.

When I arrived in Naples, Italy, five years after World War II, thousands of people were still living in caves and bombed-out ruins. Almost ten years later, when we began resettling refugees in Europe, there were 40,000 displaced persons still stagnating in camps—some authorities had given up on these so-called "hard-core." While working in Italy in the early postwar decades, we observed the communist–led coalition exploiting the wretched conditions. Beginning in the 1960s to organize projects in our inner cities, I was immersed in the poverty and racism that brought riots and violent uprisings. While doing research in Northeast Brazil—one of the Western hemisphere's most depressed regions—we confronted the brewing restless ferment there. In 1989 in Beijing, China, I was in Tiananman Square when a million students took over, demanding basic civil rights, which soon led to disaster. When in Moscow in 1990, just after the Soviet Union dissolved, we found imminent chaos in the last days of Gorbachev.

This was all in the past. Today the world is (literally) on fire. It is combustible not only because of the dry timber in our American West, the degradation of the natural environment, global warming generally, and the inept stewardship of resources. In addition, there are mini-revolutions in many places of the world. It is not only the downtrodden who are rising up, but also the middle classes. The institutions that are supposed to run things are not working very well. It does not seem to matter much if the institutions have elected governments or are more autocratic. The challenges to solve the most critical problems seem beyond the capability of the governors.

While in recent months the turmoil may have broken out in Egypt or Turkey or Brazil or China, violence can spread to any area. Usually it begins with small-scale incidents, but if not resolved eventually, the instigators go after governing structures. Each circumstance is unique in its own setting, but behind all the eruptions, the essence is the same. PROBLEMS ARE NOT BEING SOLVED. In the United States, we still live in a fairly stable environment; most of the time we don't take to the streets or start shooting.

But the protests we observe elsewhere are coming closer to home. Our national government often appears too parochially incapacitated to confront its great issues: environmental perils threatening the planet, growing economic and social inequality, the inability to handle finances, and chronic joblessness partly caused by technologies that reduce the need for the total labor force. As one sensitive observer recently summarized the situation, while the middle class revolution is now happening elsewhere in the world, "No politician in the United States or Europe should think it can't happen here."

Despite all of the above, human creativity is limitless. While the world may be a mess, there is a growing rush to design strategies to resolve problems on a fundamental level. Go to any town or city, to any community, and find people at work who are defining the challenges and coming up with solutions. Sometimes they fail, but they are out there, and there are victories. Today one can become suicidal, weighed down by the grim panorama of the realities. Or one can push through the paralysis to find hopeful directions and productive solutions. We need to know about these efforts in useful, practical experience—the successes and the struggles—to document examples of "what works." It is important to identify the emerging strategies that in due course will make a difference.

This book is one example. It is a kind of casebook in problem-solving, focusing on an array of issues. It links directly to my memoir, *Odyssey of a Practical Visionary*, published several years ago. The memoir itself ran 757 pages, but the original draft was well over 1,000 pages. It included material about my family and relatives, and many personal stories.

My wife Lisa and the "troika" team who worked with me on all of the memoir's editorial and publication aspects got me to agree to slash. We knocked out whole chapters, especially published articles, papers presented at professional meetings, and case studies from a lifetime of organizing projects.

My purpose in this book is to revisit some of that material that had been excluded, picking select samples of my thinking and representative events. From the articles and papers we're using, we've pulled out key sections of materials compiled over many years. What we have included is authentic, real-world experience. We've omitted most of the memoir's personal data.

Our journalist son Steve said this new book is valuable "because it plays up your long experience dealing with the big issues that are still with us today. It gives fresh relevance to recounting the past. You use the accumulated wisdom from working on these issues for decades. In contrast to the memoir, you now just hit the key points."

My life adventures in *Odyssey* were carved up into several overlapping themes: international, urban, community, and sustainable living. For this book, I do the same but much more succinctly.

I find that most of the issues that harnessed my full energies since college days, more than half a century ago, are still with us. The circumstances are different, and sometimes worse. The strategic solutions we came up with back then continue to show surprising relevance and applicability today.

For example, my work in the devastated World War II slums of Naples, with homeless people in desperate straits, offers similarity to the crying needs of today's areas of violence. Just look at the Middle East and the heart of Africa.

Today's millions of refugees fleeing war zones or escaping persecution or natural disasters continue to call out for creative resettlement efforts. These solutions recall my refugee work in the 1950s and 1960s. Now we also find a new category of refugees—related to climate change because of droughts, floods, and the depletion of natural resources.

During the 40 postwar years when the West faced the menace of international communism, there was the intense need to comprehend the appeal of communism among the grassroots masses. For some years, I was very active in one pocket of that milieu in Italy—the first country in the West threatened by communist-led takeover through democratic elections. Today there are other "isms" that demand not only military attention but sensitive understanding of their appeal and the values at stake.

Complex urban problems such as I coped with in the inner city culture of poverty are still very much with us. The growth of inequality of opportunity and income is becoming ever more acute.

Notwithstanding dramatic positive changes, vast areas of the world still suffer from historic deprivation and social fragmentation due to concentrations of wealth and power. I see close parallels to the places where I worked decades ago, such as Northeast Brazil.

We are far closer now to dire consequences than in the 1970s when I began dealing with the issue of creating a sustainable world. Yet there are positive efforts. High Wind, our intentional community in Wisconsin—committed to living more consciously— awakened a substantial cross-section of folks. Our seminars on sustainable futures and national conferences, which gathered assorted fertile minds, offered a few jolts to crack the cement still holding in place a dysfunctional culture begging for a new vision.

This book touches on all these themes, using brief flashes of front-line experience. Whatever the particular topic, the underlying thread has something to do with directing energy toward building a better world.

This is a time for innovators—for creative pioneers who dare to cut through whatever is holding us back. New thinking and breakthrough models from the past could contribute to a fundamental cultural shift. Such a shift would place us on the threshold of a just and thriving society. We trust that the examples given here will trigger in the reader the realization that solutions—new paths—are possible.

PART I
Creative Approaches for International Challenges

Comune di Simaxis
Provincia di Oristano

DELIBERAZIONE DEL CONSIGLIO COMUNALE

Egr. Sigg. Don Murray e Dr. Belden Paulson

Subject: Invitation to attend a Simaxis Town Council session
  Award of Honorary Citizenship to Mr. Belden Paulson

Our Municipality intends to make the community that I represent and especially the young people acquainted with your worthy and humanitarian aid. This permitted the formation of an agricultural holding to host the refugees from all over the world. Thanks to your support the refugees provided for their own needs and those of their families and perfectly integrated into our local community from a legal, economic, social and cultural point of view.

Our community was and still is culturally enriched by the presence of these people whose original background was so different from the reality of our small village.

In consideration of your great contribution, the population of Simaxis would like to invite you to take part in the extraordinary town council session which will be devoted to a reflection on your work. The event will take place in May 2013.

Bel's mother in natural dress of Poland, 1921

When growing up, I heard a lot about my mother's work in the dire conditions found in Poland just after World War I. She directed social work for the Red Cross. Later in college in the years just after World War II, I helped to run the college relief drive, becoming familiar with world needs and major agencies working overseas trying to do something about them

After graduation in 1950, I searched for a way to participate in the gigantic task of rebuilding war-destroyed Europe. I ended up volunteering with a dedicated Italian medical doctor, Teofilo Santi, in the waterfront slums of bombed-out Naples. Dr. Santi directed a small agency, the Italian Service Mission, founded and supported by the overseas arm of the American Congregational Church. One of the best local doctors, Santi gave his time to provide food, clothing, and medical care and some social assistance with people on the margin of life. They were living in caves and ruins. The doctor told me to take on small, specific projects in order not to be overwhelmed.

When I arrived in Naples, my original plan was to stay six months, but I remained for almost three years and subsequently for almost a decade in Italy. Over time, we agreed that while keeping people alive was a humanitarian act, we needed to do better. This led to our co-founding a social settlement center, Italy's first, in the worst area. Twenty thousand homeless people were packed into an ancient stone barracks where Mussolini had quartered his soldiers and horses.

I ended up directing "Casa Mia" (My Home), which served hundreds each day. Apart from the usual relief, including an excellent medical clinic, we had a literacy school, an array of efforts to help people find work and new homes, and attractive projects (such as English classes) to draw in the well-to-do from elsewhere in the city to learn about conditions. We worked with those running the last vestiges of the Marshall Plan, and members of the American Sixth Fleet headquartered in Naples, and had close contact with other aid efforts. From all of this, we learned what worked and what did not.

At this time, Italy was threatened by political takeover of a left alliance led by the Italian Communist Party. This would be the first communist triumph through democratic elections in the West. Most of the people we worked with called themselves communist although they had no idea what this meant. Often they asked us how to vote. US officials urged us to use our influence, but we steered a path as a compassionate, non-political force.

In my third year another American, one Louise Hill (Lisa) showed up, who also happened to be a graduate of Oberlin College (although we had never met). We hired her, and a year later returned to America together so that I could attend grad school at the University of Chicago, along the way getting married. The university had one of the world's premier political science departments.

Before leaving Naples, I oriented my replacement, another young American, Don Murray. When I had finished my PhD course work and was beginning my dissertation, Don Murray called. He had recently returned from Naples and now, after having previously done some acting on Broadway, had just finished the film *Bus Stop* with Marilyn Monroe. He visited us at the university where we reminisced most of the night. He wanted to use some of his new money to return to Italy and help close the refugee camps, and he wanted me to join him.

Italy was threatened by political takeover of a Left alliance led by the Italian Communist Party.

While working with Dr. Santi in Naples, we had cooperated with the World Council of Churches to provide social assistance with refugees who had been stagnating for years in camps around Naples. They were among the 40,000 so-called "hard-core"—displaced persons left over after the war's end or were escapees from communist-controlled eastern Europe. Many world authorities had given up on most of them ever again becoming self-sufficient. Don and I knew some of them personally and were convinced they should be given one more chance.

I postponed my thesis, and Don and I returned to Italy. In our strategizing, we consulted with the director of La Cassa per il Mezzogiorno (fund for Italy's poor south region). He offered us a proposition: if we were to develop a project in an underdeveloped area like Sardinia, the Italian Government would give substantial subsidies. He had no interest in these refugees per se, and the refugee authorities also had no interest in Italian development. But by interrelating the two, our strategy gained significant financial and political support from both.

We ended up buying 135 acres of more-or-less virgin land on the island of Sardinia and created a pilot community based in agriculture and small industries such as manufacturing concrete blocks for homes. Over time, we moved 15 families from the camps. The most complex piece of our work was rehabilitating the refugees. As people who had pretty much given up, and after years of dependence, they finally learned to work again and to trust in the future. Our novel strategy won widespread interest, with potential for refugees in other areas of the world.

After two years of running this project, the United Nations High Commissioner for Refugees (UNHCR) hired me for their Rome office where I served as camp clearance coordinator. In helping to design policies based on our Sardinia experience and with a detailed knowledge of the camps, we formulated a policy with the UNHCR to project a settlement solution for every refugee in the Italian camps.

Toward the end of my UN assignment, I lived for several months in a monastery in one of Italy's most communist-voting villages. It was called "Little Moscow" because its leaders had been to Moscow and had brought back a fervent ideology. Genazzano was an ancient town in the rich vineyard hills 30 miles southeast of Rome. An astute local citizen, Athos Ricci, who, with his family, had brought communism to the town, had left the Party out of disillusion with its false promises. We collaborated to conduct an in-depth study of the town's inner workings. There were long talks with the peasants on the land, old aristocrats, former fascists, artisans and small business people, clergy, students, and teachers. We were interested in why one village went communist and not a neighboring one.

By this time, I had become something of an expert on communism. I had spent years in Naples working with grassroots communists. In Sardinia, our project was based near a town with a communist mayor. I got to know intimately refugees who were mostly escapees from communism. I had lived in Little Moscow, where my ex-communist research partner had trained in communist leadership schools. And I had many contacts with American and Italian officials attuned to politics. When I returned to the University of Chicago to complete the PhD, I revised my topic to consolidate these years of overseas experience. My doctoral committee was intrigued when I chose the title, *Revolution in the Villages of South Italy.*

After finishing the PhD, I was about to join the US government foreign assistance program because of Senator Hubert Humphrey. A prominent member of the Foreign Relations Committee, he had followed our refugee resettlement project in Sardinia and also knew about my intimate contact with communism in Italy. He had placed in the Congressional Record our Sardinia example as a model of foreign aid assistance. Now he urged me to build on these experiences to play a role with the Alliance for Progress in Latin America. One of its first thrusts focused on Northeast Brazil, a vast region of poverty and historic polarization between a small landed elite and the powerless masses. Our government characterized the area as seething with revolutionary ferment in a strategically important country.

At this moment, I happened to renew contact with an American academic I had met in Rome, now a professor at the University of Wisconsin. Shortly thereafter, I attended a conference where I ran into the director of the Land Tenure Center, also at the University of Wisconsin. This was a new initiative dealing with Latin America, funded by a USAID contract. I accepted invitations to come to Wisconsin, where I could design overseas projects and also teach political science on the UW-Milwaukee campus.

I was soon engaged in research projects in Northeast Brazil, basing with a team we formed at the University of Ceará. Our first focus was to examine obstacles preventing more rapid economic development. Our initial case study was a small town surrounded by a large rural area located in the heart of the horrendous drought region of the Northeast. Ten years earlier a sizable dam had been constructed by the federal anti-drought agency DNOCS, where authorities estimated that the reservoir could irrigate some 30,000 acres of valley land. However, the water was simply evaporating under the hot sun. There was potential to lift this area from extreme poverty to become a thriving economy based on highly productive truck farming, fruit orchards, livestock, and hydro-electric power for small industries.

When we flew across the whole Northeast region we spotted other dams and reservoirs that were also not being utilized. Why? It turned out that the state deputy who represented this one region in the legislature and his brother, the local vice mayor and tax collector, more or less controlled political life. They got public works funds to create temporary jobs and relief for food distribution and some minimal medical help, but they opposed any fundamental changes and reforms. Waking people up to new possibilities through education or political action would threaten the power of the entrenched leadership.

Later, a second project analyzed the leadership class of the State of Ceará. The Brazilian authorities were very cooperative, lauding our attempt to help identify bottlenecks for regional development. This pioneer effort, never attempted before, was funded by the Social Science Research Council, a premier American academic research institution. My team consisted of seven Brazilian graduate students plus the deputy director of the prestigious Institute of Anthropology. This was also a training project, preparing a cadre of young, local researchers.

Suddenly, midway through the research, a front-page article appeared in *Ultima Hora,* the largest-circulation leftist daily newspaper, published in Rio de Janeiro. The first paragraph read: "In truth this is the renewal of the Camelot Project, destined for all of Latin America. . . . It is an investigation without limits." The piece was taken up by other major Brazilian papers, and eventually the Brazilian Government established a commission of inquiry. For a time, I was perhaps the best known North American in Northeast Brazil, even referred to as "008," working for the CIA.

The Camelot Project was a large-scale, socio-political study funded in 1964 by the Special Operations Research Office of the Pentagon in the United States. At that time, the US government was very worried about what was happening in Southeast Asia in the larger context of the Cold War. It foresaw similar threats emerging in Latin America. With a lot of money, it attracted leading social scientists; only later did the funding origin surface. Latin Americanists then came to believe that the so-called "progressive ends" of the Alliance for Progress were being subverted: "to identify action which governing forces might take to relieve conditions assessed as giving rise to a potential for internal war." Soon the project was canceled.

Our research experience revealed the intense anti-American sentiment felt in Northeast Brazil. Some intellectuals labeled America's real interest simply "to make the area a colony of the State Department and Pentagon." There was heavy pressure in the street to send me back to America. These arguments were countered above all by one of the most radical and smartest student members on my team. Wanda stood up publicly, risking her own neck to defend the work and me personally. She said: "This was my first experience of objective and systematic work in the field of social science. It showed me the possibilities of rigorous scientific research and understanding about the kind of political system we need for participation in transforming society."

Among my varied short-term assignments while at the University of Wisconsin, I served as a member of a peace delegation in Paris, to help move talks forward to resolve the explosive situation in Vietnam. In 1971, three respected peace groups assembled 171 Americans from 40 states to consult for a week with leaders of all protagonists in the war: North Vietnam, the Vietcong, South Vietnam, the United States, and various independent factions such as Buddhists and Catholics.

Although the Domino Theory still played in US policy—if Vietnam falls, communism will take over Southeast Asia—skepticism was hardening. The peace people demanded immediate or early withdrawal, while our government still wanted to keep fighting and bombing until victory.

While the dialogue continued intensely from morning to night, my most meaningful experience took place not at the conference

> In an attic on the periphery of Paris, I met a young, still unknown Buddhist monk from Vietnam. Thich Nhat Hanh and I sat cross-legged on the floor, drinking tea.

hotel but in an attic on the periphery of Paris. I met a young, still unknown Buddhist monk from Vietnam. Thich Nhat Hanh and I sat cross-legged on the floor, drinking tea.

As I listened to his powerful and wise ideas expressed in a gentle, conciliatory way, I learned that this conflict could have ended long ago. The mass of the population, he said, was Buddhist—peasants who favored neither side. They were very nationalistic, wanting independence from all foreigners. He may have sounded naïve, but in his view, we were the naïve ones.

The following chapters are a portion of what I wrote about my International experiences.

Response to War Devastation in Postwar Naples

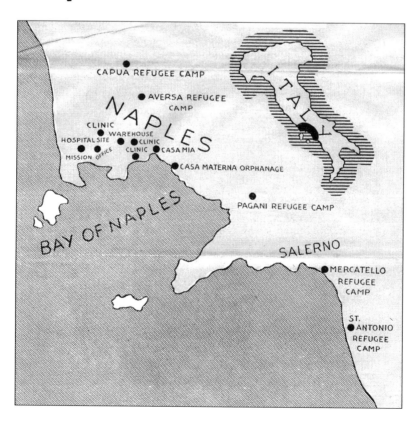

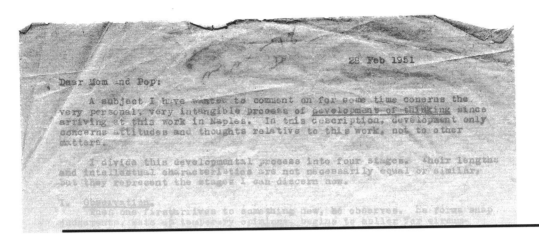

First Letters Home

I remember the day I rode into Naples. It was late afternoon of September 13, 1950. After cycling through the mountains of Italy, I was pretty well shot physically. And after living and working together for so long, strains were apparent in our small, closely-knit biking group. An ideal paradise of warmth and comfort and food and good living was all we dreamed about in this state of physical and mental exhaustion.

When we arrived, the Italian Service Mission's main focus was to provide relief to the cave dwellers and conduct a social work program to rehabilitate those who had moved out of the caves.

In one of my first letters home I described in some detail the environment of our work:

This is a wretched city with huge potholes in the streets. Packs of children roam around like animals, chasing up cigarette butts, which they "manufacture" into cigarettes to sell. They lead American sailors from the ships of the Sixth Fleet headquartered in Naples to lairs of cheap women. Their homes were shattered, literally, and also decimated because of many deaths. These children were born and have grown up in combat zones. They know the sound of bombs and like to imitate them—something they do very convincingly. The kids walk the streets barefoot or with toes sticking out of air-conditioned shoes. Naples has about a million people but little productive business and industry. Jobs are scarce. There are a few who are very well off and the rest exist in desperate poverty. Many families are huge, sex being the chief recreation, and the Church favors no birth control. There is no snow in winter but there is also no heating in most habitations. Without enough food in the body to generate some heat, the cold means stark misery.

The "sucker trade" is big business: "Hey Joe, what you want?" They say they're selling Parker 51 pens for only two dollars, but they are really "P. Arker" pens made in Milan for 50 cents. There's a flourishing black market: the sailors sell packs of cigarettes they get cheap aboard ship, and the street folks get a nice markup. A six-year-old on a packed streetcar is directed by his mother, standing at the back, toward a well-dressed passenger. Skillfully, the kid lifts the wallet, then returns to his mother where she empties the contents into her bag and then points to the next "customer."

A further word is in order about Dr. Santi. Our whole experience in Naples was directly tied to our relationship with him, his history, and his motivations. He was one of the very significant people in my life.

Teofilo Santi and his family were clearly people with a mission. As fervent Protestants in a Catholic country, they were one of the most distinguished families within this small religious minority in the Naples area. They strove to live their faith through good works. Teofilo's father, Riccardo Santi, was a Methodist pastor. One day in 1905, he had taken home a boy off the street, and over time, as the family rescued more homeless children, they created and built up an orphanage, Casa Materna, to become a major Protestant center in southern Italy.

In March 1945, just before the end of the war in Europe, a small group of American doctors was sent to Naples to study diseases caused by malnutrition. Historically one of Western Europe's poorest cities, and now badly destroyed, Naples was well known to the American troops as they moved up through Italy in the final battles. These doctors found not only disease but seven caves where many people had taken refugee from the bombs. One of the doctors had ties to the Congregational Church in the United States, and he urged that an agency be created to find homes for these cave people. Along with helping them adjust to postwar society, they would also be given immediate medical treatment and other relief. In short, he proposed a program of housing and broad social assistance. So began the Italian Service Mission.

Now and then an incident occurred that emphasized the tragic environment we were working in. One day Paul, my fellow American co-worker, and I went to distribute several large boxes of meat and bread at the worst cave, Capodimonte, where 39 families lived. I wrote home:

> They are sick, physically and psychologically and spiritually. When we show visitors around, we explain that the Capodimonte people are as low as one can go. They have nothing in life except their hordes of babies and rodents in their underground shacks. The municipal authorities have not bothered to repair water pipes, so water must be carried a long distance from beyond the cave. There are tiny strings of lights so dim that one would surely go blind trying to read for very long.
>
> Usually when we arrived to make a distribution, it was quite orderly. Anyway, on this day when we began the distribution—and this food was supposed to be just for the children—a fight broke out. Soon a woman insulted and cursed a man who had lunged for the packages. The man kicked the woman, who was pregnant, in the stomach. She fell down, unconscious. People gathered around and mass chaos ensued. Quickly Paul and I picked up what was left and escaped.

Back at the office, we all talked about the fight and were not sure what to do.

Fast-forward to a year later . . .

The Italian Service Mission Writes . . .

Excerpts from a newsletter sent to supporters worldwide, 1952.

Apart from the caves, along the sea in Naples is a poverty-stricken area called Granili. The people live in a public refuge—some 20,000 of them. They are the homeless people of Naples, and with their homelessness goes hunger, disease, and loss of faith. Outsiders who have seen Granili do not forget it easily.

With such a massive need, our challenge has been to determine what is the best approach to introduce a bit of dignity and decency into the lives of individuals in this community. The answer, we felt, was a "social settlement center," which would be a part-time home and full-time friend for these people.

Now up and running, Casa Mia concentrates our services, formerly spread throughout the city, into one center for one specific neighborhood. It gives both material and educational assistance—material because the people have empty stomachs and no doctors, educational to bring a rebirth of habits and attitudes conducive to self-help. As before, our work is without regard to creed or status because the Granili inhabitants are diverse; they are Catholic and communist, educated and illiterate.

Several members of the staff, including me, actually became a part of the neighborhood through residence at the center. The resources and help of interested people from outside the community are utilized to cultivate leadership within Granili.

The center is structured on the basis of give and take, working *with* the people rather than *for* them, getting a return of cooperation and the ability for self-help. It is the first social settlement center in Italy.

To make what we have stretch the farthest, we concentrate on family units. We organized a nursery-kindergarten for the little ones, ages three to five; group and school activities for children ages six to 15; clubs and classes for young people ages 16 to 20; sewing groups for the women; and classes of various sorts for the men. Literacy classes are for all ages because during the war schools were closed and children did not learn to read.

The various participants in the center all come together one evening each week for the movie. Now the program consists primarily of documentary films, but we're organizing evenings also to showcase skills that have been learned at the center.

By helping each member of the family in a way appropriate to that person's interests, we have developed a relationship with the family as a whole, and the whole family has slowly come to regard the center as a family friend and advocate.

Every child, youth or adult who participates in some group educational activity at the center also participates in our material services; they receive food, medical care and distributions of clothing. The children attending the daily groups eat a meal each day (often their only meal). The older groups that meet twice a week get food at their meetings. Every person receives medical care at our clinic, including medicines where necessary. Clothing is given out to the entire family of each participant according to need.

Our center is best described as a social settlement center because it draws upon the resources and interest of outsiders, some of whom become residents in order to build qualities of leadership and individual dignity within the community. In a single program to develop a healthier neighborhood at Granili, we have combined the settlement idea of community responsibility with material relief.

The influence of this settlement in Naples goes beyond its direct involvement with Granili. Its program and philosophy serve as an example—one of too few—in a country with great unmet needs. With the municipal and national social conscience tending to be backward, and a rich-poor environment with little or no middle class as a leavening force, the settlement serves as an experimenter and guide. Our activities are at Granili, but our interest is in all the homeless people of Naples and of Italy who, in their misery, have become a world problem.

The only meal for the hundreds who came to Casa Mia

Literacy classes for all ages at Casa Mia

Pilot Project in Sardinia

Bel with Don Murray and volunteer staff in Sardinia 1957.
(from left: John Earl, Bel, Don, Harold and Giles)

AMONG THE 40,000

CITIZENS OF NO COUNTRY

Refugee camp near Naples

New Lives for "Hopeless Refugees"

Taken from "Citizens of No Country," University of Chicago Magazine, February 1960

In January 1958, Mario was sitting in a refugee camp near Naples. He played cards all day, or drank wine, or slept, or just idled. He suspected everyone, had no faith in anyone, lived for the day because he could not foresee any tomorrow outside of a refugee camp. He had transferred from one camp to another since 1945 and had been rejected by 14 commissions for emigration to every country from the United States to Colombia. He knew he was no good because 14 commissions had told him so. He believed that each additional year in camp—each day—was sapping his last bit of humanity until one day he no longer could call himself a man but simply one statistic among thousands who had lived and died in a refugee camp.

There are 40,000 refugees like Mario still trapped in camps in Western Europe. They are the first generation of post-World War II refugees who have been in camps for five to 13 years. Some of them are the original displaced persons from the war. The larger number of them are escapees from communism behind the "Iron Curtain" or from Yugoslavia. Included are even displaced persons from the Spanish Civil War. They have been screened and rejected for emigration by many governments for poor health, uneconomic (large) families, inadequate skills, or a controversial past. They are supposed to be the bottom of the barrel, the "hard core."

Immediately after the war, millions of refugees found new homes, assisted by international, national, and non-governmental agencies. But in 1952, the International Refugee Organization was terminated, and governmental interest dwindled as new problems of the atomic age arose and postwar humanitarianism and the propaganda value of the first escapees from communism wore off.

The refugees still in camps are citizens of no country. They have little chance to work; must live completely off the State, which administers the camp; and must seek charity hand-outs. They cannot integrate easily into the economy of the country where their camp is situated because of local unemployment, overpopulation, no available housing, or unusable skills. They are stigmatized as rejects: "There must be something wrong with them, or they wouldn't still be in camp." Now a new generation has been born in the camps. A refugee in Italy once took his five children to Rome. Their comment: "This is a big camp, isn't it?"

Don Murray and I decided to utilize ideas we had been developing to organize a project in Italy. We knew refugees there personally and knew that they have perhaps the worst lot in Europe because of high local unemployment. Our basic assumption was that many of these "impossible" refugees still could work if they were first rehabilitated and adequately assisted at the beginning. Our idea was to tie the problem of refugees to the poverty of underdeveloped areas, thereby enlisting the cooperation of governments from two directions.

The project name we selected was HELP—Homeless European Land Program.

HELP would buy a piece of land—the most secure investment—and gradually branch out from agriculture into small industries. We would first bring single men or heads of families from the camps, only a few at a time, to transform virgin pasture into a thriving farming and diversified community. The work would be done only as quickly as the refugees became acclimated to working again. The final goal is complete independence for the refugees. They will each receive a plot of land or a share in a small industry, and a house. As a refugee is able to repay partially with a portion of his income, new refugees will be helped.

HELP would be no panacea for the total refugee problem, but would serve as a pilot demonstration. It would show that some refugees are still capable of work and self-help. It would stimulate the interest of the particular government and local population in these homeless people, not only for humanitarian reasons, but because there would also be local benefits. Through experimentation, it would develop a pattern for helping refugees that could be used by others elsewhere. Media publicity would focus public awareness on one of the great humanitarian problems of the world. These ideas had to be tested for soundness.

In the winter of 1957, several months after setting up HELP, our own faith in the project faced its most severe test. All that the critics had said about refugees seemed valid. The refugees would not work. We seemed unable to build their faith in themselves or in us or in the future. They distrusted our motivation as volunteers for helping them and speculated on our "real interest." They complained loudly that the world owed them a living; if this was not forthcoming in Sardinia, they would return to camp. The attitude of the local people

> The project name we selected was HELP—Homeless European Land Program.

toward the refugees was suspicious. The local communists called us spies and called the refugees every name except *bona fide* refugees.

It is difficult to determine the subtle forces at work that gradually changed the attitude of the refugees. Perhaps the two most important factors were being constantly near us in all of our activities, and the actual concrete results developing from each plan we laid out. When we spoke with various officials in Sardinia for all kinds of planning, usually at least one refugee accompanied us so that he could report back what had transpired. The simple ways our conscientious objector volunteers lived, in considerable part on the same level as the refugees, fostered some identification.

Along with this personal contact, words and plans became concrete. Seeds that were not supposed to grow became some of Sardinia's best crops. The concrete block industry that "would never sell blocks" landed some lucrative orders. On the basis of long-term repayment, refugees who thought that they were working for us received their own land or other property and then the first homes.

As this trust evolved, toward the project generally and toward us specifically, it brought some interesting manifestations. When the first refugees were asked to decide their future vocation, most picked the land, and not necessarily after much thought. Their desire was to get their hands on something tangible. Once they possessed it, they thought they would no longer be dependent on us or on nebulous plans for the future, because they could *see* this. Gradually, however, increasing interest has developed in such vocations as small industries. These are in their beginning stages and the ramifications are not easily visible, but now the refugees trust us more and have faith in our ideas. They see that patience may yield a more profitable future than immediately going onto the land.

HELP has had unusual opportunities to reach a wide public because of Don Murray and his wife Hope Lange. Don, in collaboration with a former German refugee, Fred Clasel, wrote a drama set in the camps of Italy describing the refugee psychology. Called *For I Loved Strangers,* it was used two years ago as the Christmas drama on televisions's *Playhouse 90*, starring Don and Hope. It was viewed by an estimated 20 million Americans. On March 5, 1958, the popular TV show *This Is Your Life* featured my life, and my wife Lisa and I were flown to Hollywood from Sardinia. A plea for support on this program brought in more than $80,000.

I am happy to report that the original objectives of the project seem to be reaching fulfillment. Begun as a small seed idea by two individuals, it has now won the confidence of governments and the United Nations High Commissioner for Refugees. The UN has decided to increase its already considerable financial participation. And it is appointing me to its staff as Refugee Consultant to help bring the project to fulfillment and to advise on enlarging the idea for a general solution to clearing the camps in Italy. Further interest has developed, not only for application of this basic pattern to other refugees throughout Europe, but as a means to attack the explosive Arab refugee problem of the Near East.

The Refugee Success Story

Taken from "Development of Refugee Attitudes: Experiences of the Sardinia Project," Research Group for European Migration Problems

Article circulated among refugee workers in Europe by UNHCR.

When the refugee leaves the camp, a characteristic trait, besides distrust, is helplessness to meet his problems. Perhaps a distrustful person is also helpless because he cannot depend on his own abilities or on anyone else, or on the straightening-out factor of time. In his years of refugeedom, he never received the help he needed to become rehabilitated. He received just enough, though, from governmental or private organizations, to appreciate the "benefits of refugeedom." Thus, while he seldom saw any important value in outside help, he came to expect it. He was a refugee, and the world owed him a living. Over the years this tended to make him more helpless, dependent, and almost unwilling to take any personal initiative to help himself.

Perhaps the ultimate degradation this brought was his growing inability to want to leave the camp. This is not to say he could have left even had he wanted to. But with virtually no confidence in anything, inevitably he tended to cling to the one security he knew: the life of the camp itself. The camp became a strange little world. Through sheer necessity, the refugee had adapted to it and in turn had been molded by it. Camp life reflected all of his frustration, and he took every occasion to say he hated it. But at the prospect of giving it up, he appreciated it merely because it existed. There were three meals a day, a roof overhead, and the little satisfactions derived from looking serious but laughing bitterly inside when emigration commissions came to inspect him, or from pitting his wits to exploit in little ways the camp administration or fellow refugees.

In the early period when the refugees distrusted the real intent of HELP, they thought of themselves as "working for us." They were guinea pigs for an academic experiment that did nothing to benefit them. Having little interest or ability to help themselves, they could not be expected to think of the problem as a whole, or of themselves as "pioneers" in an exciting pilot project.

As rehabilitation proceeded on the island, the fact that they were "the first refugees in Sardinia" not only revved up their interest but became a personal challenge for each. We found it a stimulus for each refugee to feel he was "on the block" to disprove the stereotype of being a "hard-core" refugee incapable of work and too far gone to reestablish self-sufficiency. A certain pride in the project began to evolve, and the refugees seemed to feel some importance in paving the way for other refugees. In recent months, the refugees recognized increasingly the wisdom of inviting some of the "better refugees" in the camps to Sardinia. They seem to have accepted the challenge not only to make the project on the land work, but to prove its value to the camps as well. This meant creating public opinion in the camps that was favorable to the HELP project in particular and in general that pushed the idea of refugees getting out of the camp. All of this suggests a complete cycle of attitude transformation, from no interest in helping themselves to consideration of the entire refugee problem.

> A certain pride in the project began to evolve, and the refugees seemed to feel some importance in paving the way for other refugees.

On our last visit to the camps we utilized this interesting development by bringing two of the Sardinia refugees with us. When they arrived at the gate of the Aversa Camp and saw the usual row of idle fellows sitting on the wall gazing into space, they cried out in astonishment, "My God, these people are hopeless! How could they possibly want to stay here?" They entered the camp, and many refugees crowded around as though encountering old friends after a long journey. At this point, the Sardinia refugees think much as we think, but they also are very familiar with the refugee psychology. As the camp refugees expressed doubts and cynicism about the project, the Sardinian contingent pointed out, step-by-step, what had happened. And so came about the dramatic situation of refugees, who not many months before had been too faithless to believe a planted seed would grow, now explaining to others of their kind that they too could find a new life.

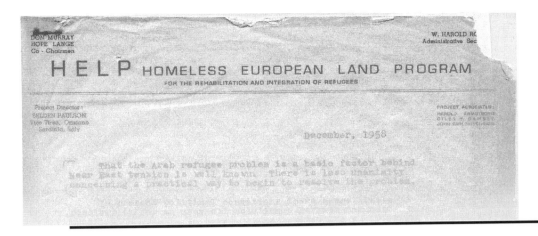

Wider Application of the Model: Palestinian Refugees

From my proposal to UNHCR and various agencies, 1958

It is well known that the Palestinian refugee problem is a basic factor behind Near East tension. There is less unanimity concerning a practical way to begin to resolve the problem.

In present political conditions, there seems little possibility for an overall solution. Perhaps the most practical course is to *begin*—in as inoffensive a way as possible. Two suggested keys are:

1. So as not to push or offend sensitive parties, begin in a small way with a pilot project.

2. Administer the project outside of Western government or United Nations auspices, preferably by a voluntary agency known to have no axe to grind.

Attached is a draft proposal that is based on the experience of HELP, with some of the European refugee families located in Italian camps who are considered "difficult to resettle." During the past year, we have resettled a limited number of such refugees on the island of Sardinia in agriculture and small industries. These refugees, like the Palestinian refugees, have been in camps for years, usually idle, often physically broken, frustrated, and bitter. Today they are becoming self-sufficient in an underdeveloped part of Italy. Simultaneously they are contributing to the economy of the area.

The Sardinia project has been examined by several former Palestinian refugees, and they offered the opinion that the pattern being evolved should be tried because it is applicable to resettlement of Palestinian refugees in an underdeveloped area of the Near East.

A Starting Point

Resolution of the Palestinian refugee problem is usually considered "impossible" because of the number of refugees involved and the negative attitude of the Arab governments.

To think in terms of planning for perhaps a million refugees requires programming and financing of vast dimensions. A more reasonable start could be made by organizing a small, carefully developed pilot project to resettle in permanent self-sufficiency a limited number of families. This would give an immediate objective, which could be realized without large expenditure or slow intergovernmental machinery.

A small-scale pilot project would not commit the Arab governments to a precedent-breaking political decision, which they oppose in principle. It would imply only a small experiment that later could be expanded. If well managed, both in its mechanics and in its public relations, it could move Arab public opinion to favor expansion, but such initiative should come from within the region.

> A small-scale pilot project would not commit the Arab governments to a precedent-breaking political decision.

As an experiment, a technique could be developed that takes account of psychological demoralization of refugees who have been in camps for many years and the economic and social conditions of the area in which the experiment would take place. In terms of the overall problem, this would minimize expenditure of resources and human dislocations.

Objectives of the Pilot Project

1. Move 25 Palestinian refugee families out of camps, permanently resettling them with completely self-sufficient income in an underdeveloped area of the region.

2. Stimulate the economy of the resettlement area, winning support of the indigenous government and local people and increasing conditions of prosperity and stability.

3. Utilize the human resources of the refugees themselves, in cooperation with local leaders and people committing their total energies to the constructive goals of the above.

4. As a pilot project, experiment to develop a refugee resettlement strategy feasible for a larger solution, should appropriate authorities one day favor an expansion.

Economic Plan for the Project

1. Procure land, through grant or purchase, in one of the land-available underdeveloped areas of the Arab States. Select an area that today is poor but that could grow with moderate capital and human investment.

2. Create at least 25 jobs in farming, raising livestock, running and maintaining agricultural equipment, etc., food processing and in small industries such as carpentry, concrete block-making, or whatever is most economic given the refugees' skills and the local conditions.

3. Allot each refugee a piece of farmland considered by the project's direction, in counsel with local technical experts, to be adequate for economic independence and for long-term repayment of a part of the assets received (the other part being a donation). The land quota would increase according to family size. Construct a house on the land. Give refugees in other activities, including small industries, a small plot of land for a house and garden, in addition to the income-bearing property.

Integration of the Refugees

1. Select refugees who are physically able to work, willing to leave the camp, and who preferably (but not essentially) have some ability in agriculture or small industry. Bring the heads of families, a few at a time, to the area to help prepare the land and develop small industries.

2. In their first months with the project, provide the refugees subsistence or, if more convenient locally, a small allowance to provide for themselves. Record their workdays to be applied against their eventual debt.

> Consider each refugee's first months a "rehabilitation period," allowing him opportunity to make the tremendous psychological transition from camp idleness to productive work.

3. Consider each refugee's first months a "rehabilitation period," allowing him opportunity to make the tremendous psychological transition from camp idleness to productive work. Let him evaluate his own abilities, the project drawing out his productive tendencies or, in instances of no usable skill, teaching minimum vocation. If there is evidence that the refugee is incapable of eventual self-sufficiency, the project leadership could return him to camp with recommendation for some other solution.

4. Project direction decides on land quotas and number of jobs to be available in each small industry. Refugees select their land or other vocation in order of arrival on the project and after successfully completing the rehabilitation period.

5. Advance necessary materials for each refugee to get started, part of which must be paid for from his first income. Advance also a small sum of working capital, with

the project at this time terminating financial assistance to the refugee, although continuing technical assistance.

6. Wait for the refugee's first income and construction of his house before bringing his family from the camp.

7. Have each refugee make a contract with the project specifying the property he is receiving and his debt and terms of repayment.

Local Relations

1. Work out carefully an approach for local relations, since the project is not only to integrate refugees but to stimulate the local economy. From the first days of the project, consult local people as to general aims and methods. Set up a local committee from nearby town or city, including key leaders.

2. With the advanced technical methods and equipment used by the project, provide an example to stimulate local economic progress. Before technical decisions are made, consult local experts, real or so-called. This is not only to utilize their experience but to enlist their participation and to stimulate them.

3. Utilize the unemployed of the nearby community when the project needs additional manpower. Purchase local food, carpentry products, etc., when needed.

4. Organize a community center, project leadership working through local leaders. Organize small-scale extension services with youth in surrounding communities to secure their interest and to teach them something technically.

5. Arrange for the refugee community to use the schools, medical facilities, etc., of nearby communities.

6. On the regional and national levels, contact key officials periodically so they are informed about the project, and so they have the opportunity to make suggestions and to learn from the project.

Dheishen refugee camp outside Bethlehem

UNITED NATIONS
HIGH
COMMISSIONER
FOR REFUGEES

Distr.
GENERAL

ORIGINAL: ENGLISH

UNHCR Proposal: My UNHCR Plan to Clear the Italian Refugee Camps

Rewritten from documents of Rome office of UNHCR, 1960

I convinced my colleagues in the office and other key actors that we could not work full throttle for camp clearance until we had carried out a refugee survey. I spent considerable time in the camps for the next couple of months with Elena Buonocuore, UNHCR representative, the camp directors, and the voluntary agencies. We collected and processed a mountain of information, after which I prepared a comprehensive report summarizing the data and reporting our conclusions. The Rome office sent this on to the High Commissioner in Geneva, specifically for the attention of Jean Heidler, director of planning.

In looking back on my two years with UNHCR, I think this survey project was one of my more significant achievements. It established a general policy for clearing the camps, challenged some prevailing assumptions, and was generally lauded by the refugee authorities. Given its importance, I include the abstract of the report we sent to Geneva. Today, decades later, there are more millions of refugees in the world stagnating in camps, and resolution of the problem will require similar kinds of hard data and imaginative policy alternatives.

My Report Began:
The purpose of the survey was to review every case in camp now eligible for UN assistance and to realistically appraise and classify each case in the framework of alternative solutions that could be offered. The assumption is that there is a solution for every refugee no matter what the situation. The seven possible solutions are rooted in the different kinds of needs and abilities of the refugees.

I.   EMIGRATION—normal emigration or special schemes where reasonable chance is given for acceptance and relocation. In instances where emigration is possible, but not too likely, a second alternative is included.

II.   INDIVIDUAL INTEGRATION—where a refugee is believed able to integrate into the Italian economy in self-sufficiency because at least one member of the family has a skill that can find a market, or has relatives or property in Italy that offer grounds for successful integration.

III.   REHABILITATION LEADING TO SELF-SUFFICIENT, PRODUCTIVE WORK THROUGH THE COMMUNITY SCHEME IN SARDINIA—where a refugee is believed capable of full-time work either managing his own small business or piece of land, or working as a wage earner for a business organized by the project and directed by able refugees or local people; and where it is believed the family could integrate socially into the ongoing refugee community and among the local people.

IV.   LIMITED WORK WITH REHABILITATION WHEN POSSIBLE, AND SOME PERMANENT CARE AND PENSION AND MEDICAL INSURANCE, THROUGH A COMMUNITY SCHEME TO BE ORGANIZED—where a case is believed incapable of productive work to maintain himself over a period of time because of physical or mental or social handicaps, or at least without a sustained rehabilitation period, but capable of some work.

V.   HOUSING WITH PENSION, MEDICAL INSURANCE AND PERIODIC SOCIAL ASSISTANCE—where the refugee is over 50 at least and is believed incapable of self-sufficient work but does not need permanent care if provided these insurances.

VI.   INSTITUTIONAL—where a refugee needs permanent care and has no work capacity without highly specialized treatment.

VII.   RESIDUE—where a refugee is believed unable or unwilling to fit into the above solutions, which will require another alternative.

The method used in undertaking the survey was: a) to discuss the cases with agency representatives in Rome; b) to hold group discussions in the camps and make decisions on each case among the agency representatives, our representative in the camps, and a UNHCR representative in Rome; c) to check with the emigration departments of each agency in Rome on emigration possibilities. The refugees themselves have not been consulted as to whether they would accept the solution judged best adapted to them. In some instances, the intentions of some refugees are sufficiently known to indicate acceptance, or in other instances rejection, but systematic counseling has not yet begun.

This kind of proposal could be considered as plans evolve for dealing with the millions of refugees now in camps in different areas of the world.

Living in a Communist Village: Early 1960s and 40 Years Later

Genazzano: Little Moscow in Southern Italy

In Oberlin Alumni Magazine, *1963*

Recently I lived for two months in a monastery high on a hill overlooking the village of Genazzano, 30 miles southeast of Rome. As I looked down on the picturesque, walled town with its surrounding vineyards in which many of the 5,000 inhabitants worked, I thought: This village, like the rest of Italy, is more than 99 percent Catholic. It enjoys free elections and gives every citizen the liberty to choose leaders and policies. Yet this village is communist controlled. Why? What accounts for the communist success in Italy, which has the largest freely elected Communist Party in the world outside the Iron Curtain countries? What effective alternatives, if any, are being presented to the people, from which they might choose?

Genazzano is a good place to seek answers to these questions. It is referred to by those in the village as "Little Moscow" where communists have steadily increased their power since taking office after their victory in the first local election following the war in 1946. What accounts for this?

My in-depth work utilized the invaluable assistance of my Italian colleague, Athos Ricci. He had recently left the Party after having a leadership role in bringing communism to the community.

The Communist Presence

How do the communists manage to hold on to power? For one thing, they communicate effectively with the people.

The communist mayor, who has held office since 1952, has a job in a bank in Rome. By law, though, he needn't show up regularly at the bank (except to collect his paycheck) so long as he holds a "public position" in Genazzano. So he drives his Skoda (imported from

Czechoslovakia) to the local *municipio* (town hall) several days a week and is seen politicking about town.

"Fellowship Meetings" are frequently held in the evenings. The mayor will address 200 or more farmers crowded into the local theater, tell them how miserable they are, lament the "do-nothing clerical national government," note the magnificence of what he calls the world's great pilot project in social justice—the Soviet "worker's paradise." Fellowship Meetings are also held in the park on festive occasions, with speeches, games, food, and a mobile library of "popular" literature.

There are other ways that the communists "get to" the people. Talks are given in the *piazza* on all local subjects. Posters depicting important current issues are put up on walls. The communist daily newspaper, *L'Unita*, is tacked on a public bulletin board so that those who cannot buy one can "get their information." The town council organizes art festivals on such "popular" subjects as "Torture in Algeria," "Harlem Slums," "Workers' (and Farmers') Portraits." The Italo-Russian Cultural Association sometimes organizes an evening of films and propaganda.

Any money that the village is able to get from the State for a school or road is presented to the population as "communist money." For example, when a new school was finally constructed, party bigwigs from Rome were on hand for the inaugural ceremony but no one came from the Ministry of Public Instruction, which had made the school possible.

Underlying all of this is the daily grind of Party activity, working through cells and sections, seeking to penetrate every residential block, each occupational stratum.

Even communism's most ardent enemies concede that the Party provides the first systematic attempt in village history at political education. It has launched the first effective drive to induce the usually immobile villagers to overcome their passivity and acceptance of archaic ways in favor of vigorous action and even personal sacrifice. It would seem as though the Communist Party in Genazzano has preempted sole rights to the bandwagon of change, which is now so much a part of our times.

La Miseria and the Communist Program

Even before fascism, a situation had developed in Genazzano and other villages that was only awaiting exploitation for political ends. This situation, ready-made for communism, can be depicted in one word: *La Miseria*—a general state of wretchedness. This is the word most of Genazzano's villagers use for their way of life.

The villager feels himself a pawn of human forces as inevitable as the physical forces of nature. Laws requiring landlords to pay him a minimum wage frequently go unenforced. Social insurance, when paid, is little help for the unemployed. Taxes are inequitably graduated, and larger earners use their knowledge of tax procedure and their political influence to evade proper payment. It is the poor who are hit. Over half of all the land is still affected by feudal rights whereby the small farmer is supposed to pay about one-quarter of his income (apart from State taxes) to the heir of the original feudal lord who "conceded" the land to him years ago.

The communists in Genazzano have never presented a platform of specific reforms aimed at rectifying gradually, step-by-step, "*La Miseria*." Their approach is always "revolutionary," not reformist. The real solution, the villager is told, is to sweep away the "system," the old class structure whereby one small class of traditionally privileged individuals dominates the rest. There is an entire system of land tenure where most of the land is owned by just a few landlords. What the communists propose is nothing less than a completely reorganized society with the masses—led, of course, by the Communist Party—in the driver's seat.

Advocating revolution instead of reform here has two tactical advantages for the Party, which is tied to the national Communist Party and to international forces of communism. First, it de-emphasizes the need to deliver any tangible gains to its mass of supporters in the village. The Party, needless to say, does not want to improve conditions. Meaningful reforms would reduce *La Miseria*, the factor most beneficial to the communists. The plan, instead, is to hold off any small (and therefore practicable) reforms until the day the communist control of Genazzano can combine with local communist control of several thousand other Italian villages and cities. This would catapult the Party into national power and make possible a communist revolution/takeover in Italy.

> **Advocating revolution instead of reform has two tactical advantages for the Communist Party.**

The second advantage in promoting revolution instead of reform is that the Party can appeal to the most discontented and frustrated of the population, the ones with little to lose and everything to gain from revolution. The inevitable result is sharp class conflict. Compromises for realizable reforms become increasingly difficult. The people are forced to choose mainly between two extremes: "rapid social progress" (led by the communists) or slow change or no change (led by the dominant government party, the Christian Democrats).

The effect is to force moderate villagers who may not like either extreme to choose one or the other. This tends to eliminate the chance for gradual, practicable reforms.

Here is what a villager who chose communism had to say. He was reluctant to talk at first, but opened up to me only after a morning spent with him in his hot, dusty little vineyard, and after considerable testing of his product, from a common cup:

> I have two hectares [five acres] of vineyard. I am better off than some, worse off than others. I have to pay 25 percent of my crop to a prince who has feudal rights on this land and lives well in Rome. I can't get a decent wine price because the buyers have a monopoly that ruins us small farmers. After paying the prince, my taxes, and expenses, I have hardly enough left to pay my own labor. My family of five must live off this. My boy has a spinal disease and can't work, but of course the government and Church do not help.

You ask if I'm a Marxist? I don't understand any of that. But I'm a communist. The communists promise that if they win, the government will lower taxes. They say that the monopolists who sell us fertilizer couldn't charge unfair prices if they [the communists] had their way. They will end all the feudal rights on our land.

The other party has been in power since the war, and conditions get worse all the time. Why doesn't anyone ever come into our fields and talk with us, except on election day, apart from the communists? I just heard that a big owner here got an agricultural loan at the special government interest rate of 3 percent, but he spent only half of it on his own land and put the other half in some speculation where he makes 13 percent interest. The communists wouldn't allow this. The big owners don't pay the same percentage of tax that we do; if the communists win, they'll tax the rich. The owners hire lawyers to get around the law. We are the ones who end up paying.

We communists don't really believe this stuff that everyone is equal. But we know there should be more equality than there is. And we know that the only ones who are fighting for us every day are the communists. No one else understands.

We are sure communism will win eventually. We don't say this just because the party is strong. We say it because the other parties can't stay in power indefinitely. It is impossible for our situation to continue forever like this. Some people are still resigned to fate, especially the religious. We go to church too. After we finish here, we want to go to Paradise. But we want something more while we're here, and we're going to fight for it.

Economic reform, land reform, social reform, political reform—whatever term you want to use—is necessary and inevitable in Genazzano. The masses want it quickly, not 10 years or a generation from now. They have begun to realize they must fight for it. They are learning to support individuals who will lead the fight.

Implementing a Democratic Alternative

Each day I would descend from the monastery into the field to talk with the small farmers. 70 percent of these farmers lived off less than five acres of land on which they usually grew grapes for wine. They told me their most urgent single problem. The wine had to be sold to middlemen who virtually monopolized the market, thereby cutting the growers' already meager profit margin.

After hearing the same story from each farmer, communist and non-communist, I began to ask, "Why don't you band together and set up a cooperative? You could buy a used pickup truck or even use some of your mule cars and haul your wine to Rome. You could set up stalls in the marketplace and create several new jobs for yourselves." We made careful calculations and figured that each farmer could increase his income by about 25 percent almost immediately.

Why no cooperative? The answer was clear. There was a lack of leadership, of initiative, of organizational ability.

In the course of my weeks in the village, I became quite close to three young men between 20 and 30 years old. One was a newly trained lawyer, a socialist, but definitely anti-communist. Another worked with his father in a small family business. The third was Athos, the ex-communist I have mentioned, former secretary of the local Party. Now he was an office worker in Rome, where he commuted daily.

The three had two characteristics in common: 1) They were thoroughly discontented with the old "system" of life in the village but lacked initiative or know-how to do anything about it; 2) They were potentially capable leaders if only "someone" would commit to teach them how to lead a program of specific reforms.

During our many discussions, they became much interested in the idea of a cooperative. The businessman made cost calculations. The lawyer figured out legal complications. Athos foresaw the possible political ramifications. Having precise knowledge as to how each villager voted, he estimated that the cooperative, once organized and operating as reasonably planned, could subtract sufficient votes from the communists to win a majority for a "reform party" in the next local elections.

There was only one thing missing. Who would convert these potential leaders into actual leaders? Even though the three individuals had good intentions, and could probably be trained to develop a self-sustaining cooperative, someone had to prepare them. This someone had to come from outside the village.

As I began to pack my bags before taking final leave of Little Moscow, two young men came up to the monastery. They asked me if I would remain with them in the village for six more months. They said that for the first time they had begun to see an exciting future for Genazzano. Once the cooperative got going, they said, it would give the people confidence to do other things to improve themselves. Eventually, if an independent "reform party" were to throw out the communists for the first time since the war, that example might be followed in other villages. It might show the government that local reforms not only help the people but also are good politics. They said that now the important thing was to get started, but they simply didn't know how to go about it.

With a wife and two children waiting for me in Connecticut, I could not yield to their plea. Yet this, it seemed, was a specific way to help the villagers help themselves, and at the same time bring political change. Once these leaders were inspired to act and trained to do so, then they could do the same for others in the village. The cooperative could well be a training ground in "working democracy." The possibilities appeared encouraging for Little Moscow, and perhaps for many other villages.

Just after leaving Genazzano and before my final departure from Rome, I summarized my findings in the village in a conversation with a high Middle Eastern diplomat. He said, "Change the words 'South Italy' to the name of my country and your observations would apply almost exactly." Subsequently I spoke with informed observers from other developing countries where most of the population still lives in villages. Their reply was the same.

C●NVERSATI●N

Belden Paulson is professor emeritus of public policy at the University of Wisconsin-Milwaukee. Athos Ricci is a writer and lifetime resident of Genazzano.

Revisiting Italy's "Little Moscow"
Belden Paulson and Athos Ricci

*I first visited Genazzano in 1961, when it was   training schools, and had become one of its most
one of Italy's communist strongholds. There I met   effective local officials in the region. Later, he be-*

Revisiting Italy's "Little Moscow"

From World Politics Journal, *Fall, 2001*

I first visited Genazzano in 1961, when it was one of Italy's communist strongholds. There I met the former Party secretary, Athos Ricci. After months of digging into the history and life of the village, together we wrote a book about Genazzano (*The Searchers: Conflict and Communism in an Italian Town*), which I came to see as a microcosm of Italy in transition. Periodically I have returned to see what was happening. This past spring I went back to renew my friendship with Athos, now 70, who has become a kind of village legend. Two days before my arrival, Silvio Berlusconi had won a landslide victory in the May 13 national elections. His presumed right-wing government, feared by many people in Europe and America, sparked a surprising reaction in this leftist village.

Athos and I spent an intense week together, talking with villagers late into the night and catching up with each other as we discussed how Genazzano had changed over the last four decades. In our conversations, we kept returning to two general themes:

1) the changing nature of communism in the village; 2) the breakup of the ancient rural culture as villagers opted for material comforts and searched for a viable compromise between the traditional and modern worlds.

I first learned about Genazzano while serving with the United Nations in Rome, after years of development work in southern Italy. The editor of an Italian political journal told me about this town, which had one of the highest percentages of communist voters in the country. The editor told me about Athos, then in his early thirties, who had joined the Party late in the 1940s, had gone through its training school, and had become one of its most effective local officials in the region. Later, he became disillusioned over the Party's inner workings, which denied the very values that had initially attracted him. Athos is probably the most informed local citizen. He's a kind of guru in the town because of his own history and his deep understanding of the changing village culture in Italy and the world. He has been asked to run for mayor, once the incumbent mayor finishes her term, but he no longer looks on politics as his primary work. Although he has only eight years of formal schooling, he reads the classics, is well-traveled, and is equally at home with a farmer in the field or a celebrity visiting the town. Members of his family make up a thread that ties together much of the village's history over the past century.

Genazzano is known for its politics and history and today draws many visitors. From 1053 onward, its castle was the stronghold of the Colonna family. One of the Colonnas

became Pope Martin V, who created a little Vatican here. High above the town is San Pio, an Augustinian monastery, now in disrepair, that once served Roman emperors as a summer resort. Most of the town's 5,000 inhabitants are snuggled inside the ancient stone walls; navigating its narrow, cobbled streets is a hazardous adventure for today's heavy automobile and motor scooter traffic. On the town's periphery, once lush vineyards and cropland are becoming subdivisions for people seeking to "have it all" by living in this picturesque, traditional village while working in Rome or elsewhere.

Bel with Athos Ricci in communist village

What follows is a dialogue between Athos and me, with some comments from other villagers.

BELDEN PAULSON: Why has communism been such a powerful force in Genazzano? And how has your family figured into this history?

ATHOS RICCI: Communism in Italy and these villages has deep historical roots; it didn't just happen. Genazzano was well-known in this part of Italy for developing a small underground during fascism, and by the end of the Second World War was helping the Allies. When the first English and Canadian trucks entered the village in 1945, the English commanding officer asked if the Red Army had arrived, there were so many red flags. The communists tried to gain control of the government at once, but the officer told my father, who belonged to no party, "You are the first mayor." My father had been a *bersagliere*, a member of the elite mountain troops, in the First World War, and was wounded three times. Because of his patriotic past, no one could touch him during the decades of fascism, so he became a leader against fascist excesses.

After the Allies left, the local communists took over in a little "coup d'etat," led by my brother Federico. He had led the underground resistance against the fascists and later the Germans. Although he never held a formal position, he was the strong force that brought communism to Genazzano. Politically he was at the opposite pole from our father. Like our father, Federico was a builder and a leader of the village's *artigiano* class, and later became a restorer of Renaissance structures in Rome. He remained a dedicated communist up to his death several years ago. He was always outspoken and critical, yet remained close to the Party's top leadership. His story relates to the origin of the Communist Party, which won the first postwar election and has controlled the village ever since. Similar experiences occurred elsewhere in Italy, which explains the strong early support of communism by the Italian people. In the 1948 election, however, the power of the Catholic Church and fear of international communism won much of the national vote for the centrist Christian Democrat Party, though not in Genazzano.

Later the wartime crisis passed and people focused on food and justice. They took over uncultivated land, eliminating the power of the big landlords and upper classes, most of whom had sided with the fascists. The communist leaders didn't wear suits and ties, and they went into the fields and piazzas preaching visions of a new life. I remember one Sunday an old fisherman speaking in a quavering voice, talking of a new faith that was beginning to evolve. Even the most timid people sang the Party ballads. The messengers of change had arrived, overturning the old status quo.

BP: It's remarkable how just a very few visionary people with organizing and communication skills, with the ability to identify the critical problems, can make tremendous headway.

AR: It's a story very common in many towns, but what actually happened depended greatly on the leadership that emerged. A few people can make a historic difference.

BP: What happened within communism was the gradual separation of the idealists, such as your brother, from the people who ran the Party.

AR: The idealists seek social justice in all its forms. They will sit up late in the cafes or give of themselves for whatever is needed. The Party functionaries, however, are no different from those of the other parties. They are petty bureaucrats, gorging themselves on the pie they are reluctant to share, throwing dust in the eyes of the citizens while grabbing, piece by piece, the material assets of society.

BP: So why didn't people leave communism in droves?

AR: They did, especially since the end of the Cold War. But there are two reasons for their hesitation. First, in its original form, communism gives a purpose, a reason for being, the kind of commitment for a better society that no one else has articulated.

Second, in Italy, there has not been a democratic alternative that is any less selfish and corrupt. This was the problem when I left the Party: where to go?

BP: When we first met in 1961, it was the height of the Cold War. Through its relatively strong leadership and the weakness of the other parties, the Communist and left Socialist coalition actually came close to victory over the other parties in democratic elections. Washington and other Western governments were worried. This would have been a first in the democratic world, a great communist triumph. I recall you and I meeting several times with my friend who was one of the political attaches at our embassy, and who was extremely interested in our information on communism at the grassroots level. He had difficulty communicating this to his peers because of the restraints in those days on American officials talking to communists.

AR: Many local governments in Italy were and still are led by Communist-Socialist coalitions, now usually called the Democratic Left in one form or another. When I resigned from the party I knew there was a fraternal relationship with the Soviet Union. However, because of the American presence, there was never expectation that there would be a Soviet military role in Western Europe short of actual war, which none of us believed would happen. A number of people from Genazzano visited Russia, and we became known there. At that time, the strength of the Christian Democratic Party came from being the main resistance to communism. The minute the Cold War ended, much of the power of both the Christian Democrats and the communists evaporated.

A good example of the new Democratic Left is Genazzano's mayor. Margherita is a smart, attractive 38-year-old, finishing her sixth year in office. She represents the new class of modern politicians and was asked to run by the left-center coalition. While the municipal building, which houses the local government, is being renovated, she and her staff are based in the Colonna castle. She is more open-minded than the rigid mayors of the past.

MARGHERITA: I have no problem saying that since the end of the Cold War we have a new politics. "Communism" is out, and "democracy" of the left or right is in. There are no longer communists or fascists; everyone is a "democrat." I believe that communism as it once was is finished, but the ideas are still there: helping with problems of schools and health and housing and poverty. I'm opposed to the right-wing coalition of Berlusconi, but I'm not as angry as some people of the past. Let's see what he can do.

The future of this town is tourism. As you see, I found money to restore the castle. Also, I'm seeking a joint venture between the town, the Augustinian Order, and private capital to restore the San Pio monastery. This would be another tourist magnet. Also, this village is the perfect distance for people to live while they commute to Rome. I'll soon be leaving because I've just been elected to the Chamber of Deputies on the Democratic Left list.

A second large change during these 40 years is the breakup of the old rural way of life in Genazzano. It was beginning to crack when Athos and I first met in the early 1960s. The village has a certain intuitive wisdom that comes from people who have lived close to the earth, lived with scarcity, and took care of themselves with minimal assistance from the state. They grew their own food, made their own clothes, often participated in building their own houses, and helped each other in times of need. They understood the vicissitudes of nature, which can be harsh.

BP: I've seen that in the old culture, there was a deep respect for the land and its use because the next generation would also depend on it for a livelihood. How different all that is from the culture of our present, complex big cities, with their ever-accelerating speed of life, high incomes, and consumption based on advanced technology and exploitation of cheap natural resources. Where mass media lets one be a spectator of the life of others. Where there is general skepticism of superstition and faith because science has increasingly mastered or discredited the unknown.

AR: As in villages throughout the world, this "archaic civilization" of material poverty and relatively few amenities is becoming history in Genazzano as well. Agriculture is dying because the land became fragmented into ever-smaller parcels when it was divided among an increasing number of heirs. Also, there are few farm laborers since higher wages in the city have lured them away.

> I've seen that in the old culture, there was a deep respect for the land and its use because the next generation would also depend on it for a livelihood.

Years ago this village, "Little Moscow," was on the cutting edge in calling for social reform to eliminate poverty and injustice. To a considerable degree, this actually did happen. Our communism threatened many people; now communism as we knew it is more or less finished, although not its higher ideals. Today the great new challenge is materialism, greed, mediocrity, and the pervasive spiritual vacuum that has taken over our culture. It's a cancer eating at our souls and our human dignity, just as in the past other forces in other circumstances were destroying us.

There are a few people in this village who are beginning to understand this. They are turning to me to talk about it. This is especially the young people, who will be our future leaders.

Seminal Ideas from Overseas Work

Spring 1962

The University of Chicago
Department of Political Science

Abstract of Ph.D. Dissertation

REVOLUTION IN THE VILLAGES OF SOUTH ITALY

by

Belden H. Paulson

I. INTRODUCTION

While the so-called underdeveloped areas are concentrated in Asia, Africa and Latin America, some are still in Western Europe. One of the largest of these is South Italy, which roughly is the Italian peninsula and islands south of Rome.

Here traditional attitudes, positions, institutions are facing rapid change or overturn. The question is no longer whether "revolution" will take place but what kind it will be and who will lead it. South Italy is appropriate for study not only because it is more accessible than some more remote areas. It is experiencing on a massive scale three main kinds of revolution to eliminate the old system of misery and immobility: revolution through withdrawal, Communist type revolution, and revolution through peaceful change. This treatise analyzes the misery from which the people are revolting, the immobility that has prevented them from helping themselves, the nature and extent to date of the three kinds of revolution, and their choices up to now as seen by political attitudes and voting.

II. LA MISERIA

Much of South Italy lives in small villages. "Village" is interchangeable with comune, which is an autarchic entity constituted by all the population residing in the territory of the lowest level of public author. Mr. Village normally means the small comune. Over 40% of the southern population today lives in villages of under 10,000 people, and over 50% in settlements of under 15,000. This study deals with these small and relatively small comuni, although the dividing line from the larger ones often is not significant.

*Bel receiving PhD degree
at University of Chicago
(with Lisa) 1962*

Concepts from my PhD Thesis: Revolution in the Villages of South Italy

University of Chicago Political Science Department, 1962

Taken from the abstract, viewed by my doctoral committee as a classic portrait of a developing area. South Italy has experienced significant change in the last half-century, but this portrait still describes much of the developing world.

While the so-called underdeveloped areas are concentrated in Asia, Africa and Latin America, some are still in Western Europe. One of the largest of these is South Italy, which comprises, roughly, the Italian peninsula south of Rome, including the islands.

Here, traditional attitudes, positions, and institutions are facing rapid change or overturn. The question is no longer whether change or "revolution" will take place, but what kind it will be and who will lead it. South Italy is appropriate for study not only because it is more accessible than some more remote areas. It is experiencing on a massive scale three kinds of change or revolution to eliminate the old system of misery and immobility: change/revolution through withdrawal, communist-type revolution, and "revolution" through peaceful change.

La Miseria

Much of South Italy lives in small villages. "Village" is interchangeable with *comune*, an autarchic entity constituted of all those residing in the territory of the lowest level of public authority. Normally village means the small *comune*. Over 40 percent of the southern population today lives in villages of under 10,000 people, and over 50 percent is in settlements of under 15,000. This study deals with the small and relatively small *comuni*, although the line dividing them from the larger ones often is not significant.

The people in the village live mainly through agriculture, now in decline. Industrialization has been mainly confined to the cities. Its major impact on the villages has been to attract migrants away from their agrarian lifestyle.

Lack of non-agricultural jobs in the villages, combined with a natural population growth, results in cutthroat competition for jobs, unemployment, and underemployment. Most of the village population lives in great poverty, with little bargaining power to increase wages and improve conditions.

Most southern villagers call their way of life *"la miseria."* There is no exact translation for the term, but it involves economic, social and spiritual depression and general wretchedness. The Parliamentary Commission investigating *la miseria* in the early 1950s defined it: "That particular level of life that does not satisfy or scarcely satisfies the minimum bare necessities of the people."

Misery involves habitations barely fit for human life, a diet based on starch, illiteracy and semi-literacy, and destitution—such as in Sicily where 47 percent of the population was so classified, and the Province of Matera, where the Parliamentary Commission estimated that 10,000 of a population of 182,000 live in "passable conditions" and the rest in misery.

La miseria has three fundamental aspects:

1. *No adequately remunerative work.* No fixed work and bare subsistence wages characterizes the mass of the population living off agriculture and affiliated occupations, and who have little land or skills. The main types are *braccianti* (dependent agricultural day laborers), *manovali* (unskilled dependent non-agricultural workers), and small farmers who rent or own tiny plots.

2. *No realizable hopes.* Without technical or cultural preparation, most villagers have little opportunity to acquire the productive and commercial skills needed for modern farming and industries. They almost never reach positions of important influence.

3. *No freedom from exploitation.* Employers often do not observe minimum wages or pay insurance. While laws protecting the villagers go unenforced, laws also discriminate against the poor. Politicians exploit misery by buying votes.

Immobilismo

In that villagers are legally entitled to the secret vote, freedom of speech and assembly, and the right to organize, why don't they use their rights to eliminate *la miseria?*

At least seven identifiable variables, which reinforce each other, explain the villagers' paralysis. This immobility, this seeming incapacity for organizing themselves to improve conditions, is summed up as *immobilismo.*

1. *Historical events.* After National unification in 1850, uniform laws hurt the South. Large southern landlords allied with northern industrial interests, supporting

tariffs in return for non-interference by the government in Southern affairs. Political manipulations gave the South a reservoir of votes for the power structure. Fascism denied the existence of a "southern question," postponing it. Most of the South never participated in the anti-fascist resistance. The tradition of the Southern masses was to serve the North and to be passive in the face of traditional forces.

2. *Class structure.* The main social strata traditionally have been: a) large landholders and intellectuals; b) middle and small bourgeoisie; and c) the disorganized mass of farmers and workers tied to a backward agricultural economy. Most of a) have been economically unproductive and try to justify the existing social structure. b) have been smaller landed also living off rents, small businessmen fearing modern industry, and most importantly, "small intellectuals" (those with at least eight to 10 years of school) who have been go-betweens for a) and c). These include professionals (lawyers, clergy, teachers), journalists, and politicians. Their main interest is state employment and influence peddling. Today the class structure is getting pressure from the mass with limited results.

3 *Political corruption and lack of social conscience.* Before 1913, suffrage excluded most of the masses. The small intellectual class voted for landlord candidates for Parliament in return for control of the *comuni* and lower governmental levels. Up to 1922, prefects often "arranged" elections. Corruption is still accepted in manipulating funds of political parties, administration of social insurance, and some taxes, and so forth. People in key positions feel little moral responsibility to the community. Solutions are marginal rather than fundamental.

4. *Village government.* There is little tradition of local government. Prefects have wide controls over locally elected officials. During fascism, local elections were abolished. Most *comuni* have funds only for bare public services, not for reform initiatives. Professionally qualified, honest local officials are rare.

5. *School system.* Many villagers have little interest in schooling compared to immediate survival needs. The few attending high school usually enter classical studies and traditional professions, not technical studies in agriculture and business. *Comuni* must provide school buildings, but these are inadequate since there are no funds. Most teachers are from the small intellectual class and too often are not interested in making the school a force for significant change and education of the masses.

6. *The family.* The villager finds his main security in the family. Extreme job competition conditions him to view others with hostility. Public morality is lax. Economic interests and status are all tied to the family. Cooperation outside the family is avoided. People conserve what they have.

7. *The pre-capitalistic system.* Most property of the masses is in tiny, uneconomic plots, and the large owners have little interest in investing for increased production. With low agricultural revenue, wages must be low. The economy cannot support the most

able, who leave. This in turn deters outside private investment. As the masses have no profit margin above survival needs, they dare not experiment with technological changes. Private investment lacking, so the state must inject its capital, which is largely administered by the small intellectuals and may benefit those least in need.

"Revolution" through Withdrawal

The villager with the drive and courage to take the future into his own hands has traditionally used one means: escape. Despite great emotional difficulties in leaving home, there was a net emigration of over four-and-half-million people from the South between 1871 and 1951. Initially they went overseas, but in recent years they have moved to European countries, to North Italy or Rome, or to larger cities in the South. A small number have moved onto small farms near their village, as a result of government land reform.

Although emigration traditionally had no political objectives, leadership, organization or ideology, it has had revolutionary effects on the economy, the social structure, and the political situation.

1. The effect on the economy is that while there are fewer people now in South Italy, they often are the wrong people needed for local development. Those who leave tend to be men of working age, and the most able and energetic. Those who stay are the better-off elements with least desire for change, or the less vigorous and able who tolerate *immobilismo*. There are more people who are politically inactive—women, elderly, children—and those who are active tend to be the less productive workers. Possibilities for capitalist entrepreneurship are reduced, and outside investors are discouraged.

2. As the most able and discontented withdraw, the villages lose potential leaders for change, making spontaneous change from within the village unlikely. However, class conflict is moderated because, on the one hand, the most discontented leave and, on the other hand, the breakdown of the old order due to emigration (along with other factors) has increasingly pushed the old, landed aristocrats to sell out. Their influence is usurped by the professional and business classes, whose attitudes toward the masses are somewhat more moderate. The small landed also can slightly expand their plots from the new lands available, moderating their revolutionary aspirations.

3. The political short-run effect is to reinforce the two staunchest forces of conservatism: women and small landholders. They are most attached to old-order values, symbolized by the powerful Church; they have proved most difficult to organize by the communists. But there are other political consequences for the long run. Emigration is breaking down the old family structure, which had provided security. Villagers who go to cities feel uprooted and become receptive to organizations advocating class solidarity. They transmit their new values back home at the same time that the old structure has been breaking down. This creates a fertile environment for new political leadership that would capitalize on it.

The Communist Revolution

Despite the large emigration outflow, in the short run, village population may increase steadily due to a high birth rate. Expectations expand far faster than an economy mired in immobility. Since feudal times, the villager has constituted a "permanent subversive minority," using political upheavals for temporary insurrections for immediate goals. His lack of solid political goals and his violent extremism usually doomed such efforts to failure. Brigandage in the South was a constant problem before there were any governors. The brigands rarely acted against the poor. Although non-political, they went after the other classes—the wealthy or those holding power.

Brigandage, like emigration, was largely individualistic. But the last quarter of the 19th century saw development of the first political organizations among the masses in northern Italy, especially socialism. In 1892, the Italian Socialist Party was formed; it was fairly moderate but Marxist; its gradualism and intellectualism weakened its revolutionary character. Socialism never won mass support in the South.

Italian communism was born in the northern industrial centers and agricultural regions of central Italy. By 1927, one of its founders, Antonio Gramsci, focused attention also on the South, but there was little systematic effort there until the end of World War II. The communist analysis of the South's problems delves with a fine-tooth comb into virtually every aspect of *la miseria* and *immobilismo*. Every person's position in society—economic, social, political, or religious—is placed in the light of the interests to which he is tied. The communist is always criticizing, asking for solutions that are unrealizable so that there is constant tension between reality and the ideal. The communist seeks to build the image that communism's historic role is to change society through identifying with the extreme aspirations of the masses. Inevitably, strong counter-forces develop, also extreme, insuring class conflict, preventing compromise, and stimulating the most discontented and sometimes most idealistic to side with communism.

Communists use the term *problema al fondo* (the fundamental problem), which, applied to concrete village problems, has two components. The first is primarily socio-economic: to bring equality by dividing existing resources more fairly. This emphasizes property and class. The second component is political: to demand a new ruling class. The premise is that equality cannot be achieved simply as a result of reforms (higher wages, more land, etc.), but only through a change of power roles between the masses and the traditional ruling class.

To implement this change, a political organization is required: the Communist Party. Communism's great innovation in the villages is that it is the first serious attempt to build a mass organization for radical change there.

Communism in the villages has not greatly penetrated among the bourgeois classes or among small landholders. It has concentrated on the most downtrodden and oppressed elements, especially the mass of *braccianti* and non-agricultural wage earners. Apart from women and landholders (large and small), the greatest barrier has been the "small intellectuals." As this group runs many aspects of village life, its unresponsiveness to communism has been the Party's biggest failure to date.

Only a small nucleus of leaders—sometimes just one individual—is needed in each village to build a mass movement.

The greatest achievement of the Communist Party in the villages is that it has built itself up as the face of dynamic fundamental reform. It has mobilized previously inert people to influence public opinion and political power. It played a central role in transforming Italy from monarchy to republic. It stimulated the government to take on reforms after World War II, such as land reform and economic development of the South. Despite this reformist image, communists nevertheless voted against most reform measures in Parliament, and obstructed their implementation when they became law. The arguments for justifying their behavior are often ingenious, but their real objective is clear: for the Communist Party to become Italy's ruling class. The Party opposes meaningful reforms because it does not want to eliminate *la miseria* until this has been used successfully to gain political power. Villagers frequently do not realize that the real communist objective is power instead of betterment of their condition. This dichotomy becomes revealed only when some other force comes to the village also bearing the message of greater equality but actually promoting concrete reforms.

Revolution through Peaceful Change

Any effective attempt to transform the village within the institutional structure of the Italian State can be considered a revolution through peaceful change. If it does not change fundamentally, then it is not revolutionary, but neither is it effective. To meet village aspirations effectively, the effort must reduce economic and social inequalities and afford larger opportunities for new strata to enter the power structure of village and state. The primary difference between a communist revolution and peaceful change is the degree of change and the methods used.

If institutions of liberal democracy are to be used to bring peaceful change, they must be relevant to the environment where they are to function. Their primary distinction from communist collectivist democracy is that they guarantee every citizen liberty to represent his needs and views before the powers who make public policy. The most important guarantee is that every bona fide citizen has equal legal rights to participate in selecting leaders and policies.

Until more recently, liberal democracy functioned poorly in the villages because neither the villager nor the ruling class, whether due to inability or unwillingness, has seriously attempted to bring village problems to the attention of the public powers to solve them. With democratic liberties unused or used corruptly, most of the population considers the political system itself more or less irrelevant. The communists exploit this by saying what is needed is not reform but a new political system that actually functions.

The mass of villagers fail to use their democratic liberties because they do not understand how democracy is supposed to function. They are relatively isolated, unschooled, and unpracticed in exercising democratic rights. They are accustomed to selling legal rights for immediate tangible benefits, interested in goals rather than means. A system of working democracy in the villages would depend on elimination of the most flagrant aspects of *immobilismo*. The villager would then be better prepared to confront his own problems and those of his community.

The Role of the "Small Intellectual" as an Agent for Political Change

Prepared for 1967 Annual Meeting of the American Political Science Association

A paper given favorable attention by national scholars

The idea for this paper evolved while I was undertaking action and research assignments in low-income areas overseas—Northeast Brazil and South Italy—and in pockets of urban poverty in the United States.

In each setting, there existed a society wracked by great internal cleavages between the major population sectors. There were different localized cultures, different value systems, and different levels of access to authoritative decision-making. They might almost be termed different civilizations within approximately the same geographic radius, but with minimal communication with each other.

In each of these settings, a particular figure performed an essential linkage role—to the extent that there was any linkage at all—between the mass of the population and the affluent and powerful classes, between people living in a culture of poverty and powerlessness and those exercising control of resources. This strategic person helped to hold the different sub-societies together to maintain the stability of the totality. At the same time, he was remarkably situated to serve as an agent for political change if strong forces favoring change understood and utilized his potential role. This class of persons is referred to here as the "small intellectual."

The small intellectual figures significantly in any society that is highly fragmented, where there are relatively undifferentiated and unspecialized social roles and institutions, where personal, subjective values rather than objective values are emphasized, where people tend to identify with primary groups rather than with secondary groups. As these are among the characteristics formulated by social scientists to describe "pre-modern" nations, it would seem that the small intellectual thrives in conditions of the "developing area."

I

The small intellectual becomes increasingly irrelevant as the total society becomes more complex, when political roles and structures of the more traditional sub-societies cut away the predominance of tightly-knit family, kinship and locality relationships. His role shrinks when pluralistic politics with competing sub-elites and participation in decision-making on the part of the broad mass of the population reduce the political cleavages among different layers of the larger community. In other words, when the larger society "develops'" from "traditional" to "modern," the small intellectual gradually loses his old job as the communicator between the social poles of the community. Or, if he does maintain important leverage, his role changes to adapt to the new milieu.

> **The small intellectual becomes increasingly irrelevant as the total society becomes more complex.**

This class of persons referred to as the small intellectual is intellectual in an essential meaning of the term. The Webster's dictionary definition: "having power or faculty of the mind by which one knows or understands; member of a class or group professing or supposed to possess enlightened judgment and opinions with respect to public and political questions; the power to perceive relationships." The distinguishing characteristic is not formal learning, although as a class, the small intellectual has more learning than the mass of the population around him. His essential quality is the ability to understand and grasp the essence of a particular person's or group's position in the larger framework of the total society—whether the person or group lives in great poverty and deprivation or belongs to the elite—and to communicate this information, or relevant parts thereof, to the other side.

The usual vocations of the small intellectual include schoolteachers, lower-level clergy, small businessmen, more skilled small agriculturists, foremen, lower-level members of the legal and medical professions, and students. The likelihood of a particular vocation and the socio-economic level of this class of persons naturally depend upon the context of the surrounding environment. But in each instance, he is in regular contact with the mass, working within the symbols and terminology locally understood and the moods felt. In exercising his role, the small intellectual may take on a bureaucratic position or an elected office. To a considerable degree, this class thus acts as a key nerve center of public life in the locality because of its strategic placement between the powerful and powerless.

This class in many, perhaps most, instances does not belong to the genuine intellectual community, which would be characterized by wide learning, advanced formal education, or equivalent development of mental skills and practice in using intellectual capacity for interests other than the immediate problems of mere existence in the place of residence or work. The small intellectual is not necessarily "well-read"; perhaps he has little contact with the modernization process occurring in the world or even in his own region.

The essential point is that he has enough formal schooling, enough variety of experience in inter-class dealings, and enough depth of perception into human relationships that he is capable of grasping the essence of the message to be communicated between the major groups of the larger totality.

While he may not be a member of the newly educated elite, in the eyes of the mass of the population around him the small intellectual is educated. He has some knowledge that is outside the grasp of the ordinary people in the rural area or urban slum. In some instances he has pushed out from the common mass, but to a certain degree, he is still felt to be one of them. He may continue to share with them a complex of economic, psychological, and family ties. Inversely, he may have reached down from the elite, for whatever motive, to try to develop links, and, in rare instances, even to identify completely with the lower class. Over a period of time the small intellectuals form a class of their own, which may occupy the same role in successive generations as long as the underlying objective conditions that create the need for their role does not change.

II

How might the identifying characteristics of the small intellectual be summarized? The following six qualifications must be considered important:

Placement in the "Strategic Middle" of the Social Structure

The critical function of the small intellectual is to serve as a bridge in a fragmented society where there is a substantial gap in patterns of behavior between the culture of poverty and that of the higher classes. Obviously the contrast is sharpest in personality traits and socio-economic criteria between the poles of the social structure, while in the middle sectors, changes in behavior are less perceptible as one moves up or down the social spectrum. For purposes of analysis, the point where qualitative changes separate the population is called here the "strategic middle."

Actual location of this point naturally varies according to the environment in terms of the proportion of the population above or below it, and the socio-economic level of each. For example, people in the poverty culture in the United States—poverty in our country is defined roughly as a family income of less than $3,000 yearly with upward adjustments as the family size increases—would be considered quite prosperous and "middle class" in certain world areas. As a developing country industrializes and public education and full employment at remunerative wages become available to all, the sector living in poverty greatly diminishes. In the United States, families with less than $3,000 annual income constitute some one-quarter of the total population, in effect, the "mass" of the population in a national sense belongs to that part of the spectrum not in poverty. In the more static, predominantly agrarian stage of development that still prevails in many countries—actually in most of the world—most of the total population lives in poverty. The degree of communication between the social groupings varies according to the magnitude of the cleavages, which in most countries is great. But in the United States, too, substantial cleavages exist. It is in this framework that the small intellectual finds his role.

Communication Skills

The small intellectual is a forerunner of the public relations man. He first seeks to sell himself to people in both cultures with which he wants to identify, and then he presents his "clients" to the other side. He provides intelligence about what the other culture is thinking and doing.

One of his outstanding traits is empathy. The man practicing empathy can withdraw enough from the rigid mold of his own little world to appreciate that everyone else also has his own little world. For example, in societies where both traditional and modern strata live geographically side by side, the small intellectual comprehends the little world of the man who basically is a non-participant in the political system and feels little interdependence with others beyond his own family and village. At the same time, the small intellectual understands the man who is urbanized, literate, and both consumes and demands mass media to satisfy his growing intellectual needs and curiosity, and who participates politically in secondary structures beyond the confines of family and narrow locality.

The small intellectual is not a specialized communicator in the sense of being a technician in a modern communications industry—data gatherer, reporter, programmer, editor, TV or radio announcer. His messages are more diffuse. They intermingle social, political, religious, and educational transmissions using a variety of media depending upon the setting, from the written word to use of the transistor radio, but above all, word of mouth. In a rural village, the small intellectual may "represent" an illiterate farmer by writing letters for him, figuring his tax payments, or formulating and acting on grievances against a landlord or employer or political authority. He may advise on innumerable personal family matters. He serves as counselor, even friend.

He may be one of the few people in the village who receives and reads an urban newspaper. Therefore, he serves as an important repository of information, and he translates this printed word—probably written for an urban-based clientele—into terms that are meaningful locally. Over time, by the nature of his established role in the locale, he is *expected* to be a source of information and advice. His messages are often accorded weight disproportionate to their intrinsic merit.

Political Skills

This individual may have considerable respect for authority. His role has substance beyond mere talk only to the extent that he can gain favors from the powers-that-be that he can allocate among the mass. Inversely, his role becomes valuable to the degree that he can speak to the powers as an authentic voice for the rural or urban poor who, while disorganized and even powerless, nevertheless represent votes and much of the labor force. Additionally, the poor become a potential revolutionary element were it to be organized and unleashed. The broker therefore becomes a bargainer in serving interests on both sides. In the process he enhances his own position individually.

The small intellectual is drawn into the political world not only because resources tend to be very concentrated in the developing area and proximity to authority is essential in order to function, but he too needs remunerative work. His level of schooling precludes his joining the unskilled labor force around him, and his antipathy to manual labor is as great as that of the upper classes. Yet due to lack of family ties or high-level connections, or lack of wealth, advanced schooling, or unusual specialized skills for which there is great demand, his upward mobility is limited. Thus, his place is to squeeze out maximum political leverage and some economic reward from exercising his mediator role.

> He knows that the upper class leader fears "revolutionaries" almost as much as the idea of "revolution."

This is enhanced by his subtle knowledge of the political dislikes of his clientele. He knows that the greatest fear of the upper classes in a fragmented society is the threat of "radical change." In one thrust this might overturn the existing order of social relationships. Moreover, he knows that the upper class leader fears "revolutionaries" almost as much as the idea of "revolution." This is because the practitioner of revolution has a style of conducting political business that is the antithesis of the ways of the more traditional political leader. The successful revolutionary emphasizes careful organizational work, articulation of problems, and large promises. He presents a new ideological framework that fans expectations of rapid justice and formation of a cadre of leaders to run the revolution. There is intensive training, and never-ending political activity and propaganda.

All of this is the exact opposite of the traditional political leader's more pragmatic, personal, easy-going style of politics with which he coasts along comfortably, accustomed to a monopoly of power. The small intellectual knows that the mere threat of such competition could irrevocably alter the leadership's style of life. He therefore offers to use his mediator role with the mass to maintain social stability in return for certain concessions for the mass and rewards for himself.

At the same time, he recognizes the cynicism of most of the lower class toward the political system and its leadership. To the extent that it is politically aware at all, the mass in the poverty culture assumes that the elite works only in its own interest, that it corruptly uses monies squeezed from the sweat of the simple laborer, and that it lacks understanding of the needs of the ordinary man. In its alienation against "the system," the mass turns away from the impersonal and distasteful mechanisms of politics to a more personal relationship with the small intellectual. Partly in genuine response to the mass, partly to satisfy his own vested interest in serving as a "protector" of the common people, the small intellectual often encourages this popular cynicism.

Thus we see him playing a two-headed game, working with both sides to maintain a system that cements a continuing role for himself. As one caustic observer of a depressed rural society put it, the small intellectual is something to everyone—democratic to the farmer, reactionary to the big property owner and the government, politically corrupt, sly. . . .

A "Community Conscience"

Notwithstanding, or perhaps because of his skill in political manipulation, the small intellectual is interested in human beings. His frame of reference is not people or classes in the abstract, but individuals. He is accepted because he is thought to be sincere in identifying with a person's hopes and fears.

Among the lower class living in the culture of poverty, there is usually little or no tendency to invest one's time and skills in the betterment of the neighborhood. Individual hopelessness and despair allow little surplus energy for thinking about "community interests." To them, "community" usually means the primary group of family and blood relationships expanded perhaps to include an inner circle of a few select friends.

Likewise, among the higher classes in a fragmented society who reside in the locality of poverty or who have a functional relationship to it, there is little tendency toward community involvement. When these people use the term "rights," the frame of reference is typically restricted to their own rights, not those of the general population. In this light the elite class has little difficulty in considering the resources it controls—including the public power of the state—to be primarily for its own personal use.

It would be unrealistic to assume that the small intellectual himself is "culture-free" from these characteristics of the fragmented community. Nevertheless, promotion of his own interests depends upon his promotion of the welfare of others, at least to the degree that anyone does this. This capacity to see beyond himself is one of the qualities distinguishing him from those around him, both in the lower and higher social strata. Empathizers within the lower class are in very short supply, while in the upper classes, being "other-directed" is fashionable but is usually limited to one's own peer group, or on a superficial level to people living on the lower societal rungs.

To communicate in depth with people in the culture of poverty, the small intellectual must seek entry inside their primary groups. He must identify with the goals they consider worthwhile and try to understand and represent the interests they consider important. Of course, in the process, he can enlarge those goals and promote new kinds of action.

Obviously this is a delicate operation, requiring not only some interest in promoting the individual welfare of a client—perhaps for meager remuneration—but large amounts of time, because in this cultural setting, little value is placed on time. A person in poverty can sense when one is not willing to engage in a dialogue on these terms. He recognizes when the "outsider" is uninterested in him as a person and that he is merely being used. The question of sincerity becomes a major test for the broker.

Non-Ideological Bargainer

The small intellectual has to be pragmatic in order to play his middleman role. His effectiveness depends on his winning and holding the trust of the different groupings with which he communicates—lower or upper class—traditional or development-oriented people. If in the eyes of either side he appears to have committed himself to only one set of interests, then he will probably lose his ability to communicate both ways. Thus, he attempts to work in a framework of economic and political issues and values that at least to some degree are negotiable, rather than in ideological terms which frequently are non-negotiable. In effect, he is the broker, giving his best efforts to the highest bidder, but realizing that his strength depends on "holding his cards close to his chest" and alienating neither side.

He performs not unlike the "balancer" in the traditional balance of power typology, with no permanent interests, maintaining a certain detachment from emotional involvement, and

> **The small intellectual doubts that complete stability is possible.**

throwing his weight to either side to maintain a modicum of social equilibrium so that neither side feels it is losing in terms of long-accepted vital interests. In principle, he prefers to be labeled neither conservative nor radical, but neutral. In this sense, he tends to support the status quo. However, he can also exercise an extremely important role as an agent for change, if and when either party presses him into this role—or if an outside force bids for his services for new policy objectives.

A Political Moderate

Although he may not be "learned," the small intellectual, more than most in a fragmented society, understands the complexity of human interrelationships. He himself is usually in perpetual fear of the potential "revolutionary" tendencies of the mass, and he has reason, being in constant touch with their daily grievances and hostilities. He also fears the exercise of arbitrary authority by the political and economic classes in whom power is concentrated. He is in sufficient proximity with them to be aware of their grip, were their full resources to be employed.

In view of the setting in which he works, he is often surprised that people get along as well as they do. He sees the potentially explosive conflict inherent in the social structure. However, a certain equilibrium—a product of opposing social and psychological forces—has come about because of constants that seem to be generally accepted by everybody. One of these constants that holds the system together is his own role as integrator of the clashing forces.

He tends to look down on the mass, harboring the unpleasant thought that misfortune might force him into this group. Nor does he love the powerful, whom he envies yet whose ranks he cannot join, and whose frequent arbitrariness he resents, although he has little recourse. At the same time, he fears that the disruption of the "system" with all of its inadequacies would probably produce something worse. He believes that severe conflict should be kept in bounds, speculating that the more the people on each side see the other side only as enemies to be destroyed, the more severe the conflict will be. Therefore, he sees a role for himself in maintaining at least minimal give-and-take to prevent this final polarization. He assumes that some stability will be maintained as long as each side feels it needs some support from the other.

The small intellectual doubts that complete stability is possible. For example, he sees mass expectations rising, which in time must force changes in roles throughout the system. To maintain agreement of both sides as to his own role, he thus must anticipate changes in expectations

> He hopes to remain in dialogue with people experiencing and demanding change, while simultaneously maintaining rapport with other groupings by interpreting events.

and behavior. In this manner, he hopes to remain in dialogue with people experiencing and demanding change, while simultaneously maintaining rapport with the other groups or groupings by interpreting events. Through this process of communication, the persuasive small intellectual may help to elicit enough flexibility on each side to prevent enlargement of basic social cleavages.

III

Whether the small intellectual emphasizes stability or change, he depends on the policy preferences of the groups utilizing his services. In the rural areas of a developing country one could generalize that members of a tradition-oriented elite will favor complete social stability, sanctified by the legal system and church. They are cautious about introducing new technology to increase production that could disrupt the whole social structure. They will not energize to broaden political participation nor prepare new leaders who could unleash new unpredictable political forces. They prefer passive cooperation by the mass rather than political competition that could force unwanted compromises. For its part, the mass tends to accept this system fatalistically. It sees its own immobility as a fact of life that is unchangeable.

Any attempt to induce change in this setting probably requires an outside force. Among other actions, such an agency would seek to attract the small intellectual into its employ. There are two extremely interesting and contrasting large-scale community development programs that are moving in this direction. One involves villages in India; the other is an attempt by the Vietcong in South Vietnam to build a comprehensive political infrastructure in villages there. In both instances, at the very heart of the program is the strategic figure we have been examining. In India, he is known as the "village-level worker." In Vietnam, he is referred to by the Vietcong as the "agit-prop cadre" (agitation propaganda cadre).

While in each instance their policy is to effect rapid social and political change in a traditional village environment, their approaches are quite different. In India, the village-level worker's assignment is to identify with the life of five to 15 villages through day-to-day direct contact and to relay local needs to the Block Development unit. This is the chief operational organ of the national ministry of Community Development and Cooperation. The village-level worker relays to the government what the villagers want and represents the multi-functional resources and skills of the government to the local people. The overall policy is to promote economic development and broaden political participation of the villagers within the established national policy of the government. The government offers pay and career incentives in recruiting individuals, often from the villages, who can function in this role of the "rural man in the middle."

For the Vietcong, the chief link between the villagers and the National Liberation Front is the "agit-prop cadre." The network of cadres that has been trained and strategically placed serves as a transmission belt for very personal, specifically oriented propaganda to develop a mass movement on the local level against the Saigon Government and favoring the NLF. This is one of the most fascinating examples on the contemporary world scene, of the small intellectual being mobilized as an agent of "revolutionary change."

We should keep in mind, however, that while the cadre may be promoting "revolution" in the terminology of international politics, in the eyes of the villagers, he may appear more moderate. In that the Saigon government had never effectively exercised authority in many of these localities, the NLF moved into the leadership vacuum, creating its own "governmental" apparatus. The agit-prop cadre served as the entity locally seen as representing the village to the outside. The cadre worked within local customs and used local terminology. Through constant socialization, it attempted to replace old political allegiances—to the extent that they existed—with new loyalty to the NLF. Like the Indian village-level worker, the cadre became a link between the traditional culture and an outside program promoting change. In this instance change is sought completely outside the channels of established legal governments.

My original paper included details on the role of the small intellectual in South Italy, Northeast Brazil, and the inner city of Milwaukee, Wisconsin.

THE OBSOLESCENT VILLAGE REBORN

By Belden Paulson

The following article serves as a bridge between last issue's theme of community and this one's theme of economics. Belden has been working with village life, both in rural Italy and in America's inner cities, for many years. He is a faculty member at the University of Wisconsin and has helped to shape mainstream attitudes

with different generations helping and learning from each other. There is a strong sense of community, where all the facets of life somehow fit together as if they were modeled by one maker. The people still marvel at the larger mysteries of existence, and they recognize their integration not only with each other but with the larger elements over which they have little control. One could say that the village is sustainable because of its closeness

The Obsolescent Village Reborn

From In Context, 1983

After a great deal of study and travel, I have become convinced that the villages of the world may be one of the last lines of resistance in preserving our planet. There are more than two million villages, although no one has really made a count. They have remarkable similarities despite differences of history and geography, which suggests a kind of universal village culture.

Much of the world's village economy appears to be on its last breath. Contemporary mass culture, based in urbanization and industrialization, was thought to make the village economy and the structure of village life obsolete. People had come to believe that there was no scarcity of natural resources; therefore, the "limits" of the village perspective, where every resource was husbanded, could be surmounted. Science and technology seemed capable of overcoming the human destruction of air, water, and soil. The care that the village took to pass down a stable environment to the succeeding generation was construed as an exaggerated concern. The modern acceptance of the materialistic ethic as life's central drive fostered economic growth in an unending upward spiral of production and consumption, and in turn seemed to advance human fulfillment and the quality of life. The village, with its intangibles and modest proportions, was left on the slow track called "pre-modern."

The village-based economy, especially as practiced in developing countries, has been seen as a major obstacle to rapid economic development. And the gap has been widening between these heavily rural areas and the industrial world, not to mention within the Third World itself. Economists point to a close correlation between urbanization/industrialization and higher incomes.

New Perspectives

My views began to shift in the 1970s and 1980s, especially during visits to Italian villages that I knew. In the earlier years, there had been no criticism of burgeoning consumer culture. On the contrary, this was seen as the model for the future. The villagers saw the city lights and all of the material progress that went with industrialization as the way out of misery and oppression.

But a few people who had left the village started trickling back to the land. Some of the youth who had gone to the city were longing to spend time on their family properties. They sent money back to put in wells, construct small buildings, replace or rejuvenate the vineyards. Bus drivers couldn't wait to finish work in evenings and on weekends to get back to work their land. Even some politicians began to admit that some of their earlier policies were in error. Far more attention should have been paid to small agriculture and the sustenance of village life. People had new respect for the land.

In the cities, former villagers reacted to the inhumanity of "modern life." Villagers, who had never locked their doors, had left their farm tools on the land, and never saw an act of violence in the community, started to worry about their safety. Part of it was simply a reaction against the disorder of the big city. Part of it was a deeper battle against the new materialism, a longing for the old village spirit.

> It became clear that the civilization of the village is not obsolete. On the contrary, it offers a radical repudiation of much that ails the modern world.

When I considered all of this within the context of my close relationship to the villages I knew, I realized more and more how much we had to learn from the village culture. "Alternative" thinkers and doers were newly searching for community. Small communities—be they residential or simply groups of people with shared commitments—were emerging everywhere.

In essence, it became clear that the civilization of the village is not obsolete. On the contrary, it offers a radical repudiation of much that ails the modern world. The "political underdevelopment" of the village can be seen to have a more positive side. For example, the lack of compartmentalized roles in the village serves individual and community self-sufficiency, since the village can virtually stand on its own with little dependence on the outside market and political systems. The village unit has a kind of internal sustenance essential for when larger "modern" systems collapse or change in fundamental ways. The fact that villagers don't invest much effort into comprehending and participating in the surrounding political culture has obvious drawbacks in the short run. This is illustrated in public policies that subordinate village interests to those of the urban industrial culture. But in the long run, assuming of course that the village itself is able to survive, this lack of immersion in the surrounding political culture makes the village more durable.

Now seen in perspective, the *immobilismo* of the village that I had once recognized and defined turns out to be a kind of protective shield from complete co-option into the modern world. Salient village characteristics are preserved.

The following village qualities are especially significant.

Spirit of the land. The land is not merely a means of production, it is a sacred living organism. The land represents the natural order, with all of its unfathomed mysteries. Mistreating the land can be worse than mistreating another human being. The villager who migrates to the city is still considered a villager as long as he retains this attitude about the land.

Family cohesion. The basis of security in the village is not primarily a governmental social security system, or some employer, but the members of one's own family. For

people dependent on agriculture, this has often meant large families—it is the family work force. However, as technology and education improve, chronic overpopulation has lessened. Economic, social, and political interrelationships begin with the family as the core. Thus the breakdown of family life, as happened with mass emigration, is a major vehicle for undermining village life.

Sense of community. Taken as a whole, the village is much like the land and the family—it is a living organism. The lines are blurred between the natural world of flora and fauna and the human world, or between families and government, or between the household subsistence economy and the external commercial economy. The village is a holistic enterprise, which can be seen as "underdeveloped" or "primitive" by social scientists whose reductionist methodology links specialization to complexity and efficiency and therefore to modernity. In actuality, the village may be the epitome of complexity.

Craftsmanship. The tradition of the village is to make things for eternity, not for the mercurial market. Value derives from the intrinsic quality of the product, not from the commercial laws of supply and demand. Village craftsmen—artisans—who erect buildings and make tools have motivations that are not primarily commercial, although monetary gain obviously has its place. A small farmer views work on the land as an artist does a painting; it is something apart from the net product. This reduces the potential gross revenue of the village, but it fits in with the village spirit.

Self-sufficiency. The village has low expectations of any outside assistance, be it from government or the private market economy. There is a turning inward—to the family and the community itself. Food production and essential crafts and accompanying services are the anchor of the village economy. Frugality and the husbanding of resources are given great importance. Renewable energy resources, such as the sun, wood, mud, and wind, are basic. A self-sustaining economy, designed to last for generations, is the goal.

Small scale. The village is a small enterprise, usually with only a few thousand people or less. It has modest resources. Some villages have a wide disparity of wealth and land ownership, with "bigness" at one end of the spectrum and "smallness" at the other end, but the totality is small compared to the prevailing scale of urban industrial systems. Villagers recognize and respect the finiteness of the material world, which can accommodate only so many people and so much land, and they tend to live accordingly.

These six characteristics are taken from a much larger listing, but they suggest the outlines of a village profile. The fact that many observers view and appreciate these qualities could represent a dramatic shift about our thinking on "modernization," and what constitutes the foundation of a sustainable culture.

Social Change Research in a Volatile Environment

Lisa and Bel at their home for one year in Fortaleza

INTER-AMERICAN
ECONOMIC AFFAIRS

The Potential Benefits of

Difficulties and Prospects for Community Development in Northeast Brazil

From Inter-American Economic Affairs, *1964*

N ortheast Brazil is an area of approximately 1.5 million square kilometers. It encompasses nine of Brazil's 25 states. Its population is close to one third of the national population. The Northeast has the single largest concentration of rural poverty in Latin America, with a per capita income of $100 to $200 per inhabitant.

Conditions have improved somewhat, but there is concentrated wealth, and land tenure is extremely polarized. There are big sugar plantations and many tiny plots. Although some industrialization is happening, in the three big cities of Recife, Salvador, and Fortaleza, the population is primarily rural. There is high infant mortality, malnutrition, poor education, and very inadequate water supply and sewerage.

This article was written after my two study trips to Northeast Brazil in the early 1960s, and this region remains the hemisphere's largest underdeveloped area.

Concept of Community Development. In order to analyze the difficulties and prospects of community development in Northeast Brazil, it is necessary to summarize briefly the term's meaning. During the last decade, community development has come to encompass more and more subject matter. Now it includes so many aspects of the development process that it has lost much of any meaning it may once have had.

Following establishment of national programs in India and Pakistan, the UN used the term "community development" to depict the processes by which:

The efforts of the people themselves are united with those of governmental authorities to improve the economic, social, and cultural conditions of communities, to integrate these communities into the life of the nation, and to enable them to contribute fully to national progress.

A capsule portrayal of community development would include the following values, principles, and basic assumptions.

- *The greatest resource of any developing country is its people, as distinct from solely material resources.* Stress is placed on human capital, the "human factor"—attitudes and values, energy and imagination, initiative and leadership.
- *The argument is that people, after all, determine development.* Whether material resources are used maximally or minimally depends on human ability and human organization; the human factor must be a point for special focus.
- *The basic unit of development is the local community.* This implies the organization of "small projects" in thousands of communities, that involve the people in the process of development, mobilizing their ideas and energies in local decision-making through government, cooperatives, schools, economic organizations, etc. The focus of this approach is considered to be in contrast to national development programs that "start from the top" using grandiose plans, although they may be complementary as well.
- *The local community, along with the family, is the most basic and universal social group in society.* The people actually live and work in the local community, and all structures—economic, social, and political—must begin at this level. The equality and vitality that is generated here greatly determines everything that is fundamental.
- *Methods for development should aim to stimulate self-help.* It is assumed that all communities have latent resources—human and material—that are idle or poorly used. These must be mobilized for economic and social production rather than the community waiting for "someone else" to give help. Substantial capital and other resources may be needed from the outside, but the initiative, planning, and much of the decision-making should originate locally.
- *Any development program must be related to the needs people feel.* The assumption is that people will get involved and mobilize unutilized resources only if they understand and want the program. Presumably most people want improved conditions of life, but the people themselves will make a maximum personal contribution only to the extent that they feel a personal commitment because of the program's close relationship to their own needs and interests. Presumably they will accept the results (if positive) of any development programs laid out and paid for by someone else. But they themselves are unlikely to contribute very much.
- *Community development must be an integrated process concerning all dimensions of the community.* An economic plan, for example, cannot materialize without due attention to malnutrition and physical maladies, which may be the primary determinants (as well as results) of low productivity. Nor can it be effected with non-existent or poorly developed skills, which the plan presupposes, or if certain leaders in the community oppose the plan and seek to manipulate the power structure to assure its failure.

Some Difficulties for Community Development

Given conditions in Northeast Brazil and the basic approach of community development, what are some of the problems facing an international community development program?

- *Lack of knowledge.* Brazil has never mounted a systematic community development program as a national policy along lines of those of some other countries. This is one reason why there is little information about the local community. Large and articulate economic development plans, which have all kinds of ramifications for local communities in the Northeast are formulated by Brazilian agencies. But there is little comprehensive data as to what is actually happening on the level of the local community. Relatively few studies have been undertaken. University curricula provide for little field research. Thus there is little specific knowledge other than some sweeping conclusions on what really are the concrete priority needs in a given community and where there are realistic breakthrough points.

- *Social structural problems.* One basic problem is that the gross economic product of Northeast Brazil is very small for the population; greatly increased regional production and income are essential. Another basic problem is that the existing product, along with all of the means of production, as well as political and social power, are heavily concentrated in a few hands. An effective development program cannot overlook the need for changing the structure of society in the area, which inevitably involves potentially volatile political factors. The fear of these political dimensions associated with structural change is a main reason for the marginal impact of many development programs.

> ... an effective community development program must have a base inside the community ... At the same time, usually there is need for an initiator and sustainer from OUTSIDE the community. The very fact that local development has not taken place to date indicates that an essential ingredient is the catalyst from outside."

- *The inside-outside relationship.* It is evident that an effective community development program must have a base inside the community: a nucleus of local leadership that has or can win some local confidence and that wants to improve conditions. At the same time, usually there is need for an initiator and sustainer from *outside* the community. The very fact that local development has not taken place to date indicates that an essential ingredient is the catalyst from outside. The job of this person is to work with the nucleus inside the community to mobilize idle or partly used resources and to present the community's needs for additional assistance to appropriate agencies beyond the community. In view of the highly nationalistic temper in Northeast Brazil, not so much on the level of the local community itself but among the intellectual groups in the universities and in some government agencies, the outside catalyst may walk a difficult road.

- *A philosophy to guide action.* There are few if any people in Northeast Brazil, whatever their place in the political spectrum, who do not admit that radical change is likely. In prevailing conditions of mass misery and semi-feudal social structure, some form of revolution is necessary. The question concerning the revolution: will it be peaceful or violent, collectivist or individualistic? Will it stress central planning or local organization, favor assistance from international sources or designate "Brazil for the Brazilians" with "no foreign capital or experts or ideas"?

    Brazil has an open society in the urban areas, especially in the South. There, change is attainable through gradualism. However, in the rural areas there is rigidity, a fairly closed society. As this is most typically the situation in the Northeast, this raises the question of the kind of change possible there.

- *Centralization.* At present, most programs that have anything to do with development in the Northeast are planned and executed from the top. It is argued that the local community is incapable of exercising substantial authority, given its inexperience and tradition of dependence. Experts are scarce. The Northeast is so vast that a centralized authority is essential to prevent the anarchy of many overlapping local programs. The problems are so complex, also involving such factors as inflation, international trade, drought, and regional infrastructure, that overall plans must be centrally formulated into which the community will of necessity fit.

Some Prospects for Community Development in Northeast Brazil

What is the capacity of a community in a region—that has a low level of per capita income; has backward educational, health, and welfare facilities; has property, power, and social privilege concentrated in a small segment of the population—to mobilize its own human and material resources for rapid improvement of community conditions? Five prospects for community development in this region are summarized:

- *The community, an untapped resource.* There is something missing in the aid programs. One recognized failing has been the lack of a dynamic philosophy that could elevate the diverse partners above their often petty squabbling and politicking to work together as true allies in a challenging task. Another deficiency has been inability to get down to the people so that aid program benefits can be widely seen and felt.

Given Brazil's huge area, not to mention the expanse of the Northeast itself, international or Brazilian government money can make only a bare beginning. Yet in almost every local community in the Northeast, there is idle land, and land in production reaping only a fraction of its potential, and a labor force that is chronically unemployed and underemployed. There are water resources in this drought area that have been little used.

- *Involving interest of intellectuals and business community.* Perhaps the people most hostile to North Americans are some intellectuals, such as faculty and students in the universities. Their arguments are mostly theoretical, and their stock in trade is speaking, writing, and armchair planning. Apart from those engaged in political organizing, few of them have actually worked in the community to apply their skills and energies to concrete development problems. But there are small pockets in the universities and assorted agencies, which offer a huge resource if and when creative relationships can be forged.

  The business community is another prospect for community development. Despite popular stereotypes, there are a number of landholders and business leaders who are interested in transforming the region and in committing their resources and talents. There are examples for establishing revolving capital funds, and organizing experiment stations to increase productivity on the land, and testing methods to prepare landless laborers to own and manage small plots. In sum, the "community" is not only the local community but the larger intellectual and business communities, which, through creative interrelationships, could assist the local community to realize its potential.

- *Capital available in the area.* It is clear that the shortage of capital is not necessarily the priority breakthrough problem even in capital-scarce Northeast Brazil. Officials of the Northeast Brazil Bank, for example, made known that billions of cruzeiros were available for investment but that few sound investment proposals had been presented. The administrations of two state governments, while emphasizing their small budgets, noted that their most significant problem was lack of carefully-thought-through projects and qualified specialists to implement them. The greatest bottleneck appears to be the catalysts to stimulate community development.

- *Opportunity for creative federal relationships.* The US governmental structure realized its first vitality is on the level of local government. Strong centralized government was a phenomenon primarily of the twentieth century. In much of Spanish Latin America, roughly the reverse took place, with central governments emerging in the colonial period. But in Brazil, due to its vastness of area and lack of communication, there was and still is much local autonomy. This, however, was not based on local self-governing units involving popular participation but on the domination of a plantation family or a relatively small group of local elite, which controlled the particular areas—almost like fiefdoms. Actual participation of the local people in decision-making was and still is very limited. As the local government usually does not have enough revenue even to maintain satisfactory public services, not to mention embark on a development plan, it greatly depends on state and federal assistance. The need is to work out an arrangement whereby the local government and newly created local organizations seeking to mobilize community resources can tie in with appropriate authorities and agencies on the state and federal levels outside.

- *Twofold goal of community development: increased productivity and viable institutions.* A common criticism leveled at community development programs, which the evidence frequently supports, is that some "good community spirit" may have been generated but there is little impact on production. Existing resources must be identified and analyzed, realistic technical plans laid, specialized training established, persuasive approaches made outside the community for capital and know-how to supplement those locally available. The essence of community development is to prepare people for these jobs.

At the same time, institutions must be established or strengthened so that the economic result has widespread social benefits for the local populations. Otherwise the gains become concentrated, the socio-economic class gap widens, and tension and political instability deepen.

A Research Paper

LAND TENURE CENTER

University of Wisconsin, Madison, Wisconsin 53706

Local Political Patterns in Northeast Brazil: A Community Case Study

Taken from a 58-page research report recognized by USAID as a model for understanding complex political cultures overseas

Research based on two study trips to the state of Ceará in Northeast Brazil.

The present study is a summary and analysis of political data gathered in one community in Northeast Brazil. The area selected was a representative *municipio* (corresponding to the US county), normally with one or more urban centers surrounded by a sizable rural area.

This *municipio* was selected because of accessibility to the capital Fortaleza, representativeness in terms of basic socio-economic conditions and population, and the expression of willingness of a number of local leaders in the *municipio* to cooperate. This *municipio* is extraordinarily interesting because of the existence of a sizable dam adjacent to the *municipio,* which, if fully utilized, might rapidly and profoundly change the economic, social and political life of the area. The dam was constructed 10 years ago by the federal government anti-drought agency (DNOCS). Authorities estimate that its waters have the potential of irrigating some 30,000 acres of valley land in this and neighboring *municipios*. This could transform the area from a very low-income agriculture characteristic of semi-arid parts of Northeast Brazil to a high-income intensive agriculture based on truck farming, fruit and livestock. Since construction of the dam, less than 5,000 acres actually have been irrigated. Income on these particular acres apparently has increased greatly. The dam also has potential for hydroelectric power for small industries.

The study included a questionnaire, collecting comprehensive data on a selected sample of families in the community. It was administered to 79 heads of family in the urban sector and 104 heads in the rural sector.

A "leader questionnaire" was also used for more open-ended, separate interviews with a small, predetermined panel of people. Included here were those holding formal positions of authority (e.g. the mayor and vice-mayor and the priest and key officials of two entities working in the *municipio* with authority and funds from the outside), plus various people with reputations of local influence.

This was a cooperative project with a Brazilian university, the University of Ceará.

The population of the *municipio* is slightly less than 30,000, with about six people per household. 90 percent of the population is rural. The dam was promising new opportunity and drawing migrants from other *municipios* deeper in the drought-ridden interior. 10,000 people live in the main urban center.

> There is no enterprise that could be called an industry and virtually all private enterprises are family-oriented.

A state deputy is a dominant power in this sub-region, representing it in the state legislature. Likewise, the important federal anti-drought agency, DNOCS, has a decisive role in several *municipios* served by the dam.

The urban center is subdividing into two main sectors: the "old town" and the "new town" located directly next to the dam. The "new town" is only a few years old and is strictly a result of the dam being built. Already it has a population of about 2,000. Many of the men here are construction day workers employed by the federal agency, DNOCS, which not only built the dam but has other public works projects under construction. A number of small shops have opened to service this growing complex.

The *municipio* encompasses 1,000 square kilometers, much of which is semi-arid land characteristic of much of the Northeast. Large farms hardly exist here. The lack of a striking latifundio-minifundio, (huge land holdings/tiny holdings) contrast in this *municipio* has tended to minimize rural social tension, in contrast to the humid areas on the eastern coast where violence between the large owners and landless tenants periodically erupts on the sugar, cotton, and pineapple plantations.

Although the mass of the active population is in subsistence farming, there is an array of people in occupations in the urban center, such as shopkeepers, cattle brokers, laundry women, masons, carpenters, shoemakers, artisans, bakers, barbers, and police. But the largest category is manual laborers working for DNOCS in construction projects.

There is no enterprise that could be called an industry, and virtually all private enterprises are family oriented. There is no bank, no food processing activity, no wholesale warehouse or retail store of any consequence.

It would seem that the *municipio* has a bright economic future if and when all the irrigable land is transformed for fruit and vegetable farming, a livestock industry is established, and favorable market possibilities in Fortaleza are utilized. But these developments require new initiatives, preparation of people with technical skills to carry out these tasks, and a political system that encourages the population itself to bring its economic needs and views into the decision-making process.

The needs most urgently felt by the local people are in the fields of health and education. In this community of nearly 30,000 people, there is no hospital, no maternity center, no full-time trained medical personnel.

The poorer rural people live in mud huts that have no floors and no bathroom or toilet facilities. (A typical house for a family of eight or nine consists of a sitting room, bedroom and kitchen.) The diet of the lower classes is principally beans, manioc flour, and cornbread, with extremely little protein.

The people feel strongly about local educational deficiencies. Schools are of extremely low quality. There is no high school. Vocational schools are nonexistent. None of the more than 70 primary school teachers in the *municipio* has a teaching diploma. Some 80 percent of school-age children do not attend any school. The rural child may have to walk many kilometers to the nearest classroom—if the parents spare him from working the land.

The main channels for information come less from the school than from informal contacts and from radio and television. There are some 200 radios in the *municipio*, mostly in the urban sector. Given high local illiteracy and no local newspaper (the closest center for publications is the capital city), radio is necessarily a principal line of communication for what is happening in the world. There is no movie theater.

The local government consists of a mayor, vice-mayor, and nine aldermen.

The Church, too, is poverty-stricken, with a congregation mainly of non-contributors. As the one priest in the *municipio* serves a large territory with very meager means, he is seldom seen in much of the parish.

Material resources for any local development work by a public entity are concentrated in one agency—DNOCS. All important material changes—the dam, some irrigation, houses for DNOCS employees, water systems, electrification—wrought in this community by a public agency have been DNOCS-financed and initiated. DNOCS also owns a farm administered by two government agronomists. This farm has possibilities for experimental work, but it is largely unutilized.

Organized associational life is almost nonexistent in the community. The main occasions for a sizable number of people to assemble are the public markets, or the weekly *feire*.

The community has many types of stratification, not only urban and rural, but according to economic class. Most important, maybe, is the realm of attitudes—for example, the attitude toward manual work, which sets apart the classes distinctly, and toward change. There are no Peasant Leagues here yet, and not much talk about land reform. There is still the amorphous mass of people on the land, resigned to their fate.

There are six informal leaders, cited by people from both the urban and rural sectors of the *municipio*. Again, however, confirming that the local political center of gravity lies in the urban sector, five of the six pull their major support there.

There are at least seven key formal positions of influence in the *municipio*. Six of these were also mentioned on at least one of the lists indicating informal leadership. They are the mayor, vice-mayor, priest, DNOCS engineer, DNOCS agronomist, DNOCS medical doctor, and ANCAR agronomist.

The vice-mayor has a very special function in the *municipio* and it is not wholly by chance that he is vice-mayor and tax collector. He is the brother of the deputy in the state legislature, who is the dominant political personality representing the *municipio* in the outside political world.

From the complex of data about the leaders—each interviewed—they can be classified as follows.

Traditional leaders: state deputy, vice mayor and tax collector, and the priest.

Change-oriented leaders: DNOCS agronomist, DNOCS engineer, and ANCAR extension service agronomist.

More or less neutral leaders: DNOCS doctor, self-employed landholder/businessman, DNOCS agronomist, and the mayor. The first three of these are very part-time, spending much of their time in Fortaleza. The DNOCS technicians have access to the most resources, but their headquarters agency in the capitol is itself part of the traditional culture. The ANCAR agronomist is unique, representing one of the most change-oriented agencies in the Northeast. He is outspoken, but must be cautious in order to maintain his good standing locally.

In essence, the *traditional leaders* desire to exercise their influence to maintain local political stability, minimizing any fundamental changes toward redistributing economic and political power and discouraging any efforts to develop new local leadership. They favor the traditional pattern of acquiring and using influence.

The *change-oriented leaders* desire to use their influence to improve local conditions by means of social and economic changes—a principal means being to develop new leadership with specialized skills. They are above all technicians; they favor "technical leaders" as distinct from "politicians." They would emphasize increasing production rather than simply redistributing property; they favor land reform *if* it is associated with technical assistance so that production is enhanced. Their method of exercising influence is by doing technical jobs (such as bringing drinking water to the urban center, extending better agricultural methods to the farmers, etc.).

Given that the single dominant political force in the community is the state deputy and his brother, what are the characteristic means used to gain and exercise power? What factors affect their influence?

They "inherited" their position from their father who is considered to have "unofficially" ruled the area. However, as the Brazilian government has gradually extended its authority throughout the land with the aim of integrating the vast northeastern region into the modern federal state, these leaders, as their counterparts elsewhere, no longer can govern quite as did their father—by use of violence. Homicides have continued, and the fear of bodily harm is one reason their rivals move with caution. At the same time, traditional leaders have developed more "acceptable" methods of exercising influence.

This points up the great importance of family heritage in a society that is relatively immobile and where traditional politics facilitates the passing down of prestige from generation to generation. New competitors for influence start at a distinct disadvantage.

This dominance is recognized by the other leaders themselves. The state deputy and vice-mayor, plus the priest who is rather close to them politically, were widely selected by the other leaders.

The deputy is one of the real powers of his party in the state, but this party like the others, has little organization. Party victories at the polls, especially in the more rural areas, result more from the strength of important individuals.

While the deputy is primarily interested in his own power rather than that of his party, he would not tolerate, unless he had no power to resist, the election of a mayor and town council in his *municipio* of a party other than his own. This would be a major step toward the disintegration of his influence. It is not by accident that the mayor, vice-mayor and eight of the local councilmen are of his same party.

> The deputy is one of the real powers of his party in the state, but this party, like the others, has little organization.

Because the deputy's chief source of power is political rather than economic, it is useful—maybe absolutely essential—for him to hold a major elective office so that he can integrate the traditional influence of his family into the constitutional democracy of Brazil. As he cannot exercise influence quite as his father did, he must legitimatize his power. He has satisfactorily resolved this for the present due to his own position in the state legislature and his brother's post as vice-mayor.

The great importance to him of these elective offices is a system of politics that virtually guarantees him, and any other candidate he chooses to support in the *municipio*, victory at the polls.

Traditional politics, as characteristic of developing areas throughout the world, work within their own particular setting. In Northeast Brazil, the most significant feature of most of the region is the periodic drought. Drought affects not only the rural areas where people on the land feel the first and most direct impact. It also hits the cities, which face food shortages and soon feel price rises as food imports are augmented from outside the region. The drought is not only a physical and social factor but it has become integrated into the political system. The state deputy's present influence is not unrelated to the anti-drought agency, DNOCS.

Historically Northeast Brazil's experience has been that each drought—the interval between droughts varies—brings a massive outlay of public resources to the Northeast.

Existing agencies have administered this influx of resources, and frequently new ones have been created. A common result has been personalized political profiteering.

Apart from direct relief, the main type of public expenditure has been for public works projects especially dams and roads. These activities can become highly political.

"Dams and roads were built to benefit properties of friends or to consolidate the political influence of some political chief in the interior."

Politics becomes "the politics of drought."

For a person such as the state deputy who wants influence, but has limited economic resources himself, access to these public resources flowing *abundantly* in time of drought has become a key to power. Through "properly distributed" use of assistances and favors, whether they be the strategic placement of a road or locational plans for an irrigation aqueduct, a job with one of these governmental agencies, or simply drinking water for the town, or money or manioc flour, the deputy can build up and solidify a clientele loyal to him personally. This system of personal loyalties in return for services rendered appears more satisfactory to him than influence based on a strong political party organization. Parties have advantages of mobilizing large numbers and enforcing discipline. But organizations require organizers who gain experience in leadership and develop their own centers of influence. They breed potential rivals.

> This system of personal loyalties in return for services rendered appears more satisfactory to him than influence based on a strong political party organization.

Once the traditional leader has built up his loyal following in the *municipio*, in this case over a sub-region of several *municipios*, so that he is the dominant influence over local public authority, he then has access to state powers to protect his interests. The lines of communication between the legally constituted public entity, the *municipio*, and the higher levels of public authority pass through him or his representatives in the local government. It becomes extremely difficult, if not impossible, for the *municipio* to take actions or formally make reports that jeopardize his position.

To maintain his dominance, the deputy favors one general policy: discourage any fundamental changes in the economic and social organization of the community but, at the same time, "do something" to combat local misery. The deputy has sought to win sizable public funds through DNOCS for temporary increases in work—at present to install drinking water in the urban center. He recognizes the need for medical facilities. He endorses food distributions handled by the priest (mostly US surplus). All of these activities not only improve local welfare somewhat, they are excellent means for exercising his influence through distributing jobs and largesse of all kinds.

In contrast, he discourages attacks on more "fundamental" problems. The above assistances are remedial actions that deal with recurring needs, although in the long run they may help somewhat in dealing with fundamental problems. He is unreceptive to such "reforms" as redistributing land, the training of specialized labor, or the development of local groups to plan for irrigation or better schooling.

Above all, he would be unreceptive to efforts for "leadership training," for preparation of a leadership class with technical skills, initiative, and broad outlook. Several cooperatives have been attempted in the *municipio* but are yet to function effectively. The traditional leader's rule-of-thumb guide must be highly pragmatic: support any action unlikely to have consequences that challenge his own position; oppose any action that seeks to redistribute power or prepare people who will recognize that the only means to enlarge their opportunities is by changing the status quo.

The type of program that the traditional leader can heartily endorse is precisely the kind of public assistance that has been channeled into the Northeast during most of this last century. Apart from actual relief, this approach has mainly concerned "physical solutions"—dams, roads, and other public works. Their construction implies large sums of money for temporary jobs and for temporary stimulants injected into local economies.

As in this *municipio*, it is apparent that throughout the Northeast, there are reservoirs whose waters have been little used for irrigation or power. It is not surprising that upon completion of the dam in this community, the utilization of its tremendous potential has been mainly by DNOCS itself. Little local leadership has materialized in the *municipio* of almost 30,000 people to plan how to take full advantage of this significant resource.

Departamento de Sociologia
Faculdade de Ciências Sociais e Filosofia
Universidade Federal do Ceará

2.º Semestre 1970

Revista de

CIÊNCIAS SOCIAIS

1
Volume

1
Número

The Role of the North American Political Scientist in a Foreign Area of Social Change:

A Political Research Project in One State of Northeast Brazil

Prepared for delivery at the National Meeting of the Latin American Studies Association, New York City, 1968

My original intention for this paper was to summarize and interpret the substance of findings on politics in one state of Northeast Brazil. This material was collected on a research project implemented cooperatively with eight Brazilians connected to the Institute of Anthropology of the Federal University of Ceará during 1967-68. Instead, I am referring where appropriate to findings, but am focusing specifically on the *process* by which the research was carried out, stressing experiences and learnings. Since my return to Wisconsin after one year of considerable adventure, I have found this subject of special interest to colleagues committed to research in areas of rapid change and especially in countries of Latin America.

First a word about the environment. Ceará is the second northernmost of Northeast Brazil's nine states. Its population of some 3,600,000 is about one-fifth of this region.

Fortaleza, the state capital and dominant city, is the third largest city in the Northeast with almost a million people and is the fastest growing. The *sertao* is known as the backlands. It is Brazil's second most drought-afflicted state in terms of area.

In characterizing the changes now taking place in Ceará, the following five factors should be included:

Persistence of Chronic Poverty: Communications and Electoral Participation Are increasing at a Faster Rate than Production and Income

Despite this low economic level—with all the social impacts in terms of inadequate housing, malnutrition and lack of medical care, illiteracy and limited educational opportunity—modern mass communication is rapidly beginning to penetrate formerly isolated people who still today are often unable to read. The transistor radio is becoming a common sight even in the poorest, most isolated rural *municipios*. Virtually every *municipio* that receives TV signals has a large TV apparatus set up in the main square, which draws a nightly crowd. Construction of roads linking the isolated areas to the state capital and to the larger interior centers has facilitated one particular form of cheap mass transporation: the bus.

Political participation, as measured by the vote, has doubled, while per capita production in much of the state has barely increased, and in some important instances, such as in the capital, it has decreased.

The people, particularly in the urban areas, face a growing gap between rising expectations and the material basis for fulfilling them.

Urbanization without Industrialization

A corollary of the first factor relates to the breathtaking growth of certain cities, especially of the capital, while the economy has not yet been geared up for industrial take off. Suddenly the capital had an unprecedented number of people without jobs that produced a minimal family income, and it lacked the social overhead to serve its big-city needs. There is massive unemployment, and *favelas* (slums), by conservative estimate, encompass at least one-third of the city. That more unrest has not been evident would seem related to the often-overlooked fact that for a good part of this new population—namely the migrants from the rural interior—movement to the city is considered a step upward. The city offers certain comforts even in the lower class quarters compared to the isolated village.

Shift of Power from Interior to Capital

In less than a generation, the capital has moved from a relatively small city to large metropolis that dominates the state's economic and political life. It has almost one quarter of total population of the state, and production that is more that seven times larger than of either of the two next strongest *municipios*.

The new role of Fortaleza is to force the inevitable conflict between the formerly powerful forces still controlling the land and newly emergent forces embracing another way of life. The most dramatic confrontation is between the conservative, rural-based coalitions and the "progressive" university students and left-wing clergy.

Ending of the Old Rural Civilization

One of the fundamental changes is the decline of land in economic and social value. While agriculture is still the main productive base in most of the state's *municipios*, and therefore still provides the livelihood for most of the state's population, the rate of increase in industrial and commercial production is larger than in agriculture for the majority of *municipios*.

The present-day leaders derive drastically less income from agriculture and commerce. Only a few of them still live on the land. The major sources of income are the professions and government service. Most of the leaders, including those in the interior, consider themselves "urban." Their educational level has drastically increased in one generation.

Increased Governmental Intervention but Low Evaluation of Governmental Action

The major governmental intervention to improve conditions in the state was the federal anti-drought agency, DNOCS. This agency built more dams in Ceará's *sertao* than in any other state in the Northeast. Dams usually also meant the construction of roads, and in some instances development of town water and electric systems, and a limited amount of irrigation. All of this provided public works jobs, which accounted for a major source of income in the poverty-stricken interior.

The beginning of the 1960s marked a tremendous increase in governmental activity. The Superintendency for the Development of the Northeast (Sudene) was established to move beyond the heavily criticized "hydraulic approach" of DNOCS, which had concentrated on construction of dams and related public works and relief, to confront the causes of poverty with a regional development policy. Sudene received unprecedented public resources to promote industrial investment and intensive land utilization. The Northeast Brazil Bank, headquartered in Fortaleza, gained new resources for regional development. Sudene and the Bank also augmented their resources through foreign aid especially from the US government and the Inter-American Bank.

> Political participation, as measured by the vote, has doubled, while per capita production in much of the state has barely increased. . . . The people, particularly in the urban area, face a growing gap between rising expectations and the material basis for fulfilling them.

It is important to keep in mind the low evaluation that the people seemed to place on the government's output. It was difficult to find people with a positive view of government action. Among the university students, the air was revolutionary. "The government must go," they said.

Although government on all levels had begun to confront the historic misery and underdevelopment of the area, its actions thus far seemed almost trivial.

As a minimal temporary expedient, the government was at least expected to provide employment in a public agency, until the economy opened new opportunities. This in turn led to rapid expansion of public employment, with personal favoritism often the basis.

Not unexpectedly, disillusion set in, not only with government, but to a growing degree, with the political system itself. One of the most readily available, and not altogether unjustified, forms of articulation of this alienation from this whole complex translated as "the system," or status quo, is to place the blame on "outsiders." This included Brazilians from the South and above all those from Sao Paulo. An even more satisfying outside target was "foreigners," especially all North Americans, because they were felt to be continuing a pattern of colonial bondage through manipulating the terms of international trade to the region's disadvantage by supporting the national government. In the eyes of the Northeast, the foreigner perpetuates the national status quo, which is, in short, a strong South allied to international interests.

My collaborating Brazilian research group and I decided to focus our attention on a substantial study in the state of Ceará. We defined "leadership" broadly, a leader being a person who exercises power, influence, and authority in the state's sub-regions and/or the capital city. Our project was part of the ongoing work of the Institute of Anthropology of the University of Ceará where we were based. It was a training as well as a research effort: to prepare by means of seminars and fieldwork a cadre of people with experience in social science research.

The state legislature urged us to formulate a questionnaire to be administered to a substantial sample of the state's leadership class. This we finally agreed upon.

Given limited time and resources, we decided to interview some 400 people in the state. These included: federal deputies from Ceará, senators from Ceará, deputies in the state legislature, and "leaders" in six key interior cities and in other areas as well as in Fortaleza and its environs.

A professor of social sciences, who also served as deputy director of the Institute of Anthropology, was administrative coordinator of the project. I served as scientific adviser. In consultation with the director of the Institute, shortly after my arrival in Ceará we organized a seminar on political science. A small, selected number of recent graduates of the University of Ceará from several academic disciplines were invited, after having been interviewed by us. Each of them had indicated interest in social science and in the prospect of involvement in field research—to study political behavior in the state. As a result of the interviews, participation in the seminar, and other academic consultations, we decided to select six people, later increased to seven.

Of value was the opportunity provided to all of us—the eight Brazilians as well as myself—to travel through the state. The main training took place through the regularly organized seminar held from October to December 1967, and in informal, seminar-type sessions held at least once a week throughout the course of the project. These were problem-solving meetings where each step of the research was discussed and sometimes intensely debated. All decisions regarding the design of the research, the timetable, coding, and interpretative summary were made by the total group.

On January 6, 1968, our research project was attacked in *Ultima Hora,* Brazil's largest circulation leftist daily newspaper, published in Rio de Janeiro. This was a major front- and second-page story: "Camelot is Repeated in Ceará." The first paragraphs read as follows:

Fortaleza-Ceará — Quinta-feira, 18 de abril de 1968

Professores Contestam Projeto Camelot e Reclamam Inquérito

Dentre os últimos acontecimentos, que têm agitado a vida universitária cearense, figuram as renovadas denúncias contra a possível execução, por parte da Universidade Federal do Ceará, de um projeto de pesquisa que estaria vinculado ao chamado Projeto Camelot.

Sôbre a matéria, professores do Departamento de Ciências Sociais, da Faculdade de Filosofia, Ciências e Letras, enviaram-nos os seguintes esclarecimentos:

1. Os projetos de pesquisa do Instituto de Antropologia inserem-se no Plano Geral de Pesquisas, formulado em 1958 para êsse órgão pelo então Diretor, professor Thomaz Pompeu Sobrinho, com o objetivo de configurar a realidade sócio-cultural do Estado. A pesquisa sôbre o Comportamento Político no Ceará tem como Coordenador o professor Paulo Elpídio de Menezes Neto, do Departamento de Ciências Sociais, da Faculdade de Filosofia, Ciências e Letras, não estando vinculado a nenhum organismo nacional ou internacional, a não ser, como é óbvio, ao próprio Instituto de Antropologia que, pela sua natureza, se dedica, no âmbito da Universidade, a pesquisas e investigações no campo das Ciências Sociais.

2. A SUDEC, solicita a financiar o aludido projeto, a exemplo do que se tem feito anteriormente, recebeu com indiscutível interêsse o pedido formulado, em virtude de se tratar de um estudo acadêmico de inegável nível científico. Todavia, constatadas pela própria Superintendência daquela entidade governamental as dificuldades financeiras em que se debatia, comprometendo, inclusive, algumas de suas pesquisas prioritárias, tal financiamento não pôde ser implementado. No ano passado, contudo, a SUDEC havia ll capazes de subvencionar, em virtude de convênio firmado com a Universidade, outro projeto de pesquisa do Instituto de Antropologia, em fase de acelerado desenvolvimento, o que vem comprovar o interêsse que as atividades científicas dêsse Instituto sempre despertam junto ao próprio Govêrno do Estado.

3. A presença do professor Belden Paulson na Universidade do Ceará não é desconhecida pela Reitoria. A Universidade Federal do Ceará dispõe de documento oficial, firmado pela alta direção da Universidade de Wisconsin, apresentando o professor Belden Paulson, cuja presença no Instituto de Antropologia tem por objetivos o treinamento de técnicos em Ciência Política, através de Seminários e de orientação científica no campo da pesquisa. O reitor Fernando Leite tem conhecimento das démarches, ainda não concluídas, para a efetivação de convênio en-

4. Quando apareceram as primeiras denúncias contra o Projeto, supostamente Camelot, em matéria publicada na imprensa do Sul do País, constante de entrevista concedida pelo Sr. José Alencar, a direção do Instituto de Antropologia dirigiu-se à Reitoria pedindo para que apurasse a veracidade dos fatos, em janeiro do corrente ano, três meses antes, portanto, do pedido de informações solicitado pelo deputado Levi Tavares na Câmara Federal. Respondendo posteriormente ao pedido de informações da Reitoria, o professor Luiz Fernando Raposo Fontenelle, Diretor do Instituto de Antropologia, encaminhou à administração central da Universidade documento amplamente esclarecedor, acompanhado de farta documentação.

5. Finalmente é do nosso interêsse, na qualidade de professôres da Universidade do Ceará, expressar neste documento, de forma inequívoca, a nossa posição. Defendemos e continuaremos a defender sempre o bom nome de nossa Universidade, numa tentativa de mantê-la livre da presença de elementos e de crises nocivas.

Queremos ver apurados, em profundidade com urgência, os fatos e as denúncias. Defendemos tão só a instituição e os supremos interêsses do Ensino e da Pesquisa — enriquecido pelo exercício sadio do intercâmbio entre cientistas.

Se confirmadas tais denúncias, seremos os primeiros a cerrar fileiras ao lado dos que defendem honestamente a dignidade da Ciência e os interêsses nacionais, consoante pode atestar a nossa conduta profissional e cívica até o presente momento.

Fortaleza, 17 de abril de 1968: Hélio Guedes de Campos Barros, Luiz de Gonzaga Mendes Chaves, Eduardo Diatay Bezerra de Menezes, Geraldo Markan Ferreira Gomes, Paulo Elpídio de Menezes Neto, Pedro Alberto de Oliveira Silva, Maria Luíza de Almeida, Maria Laura Pinheiro Rêgo e Elias de Oliveira Motta.

NAVIO OCEANOGRÁFICO ALMIRANTE SALDANHA NO PÔRTO ATÉ SÁBADO

Realizando pesquisas oceanográficas no trecho Recife-Cabo Orange, em continuação aos trabalhos executados na "Operação Nordeste I", o navio-oceanográfico "Almirante Saldanha", comandado pelo capitão de mar e guerra Paulo Gitahy de Alencastro, estendeu sua viagem até Fortaleza, tendo chegado ontem à tarde. Nesta capital aquêle navio-oceanográfico, que é um grande laboratório flutuante, permanecerá até sábado. O comandante Gilberto Amary Aché Pillar, da Escola de Aprendizes Marinheiros do Ceará, estêve no pôrto do Mucuripe para recepcionar a guarnição do "Almirante Saldanha" e hoje, pela manhã, foi visitado naquele estabelecimento pelo capitão de mar e guerra Paulo Gitahy.

"Almirante Saldanha" permanecerá realizando pesquisas até o dia 31 de maio, quando retornará à Guanabara.

CARTA DE PESCA

O trabalho que vem realizando, e planejando aquêle navio-oceanográfico servirá para elaboração da primeira carta de pesca do Nordeste. Recentemente, em estreito contacto com a SUDEPE e após consulta a órgãos e técnicos especializados a diretoria de Hidrografia e Navegação elaborou a primeira carta de Pesca do Brasil, primeira de uma série de onze, contendo dados oceanográficos e meteorológicos de interêsse da pesca, além de dados de estatística pesqueira.

REALIZADA EM RECIFE A I SEMANA ANTICOMUNISTA

A "I Semana de Formação Anticomunista para estudantes do Nordeste" realizada em Recife de 9 a 14 dêste, encerrou-se com sessão solene no auditório da Seção de Pernambuco do TFP.

O certame reuniu 60 jovens dos estados nordestinos, desde a Bahia até o Maranhão que durante cinco dias estiveram naquela capital pelos principais pontos da cidade, tendo como ponto principal a calçada da Igreja de Santo Antonio, distribuíram obras anticomunistas. Essa campanha de difusão foi caracterizada pelos estandartes rubros com o leão dourado, símbolo da T.F.P., tendo as obras mais vendidas de autoria do professor Plínio Corrêa de Oliveira.

The federal University of Ceará is furnishing all the material necessary for Professor Belden Paulson of the University of Chicago and the Department of Political Science of the University of Wisconsin to realize an extraction of socio-economic, political and culture material from the State of Ceará, research whose results Brazilians will not have access to.

On January 6, 1968, our research project was attacked in *Ultima Hora*, Brazil's largest circulation leftist daily newspaper, published in Rio de Janeiro.

What it is, in truth, is the renewal of the Project Camelot, destined for all of Latin America after it had been previously suspended. . . . It is an investigation without limits.

The article was soon taken up by *Jornal do Brasil*, one of Brazil's most important newspapers, and by papers in Sao Paulo and the Northeast. Regular news reports on the subject were also transmitted by radio and television in Ceará.

Some University of Ceará students now approached the director of the Institute of Anthropology demanding that the project be terminated and the North American professor asked to leave Ceará.

On January 9, 1968, *Ultima Hora* published a second article, according to "the right of reply," which denied existence of any Camelot Project in Ceará. It was written by the deputy director of the Institute of Anthrology and my close colleague running the project, backed by the director. It read in part:

> The project of research about 'Political Behavior in Ceará' under my coordination is a program of investigations essentially Brazilian, executed and directed by Brazilians, and financed by Brazilians. Whoever asserts the contrary is speaking from bad faith or ignorance.

His piece was not completely truthful, because I did provide some funds from my grant provided by the prestigious Social Science Research Council. Subsequently, off and on until my final departure from Ceará as originally planned in August 1968, an intermittent battle was waged. For lack of better identification, it was between the forces that defended the research as a genuine scientific program and those who attacked it, giving it overtones of espionage. Without entering into excessive detail, this included: denunciation and defense of the project on the floor of the state legislature in Fortaleza; denunciation by a federal deputy from Sao Paulo on the floor of Congress in Brasilia; suspension of funds by a development agency of Ceará that had committed itself to subsidize part of the fieldwork; appointment of a Commission of Inquiry by the *reitor* (chancellor) of the University of Ceará; and confiscation by Brazilian federal customs at the time of my departure of two boxes of my private books in English and Portuguese and some research material, including 49 of the 210 interview schedules.

There was ample coverage of the whole incident in major Brazilian newspapers, including editorials, signed articles by columnists, references in "gossip" columns, and regular coverage on radio and television in Ceará—as well as radio transmission in Europe and Radio Moscow.

The original Camelot Project came into being in 1964 as an offspring of the US Department of the Army's Special Operations Research Office (SORO). It was a large-scale socio-political study, which supposedly was to receive the largest single grant ever provided a social science project—an initial $6,000,000 for three to four years. The purpose was to assess "the potential for internal war within national societies." At this time, the US government was very concerned about counterinsurgency in some Latin American countries before they might reach proportions similar to what had happened in Southeast Asia. As this was a richly supported study into the conditions for social change, including the subject of revolution, leading social scientists were enlisted. Soon serious questions were raised in university circles in Chile where the first investigation was planned. Once the Camelot Project took on the appearance of a North American manipulation—espionage if you will—it was canceled.

We have already mentioned that in Northeast Brazil suspicion of "outsiders" had been growing. One frequently heard the region referred to as a "colony" of more developed southern Brazil, which, in turn, in some eyes, is a colony of Washington.

There was a growing suspicion that the "Yankee faces" in the Northeast were "CIA faces." In Ceará, the North American physical presence was not unnoticed. In Fortaleza, there were some eight American professors and their families from the University of Arizona, contracted by USAID to assist development of the School of Agronomy of the University of Ceará. Some 50 Peace Corps volunteers were scattered throughout the state. In Ceará there were at least 100 American missionaries, counting families.

In addition, there were several USAID officials involved in road construction, internal security assistance, industrial development, and Food for Peace. There was a USIA officer, and also a number of businessmen. The North American presence was "seen" behind brands of products labeled "*Industria Brasileira*," which ranged from automobiles manufactured in Brazil to appliances to drugs—the companies being subsidiaries of American-based corporations. While many of these personnel were performing useful individual services, in local eyes, they were symbols of "the Yankee stranglehold."

In my own case as a political scientist, I represented one of the more mysterious professions. A political scientist going into the field to study political behavior, traveling the state from end to end, was something very unusual and unknown, even when I held documented credentials and was working under the auspices of a Brazilian university and with respected Brazilian colleagues.

I quickly became aware of the sensitive nature of my mission at the time that we interviewed the first recently graduated student who was to join the project. She had been a vice president of the university student government, and, as most of the politically involved students, was "anti-American." She told me that the mere fact of her working with a North American in research would cause her to be suspect, no matter what my credentials and scientific competence. She said she would be subject to—as she put it—"the coercive power" of her student friends and even her own family and relatives. She could even be labeled *traidora*. Despite these pressures, she risked her reputation in her own words for the following reasons:

- I was invited by a representative of a group in which I held confidence [the director of the Institute of Anthropology];
- It was an unusual opportunity, the opportunity for entrance into professional social science training;
- If an American were intruding into the political reality of Ceará, he should not be left alone; I had a duty to be there;
- Given our own lack of know-how, it would be foolhardy to refuse an opportunity to learn something.

For a number of months she, and most of the seven graduate students, suffered personal crises due to self-criticism or outside pressures because of their "close identification" with a North American political scientist.

Thus these several factors—with memories still fresh of the Camelot Project, growing anti-Americanism, and suspicions harbored by ignorance and fear of political science—made our research an easy target for attack.

This "Camelot Project Affair," as it became known, evolved from a single isolated news story in *Ultima Hora* into a situation that directly involved the *reitor* and numerous faculty of the university. It stirred up discussion in the state and national legislatures and attracted some attention at high levels of the American government in Brazil and the Brazilian authorities. It turned into an issue of some importance in the university's internal politics. The University of Ceará, as also the state, was in a period of great flux.

> There was a growing suspicion that the "Yankee faces" in the Northeast were "CIA faces."

Student pressures were ever increasing, pushing for "modernization" of the university.

One component of the "university reform" scheduled to take place at the University of Ceará, as elsewhere in Brazil, involved restructuring certain subject areas for formation of new departments and schools. Such a process had brought endless jockeying as decisions were being made for the final resting places of particular disciplines, courses, and professors.

The present director of the Institute of Anthropology was in line for a new position to be created—that of dean of the social sciences faculty. The most viable means for eliminating the likelihood of appointing this person of prestige as a scientist and as an administrator of forward-looking views—was to discredit his administration in the Institute of Anthropology. The instrument for doing that: "Camelot Project."

As the conflict and discussion broadened, the social sciences gained a new priority in intellectual circles. The director, who heretofore had been relatively unknown, was becoming "a voice to be heard" in the university. Even those professors who might have disagreed with his stance tended to agree with his view and that of the social sciences faculty that each faculty member must preserve his independence. They also tended to respect his courage in defending an "unpopular cause"—a North American-related project—because he believed in its integrity.

As for the student body, the complex of circumstances that had enveloped the "Camelot Affair" was perplexing. The students were committed to an uncompromising hostility toward all North American-related endeavors, including that of scientific research. However, they became aware that there were larger stakes than the fate of one North American professor. They knew that the defenders of the research were also the chief promoters of the social sciences in the university, the ones who had been advocating for an independent faculty, more courses, more professors, and more openings for students. The student forces mostly remained neutral, therefore depriving the attackers of their main potential body of support.

The students with whom I had most contact remained loyal throughout. When their peers were urging them to leave the project, they not only continued to work but became more cohesive in defending it. They were its best propagandists. When they were told that they were participating in "espionage," they began asking serious questions that had not been raised: What is espionage? Where is the line between scientific investigation and spying? When the students were told that "secrets were being withheld from the public," they invited in anyone so interested to inspect the research materials.

In the process, they became familiar with political science, not only as researchers but also as its "public defenders." In a way they became "teachers" of political science. One of the group, who was considered the most "anti-American" of the seven, wrote in her final report:

> It was my first objective and systematic experience in the field of social sciences. It introduced me to a new kind of political science, much broader, opening up economic, sociological and anthropological aspects of political relationships, and of the distribution and use of power in human groups. This experience showed me the possibilities of rigorous scientific work. We could define the types of forces that determine why some people govern and others are governed, and of the possibility for people themselves to become determiners of their fate rather than having it determined by others. It gives scientific understanding about the kind of political system that could be instrumental for effective participation in transforming society.

As a final word, the full research that I intended was not completed, although we produced enough good data for several publications. On the other hand, as one faculty colleague back home put it, if you had sat in your university office to diagram an imaginary project in order to comprehend what it's like to operate in a restless place such as Northeast Brazil, you would be hard pressed to come up with what actually happened.

Vietnam Conflict:
A Voice of Wisdom

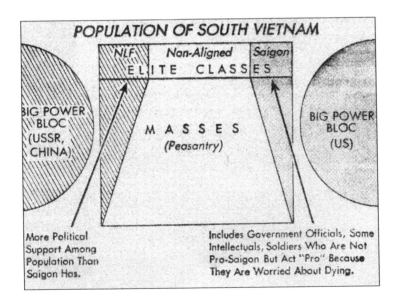

POPULATION OF SOUTH VIETNAM

NLF | Non-Aligned | Saigon

ELITE CLASSES

BIG POWER BLOC (USSR, CHINA)

MASSES (Peasantry)

BIG POWER BLOC (US)

More Political Support Among Population Than Saigon Has.

Includes Government Officials, Some Intellectuals, Soldiers Who Are Not Pro-Saigon But Act "Pro" Because They Are Worried About Dying.

Thich Nhat Hanh,

Buddhist Asks: "Not Peace Solution but Peace"

The fourth in a series of six articles I wrote for The Milwaukee Journal from the Paris Peace Conference on the Vietnam War, April 1, 1971

Thich Nhat Hanh was a young, relatively unknown Buddhist monk. Today he is an internationally celebrated leader.

As our days in Paris rapidly came to an end, a gnawing question became ever more persistent in our peace group: What is the United States doing in Vietnam today? Why are we there now?

At the conference were businessmen, attorneys, housewives, students, educators, people employed in state and local government, and clergy. There were Republicans as well as Democrats. There were 15 blacks from a number of states. There were not very many "hawks," but a good number of the delegates could not be characterized as "doves." I collected more than 20 hours of taped speeches, interviews, and conversations with various points of view. Probably half of the whole group also carried tape recorders. Scores of yellow tablets were filled with notes, and our briefcases were stuffed with historical statements about Vietnam and the various ten-point, eight-point, six-point, five-point plans to end the war.

A Different Question

The question "Why are we there now?" is different from "Why did we go there in the first place?"

The discussions with the DRV (North Vietnamese) and PRG (Vietcong) on the one hand, and the Saigon government on the other hand, made clear their fundamentally different views of history. Many Americans—including some scholars—are as divided on this point as are the Vietnamese. To imply, as some peace workers do, that every American is naïve and simple minded who thinks the United States ever should have intervened in Vietnam may have as little validity as to imply, as do some fervent "patriots," that every American who thinks our policy is grievously wrong is "pro-communist" or is at least "weak and spineless" in shirking legitimate US international obligations.

The fact is, as Kahin and Lewis point out in *The United States in Vietnam*, one of the better books on Vietnam, that US entry into Vietnam was based on numerous decisions stemming from World War II and the first decade of the Cold War. At that time, most Americans were genuinely concerned about Soviet and Chinese expansion.

Mistakes Evident

Today the grandstand quarterback, using two decades of historical perspective, may conclude that after World War II, the United States should have carried through on President Franklin Roosevelt's wartime pronouncements for "self-determination of colonial peoples" instead of backing French aspirations in Southeast Asia in return for French support to "stem communism in Europe."

Likewise, it is not difficult to look back to the period immediately after Dien Bien Phu and the French defeat, and conclude that the United States should have interpreted the Geneva Accords in terms of reunifying all of Vietnam, which would probably have been under the leadership of Ho Chi Minh, the most respected Vietnamese nationalistic leader.

> The way to end the war is simply to stop the fighting and withdraw.

But President Dwight Eisenhower and Secretary of State John Foster Dulles had just then emerged from the Korean War, which was considered a struggle to stem communist aggression in Asia. At that time, the clash between the Soviet Union and China was not yet evident, the brutalities and expansionism of the Stalinist era were still fresh in memory, and people were only dimly aware of the likely balance of power that was beginning to crystallize out of the chaos and socio-political revolutions in postwar Asia. This is relevant history that cannot be ignored. From it stems the increasingly sterile debate about why we are in Vietnam.

Whatever the motives and policies in the past, is the primary thrust in Vietnam today a war about communism or a war about foreigners—meaning non-Vietnamese?

During a break in the conference, I went to the attic of Thich Nhat Hanh, the Buddhist who has suffered repression from Saigon but who is non-communist, says the overwhelming need now is to remove all non-Vietnamese from the country and permit the Vietnamese people to resolve their affairs in their own way. Is this an unreasonable request?

The United States already has dropped almost three times the bomb tonnage in Indochina that it did in worldwide bombings in World War II. Must we continue this bombing? One hears much talk among the Vietnamese, Cambodians and Laotians that a main result of the Vietnamization program (the training and equipping of the South Vietnamese forces to assume the burden of the war) is that it "changes the color of the dead." US withdrawal of combat troops drastically reduces American casualties, but continued US presence in Vietnam, which includes heavy air support, brings mounting Vietnamese casualties, not to mention Cambodian and Laotian.

Hanh said the United States was the most responsible for the war now because it had the most power to end it. "If the American people want to, they can end it," he said. "It does not require defeat or the losing of honor. But it requires creative effort. The way to end the war is simply to stop the fighting and withdraw. Let the Vietnamese people have their own government. The Americans don't have to negotiate with Hanoi or the National Liberation Front. They don't have to negotiate with anybody. They just have to stop the fighting and leave. Then the Vietnamese will make their own government. I think maybe this has never been said—that the Americans do not have to negotiate. Let the Vietnamese negotiate among themselves."

These points are, in effect, the essentials of the six-point proposal made by the Vietnamese-Buddhist delegation to the World Conference on Religion and Peace in Kyoto, Japan, on October 20, 1970. An immediate ceasefire and a Ceasefire Control Commission were the first two points. Next, the government of South Vietnam should release "all political prisoners, students, intellectuals, monks, priests, and all persons imprisoned because of their struggle for peace and for national sovereignty." The fifth and sixth points asked the United States, Soviet Union, China, and the world religious communities and all humanitarians to help end the conflict.

Not Just a Church

The fourth point returned to the "essential details" that have blocked ending the war thus far: US withdrawal from Vietnam and the formation of the next government. Regarding withdrawal, the proposal calls for "speedy total evacuation from Vietnam of all US armed forces." According to Hanh, this would mean, in effect, the United States "bringing an end to the condition of powerlessness created by the corrupt and oppressive dictatorship currently in South Vietnam. It would let the Vietnamese people choose freely for themselves a government that is representative of the majority of the population, a government that is nonaligned and reconciling in its nature."

There would be general elections and all political forces of South Vietnam should be represented. Elections would be organized under international supervision. What role would the Buddhists play in postwar Vietnam? Hahn discussed the nature of the Vietnamese Buddhists—their power and the limits of their power:

> The Buddhists are not just a church; they are most of the Vietnamese people. No political party really exists in Vietnam. The only community that exists, which has popularity and that politicians are trying to use, is the church. Most of the writers, intellectuals and artists have sympathy for the Buddhists because Buddhism represents the traditions of Vietnam. The monks are very popular in each village. The people don't believe in the politicians. They believe in the clergy. However, the people don't like the clergy to be in the government, so we rely on laymen.

If the Buddhists have no political party and there are no significant political parties in South Vietnam (other than the Saigon government and the PRG), who, I asked, would organize the elections once the fighting stops?

May Reject Both Sides

"Maybe Saigon will organize one set of elections and the PRG another set," said Hanh. "The PRG cannot hold elections in the cities because these are controlled by Saigon. Maybe it would be good if there were two elections and two governments. Then they would come into one."

Is the real power in the cities or in the villages? "It depends on the meaning of power. Military power? We will see where the power is only when you remove the guns. If the Vietnamese choose freely, they may get rid of both sides because they have suffered under both. If the guns were removed, the two existing powers might both be eliminated."

Does the PRG represent the people? "The PRG represents the PRG. How many people back the PRG? It is very difficult to determine if a person is for the PRG or Saigon. He might have a brother in the Saigon army, and he doesn't want his brother to be killed. Sometimes he gives rice to the PRG soldier because the soldier lives in the village and his sympathies are with the Buddhists. So how can you say? There is little individual loyalty to one group."

Communism Changing

Hahn said Buddhism in Vietnam was uniquely part of Vietnamese culture:

> The Chinese discovered that bringing Chinese Buddhism into Vietnam did not help them to conquer and assimilate the Vietnamese. Instead, it helped the Vietnamese to build the self-reliance and independence to resist invasion from the north. After liberation from Chinese domination, the Vietnamese were more determined than ever to develop an independent culture.

He believes that communism in Vietnam is also being "Vietnamized:"

> Communism entered Vietnam as a western weapon to oppose western colonialism following the French occupation of Vietnam. When it was found to be effective

in combating colonialism, some Vietnamese embraced communism in a fanatical way, until it became to them more important than the values of traditional Vietnamese culture.

But suffering has helped us to see that we cannot apply western thought to an analysis of Vietnamese problems. Americans failed in Vietnam because they came with knowledge obtained in western schools and western books to try to solve Vietnamese problems. Attempts to force western democracy upon us ended up creating comical activities labeled 'democratic ways of life.' Communists, too, tried in a very unnatural and awkward way to fit the social, cultural and historical realities of Vietnam into Marxist patterns of thought.

> "But suffering has helped us to see that we cannot apply western thought to an analysis of Vietnamese problems. Americans failed in Vietnam because they came with knowledge obtained in western schools and western books to try to solve Vietnamese problems."
> —Thich Nhat Hanh

Basis for Reconciliation

Hahn believes Vietnamese Buddhism can provide the basis for national reconciliation between ideological groups after the war:

"Since the Buddhists are close to the resistance movement for independence, they have the opportunity to understand their communist countrymen. The Buddhist attitude is not antagonistic, but cautious. While they are aware of the anti-religious nature of communism, as well as its dogmatic tendencies, the Buddhists also see the efforts of the communists in the struggle for independence and social progress. That is why they keep the door for dialog wide open.

The struggle by the communists should be understood in the light of the struggle of the whole population for survival, for a progressive, humanist way of life, and above all, to remain Vietnamese.

Hahn again emphasized the conciliatory nature of Buddhist thought with this comment:

Each effort to achieve peace and harmony made by Vietnamese, whether communist or Catholic, in the North or the South, is in harmony with the non-violent struggle by the Buddhists. The non-violent struggle rejects fanatical communism and fanatical anti-communism. It stresses harmony, open mindedness and humanism."

The humble monk, who would one day spread his gentle wisdom worldwide, smiled and ushered me out of his attic.

International: Postscript

Relief needs in today's world are gigantic and far more visible compared to when I worked in the caves of postwar Naples. Natural disasters from earthquakes, floods, tsunamis, droughts—in part related to climate change—and extreme poverty combine with death and suffering caused by multiple wars. But we can learn valuable lessons from past experience.

Relief interventions respond to immediate emergencies. They bring in new resources and talents from outside the area. The essential lesson is that while the relief should be relatively short term, if used creatively, it can stimulate significant longer term strategies with huge positive results. In Naples, we soon joined our food, clothing, and medical programs with education at our Casa Mia center, along with hunting for housing and jobs. The Haiti earthquake, for example, brought a massive relief operation and offered a historic, strategic opportunity to reduce Haiti's chronic poverty and corruption. Too often such opportunities are wasted.

In moments of dramatic human disaster when people respond, new agencies are created. Once the immediate problem is taken care of, either the agency should terminate or redirect its resources to confront the more complex challenges that merit its continued existence. Often, however, the agency may continue doing the same thing, more or less, for years after needs have changed.

The world's largest refugee camp today may be Dadaab in Kenya. If reported numbers are correct, more than 400,000 people are collected there, drawn from around the Horn of Africa. This one camp holds ten times more than all the 40,000 hard-core refugees in Europe when I worked in Italy in the 1950s and '60s. A "refugee," as originally defined by the Convention establishing the UN High Commissioner for Refugees (UNHCR) in 1951, is a person who flees his home country due to fear of persecution. This definition continues, but world conditions have drastically expanded the numbers caused by wars, autocratic regimes, and natural catastrophes. There is the constant challenge to determine whether the individual or family merits international assistance or is simply seeking a better life.

When people are forced to leave their homes with no ready destination, they end up in a camp. Usually this is seen as temporary, but some camps become more or less permanent. Today refugees resulting from natural disasters and wars will eventually end up in their own country. This should push their government to become innovative in creating jobs and new living situations. Our HELP model in Sardinia offered an exemplary strategy; it solved two disparate problems with a common solution: resettling refugees in an underdeveloped region while contributing to regional economic development. We proposed similar strategies for other areas, including a pilot effort to move families from the crowded Palestinian refugee camps into lower density areas of the Arab world.

We learned that refugees who spend years in the camps take on a special "psychology" of dependence. The camp culture becomes its own little world, where people lose trust in everything. Smart camp-closing strategies need to include rehabilitation efforts that lead to successful independent living.

Young people today have little concept of the fears generated by the Cold War—the period from the end of the 1940s to the end of the 1980s—the mortal worldwide standoff between the communist bloc and the West, both armed to the teeth with nuclear weapons. In the early 1980s, the eminent pollster Lou Harris noted that something dramatic had happened to public opinion: Americans thought we were on the verge of a nuclear war—humanity could be wiped out. I also recall talking at a high school assembly in Wisconsin about peace strategies. Most students had become convinced they would never live to become adults.

When I arrived in Europe in 1950 just after college, the thousands of homeless I worked with in Naples called themselves communist, but they had no idea what this had to do with the USSR. So it was also in the villages of Italy, such as Genazzano. As my intimacy with grassroots communism deepened, I was consulted by the US Embassy and foreign aid officials who feared the march of communism. Later Senator Hubert Humphrey urged me to join the Alliance for Progress, a new American initiative in Latin America, at the time focusing especially on Northeast Brazil, one of the poorest, most restless and anti-American regions in the Western Hemisphere. I did end up there but through the University of Wisconsin.

In my various international assignments, I mingled with researchers and practitioners from the UN and many public and private entities, and consolidated my thinking and experience with my political science PhD at the University of Chicago. As communism was replaced by other "isms," the challenge was to comprehend different cultures and the worldwide movements of rising expectations.

I wrote about *miseria* and *immobilismo* in explaining conditions in developing areas. Students of "modernization" theory found intriguing my discussion of the role of the "small intellectual," a figure with special skills in bridging the different sectors in fragmented societies. After examining why one village in Italy decided to vote communist while a similar nearby community did not, I wrote articles about "A Man in Every Village." This meant that one person or a small nucleus of astute people who understand village dynamics and communicate persuasively with the population could play a decisive role in local politics while creating a linkage between a force (resource) outside the community with the nucleus inside.

While working in areas of high political volatility, I discussed a concept that triggered surprising respect. I said we needed a cluster of people I called "Soldiers of Understanding"—highly skilled in comprehending and communicating compassionately with other cultures and with varied kinds of expertise. This could be risky and would require advanced training. General Stanley McCrystal, former commander in Afghanistan, recently said we'd have a different outcome in Afghanistan if we had 10,000 Americans who had learned the language and knew the local history.

As a final word, our Casa Mia center in Naples continued to expose the needs until the caves and the Granili public refuge were closed. Decades later my Naples colleague Don Murray visited the area where we once operated. By chance he met an elderly man who said, "When I was a kid, Casa Mia saved my life."

Our Sardinia project continued for a number of years, until the refugees took full control of the land and buildings. I joined the UNHCR Rome office as camp clearance coordinator to help plan closing the camps in Italy. Although our pilot project had been approved to greatly expand, it remained a pilot model, still a beacon for refugee resettlement and rehabilitation.

The research in Brazil led to my forming a team for a major research and training project in the Northeast. Although political obstacles blocked this next big step, I was pushed to redirect my next efforts into urban poverty and racism. I was finding projects in Italy, Brazil, and Wisconsin had interesting comparability.

PART II
Urban Poverty and Racism

Distinguished Service

Ayse Somersan
Emeritus Professor and Dean, UW-Madison/UW-Extension

UNIVERSITY OF WISCONSIN FACULTY AND STAFF
HELPING TO BUILD ORGANIZATIONS IN THE STATE

*Bel with
Agnes Cobbs,
1992*

Urban: Introduction

For decades, University of Wisconsin Extension had become world famous for its work with agriculture and small towns. It had organized an office in each of Wisconsin's 72 counties. The "Wisconsin Idea" meant to extend university knowledge throughout the state. It was not until the early 1960s that urgent urban problems were forcing the university to expand its attention. Then, when I joined the university, I participated in a small seminar exploring how faculty and students could get more involved.

A leader from Milwaukee's inner city came to the university seeking help and ended up with me. Reuben Harpole had been pushed by the city's then-mayor and civic groups to find new resources to address the seemingly intractable problems of poverty and deterioration. Milwaukee was known as one of America's most racist urban areas; the lower income black population was concentrated north of downtown, and there was an expanding Hispanic population on the south side. Reuben had grown up in the city and knew every street; he helped run Milwaukee's only black newspaper.

Reuben invited me to meet people in the inner city: in the shops, schools, churches, and homes, and to sit in bars. I enlisted the university's survey research lab to assist us in designing a scientific survey on a sampling of 60 blocks. We recruited and trained 30 volunteers to conduct 260 one-hour interviews with every family that included youth, to learn the most pressing needs felt by these people. Again and again, we found that when a youth's grades had fallen way behind in reading by junior high, everything else started to go wrong.

We got the university reading clinic to assist in running a summer demonstration reading project for low-achieving youth, ages 12 to 16. Amazing results accrued, not only because of the four professional teachers but in particular because of the six community workers. These key people had participated in the survey, recruited the students, involved the parents, assured attendance (often "kicking kids out of bed"), and prodded every day to make sure everything worked.

In many later programs, the teams we organized found that these grassroots leaders were essential ingredients for success. Our programs were unique in building bridges between people living in the culture of poverty and powerlessness, and the resources of the larger community. Although often the neighborhood residents were angry, both sides were able to win trust and translate and transmit their needs and views to each other. These grassroots leaders were invaluable in many subsequent projects.

The reading program was merely the beginning of a wide range of efforts with the schools. We implemented a government-funded experiment to build communication between the inner city community and the schools that was to encompass one-quarter of the inner city schools in Milwaukee. We organized a network of 25 tutor centers, mostly in the basements of inner city churches, with volunteers trained by the university's reading clinic.

As our efforts quickly expanded and our contacts multiplied—not only on the grassroots level but with public agencies and the business community—the university in 1967 recognized the need to establish a new department. The focus: organize education and experimental programs to deal with inner city poverty and racism. This was the first such unit in the University of Wisconsin; it was later known as the Center for Urban Community Development (CUCD). I was selected as department chairman and served for 22 years.

> ... the university in 1967 recognized the need to establish a new department. The focus: organize education and experimental programs to deal with inner city poverty and racism. This was the first such unit in the University of Wisconsin ...

Every need or problem we encountered sooner or later seemed to have something to do with education. With the world in rapid change, a new context for education not only meant new courses but also the use of advanced technologies, the rewriting of textbooks, and the retraining of teachers. There was need for a uniquely radical thrust. Schools had to empower our youth and provide the knowledge and skills to cope with the new world they were entering.

We constructed seminars on new thinking with teachers and administrators on such subjects as "Applying Future Education in the Urban Classroom," "Educational Innovation—Designing Models that Work," and "The Learning Revolution and School Policy." We cooperated with public school superintendents in exploring what new-paradigm thinking in education would look like.

Some of these courses had action consequences. One series of classes that focused on beginning to prepare middle school inner city students to become global citizens led to the establishment of a new school, the Global Learning Center. This was authorized and funded by the Milwaukee Public Schools. Its innovative model did not use the traditional big school building but six small cluster centers scattered around the city. Academic achievement soared, as did attendance.

Another series worked with a group of committed teachers in a comprehensive sequence of graduate courses on Waldorf education, so they could become certified for another new school, the Urban Waldorf School. Again sponsored by the public school system, this was the first public Waldorf school in the United States, and located in the heart of the inner city. (All of America's Waldorf schools had been private and not in inner city environments nor with minority students.)

In the mid-1970s, a federal court labeled the entire Milwaukee public school system "unconstitutionally segregated." This brought the city into the middle of that great national civil rights battle. We were involved with civic and church leaders to create a citywide dialogue that, in due course, was to bring desegregation without the violent turbulence of some other cities. One related effort we also helped to organize was the Riverside Educational Improvement Project. It designed a strategy for school integration while maintaining learning quality. This whole desegregation episode had to be understood in the broad panorama of urban development occurring in America's cities, including Milwaukee—segregated schools were linked to segregated housing and urban decay.

As economic development—the construction of housing and the establishment of industries—had been taking place on more or less vacant land on the city's fringes, higher income families had been moving away from the older, deteriorating inner city. Once the new occupants who moved in were unable to maintain the quality of the property and neighborhood, all of the characteristics we have come to know as inner city pathology crystallized: less home ownership, higher mobility of residents, exodus of businesses, family instability, more people on welfare, higher crime, and fewer resources for community problem-solving. Income and racial polarization resulted, with massive impact on the schools. This inner city malaise was the stimulus mentioned above that brought Reuben Harpole to the university for help, and pushed me from my previous international focus to urban.

The Harambee Revitalization Project (HRP) that Reuben and I organized with inner city residents was one of the more comprehensive community development efforts the university and Milwaukee had seen. The leaders of the Harambee Community School, a private community effort, contacted Reuben and me, desperate to find resources to save their school. Since it was located in the center of the area where we'd been working, we volunteered to assist.

Because this was a *community* school, we insisted that the group must empower the local area itself to provide support. Our combined network set up the Harambee (Swahili for "Let's Pull Together") Revitalization Project, using some public money and small grants. It formed a broadly based policy board and task forces, and mobilized four interrelated community initiatives. The project began in 12 square blocks, but over time encompassed a sizeable chunk of the inner city. This effort has lasted for more than four decades and has won national recognition.

The Harambee Ombudsman Project evolved from a political science class I offered with residents from the area. We invited Ben Johnson, the local alderman who also was the elected president of the city's governing council, to co-instruct with me. The residents wanted to create a "political base" to empower citizens to get governmental bodies to serve their deteriorating neighborhood like any other city area. Meeting in the local library, class participants learned how to articulate problems (inputs) and understand the political process to produce results (outputs).

Over time they established a very effective community block organization, with more than 200 trained block leaders operating on more than 50 blocks. Agnes Cobbs, a local community leader we hired in CUCD, coordinated and worked with me as trainer. Each block leader served as an ombudsman to process local needs. This neighborhood political system evolved a model that became a replica for many others.

The Harambee Development Corporation responded to the need for home maintenance and repair, preventive care of housing stock, and generally confronting housing deterioration in this decaying neighborhood. It included technical counseling, small home repair loans, operating a "paint-up" program, dealing with city and county on vacant lot and zoning issues, and general economic development.

> The residents wanted to create a 'political base' to empower citizens to get governmental bodies to serve their deteriorating neighborhood like any other city area.

The Harambee Health Committee detailed the dreadful status of health in the black community. Reuben and I enlisted government and university health officials, along with the block leaders, the city's health commissioner, and the Medical College of Wisconsin, to think through a comprehensive health delivery and preventive care system. Later a national foundation founded and funded a Community Health Center in the area.

The Harambee Human Services Project stemmed from the State of Wisconsin's interest in creating pilot decentralized human services efforts. We formulated a comprehensive proposal that could affect some 8,000 families in the area, more than one-third of them receiving some public benefit from a maze of different agencies. This was considered something of a "revolutionary" opportunity to rationalize human service delivery. After our comprehensive survey in the area and close links with the alderman and county supervisor, we got resolutions passed, and I ended up serving on a county policy-making advisory committee. The final county plan included some of our proposals.

All of these projects had broad ramifications and involved various members of our department and the broad university. They linked community to government, and local to state and national entities. They used little money but maximized voluntary community effort. They provided rich experience useful in teaching.

Since the overall goal of all of this activity was to create a healthy urban community, we decided to explore in depth: what is a healthy community? We defined "health" broadly, not only physical health but economic, educational, environmental, and political health. By fleshing out what each of these meant, and developing yardsticks (social indicators) to measure progress, we could begin to assess what the work of us and others was accomplishing. Since national critics were arguing that the whole "poverty war" was a waste of time and money, these yardsticks helped to measure results.

We recruited an array of faculty and grad students eager to participate over a couple of years, in what turned into a seminal intellectual enterprise. The resulting model was used in several practical settings, including the Harambee community. This project generated fascination in university and public circles, including the National Institute of Mental Health (NIMH).

These programs had broad ramifications that attracted local and national attention. This work, beginning in one small inner city community, offered a microcosm in helping to deal with a great unresolved American social dilemma. By sharing findings at professional meetings and in writings, some learnings were incorporated into policy-making, and our teaching was enriched as we interrelated conceptual ideas with real world field experience.

Evolution of Work

Promoting Change in the Central City

Taken from document published as a joint project of:

- *Cooperative Educational Service Agency No. 19, U.S.O.E. Project No. 975, PL 89-10, Title III*
- *Milwaukee Public Schools*
- *University of Wisconsin Extension and University of Wisconsin-Milwaukee*

This project cemented the cooperation of the public school authorities to work with the university. This first relatively small effort soon expanded to affect a significant part of the school system. It had multiple benefits, including building school-community communication, improving teacher quality, and pointing up system inadequacies that demanded attention. This initial phase is discussed in some detail, because by the third year, it encompassed 200 teachers, 1500 families, and 40 community representatives. The project became known nationally.

Summary of the Central City Teacher-Community Pilot Project
Origin and Development of Project

Innovations stemming from carefully designed pilot projects usually do not come about as suddenly formulated ideas or as mere strokes of luck. They are more likely the result of a prior background of experience that convinced a group of people of the need for the pilot project in the first place in order to cope more adequately with a particular set of problems. Analysis of the project therefore requires at least a cursory outline of the problem framework to which the project is addressed, and the background of experience on which the project design is based.

Specific Problem Framework

The general area where this project is located is the central city, north of downtown, the most depressed part of metropolitan Milwaukee. The city's lowest-income families are concentrated here: the highest percentage of families receiving assistance from the County Department of Public Welfare, the highest unemployment rates, the highest percentage of physical and environmental blight. Most of Milwaukee's non-white population lives in this area.

The schools of Milwaukee's central city, like those in similar areas of every major city, present unique problems. There are at least four characteristics that summarize the differences between these schools and their students and the schools and students of outlying areas:

- Significantly lower achievement in the basic academic skills;
- The tendency of students to react to situations of stress with various forms of overt behavior;
- The extremely poor motivational level as shown, for example, in significantly high rates of absenteeism and tardiness;
- The hostility that many Negro [In these early reports and papers describing my inner city work, the term "Negro" was normally used, soon replaced by African American or black.] parents and children feel toward authority in general and white authority in particular.

The causes of these differences are many and complex. Ample research demonstrates the following: a high degree of de facto racial segregation due to place of residence, low-income level, and lack of participation in the decision-making structures of the political system due to low cultural achievement. At least two other major factors must be included as particularly critical. The first, which contributes to the second, is the failure of universities, colleges, and school systems to prepare teacher trainees and candidates for teaching in disadvantaged areas. All of the teachers directly involved in this project stated in interviews that their training was woefully inadequate to cope with the needs they face at Robert Fulton Junior High School, the inner city Milwaukee Public School where we were working. Thus the school is staffed with faculty who, even if well intentioned, are frequently ill-prepared to confront the demands placed upon them.

> **The school is staffed with faculty who are frequently ill-prepared to confront the demands placed upon them.**

The second factor is the lack of full support and mutual understanding between the school and the families. With the tendency for breakdown in communication, a feeling of alienation on the part of the local population arises toward the school and toward other authorities. The school's personnel, in turn, lack feedback as to the community's seeming inability or unwillingness to utilize fully its facilities and services.

This project, therefore, is designed to attack creatively certain aspects of central city teacher training and the problem of alienation between children and parents and the school.

Project Objectives

This project's objectives can be summarized as follows:

- To upgrade the academic preparation, community sensitivity, and communication skill of the selected teachers presently at Robert Fulton Junior High School. An assumption underlying the project is that 20 percent of Fulton School's total professional staff is sufficiently large to produce an impact on the school.

  The teacher signs a statement agreeing to the following: to accept no other remunerative employment during the eight-week summer program; to commit him- or herself full time to the summer project, with at least half of that time devoted to fieldwork in the community; to remain at Fulton School for two years unless transferred by the school administration; to return for a similar project in summer of 1967 if requested; to participate in a 10-week seminar during each semester of the 1966-67 school years; and to assist the principal at Fulton in the orientation of new teachers.

- To upgrade the desire and the ability of children of 150 families attending Fulton School to reap maximum benefits from the educational programs of the school and other opportunities in the community. It was desired that children reflect a cross-section of the school: some were straight "D" and "F" students, some were school "troublemakers," others were neither of the above but were youngsters who indicated unused potential ability.

- To upgrade interest of the parents in opportunities offered by the school and other agencies for their children and also for themselves. This includes developing an understanding of ways and means of parent access to school staff through parent-teacher and other communication channels.

- To design, test, and demonstrate methodology for implementation of the above objectives by utilizing specialized resources of the University of Wisconsin Extension and the University of Wisconsin-Milwaukee, the Milwaukee Public School System, the Cooperative Educational Service Agency, the neighboring community, and any other relevant resources. The process of carrying out the project is in itself a process of communication, of developing a coalition of representative interests, which are coming to agree on certain needs and possible solutions. This provides a political basis for subsequent larger programs.

The Teacher Interviews

The teachers were initiated into the project through an interview conducted with each one by myself. The replies, which illuminate the nature of the needs with which the project deals, could be summarized as follows:

- Central city schools are different. There are many kinds of social and emotional problems resulting from all sorts of deprivations: large families with poor parental control, little study space at home, little practice in verbalization and listening and concentrating on a definite goal, broken homes, rebellious parents who have suffered indignities due to race, limited exposure to a variety of cultural experiences. The children tend to be promoted in school notwithstanding poor academic records. By the time they reach junior high school age, they are mature beyond their years in some respects, but academically they may be several grades below their reading level. Failure then becomes increasingly likely, and their behavioral problems are compounded.

- We were (the teachers speaking) prepared fairly well in subject matter, but we were definitely not prepared to cope with behavioral needs in our school. Everything in our school is different from the norms of the School of Education. Much of what we had been taught was wrong; our professors obviously had little experience with the disadvantaged. For example, you cannot coerce our kids; they simply will not come to class anymore because their motivation to learn is low. We were prepared to teach in an all-white school in a decent neighborhood. We were to assume that the children could read and follow directions, that they would respect the school and teacher, that they understood the democratic process, that they would put supplies back on the shelf. The kids know we were not prepared to work with them, so they take advantage of us, or call us phonies due to our ignorance or patronizing intolerance of conditions we were never helped to understand.

> There should be encouragement of new ideas of "creative research" to deal with inadequacies, rather than "following the book."

- Most personally satisfying is to teach a non-reader to read. This requires working with the individual child or a small group, continually stimulating them. Many of them are given no aspirations at home. In effect, the child is now saying to the teacher, "You come to school because you really are interested in me, not just to collect your check."
- Most personally dissatisfying is when the child fails a test he could easily pass because he didn't take his books home and study. In other words, he had opportunity to learn but didn't. When he gets three correct out of 20, you ask him what happened. "I didn't understand." Why didn't he ask? You get "the shoulder" and complete silence. Apart from the ever-present job of keeping discipline, there is the constant strain of repeating everything four or five times, explaining things with a few key words you know are understood. It is also demoralizing to see the prejudices of many of the teachers. They do nothing but complain. They rarely visit the homes and have little positive to say about their students.
- The majority of the teachers interviewed, especially the Negro teachers, stated emphatically that they would not want to transfer out of the central city school. They are held there by the challenge and desire to contribute to the needs, plus

a feeling of responsibility to help "their own people," in that Fulton School is mostly Negro. Most of the teachers stressed that many teachers in their school—in all central city schools—would prefer moving out. They suggested this to be true for most of the whites and a good many Negroes. The main reason for this large desired exodus is that the teachers are unable to cope with the complex of problems for which they are ill prepared. In addition, in the case of some whites, it was felt that there is prejudice against them.

- The teachers stressed again and again the following factors required to improve their school: far more comprehensive training so that the teachers better understand the special variables in dealing with a disadvantaged neighborhood, and special incentives to motivate teachers to give the essential "extra push." If the teacher is apathetic or discouraged, the child is almost sure to be also. More careful screening is needed of central city teachers, and those who are especially unprepared or biased should be transferred. There should be encouragement of new ideas in the school, of "creative research," to deal with inadequacies, rather than "following the book" and fearing that "changes" will overturn the system and reflect critically on the administration and School Board. Also helpful would be smaller classes and more homogeneous grouping so that teachers can develop more individualized programs for each child, including personal attention to help the child develop aspirations, set learning goals, form study habits, and build confidence that he or she can achieve.

Program Implementation during Summer 1966

- Academic. Each of the 15 teachers worked a regular 40-hour week, focusing on the following: a three-hour credit course at UWM, a five-session reading workshop developed in cooperation with Alverno College, an afternoon seminar one day each week, and roughly 20 hours a week in fieldwork with 10 families assigned from Fulton School.

- Community Fieldwork with the Families. The teachers spent approximately one-half of each week in close contact with 10 families having children at Robert Fulton. The fieldwork was open ended, and because of its novelty for some of the teachers, several weeks were required before it was systematized into a workable routine. Each teacher could approach this activity, which normally was carried out in the afternoons and on weekends, in an individualistic manner, as long as actual contact was made with the family, particularly the Robert Fulton child, and also the parents. Each teacher accounted for time use with a daily log that was submitted to the project staff at the end of each week.

As part of its staff, the project had five parents from the community who had had experience in previous grassroots programs with the University. They now served on a part-time basis. Their job was to facilitate contacting the families, especially valuable for the new teachers and the white teachers who were less familiar with the central city.

The purpose of the fieldwork was for the teacher to win the confidence of the children and parents and to convince them that he was not arrogant or condescending but genuinely interested in helping each person to realize the full potential of his abilities. Once communication was built up, then activities could be developed of educational significance. Frequently the order was reversed, whereby concrete activities, whether a softball game or a fishing trip to a nearby lake, was the pre-condition for building rapport.

Weekly Seminar

Every Wednesday afternoon at 1:30 the 15 teachers, the community reps, and the four general staff met at the UWM Union for a freewheeling discussion. Insights from the academic coursework and reading workshop were shared. Problems stemming from the fieldwork were discussed in detail. All participants treated one another as equals: principal and teachers, community reps, and staff. No person, idea, or gripe was immune from the focus of the group. At times the discussion became sharp and sometimes even descended into personality conflicts.

Innovation—a search for new methods to deal with old problems—was the thread running throughout. Numerous concrete recommendations emerged, some of which are being implemented in Robert Futon this academic year. The process was an intense growing experience for all concerned. By the end of the summer, it had built up an esprit de corps among the teachers and principal, which carried into the school in September.

Apart from material incentives, a certain intangible began to characterize the teachers as the project evolved. They began to question the usual fatalistic conclusion that "change is impossible." They began to demonstrate a collective pride in realizing that if particular innovations were to be realized, these might have to depend upon themselves. While many changes required structural modifications of the "system" itself to be made by the School Board and central administration, there were numerous improvements that could be implemented in their school.

Personalized Relationships

The fieldwork created a highly personal relationship between teacher and parent and child. The teachers spent considerable time at the homes of the families. They learned much about the milieu in which the child was growing up. They found out that some of the parents were very interested in cooperating closely with the teacher in the future, while in some instances, parental guidance was altogether lacking and substitute stimuli were required.

This work in the community emphasized the uniqueness of every family and child. The "problems" of the school tended to submit somewhat more readily to solutions when translated into terms of individuals who could be approached on a personal basis.

ADULT *leadership*

VOLUME 15   NUMBER 10   APRIL, 1967

Research, Training, and Action in Milwaukee's Inner Core: A Case Study about Process

Prepared for the Annual Conference of Adult Education Association of the USA; taken from
Adult Leadership, *1967*

This study describing our first period of urban work in the university was awarded the Association's "Best Case Study of all those submitted." The details of the projects are written about elsewhere. Our early efforts started small and built strong local buy-in. This contrasted with some much larger bureaucratic operations of the "poverty war."

Reviewing these first months, we began to conceive the project around several simple anchor points:

- The first step to effectiveness had to be an accurate assessment of the real needs—what the people on the blocks perceived their needs to be, not what did some professor at the university, or some official at a poverty office who rarely had time to get into the homes, wanted for them. The ideas might or might not be synonymous. We found, for example, that many parents tended to be more interested in improving their children's reading skills than in integration or bussing. Therefore, our educational projects might well start with the "here-and-now" reading problems rather than the more abstract social goal of integration. At a certain point, of course, the two might well intersect and the people would realize their interrelationship.

- A small, informal coalition of interests was beginning to form from the larger community that had interest in dealing with particular needs in the Inner Core through manageable projects. Included were several people from business prepared to contribute time and money, a number of churches and clergy, several people from our university, and a beginning cooperation of the public schools, all working on a partnership basis with people from the Inner Core community. It was assumed that significant change could be realized only through such a broad alliance of representative interests, and that decisions on activities would require some consensus if later they were to be considered models for larger programs.

- Our efforts should concentrate on a series of projects limited in scope, all interrelated, through focusing on certain basic goals that we had decided should be in the field of education. The projects should require limited expenditure and personnel, or else a sizable number of workers but with limited time involvement per capita. Either way they should produce short-term, tangible benefits for the participants.

- There was also a feeling that the organizational framework should be held to a bare minimum. The people on the blocks had negative thoughts about a number of organizations that to them were mere "talk agencies," organizations that elected officers and advisory boards and held meetings but had little noticeable impact on the Inner Core community. We felt our efforts should remain as informally structured as possible. Most communication among ourselves should be through personalized verbal relations rather than written memos that smacked of bureaucracy. The less publicity the better. It was felt that publicity would lead to struggles about who would get "credit" and would bring to the fore all kinds of factional bickering that would best be laid to rest. In addition, as one person put it, "Once you raise your head in the Inner Core, some agency will inevitably say, 'We are already doing this. Go away.'" In the one or two instances where we overlooked these simple rules, the program suffered.

University Urban Extension in Milwaukee

Taken from UWM Magazine, *1970*

This article briefly describes our efforts to establish the first department in the University of Wisconsin-Extension to focus on problems of urban poverty and racism. The piece also mentions my overseas experience with the "small intellectual," for which we were now using the term "community representative," who plays an increasingly important role in the work. I also helped the university expand the meaning of "student" to increase the relevance of traditional campus-based teaching to the inner city environment.

I n the early 1960s, America only dimly perceived the urban crisis that lay ahead. The University of Wisconsin-Milwaukee and University Extension were then in the very initial stages of confronting urban problems. When I joined the faculty of both as a joint appointment, I began an immediate search for other faculty members in Extension who were interested in the multipurpose, if often vague, field of community development, a specialization in which I had overseas experience. Such interest was widespread but almost totally rural-oriented. There was surprisingly little focus on city and metropolitan government; urban poverty; the needs of the urban black, Spanish-speaking, or Indian communities; urban education; and present or threatened violence and disorder.

Rural development had been the major concern of University Extension for decades—the "Wisconsin idea" of extending the knowledge of the university into communities to the outer boundaries of the state. One of Extension's major successes had been its agricultural plan, duplicated across the country by other universities with historic results. The plan placed agricultural representatives in each county of the state so that university knowledge and research could be of benefit to farmers. It was now understood that the focus of attention must also switch to the crowded urban centers. Since it had taken decades for the university to create a workable system to aid agriculture, it might take 10 or 20 years before the university might be able to work effectively in urban areas.

In 1963-64, a small group of us began to meet to define urban needs, particularly in Milwaukee, and to discuss the role of the university in the community. The group rarely numbered more than 10, most of whom were joint appointments between UWM academic departments and Extension. This became the nucleus for a series of urban seminars, which broadened into wider faculty and Milwaukee community participation.

In the spring of 1964, two young men from the black community came to the university seeking support for new programs in their area. They explained that despite some worthy public and private projects, the schools were deteriorating, crime and vandalism were on the rise, businesses were closing, and, above all, racial friction was increasing and the spirit and hope in the community were being crushed. They thought that more direct university involvement might alleviate some of these problems. One of these men was Reuben Harpole, at that time assistant advertising manager of the Milwaukee Star, then the main newspaper for the black population in the state. We went into the Central City as a team and began to talk directly to the people.

> The community representative, combines a special set of traits that enable him or her to act as a mediator.

Our early projects grew from the insights we gained from conversations with Inner City residents. As time passed, the projects multiplied, merging from one into another. We soon found ourselves working not only in the black community but in the white and Spanish-speaking communities as well.

In July 1967, our Center for Community Leadership Development (CCLD) was established. It was a statewide Extension department that joined together the group in Milwaukee with a nucleus of people in Madison who had organized the Center for Action on Poverty. This was initially financed by the United States Office of Economic Opportunity. The Center was to work with minority groups on the problems of poverty and prejudice through research, experimental action projects, formal and informal training, and evaluation of program results.

The Role of the "Small Intellectual"

One of the most fundamental problems in the Central City was poor communication. In the simplest terms, this meant ineffective communication between the mass of the population on the blocks and the individuals, agencies, and institutions exercising authority in the Milwaukee area. We knew that there were considerable opportunities and assistance available to the people but that they were minimally utilized. Above all, there was a feeling of alienation against those in authority—whether in the public schools, police department, welfare agencies, or our university—because those resources "were not working in the interest of the community." Whether or not this was based on fact, it was strongly felt and therefore it had to be dealt with as if it were a fact.

The key question was: who is capable of building understanding and promoting communication in a society wracked by sizable cleavages between major population groups? Within the confines of Milwaukee, there are different levels of access to authoritative decision-making that are not merely contrasts in quantity but in quality. In some cases, they are almost different civilizations within approximately the same geographic radius, but there is minimal communication between them. For example, a minority person of low income with little schooling and another well-off, educated white person from a suburb, or even an official or business person in a downtown office, may face a huge communication barrier.

A person working in this setting must be able to bridge the gap between the people living in poverty and powerlessness and those controlling economic and political resources in great disproportion to their numbers. A unique quality of this person is his/her ability to explain the views and needs of each side to the other in meaningful terms. This person, the community representative, combines a special set of traits that enable him to act as a mediator.

Though he may have somewhat less formal education than certain other professionals with whom he would work in the larger community, his education is normally in correlation with the environment in which he works. A quality that distinguishes him is his ability to avoid irreconcilable conflict with the values of the cultures with which he must communicate. Instead, he is able to identify with the people, understand their nuances of language and lifestyle, and define and verbalize their interests.

Representatives of the people for whom a project is designed are essential to the planning. The community representative is frequently "fed up" and wants to try new initiatives to "make something happen." He is usually not interested in "more meetings and memberships" but in concrete results. Neither a member of the lowest socio-economic level nor of the power structure, he is usually a long-term resident of the area and has a personal interest in improving the quality of life in the neighborhood. Frequently he is a homeowner.

Both the least educated and the highest salaried and professional groups of the two neighborhoods often lack interest in playing this role. People from the middle social strata have been the driving force behind most of the projects. They favor some interracial and inter-ethnic contact and cooperation, whether for pragmatic or ideological considerations. They understand the long-run implications of social change induced through education, employment, and entry into the political system. In this sense, their view of social change could be described as moderate. Yet they can identify with the frustrations of low-income residents, and they are aware of the growing alienation against unresponsive institutions. Recently they have become increasingly interested in institutional change.

Thus the community representative has come forward as a major force in providing leadership in America's poverty programs. These people have been called "sub-professionals," "lay aides," "indigenous workers," and so forth. Their usual assignment has been to communicate with people in the lower economic groups on behalf of some agency: the public school, the welfare department, a university. A commonly used job description states: "Sub-professional jobs consist of sub-sections of work, heretofore done by professionals, for which full professional training is not necessary, or of new functions that expand the scope of professional service."

Based on an erroneous assumption, this definition of sub-professional jobs runs contrary to our experience. The assumption was that professionals were able to play the role of the "small intellectual" (as described in the "International" section of this book), and that the reason for the advent of the "sub-professional" was the scarcity of professionals, not the inability of professionals to do this job. It is quite clear that few professors, for example could play this essential role of communicator even if they were available. They lack the experience and skill required to understand the life reality of certain populations and to frame programs that would be relevant.

A body of evidence about poverty and welfare programs, not to mention the educational efforts of public schools and institutions of higher learning, suggests that the essential missing ingredient may not be knowledge, or in some instances even resources, but delivery systems capable of carrying them to the right people in the right way.

> The key to the program is the "trainer of trainers" concept: . . . multiply the learning experience by training others.

This raises the question: Why are "sub-professionals" so categorized when only they may be able to fulfill this function? They are "professional" in carrying out their tasks; the proper implementation of their role requires a high level of skill as well as a special set of background traits. At an early stage in the activities of CCLD, this question was raised because of the long hours of voluntary work put in by Reuben Harpole on projects that were University and community sponsored. It seemed appropriate that he be appointed to the Extension faculty. His appointment opened the door for other professional-level appointments of people based on the expected contribution they could make toward University effectiveness. These community representatives have become invaluable elements of my department.

A New Meaning for "Student"

Students are at the heart of much of the campus unrest today. This unrest may well be a necessity to shake up higher education. If the university is to understand the needs of the city, especially issues related to poverty and racism, then people who experience these conditions are essential in helping to shape the educational program. They are students in the usual sense as learners but they also serve a vital role in defining what is to be learned.

Student involvement is critical in development of Extension programs, but it is equally critical to the whole philosophy of planning and implementing educational offerings.

After a contingent from the community has identified educational problems labeled "important," they become "students" in the sense of thinking through with us the design of an educational program to deal with the problem. They help to figure out the curriculum and often have an important role in determining the instructors, and then they usually evaluate the impact of the effort. Although they may not sit at a classroom desk and put in a specified number of hours on campus, they are students in the total process as defined by Webster: they are "learners, attentive and systematic observers." The terms "curriculum," "instructors," and "students" may be quite different from their usual meanings.

"Student" in this context has at least three meanings: a person involved in learning situations that have been structured toward educational goals but cannot be considered usual classroom instruction or courses; a person in organized classroom instruction that is problem-oriented rather than degree-oriented; and a person in regular classrooms taking credit courses, usually toward a degree. Informally structured learning may take place in a church center, a TV studio, or even on the street, and the people in the role of students may simultaneously serve as leaders or trainers of others. In this setting, education, action, and sometimes research may be merged into one program organized by the university cooperating with people in the community.

An example of problem-oriented rather than degree-oriented instruction was a series of seminars in understanding minority groups and the urban crisis that our university department began offering four years ago. Originally set up for suburban housewives, the "Afro-American in Contemporary Society" was expanded to include business and industry executives and, more recently, key people in local congregations of one statewide church organization. The seminars are held at the university, businesses, or churches. The participants establish the rules for conducting the sessions. The program is carefully evaluated, and with the instructor, the participants develop a meaningful community effort to solve a problem.

The seminars often have participant observers from the outside—sometimes UWM graduate students. The key to the program is the "trainer of trainers" concept: key people from the organization are prepared to multiply the learning experience by training others. Many of our grassroots community representatives are trained as effective community organizers who then prepare others on their blocks.

In the spring of 1969, there were no student majors in the UWM Department of Political Science from the black or Latin communities, despite the interest and the need for such people to understand the American political system. In the fall of 1969, I developed an introductory political science course in close consultation with several people from the black community. 29 of the 32 students who registered were black or Spanish-speaking, many of them mature adults in leadership positions in their communities. They played a major role in running the class: they summarized readings, presented papers that analyzed political questions in problem areas of interest, and they selected outside consultants to address the class. This was merely a model, later duplicated.

Harambee Project: Comprehensive Community Development

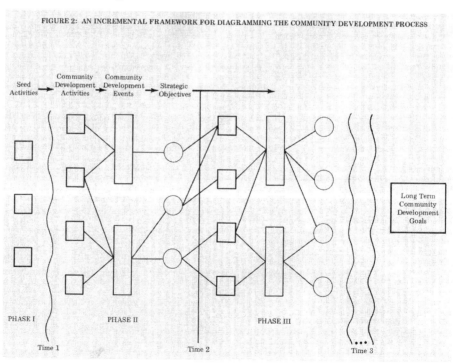

FIGURE 2: AN INCREMENTAL FRAMEWORK FOR DIAGRAMMING THE COMMUNITY DEVELOPMENT PROCESS

From A Reporting and Planning Model for Urban Community Development *by Belden Paulson and Daniel Folkman, 1978*

A Reporting and Planning Model for Urban Community Development:

A Case Study in Community-University Participation

A study of an inner city revitalization project partially funded by Title 1 of the Higher Education Act of 1965, 1976

Co-authored with Daniel Folkman

The Harambee Revitalization Project, organized by our department with inner city residents, had multiple dimensions as a comprehensive planning effort. It impacted different community needs.

Further, it played an array of roles in the university. Since it was partially funded by Title I of the Higher Education Act of 1965 to enhance university-community relationships, and it was receiving national attention, my colleagues and I were asked to develop a detailed analysis of this model.

If the university is to involve itself in seeking solutions to complex urban problems, as prescribed by Title 1 of the Higher Education Act of 1965, then it faces the need not only to get out into the community but also to be able to describe what it's doing there, what it hopes to achieve, and the process it plans to use. Many persons today who are associated with university community service work are particularly sensitive to these kinds of questions. The tightening of university budgets and the growing public concern for accountability have provided mounting pressure to do what should have been done anyway, that is, to examine the university role in the community and profile community service activities within the overall functions of the university.

The Center for Urban Community Development (CUCD) has been developing two conceptual approaches for describing its activities, which can be broadly called urban community development. The Center wanted to look beyond the minutia of the operational details of its projects and extract from the data certain general, realistic statements about its community activities and the process used. The particular project under discussion was one of the major stimulants that encouraged the Center to undertake this conceptualizing task. This project, it was felt, was so complex and long term that everyone who was in some way involved—Center staff themselves, university administrators, community leaders, government—needed a descriptive picture of the nature of the project and their involvement in it. With this clearer understanding, they would then have a basis for making policy determinations as to the extent and duration of their commitments.

The first approach is a typology that interrelates the university's educational functions with the type of changes being sought in extension community development work.

The second approach examines the community development process within an incremental framework. This framework is used in diagramming the activities and events that take place in a project over time and shows their relationship to identified strategic objectives and long-term goals.

The CUCD uses these two approaches in profiling its various community development projects, irrespective of their diverse nature. Given the great complexity of many of the urban problems the CUCD attempts to address, the staff has found that these two interrelated approaches have enhanced their ability to plan and communicate what they are doing, what they hope to achieve, and how they plan to achieve it.

> This project can be seen as performing one or more of three fundamental educational functions: continuing education, service, or experimentation.

A university-related community development project can be seen as performing one or more of three fundamental *educational functions*: continuing education, service, or experimentation. A project can also be seen as working toward one or more of three basic *types of change*: individual change, agency/organizational change, or policy change. These two perspectives can be combined into a typology that is useful in profiling one project or a set of projects of an extension unit by interrelating the different educational functions performed with the types of change being sought.

The three educational functions are here defined:

- *Continuing Education:* the transmission of information and knowledge through classes, workshops, conferences, institutes, and similar activities. This may take the form of formally organized credit or noncredit courses or meetings or informally structured learning. Continuing education should contribute to the knowledge and understanding of people and assist them in fulfilling their individual or group goals. It is assumed that information and knowledge is presently available to do this.

- *Service:* the application of skills, expertise, and knowledge as a method of problem-solving. This may take the form of consulting and technical assistance, or directly carrying out a task to meet a need. Service implies the actual involvement of the community developer in some way in carrying out a problem-solving activity, usually working with persons in the community and/or power structure. This contrasts with continuing education, which has the primary function of teaching others.
- *Experimentation:* the designing of possible solutions to a community problem for which there is presently no adequate knowledge and/or experience on how to best solve the problem. The conceptual design of the community development project represents a new model for solving the problem. The community developer takes an applied research approach in formulating this model and plays a participant-observer role in implementing and evaluating a trial program. The experimental solution that has been shown to be successful (or sometimes unsuccessful) can then be moved from the experimental to demonstration stage, where the model is demonstrated and applied on a broader basis. Finally, the knowledge that has been generated can be used in carrying out continuing education and service functions.

The three types of change toward which university-related community development projects aim are here defined:

- *Individual Type:* change that impacts upon individuals to bring about benefits that in some way may contribute to improve their lives. The focus is upon direct delivery to individuals, which in turn is related to improving community well-being.
- *Agency/organizational Type:* change that increases the effectiveness of agencies or organizations, private or public. Community development activity can assist agencies in developing the capability to assess needs, set goals, develop human resources, mobilize material and political support, and design, implement, and evaluate programs. Presumably the agencies in turn will contribute to the well-being of individuals in the community.
- *Policy Type:* change that influences a body of government or other entities that have significant power in the resource allocation process to either improve the delivery of services or to provide new services. Presumably such policy changes in turn will contribute to the well-being of individuals in the community.

The typology may be visualized as a nine-cell matrix. This can be used to identify and clarify the major thrust of a community development project by placing the project in one of the nine cells. The cell or location in the typology shows what overall educational function is being performed by a university-related project for the purpose of achieving whatever type of change.

The process of identifying the appropriate cell for a project may be difficult, because the distinction among the three educational functions is not always clear. A particular community development project may appear to perform more than one function. Likewise, a particular project may have an impact that brings about more than one type of change. This difficulty can be surmounted by distinguishing between the *primary thrust* of a community development project and its *supporting thrusts*. The primary thrust is identified by stating the long-term goal(s) of the project—that is, its essential significance, what it is really trying to accomplish. The agent does this by selecting the single educational function and the single type of change that best characterize the overall emphasis of the project in view of its long-term goal.

While the typology displays the primary and supporting educational thrusts of a university-related community development project, an incremental perspective views the project as a sequence of activities that flow from one to the next through time. This process can be described in a framework that reflects the incremental movement of successive phases of activities and events aimed at meeting certain immediate strategic objectives that are related pragmatically to achieving long-term goals.

The key terms of the incremental process are defined as follows:

- *Seed Activities* are those preliminary meetings and discussions that take place between the community developer and community people on the one hand, and influential persons having access to political and economic power as well as to the technical knowledge, information, and skills necessary for decision-making on the other hand. These seed activities act as catalysts. Some seeds never grow.

- *Community Development Activities* are the inputs of time and energy required to generate the involvement of community people and influential personas in planning, organizing, and implementing events. Many of these activities lack structure, but they may require enormous amounts of time and often a high level of skill.

- *Community Development Events* are structured activities that occur in an identifiable time frame and are designed to create one or a number of strategic objectives. An event may be a brief occurrence representing only a moment in time, such as the submission of a proposal, the creation of a policy committee, or the establishment of a community organization. An event may also be an ongoing process lasting for days, weeks, and months. The important characteristic is that it fulfills a strategic objective.

- *Strategic Objectives* are the results that are expected to accrue from the community development events. Achieving these objectives represents concrete steps toward realizing the long-term goals. They should represent sufficiently tangible achievements so that community people and influential persons can accept them as "landmarks" for meaningful progress.

- *Long-term Community Development Goals* are statements of purpose aimed at improving certain aspects of the quality of life in the community. While they are long term, they should be feasible. Their achievement will depend upon the degree to which their strategic objectives are fulfilled. The long-term goals are also used in defining the primary thrust of the community development project.

> **What are we really trying to accomplish? How are we going to do it?**

- *Phases* of the community development process mark the evolving nature of the work. Phase I encompasses the seed activities, which set the stage, enlist the commitment of participants, and determine the early direction of the process. Phase II encompasses a sequence of activities, events, and objectives within a given time period. Phase III and subsequent phases have the same sequence of activities, events, and objectives. As the process evolves with one phase leading to the next, new directions may be charted out, and the long-term goals will be refined or even redefined until they are achieved or until the project terminates.

- *Unanticipated Events and Results* are happenings that occur during the community development process that are not planned but nevertheless have a significant impact. An unanticipated event normally occurs as a failure of a planned event to achieve its objective. The result may lead to "backtracking" to try again, or to planning alternative strategic objectives, or to a fundamental rethinking about where the project is going.

The process of diagramming a project can in itself be an important community development activity. The exercise forces people who are so engrossed in the particulars of their projects to take the time and answer the questions systematically: What are we really trying to accomplish? How are we going to do it? This situation gives everyone the opportunity to begin examining the "latent strategy" that they have been using, although not adequately articulating, and to decide whether the formulation of a more "objective strategy" is needed.

THE MILWAUKEE JOURNAL

INSIGHT

Sunday June 19, 1977

Block power

Getting it together, Harambee style . . . .

Harambee — Swahili for "pulling together." Which is what neighbors in a 170 block area on Milwaukee's North Side have been doing with the help of Harambee's Ombudsman Project. It's a small operation, to be sure, with meager funding, but it seems to work.

Block Power

Excerpts from the Sunday Milwaukee Journal, *June 19, 1977 by Don Olesen*

This article was not written by me, but lends a personal touch to a project I was heavily involved with. Harambee's block work, known as the Harambee Ombudsman Project, became quite famous. It evolved a strategy for using education and block-level organization in winning political support to improve local conditions. It was a classic example of maximizing results at minimum cost, because both the community and politicians found participation to be in their interest.

Harambee is Swahili for "pulling together." Which is what neighbors in a 170-block area on Milwaukee's North Side have been doing with the help of Harambee's Ombudsman Project. It's a small operation, to be sure, with meager funding, but it seems to work.

Jesse Jones is part of Harambee's outreach arm. She goes door-to-door bearing questionnaires, an open mind and a warm heart. She and Elizabeth People, the other interviewer, are not Lady Bountifuls from another culture; they *live* among the people they visit. They try to identify their neighbors' problems and pass along these muddles to Harambee's two ombudsmen for solution.

Mrs. Jones and Mrs. People also pick leaders in the blocks they visit—stable residents who command respect. Harambee now has more than 100 block leaders. They often relay problems directly to the ombudsmen, using the Harambee "hotline" telephone. And the two ombudsmen plunge into the thicket of public and private social agencies to try to solve these problems.

Jessie Jones is a warm, attractive, energetic woman who could charm the rattles off a rattlesnake. She is smartly gotten up today in a black knit suit and leatherette coat. She carries a briefcase full of her Harambee questionnaires and literature, plus a purse large enough to hold a complete set of the Encyclopedia Britannica.

In almost five hours one day Jessie calls at 26 different homes. She knows this neighborhood; she lives only three blocks away. 15 years ago, it was an area of "stately homes," she says. Today the houses in this block range from immaculate to disastrous with all gradations in between. Some residents own their homes; more are renters. Several places are boarded up—vacant, with raw plywood covering doors and windows.

"You know," Jessie says, "with all the places boarded up and all the people needing a place to live, it would be better for the landlord to let somebody stay there without rent. At least that keeps the vandals out and protects his property."

One house has broken windows on both stories. You can see the cardboard tacked over the gaps, flapping in the wind. Jessie has been inside. A woman lives there with seven kids, she says. The rent is $140 a month. The interior is disaster; cracked and fallen plaster everywhere. The kids eat the plaster.

Across the street is another calamity. On the porch is a shattered full-length mirror flanked by a soggy mattress oozing ticking. The porch deck sags; the roof above is rotted and leaking.

A woman answers Jessie's knock. She lives here with her two children, both nicely dressed and polite. The living room is tidy; the furniture old and battered. The rent is $140. "If your landlord don't do more than he has done, you call Mrs. Cobbs on the hot line," Jessie says, handing over a leaflet with the number. "A house is just like a body—if you don't keep it up, it goes down."

Mrs. Agnes Cobbs is the ombudsman coordinator. The other ombudsman is Todd Honeyager, who deals with the social agencies.

Jessie gives her spiel at another door. "I'm from Harambee," she says, "that means 'pulling together.' Let's pull together to keep this area together—keep it from getting blighted."

This ombudsman approach to community uplift got its start, oddly enough, in a classroom. First came the Harambee Community School, begun when the old parish school closed in 1969. One day, the Harambee leaders sat down with Belden Paulson, a professor of political science at the University of Wisconsin-Milwaukee. Leaders hoped to develop a little political awareness and clout in the community.

What emerged in 1974 was a special course for community people, taught by Paulson and held at the Martin Luther King Library. By careful design, Paulson's co-instructor was Ben Johnson, alderman of the Sixth District, which embraces the area. Johnson now is president of Milwaukee's Common Council.

County Supervisor Emil Stanislawski, whose District 13 also includes the Harambee area, appeared for several sessions. Rep. Henry Reuss (D.Wis.), the area's congressman, attended one class and talked up the ombudsman approach, which he had studied in Scandinavia.

Before long, students were out of the classroom and into the community, going door-to-door, trying to pinpoint the things that *really* bothered people. This was not always easy.

A case in point: Residents in the vicinity of Fulton Junior High complained of "crime" in their neighborhood. Students brought 20 residents back to the classroom, sat down with them and talked it over. What really troubled the Fulton area people, it developed, was the tall grass on a hilly vacant lot known locally as "Goat Hill." Kids hid in the grass of the city-owned lot and harassed passersby. The grass also screened all manner of illicit activities, both real and imagined.

The solution to "crime" was obvious—cut the grass. Alderman-Instructor Johnson was present, so they put it to him. Johnson had to call half a dozen different city agencies before he found the right one. The grass was cut.

Out of the classroom came the Harambee Ombudsman Project. One of the students in that inquisitive 1974 class was Agnes Cobbs, herself a resident of "Harambeeland" and now the ombudsman coordinator.

The project grew, taking in more and more territory. Today it covers an area of 170 blocks, embracing 32,000 people. About 75 percent are black.

Harambee has more than goodness to dole out. For block leaders and their neighbors, there also are modest "goodies," a term frequently used by Ms. Cobbs, Honeyager and Prof. Paulson.

> **Harambee has more than goodness to dole out.**

Examples

There were 40 openings in the Department of Natural Resources' summer youth camp program this year, with pay at $2.30 an hour. DNR wanted more black kids in the program and asked Harambee to help. Agnes Cobbs passed the request along to her block leaders, who recruited the campers. Block leaders like having favors to distribute. The kids love it. Their parents are grateful. So is the DNR. Everybody's happy.

Harambee also gets to fill 10 jobs in the summer work program of the Community Relations-Social Development Commission—cleaning up neighborhoods, maintaining community centers, painting homes.

If the school system needs teacher aides, if a private firm needs workers, the request often is funneled through the ombudsmen. They keep a list of jobless and deserving residents, often recommended by block leaders.

There are "goodies" for the block leaders, too. Last November they toured City Hall and met their alderman. In March they visited the County Building and met their supervisor. In May, they visited Madison and called on Rep. Marcia Coggs, their state representative and resident of Harambeeland.

Block leaders also get 8 by 11-inch signs reading "Harambee Block Leader" to post at their homes. They proudly display wallet-sized cards, sealed in plastic reading, "Harambee Ombudsman Project—Block Leader," signed by Ald. Johnson and Supervisor Stanislawski.

In the old days city political wards once offered similar rewards to the faithful—jobs, status, help with personal problems. In a sense the ombudsman project fills this gap.

All of this has the earmarks of an incipient (and possibly rampant) grassroots political organization. You'd expect the politicians to be intimidated. Indeed, the opposite seems to be true. From its beginnings in Prof. Paulson's classroom, Harambee has consulted with and cooperated with Inner City political leaders. Their names are prominently displayed on Harambee literature. In turn, the leaders seem delighted with Harambee. They help it; it helps them.

The project has developed "a very strong and very healthy interest in politics," Johnson said. It has helped register Inner City voters. He feels that new political leaders may be emerging from the ranks of block leaders.

Cutting Through the Maze

Harambee is *unusual* because it starts from the bottom and works up. It goes where people are to find out what troubles them. It hands out its "hot line" number to call. It sets up an ongoing block leader organization to keep the blocks and ombudsmen in touch with each other.

Harambee is a middleman in the vast, confusing sprawl of Milwaukee social agencies, private and public. It cuts through the agency jungle and does its damnedest to help those in need get the help they need.

Todd Honeyager, the "agency" ombudsman, usually knows which buttons to push at City Hall, the County Building, Madison or even in Washington when he needs to solve somebody's problems.

But the most *exciting* thing about Harambee's Ombudsman Project is the block organization—those

In the old days city political wards once offered similar rewards to the faithful—jobs, status, help with personal problems. In a sense the ombudsman project fills this gap.

100 or so solid citizens who serve as eyes, ears and voices…down at the grassroots. If the project endures and builds, block leaders may help bring new clout and political awareness to the Inner City.

Neighborhood Pillars

They call her "The Top Sergeant." Not to her face; then it is "Mrs. McGrew." Ethel McGrew has been a Harambee block leader for more than two years. She is a feisty, warm, square-jawed, firm-voiced lady with short graying hair. She is 75 but looks at least a decade younger. The McGrews have a tidy, comfortable, nicely furnished home. When she and her husband, Bennie, moved here 26 years ago, she said, "We were the only colored in this neighborhood."

The Harambee Project tends to pick stable, long-time residents like Ethel. They help to "anchor" the neighborhood.

This block, like many in the ombudsman project, has an annual block party. ("Last summer I told them, 'No beer—nothing to drink!' They know I mean something when I mean it!")

Neighbors also hold an annual block cleanup drive in which they pick up and rake trash. (The cleanup is carefully orchestrated with City Hall; sanitation trucks and crews follow to collect the debris. A mechanical street sweeper may follow. A rodent control crew moves through, looking for rat burrows. None of this is accidental; for their efforts, block residents are getting *visible* results from the bureaucracy.)

Block people look after their own. When a neighbor dies, residents take up a collection for the survivors.

Neighbors sometimes call Ethel McGrew in the middle of the night with their troubles. "I tell them my phone's right by my bed and I don't mind being called at any hour. One woman she just told me to my teeth, 'I wouldn't take your job for nothing in the world.' But I just naturally know how to approach people. My life is going. Younger people are coming along. I want to do something for somebody else."

THE ROLE OF CITIZEN ELITES IN EFFECTING MORE RESPONSIVE BUREAUCRACIES
(A Hardheaded Perspective on Community Development)
Belden Paulson
and
Daniel Folkman

The Role of Citizen Elites in Effecting More Responsive Bureaucracies:

A Hardheaded Perspective on Community Development

Taken from Urban Community Development: Case Studies in Neighborhood Survival
Published by the National Community Development Society
Co-authored with Daniel Folkman

One of the Harambee Project's most complex interventions was to improve human services—a maze of bureaucratic agencies. Here is a case study. I was the CUCD member referred to, and eventually was appointed to serve on the county steering committee as one of two university representatives.

Perhaps nothing is more strongly emphasized in community development literature than the necessity for broadly based popular participation—to be as inclusive as possible in involving people.

To the skeptic, the difficulty with the theory is that it does not necessarily conform to the real world. In particular, it simplifies the extraordinarily complex milieu in which people who live in big cities find themselves, characterized by the bureaucratic machinery that dominates the urban scene. This machinery is virtually unmanageable by the bureaucrats themselves, and unaccountable to the citizens whose needs are supposedly being served and whose taxes are footing the bill.

Worse still, as the trend for more bureaucracy continues, the average citizen is losing the capacity to understand the overall system in which he lives, and is withdrawing from participation in community decision-making. As a result, the citizen is losing access to public policy-makers, while most of the public's business is being conducted by elites: appointed officials, planners, experts, corporate leaders, and the like.

Involving citizens in welfare or human services reform is an excellent case in point. The bureaucracies are so specialized and fragmented that the average citizen is baffled by the whole collection of agencies that make up the human services network. There are simply too many separate agencies and officials, with overlapping responsibilities and jurisdictions, to comprehend who is responsible for what happens and to determine what actions are needed to bring desired changes.

> **Making bureaucracies more responsive, accessible, and accountable to people is one of the most challenging problems facing our political system.**

Reform-minded citizens see the quality of service delivery as appalling in human and cost-benefit terms and are angered by the lack of direct public control over specific agencies. They are frustrated about knowing how to begin solving the problems. It is doubtful that many are prepared to invest the time and energy needed for involvement given the dubious expectation of results. This reluctance is accentuated in low-income communities, which are most familiar with this problem but have been traditionally powerless and apathetic. The effect is to leave unchecked power in the bureaucracies themselves.

Making bureaucracies more responsive, accessible, and accountable to people is one of the most challenging problems facing our political system. It is an immediate problem facing inner city neighborhoods.

The Harambee Human Services Case Study

Problem: Presently, numerous public, quasi-public, not-for-profit and proprietary agencies are delivering human services in Milwaukee County, and substantial amounts of public and private funds are invested in the county in a highly categorical and fragmented manner with no effective means of determining whether such programs and funds are meeting the needs of the citizens.

Mission and Goals: The mission of the Milwaukee County Human Services Project is to plan and design an improved community human services delivery system for the citizens of Milwaukee County, which optimally meets citizen needs and maximizes independence of consumers.

Recommendation 45: The Milwaukee County Board of Supervisors should direct the Director of Institutions and Departments to assist the Harambee Human Services Project with obtaining of Federal and State funds to pilot-test certain delivery aspects within the Harambee area. In addition, Milwaukee County Human Services programs should be requested to cooperate with the Harambee Human Services Project in the pilot delivery of coordinated services.

These statements are taken from the final document of the Milwaukee County Human Services Project. This report is the culmination of a long process that could conceivably lead to some reforms in the human services field in Milwaukee County. The project's recommendations have been submitted to the Milwaukee Board of County Supervisors and the Wisconsin Department of Health and Social Services.

The story behind the development of this model is just now being completed after five years of effort.

It has important implications for the theory and practice of community development in seeking change in complex bureaucratic systems.

In the spring of 1973, "A Discussion Paper on Community Service Centers for Wisconsin" was circulated by the Wisconsin Department of Health and Social Services (HSS). One of the readers was a member of the Center for Urban Community Development (CUCD). He discussed the paper in detail with a colleague, and then brought it to the attention of a nonprofit community development corporation in Milwaukee's inner city that CUCD had helped to organize.

In 1973, HRP (Harambee Revitalization Project) was completing a comprehensive blueprint for neighborhood revitalization. One major part of this blueprint focused on the delivery of health and social services to local residents. Without delay, two CUCD members and the HRP project prepared a detailed statement titled "Draft Proposal for Creation of a Viable Community Service Center for the Delivery of Social Services in an Inner City Neighborhood of Milwaukee." This statement laid out a number of innovative ideas for addressing human service deficiencies in low-income urban neighborhoods such as Harambee and was submitted to the Bureau of Planning and Analysis of the Department of Health and Social Services.

The upshot was that the county supervisor representing the Harambee area would try to have the County Board formally request that the Department of Health and Social Services accept Milwaukee's participation as one of three pilot sites in Wisconsin and to designate the Harambee community as the test area.

In January 1975, the County Board passed this resolution:

- Be it resolved, that the Milwaukee County Board of Supervisors, recognizing the need for better coordinated and integrated human services, hereby authorizes the Director of the Department of Public Welfare to prepare and submit to the State Department of Health and Social Services an application requesting that Milwaukee County be included as a pilot program in the Community Human Services Project; and

- Be it further resolved, that the Harambee area be designated in Milwaukee County's application as the geographic area in which this pilot program would be initiated.

It was soon apparent that the Harambee initiative had taken the human services bureaucracies somewhat by surprise. The thrust of a newly formed "Administrative

Study Group" was to re-focus the county pilot project from the Harambee neighbor-hood to moving countywide. Its resolution:

Whereas the Harambee neighborhood has been designated the geographic area for a pilot project under the Wisconsin Department of Health and Social Services Community Human Services program by the Milwaukee County Board, there is a need for interfacing and relating such local sites to the broad county-wide issues of services integration; in addition to the existing pilot project committee, there is a need for a county-wide coalition.

> ## Harambee had taken the original initiative in getting Milwaukee involved in the pilot project, and because of its close ties to the county supervisor had pushed the resolution through the County Board.

Harambee had taken the original initiative in getting Milwaukee involved in the pilot program, and because of its close ties to the county supervisor had pushed the resolution through the Country Board.

Milwaukee County entered into an agreement with the Wisconsin Department of Health and Social Services to establish a 17-member steering committee for:

- Increasing responsiveness of human service agencies and programs . . .
- Increasing accessibility and use of the services needed . . .

The agreement had one important concession for Harambee:

> A specific component of the Planning/Design stage will focus on the Harambee community....This component will focus on the specific problems and needs of that community and develop recommendations and designs for achieving the above-specified goals within the Harambee community. The Harambee community is expected to offer a useful testing ground and reference point against which proposed county-wide policies and mechanisms can be tested.

It did not take long for a Pilot Site Subcommittee to become embroiled in four issues:

- Why was Harambee identified as the only pilot site area and not some other communities in Milwaukee County?
- How should human services be defined? Should the definition be broad enough to include issues of economic development, unemployment, housing, education, etc.?
- What is the relationship between the Pilot Site Subcommittee and the Technical Base Subcommittee that had just hired an out-of-state consultant?
- What should be the proper role of citizen participation in the test community?

Where did all this discussion lead? There was no unanimity as to how to proceed. Within the Harambee community itself, almost everyone had long since lost interest in the human services program. The general belief was that the bureaucrats had taken over.

Now the CUCD member and the two Harambee residents decided to prepare a detailed Harambee plan for action to be submitted to the whole Steering Committee. A coalition would design a neighborhood-based human services model for testing in Harambee, and $20,000 should be allocated for planning. The plan was approved, including the $20,000 allocation.

The CUCD member and the two Harambee residents met on their own to prepare a more operational proposal titled "Suggested Steps for Action on Harambee Community Proposal." This proposal specified the creation of a Harambee Human Services Task Force that would be responsible for developing the Harambee model. The Task Force would have 10 Harambee residents, three elected officials (the supervisor, alderman and state representative), four service providers (including the three major service providers represented on the Steering Committee), and two representatives from the university (the Steering Committee chairperson and the CUCD member.)

The Steering Committee approved the strategy. Its main fear was that Harambee would become an entity unto itself. Harambee, after all, had the advantage of a clearly delimited population and goal, in contrast to the continuing vagueness of the overall county project. It had its own constituency and assured political support from its elected officials.

One final hurdle remained: Who would administer the $20,000? The Harambee work plan called for a project coordinator, two assistants, two outreach workers, four university students, and a university technical consultant—all part time. There would also be a community office and the enlistment of up to 120 neighborhood people who would be compensated for their time as consultants. Because Harambee's nonprofit corporation was not in a position to contract with the county for this effort, and endless delays were anticipated if the county itself administered the $20,000, the CUCD member offered the services of the University of Wisconsin-Extension for administering the funds at no cost to the county. Operations began in late March 1977, for a period of seven months.

The process of designing the Harambee model can be described quickly. The first phase had four components: (a) developing a community needs profile through interviews with residents; (b) assembling an inventory of services available in the area; (c) compiling census data on the area that would be essential for planning human services; and (d) reviewing the literature and comparative experiences. The literature review included over 154 separate projects, which represents one of the most complete compilations of experiences relevant to the designing of a decentralized human service system.

The second phase was model-building: utilizing all the data to formulate a testable plan.

The Harambee model was submitted, but this was largely a formality. Now the atmosphere was strikingly cordial and decisive. It was generally recognized that the Harambee effort was the only dimension of the total county project that had developed significant community involvement and dealt with human needs and services "on the front line," as distinct from dealing with administrative structure and planning models.

After making several final suggestions that strengthened the model, the subcommittee delivered the Harambee report to the County Steering Committee. Here, too, the report was received with relatively little discussion, for by the time the Steering Committee was fighting a deadline to complete its work by the end of 1977, the overall County Human Services Project report was being prepared for submission to the County Board and the state government. After public hearings and final modifications, its recommendations would run the legislative gauntlet.

> "Harambee had influence not only on what will happen in its own pilot area. It influenced the whole Project in more ways than you think."

The final recommendations by the Steering Committee contained a heavy emphasis on reorganizing county government. The fundamental premise was that administrative reorganization would improve the delivery of human services. Other than the Harambee Task Force efforts, however, there was no attempt to assess actual needs in the Milwaukee community, nor to look at actual services.

Nevertheless, sprinkled throughout the final recommendations are references to the Harambee neighborhood and to ideas and recommendations laid out in the Harambee Task Force Report. Recommendation 45 stated that the proposed system should be tested in the Harambee area and special monies should be obtained for this purpose. A well-informed observer of the Project concluded: "Harambee had influence not only on what will happen in its own pilot area. It influenced the whole Project in more ways than you think."

Conclusions

What does this case study tell us about the role of ordinary citizens in changing a complex bureaucratic system? Bureaucratic change is essentially a political process: select elites are the primary actors in this process; the community development agent, along with key community representatives, have to perform within this elite setting—as either appointed or self-declared community representatives.

- Bureaucratic change means *political* change, because any reform will affect the allocation of scarce resources, which is what the political process is all about.

The Harambee actors in the Milwaukee County Human Services Project were acutely aware of this politicized change process. From the beginning, every effort was made to maximize Harambee's political strength as a strategy to assure its inclusion in the county's human services planning agenda.

This included investment of substantial time and developing an understanding of the complexities of the issues at stake.

- Only a few citizens are likely to become effective change agents vis-à-vis powerful bureaucracies like those in the human services network. This suggests that major initiatives for reform will either come from within the system itself, or from within broader orbits of government, or from small clusters of citizens with exceptional characteristics.

The initiative to locate one of Wisconsin's pilot projects in Milwaukee, and in particular in a low-income Milwaukee neighborhood, came from two university faculty (CUCD), two members of a community organization (HRP), and one official of the Department of Health and Social Services located in Milwaukee and working with the community organization. This group cooperated closely with the county supervisor, who took leadership in passing the first County Board resolution in January 1975. This small group also organized a community seminar on the politics of human services delivery that was offered through the University of Wisconsin-Milwaukee and involved some 25 residents. From this class came the two Harambee residents who later served on the Milwaukee County Project Steering Committee.

The Harambee person who was elected as state representative from the area and was appointed to a key legislative committee, found that her legislative positions made her role as vice-chairperson of the County Steering Committee of uncommon importance.

The above small number of individuals could be characterized as a "community elite." The influence Harambee generated in the County Human Services Project was not the result of any broadly based citizen participation. The outcome was produced by a very small group of individuals through slow, meticulous work over several years. The core of this group invested much time and energy and displayed considerable sophistication in the process of trying to improve human services delivery.

Transcending Symptoms to Community Fundamentals

Bel and Reuben

Rueben Harpole

The New Community as an Application of Community Health

Authored with Reuben Harpole

Prepared for presentation at the Annual Meeting of the Adult Education Association of the USA, Atlanta, Georgia, October 1970

A Time for Questioning

Those of us educators and community developers interested in the needs of low-income urban populations should have great concern in responding effectively to such basic questions as the following:

- In identifying the problems that serve as the framework for our policies and programs, have we been dealing mainly with symptoms *or* with fundamental problems?
- Have we tended to define "problems" as single variable and failed to interrelate the one or two factors or variables of our immediate interest to the system of which they are a part?
- As a result, have we become so wedded to projects—sometimes very good ones in themselves—that we neglect comprehensive planning, which necessitates the integration of individualized projects?
- In a society that emphasizes speed, and as programmers living in the shadow of constantly changing governmental policies and resource availabilities, have we come to program in terms of quick results and to analyze problems as if cause and effect are closely related in time?
- Have our program evaluation efforts involved us in investing more and more resources to measure results having less and less significance?

- Have our goals become a function of programming capacity and available technology, instead of being a function of goals that need to be achieved and our technology being designed as the means to achieve those goals?

These could prove hard questions, even for people who are noted for diagnosing and resolving community ills. They could be addressed equally to universities, government officials, businessmen, church leaders—anyone who has accepted responsibility for upgrading the quality of life in our communities.

Those of us working in the context of Milwaukee's central city have begun applying this type of questioning to our own activities. Despite a number of years of vigorous work, we have become ever more aware of the limited impact of our efforts and other initiatives with which we are familiar. A couple years ago a PhD candidate at Marquette University made a survey of the agencies "serving Milwaukee's central city," and he identified at least 500 entities. Yet one must stretch his imagination, or "play with the facts," to find major significant impacts resulting from these initiatives.

We are proud of our achievements, gratified to know that people have benefited in some way from concrete efforts. As we thumb through clippings and reports dealing with particular projects in which we played a role, we may have some regrets as Monday morning quarterbacks, but we are convinced that, by and large, our commitment was well made and our small resources well invested. We do not, therefore, feel particularly threatened.

Nevertheless, we have become increasingly conscious that the fundamental weakness of most efforts is an overly simplistic analysis of the needs that the programs are designed to confront. The problems of the city are rarely isolated difficulties but are composites of many causes. There are whole systems of problems. For example, what could appear to be a "reading problem" facing central city school-age youth may in fact involve a whole package of factors, including the following:

The school system—The ability and training of teachers and administrators to reach the child, relevance of the school curricula to the child's background and interests, school-community relations, school board policy;

Home environment—Parental interest in education, presence of one or more parents at home to supervise the child, including his studying; physical health of family members, including nutrition level;

Economic system—The degree of necessity for the child to work at an early age; the opportunity to buy books and reading matter, not to mention clothes and other necessities;

Housing—Condition of the home in terms of space, sanitation, heating, and study area without distraction;

Political system and the efficiency and responsiveness of government—Family's acceptance of the legitimacy of authority (including the schools); participation in the political system, including selection of public officials such as school board members.

This is the background behind our desire to work toward developing a concept of the total health of the community.

Designing a Community Health Model

Taken from Odyssey of a Practical Visionary, *2009*

From the first days of our work with Harambee, and now with new communities, our overall objective was to create healthy communities. Since that vague, indefinable goal surfaced in countless conversations and at my university department, one of our fun pursuits was doodling at the blackboard with whatever far-out idea someone came up with.

One afternoon my experiences with the Sardinia project entered the conversation. I referred to our *Piano di Massimo*, the requirement imposed by the economic development agencies of the Italian government that stipulated that in order to receive funding for building houses, irrigating the land, and bringing in electricity, we had to prepare a Master Plan. It had to describe how each of these specific projects fit into the overall goal of creating a viable refugee community.

Maybe now, as we focused on new urban communities, we should conceptualize a *Piano di Massimo* for community health. What would a healthy community look like—the essential factors that we called variables? For operational simplicity, we thought of four essential variables: economic health, educational health, environmental health, and political health. What if we were to recruit the most knowledgeable and creative minds we could find in the university to work with us to figure out what each of those meant in describing a healthy community?

And so was born one of the more intellectually stimulating projects I worked on in my years at the university. We've already referred to the social ferment in America at this time, the late 1960s and early 1970s: the assassinations, the war in Vietnam, the War on Poverty. It seemed that the one popular success story was the US space program, which demonstrated our ability to master the complex undertaking of landing a man on the moon. Now people were asking: why can't we use such rigorous methods to achieve other goals? MIT Professor

Jay Forrester's book *Urban Dynamics* used systems analysis to think about an urban area—its system of interacting industries, housing, and people. Unless there is the right mix, stagnation and deterioration will result.

Along with fleshing out the variables to determine what makes for a healthy community, we'd also need to develop yardsticks to measure progress. These social indicators would provide a conceptual framework for telling us how well we're doing—if the community is moving in the right direction. For example, in physical health, we can measure one's body temperature, blood pressure, heart rate, and so on. In the social context, we'd identify community needs or problems by measuring levels of unemployment, illiteracy, school dropouts, political participation, dirty air and water, and so on. Obviously equating different levels of measurement to health is a delicate process. For physical health, the World Health Organization and the medical profession play critical roles; in the social arena, we define poverty, quality education, and so on. These expectations become goals for how we define a healthy community, be they established by officials or citizens at large.

Since now our task was to form a team to develop this analytical framework, I contacted faculty members we thought to be among the more intellectually able to represent their respective fields in this exploration. Even though compensation would be minimal, I was delighted with their eagerness to participate. Martin Haberman, on Education Health from the School of Education, was a radical thinker challenging traditional education. Bob Beckley, on Environmental Health, was one of the founders of the UWM School of Architecture and had been involved in inner city planning projects. Gary Gappert, on Economic Health, was an economist in the new UWM urban affairs department, with futurist visions for metropolitan areas. Neil Reimer, on Political Health and a colleague in the Department of Political Science, had already done work on the health of societies. I also involved Mark Tessler from the Department, whose specialty was social and ideological diversity, and then Dan Folkman from my department, interested in community political analysis. Later Jonathan Slesinger also joined us from Sociology, a student of policy analysis and complex social systems and expert in survey research. I got all team members to share their first musings in my Urban Politics seminar.

My University Extension Dean, Glen Pulver, indicated great interest in the project, concluding that it might provide what he felt was the missing component for Harambee, a

> The US space program . . . demonstrated our ability to master the complex undertaking of landing a man on the moon. Now people were asking: why can't we use such rigorous methods to achieve other goals?

clearly stated goal for all of this effort: to build healthy new communities. He was happy to provide the small funding I requested to pay consulting fees to the team members. We presented the initial ideas to leaders in Wisconsin's state government, which led to a proposal Pulver submitted to the governor asking for money to use the community health model to serve the state.

Acting Chancellor George Strother also saw "great potential . . . I am wondering if there are any ways in which we can do more in the chancellor's office to strengthen your efforts—assistance with drafting of proposals, contacts with agencies, letters of support . . . I see this as an area in which we have an opportunity to make a significant breakthrough."

Our team members quickly put together their own small groups to carry out the work. People in the Harambee community began using the community health framework, and the affluent Milwaukee suburb of Whitefish Bay had a prominent Episcopal church that wanted to look at its own health. We led an eight-week seminar at the church that generated a huge amount of creative energy in the North Shore parishes.

By chance, I met a member of the National Institute of Mental Health (NIMH), who was in Milwaukee. He urged us to seek financing with the NIMH section dealing with Metropolitan Mental Health Problems. Our team agreed that if we received a sizable grant, each of us would commit one-third of our time for two years to fully develop this project. We banged our heads together to prepare a proposal with references to the cutting-edge literature. To assure NIMH that this was not an ivory tower research exercise, we linked the project to four diverse settings in the Milwaukee metropolitan area as community labs: Harambee, inner city; Whitefish Bay, suburb; the Riverside interracial school district; and a new town site out of the city being planned from scratch.

Our whole team, including representatives of the four community labs, met with university officials for a trial run. The purpose would be to prepare for the five eminent national scholars from NIMH when they visited Milwaukee to review our proposal. Several UWM administrators were so excited they said they'd be surprised if we did not get funded. Our team also offered a seminar that had our whole group of professors, community lab representatives, and interested graduate students from several departments participating. We concluded that this kind of seminar was an ideal format for real learning: intellectual explorations, literature across disciplines, practical applications for problem-solving, minimal attention to the usual routine of tests and grades.

We also learned that the US Department of Agriculture was awarding us a small, two-year grant for Development of Indicators of Community Health. The big question: where would this whole endeavor end up?

Although the model was used in various community settings and generated widespread professional interest, it was not funded by the federal government.

Promoting a Healthy Community

1973

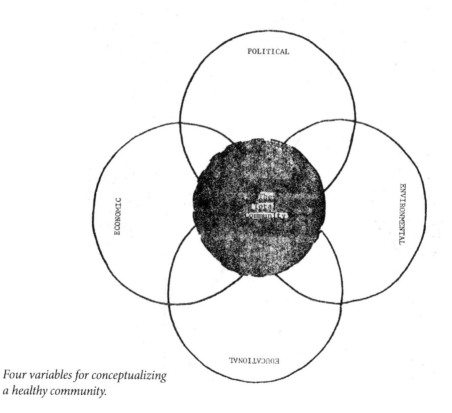

THE TOTAL HEALTH Of The COMMUNITY

POLITICAL

ENVIRONMENTAL

ECONOMIC

The Total Community

EDUCATIONAL

*Four variables for conceptualizing
a healthy community.*

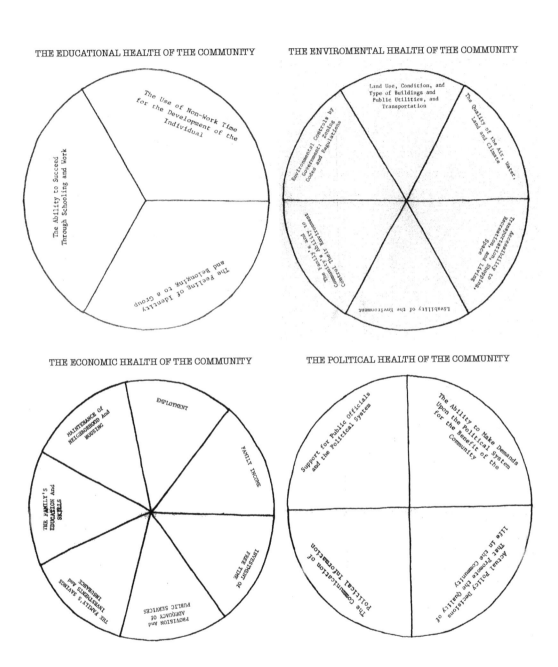

THE EDUCATIONAL HEALTH OF THE COMMUNITY

The Use of Non-Work Time for the Development of the Individual

The Ability to Succeed Through Schooling and Work

The Feeling of Identity and Belonging to a Group

THE ENVIROMENTAL HEALTH OF THE COMMUNITY

Land Use, Condition, and Type of Buildings and Public Utilities, and Transportation

Environmental Controls by Government: Zoning Codes and Regulations

The Quality of the Air, Water, Land and Climate

Transportation and Accessibility to Space

Accessibility to Transportation and Layout of Space

The Family's Ability to Control Their Environment

Livability of the Environment

THE ECONOMIC HEALTH OF THE COMMUNITY

EMPLOYMENT

MAINTENANCE of NEIGHBORHOOD And HOUSING

FAMILY INCOME

THE FAMILY'S EDUCATION And SKILLS

INVESTMENT OF FREE TIME

THE FAMILY'S SAVINGS INVESTMENTS And INSURANCE

PROVISION And ADEQUACY OF PUBLIC SERVICES

THE POLITICAL HEALTH OF THE COMMUNITY

The Ability to Make Demands Upon the Political System for the Benefit of the Community

Support for Public Officials and the Political System

Life in the Community

Actual Policy Decisions That Promote the Quality of

The Communication of Political Information

Major components developed by task groups for defining the essential elements of the educational health of a community, environmental health, economic health, and political health.

Coping with School Desegregation

After Federal Judge John Reynolds decided in January 1976 that the entire Milwaukee Public School System was unconstitutionally segregated, John Gronouski was appointed as Special Master to develop a desegregation plan. There was a period of turmoil in Milwaukee and strong resistance to the order. We became involved in building citizen coalitions to prevent violence, and I spoke with groups around the city to discuss the complex issues that went beyond education.

These first papers were presentations that discuss the metropolitan context of school integration

The Process of Urban Development, Its Impact on Public Education, and Some Implications for City-Suburb Interdependence

Presented at The City-Suburban Connection, UWM, 1975

People continually talk about urban sprawl and the lack of any planning in urban development in our country. In certain respects, this is quite untrue, because there is a definite logic and much predictability as we chart the course of urban development in the United States and Milwaukee.

New development takes place mainly on vacant land around the fringe of the city because there is both space for growth of population and because the cost of land is much lower than in the older, built-up areas while the rate of return on investment in new buildings is higher. This leads to the "trickle-down process" whereby higher income families tend to move away from older, deteriorating neighborhoods, located usually in the center of the original city, later known as the inner city. Lower income families gravitate toward the deteriorating area because the housing and accompanying facilities have lower cost. Thus, what was once a new and fashionable neighborhood gradually sees its occupants move away. These facilities trickle down to successive occupants.

As long as the new occupants have income adequate to maintain the property, the neighborhood will remain in good physical condition, and there is reasonable chance that it will stay socially healthy. But once incomes are too low to keep up the housing, then the overall quality of the neighborhood drops, with consequences such as: less home ownership, higher mobility of residents, higher family instability, higher density of residents, exodus of business, higher proportion of people living on welfare assistance, higher crime, and fewer people with the political and economic resources needed for community problem-solving.

Minority populations have become concentrated in these lower-cost, older neighborhoods for at least two reasons. First, the black and Spanish-speaking populations, which are the main nonwhite urban populations, have lower average family incomes than the national median, and therefore they seek lower-cost facilities. Second, as higher-income families move into the new developments away from the deterioration, they create barriers that prevent lower-income families from living in their communities.

> The net impact is that the public schools are becoming the schools of low-income people—the people who can afford no alternative.

These barriers take the form of zoning regulations and carefully enforced housing codes, which have the effect of increasing the cost of living in the community beyond the point of low-income family accessibility. One result is the effective exclusion from new developments of most of the minority population located in the city, although this is now beginning to change somewhat.

The effect of this process over the years is obvious. The communities located around the periphery of the city—suburbs and exurbs—are mostly populated by families with middle income or above, who for the most part have adequate housing, the accompanying amenities, and viable neighborhoods. The inner city, in contrast, tends to concentrate the lowest income people of the metropolitan area. While this trend has been occurring for years, its full proportions were starkly brought out in the 1970 census. This showed statistically that the suburbs had taken over the largest share of national population as compared to the central cities. It was clear that all the factors of urban deterioration were most blatantly present in the inner city.

With this shift in population to the suburbs has gone a massive outflow of economic growth from the cities to suburbs. As Anthony Downs points out in his book *Opening Up The Suburbs*, ". . . the vast majority of new homes, new apartments, new shopping centers, new schools, new streets, new parks, new roads, new highways, new public buildings, new factories, new sewer and water systems, and other new structures built in the United States in the past 30 years have been in the suburbs." Also, a preponderant majority of the net new jobs have been located in the suburbs.

What is the impact of all this on public education in the Milwaukee area? Through suburbanization, more and more middle- and higher-income families have left or are leaving the city. This has two immediate impacts. On the one hand, children of lower-income families make up an increasing percentage of total enrollment in the public schools.

To upgrade their level rapidly, large inputs are required. Also, to keep the middle- and upper-income families who reside in the city to continue to believe in the public school system, quality efforts are demanded.

On the other hand, large amounts of money are needed to maintain or increase educational quality. Yet with declining population in the city, and with many other costs to be met in the myriad of social problems faced by the city—all of which compete for scarce money provided by the property tax—it is ever more difficult to find the wherewithal.

One overall result is the dissatisfaction of much of Milwaukee's population with their schools. The dwindling middle-to-higher-income population observes less and less likelihood for quality education in the public schools and therefore seeks to withdraw. Some of them simply move out of the city. Others who desire to reside in the city arrange alternative schooling for their children, be it in parochial schools, enrollment in a suburban school with tuition, or various types of community or private schools. The net impact is that the public schools are becoming the schools of low-income people—the people who can afford no alternative. We can assume that the parents of the minority student population who can afford alternative education act approximately the same as white parents. This has nothing to do with racial or ethnic background. However, in that few minority parents have the financial possibility, the percentage of total public school enrollees becomes increasingly minority. Thus, low educational quality and increasing school segregation easily go hand in hand.

Implications for City-Suburban Interdependence

What does this whole process of urban development have to do with interdependence between city and suburbs—the theme of this seminar? I would like to suggest four propositions for your consideration.

- *Metropolitan areas cannot function well in the compartmentalized isolation of the political jurisdictions in which they are subdivided.* The 19 municipalities in Milwaukee County are interdependent in innumerable ways. Many people living in the suburbs are employed in the city, and vice versa, and therefore are financed in various ways by property taxpayers in jurisdictions other than those that they themselves sustain. The infrastructure of roads and public utilities recognizes no political boundaries, nor do the "people problems" related to the effectiveness or ineffectiveness of systems of police and fire protection, primary and secondary and higher education, welfare, the arts, and the like. To prevent waste and duplication in a period of increasingly scarce resources, some common planning is necessary. This involves the whole metropolitan area.

- But at the same time *we demand responsive government.* This involves neighborhood-level decision-making, accountability of public officials, and flexibility for change according to the needs of the community. It is recognized that these characteristics are facilitated through small size and closeness between citizens and government. Thus, on the one hand, there is need for a level of planning for needs and problems that can best be cared for on a metropolitan or county level. This encompasses city and suburbs and therefore is larger than any one jurisdiction. On the other hand, there is need for strong local community control to assure that local officials are responsive in carrying out the wishes of the local communities and neighborhood within the larger framework. These are complementary, not contradictory.

- One of the best means to improve the economic and social health of the metropolitan area is to *de-concentrate the low-income and minority populations now located in the inner city.* And one of the best ways to do this is to create alternative places for people to live if they choose to do so. We have discussed that a major reason why low-income people and also minorities are concentrated in the inner city is because they cannot afford the high cost of housing elsewhere, especially in the suburbs. We need to develop a strategy whereby low- and moderate-income families can be assisted to live in other parts of the metropolitan area if it is their wish to do so. This would break down concentrations of poverty, reduce racial segregation, and enrich suburban communities through opening them to the heterogeneity of the metropolitan population. It would also facilitate the bringing together of place of residence and place of work for some families. City and suburbs would need to cooperate in developing this strategy. Certain social benefits should be made available by government to facilitate this.

- One solution to the big fiscal disparities between city and suburbs in making money available for education, and to the big differences in level of achievement between city and suburban public schools, would be to "*metropolitanize*" *public education.* The premise here is that good schools serve the needs of the whole metropolitan area. Bad schools hurt the whole metropolitan area. One way to metropolitanize education is to arrange for a countywide sharing of revenue for schools, but at the same time for each community to continue to have major decision-making control on educational policy within the broad guidelines that the communities would develop jointly.

We could ask the question: How can *we,* whether we live in the city or a suburb, contribute to making our metropolitan area a healthy place to live and work?

Still separate, still segregated

White Flight and School Desegregation

Presented at The Research Clearinghouse of Metropolitan Milwaukee, 1976

There is interest in relating "white flight" to school desegregation for at least two reasons:

- School integration requires enough of a balance between majority white and minority populations so that the ingredients for integration exist. School integration in Washington, D.C., for example, is impossible because there are few white students attending the city's public schools.

- Data on socioeconomic status continue to give evidence that the white population in the United States has a considerably higher average income and educational level than does the minority population. For urban planners, white flight implies the loss of a property tax base, which is the main source of revenue for schools and other public services; the loss of professional and technical resources that are needed to help solve complex city problems; and the reduction of political power as population and the economic base leave.

In short, both school planners and urban planners are extremely interested in the phenomenon known as "white flight."

White flight implies different things to different people.

Conventional wisdom has it that school desegregation—especially court-ordered bussing—ends up in pushing many families out of the community that is implementing the court order. As it is usually assumed that the whites are the ones who are escaping, logically there is close identification of desegregation and white flight.

Last spring one of America's best-known sociologists stirred up a hornet's nest. Dr. James S. Coleman was given the ambitious assignment, after Congress passed the Civil Rights Act of 1964, to supervise the organization of a comprehensive national survey on lack of equality of educational opportunity due to race, national origin, and religion.

The basic question he addressed in the famous Coleman Report of 1966 was how the differing distribution of resources in schools attended by blacks and schools attended by whites affected children's behavior. He concluded that children from disadvantaged backgrounds did somewhat better in schools that were predominantly middle class than in schools that were homogeneously lower class.

Because residential patterns in our big cities have tended to concentrate blacks in older and deteriorating areas of the central city, he argued for transporting children among schools as a means to achieve more racial balance. This in turn would promote more equality of educational opportunity. In the late 1960s, Coleman thus found himself as having provided the intellectual justification for the subsequent series of court decisions that used forced bussing as a remedy to integrate public schools.

> To the degree that schools play a role in withdrawal, the important factor behind whites leaving may in truth be less race than other factors that relate directly to school quality, such as the income and educational levels of the school families (whether white or minority), and the intangible qualities that make for a "good school."

Last spring, 10 years later, Coleman gave a paper at the American Educational Research Association. Given his reputation, plus his important earlier study, his remarks quickly hit the headlines, especially because it appeared that his views had changed over the decade.

He had become involved in a research project, which, among other things, examined whether those cities that had experienced some desegregation during 1968–1973 had lost more whites than cities that did not experience desegregation. He concluded that the loss of whites did in fact increase faster in the large cities that had desegregated. He cited eight cities that experienced a fourfold increase in loss of white students after desegregation began.

He concluded that whites who could afford it were moving out, and as school systems became more black, still more whites moved out. It became a vicious circle. The result, he said, is that big-city school systems are becoming systems of blacks and low-income whites. The major justification for integration, using his earlier arguments of the Coleman Report, then disappears.

He further points out that the black middle class is just as interested in escaping from the city as is the white middle class. So we are not really discussing *white* flight but *middle-class* flight. But because the great majority of the middle-class population has been white, the flight in large part becomes white flight. Thus white flight takes on racial characteristics as distinct from only socioeconomic factors.

He thinks the courts could find other remedies than forced bussing to bring about educational opportunity, such as redrawing school boundaries and eliminating gerrymandering to promote integration, as well as enlightened policy for construction of new schools and voluntary programs, which make the schools attractive to attend.

A still unanswered question: What significant role, if any, does the racial makeup of the school population really play in whites leaving the community? Here is where Coleman may have drawn superficial conclusions: that increasing black presence in school enrollment automatically brings white withdrawal. To the degree that schools play a role in withdrawal, the important factor behind whites leaving may in truth be less race than other factors that relate directly to school quality, such as the income and educational levels of the school families, whether white or minority, and the intangible qualities that make for a "good school." This is what increasing numbers of people are looking for and not enough are finding.

State Representative Dennis Conta, from Milwaukee's East Side, had introduced a far-reaching piece of legislation, as previously mentioned. It called immediately for voluntary movement of students between two MPS school districts and two suburban districts, with significant financial support from the state for incentives. It focused not only on integration but on the quality of education, which MPS desegregation activity did not do.

On a broader scale it was also a first step toward generating discussion about metropolitan government, a scary concept for parochial thinkers, although considered the wave of the future. The city's racial segregation in housing and education and its concentration of poverty could then be dealt with through some mixing of the richer suburbs and poorer city.

Because Conta's plan included the Riverside Cluster area as one of its two city districts, we arranged for key people in the Riverside Educational Improvement Project to meet him for detailed discussions. Eventually the state approved a compromise bill, which became known as Chapter 220 (of the Wisconsin state statutes); it did not create a new school district but did provide funding to bus students between cities and suburban schools.

Innovative State Legislation for School Integration

Taken from "A New Legislative Framework to Facilitate School Integration"

Comments at the Workshop on Community Involvement in Desegregation Planning, Alverno College, 1976

Anyone who participated in the open meetings held last winter to hear State Representative Dennis Conta discuss his East Shore District Plan (A City-Suburban School Merger Proposal) could conclude that our Greater Milwaukee community has come quite a way during the last year. The so-called Conta Bill was introduced into the Assembly and was finally tabled for lack of support.

It is rather remarkable, therefore, that Assembly Bill 1040 was recently approved by both houses of the State Legislature, and is expected to be signed by Governor Patrick Lucey at any time.

This bill is important and innovative, not only for Wisconsin but for the United States. There are very few examples of legislation by state governments to promote integrated education. This bill declares that:

It is the announced policy of the state to facilitate the transfer of students between schools and between school districts to promote cultural and racial integration in education where students and their parents desire such transfer and where schools and school districts determine that such transfers serve educational interests. The state further declares that it is a proper state expense to encourage such transfers through the provision of special aids.

The central intent of 1040 is to facilitate the transfer of minority pupils—"minority" defined as black American, Native American, Spanish-surnamed American, or Oriental American—who are now in schools that have 30 percent or more minority enrollment to schools where minority enrollment is less than 30 percent, and also to facilitate transfer of non-minority pupils from schools that have less than 30 percent minority enrollment to schools that have 30 percent or more minority enrollment.

These transfers can be done in two ways: inter-district or intra-district. Inter-district transfers would involve pupils attending a school that is located in a different school district than the one in which they reside.

Intra-district transfers would involve pupils who reside in a particular attendance area within a district to enroll in a school in another attendance area of the same district.

The bill provides that both inter-district and intra-district transfers will bring state aid to the participating school district or districts *if* the transfer has the effect of promoting cultural and racial integration. In the case of inter-district transfers, the sending district can count each student transfer as one pupil for purposes of state aid, even though the pupil is no longer enrolled in its district. For the receiving school district—where the pupil will actually attend school—state financial aid will be figured in one of two ways. If the number of pupils transferring to the receiving district in order to promote integration totals at least 5 percent of the total pupils enrolled in the district in a given school year, then that district will receive 120 percent aid for the cost expended on the average pupil in that district. If the pupils transferring are less than 5 percent of enrollment, then the receiving district will be reimbursed for the actual cost of educating the average pupil in its district.

In other words, the receiving district will get reimbursed for at least

> Both inter-district and intra-district transfers will bring state aid to the participating school district or districts *if* the transfer has the effect of promoting cultural and racial integration.

the full cost of what it pays for one of its students. And if it makes a significant effort to integrate, which involves at least 5 percent of its total enrollment in one year, then it gets 20 percent more than actual average cost of one of its pupils.

In the case of intra-district transfers that promote integration, each pupil who transfers will be counted as 1.2 pupils enrolled compared to the usual state aid the district receives. In other words, the district gets 20 percent additional aid for every intra-district transfer that promotes integration.

All of the transportation cost, which is required both for the inter-district and intra-district transfers promoting integration, would be covered by state aid.

It is to be emphasized that this is a *voluntary program*—and in the best interest of both the sending and receiving districts. For example, the city schools will want to be careful to prevent only the best students transferring out of the city, while the suburbs will seek to enroll not only the city's lowest achievers. The bill calls for establishment of planning councils within 60 days after the legislation goes into effect.

This legislative framework brings together several good ideas into one package:

- **Fiscal incentives are made available to involve the suburban districts** in integration efforts, which historically have been mainly a city concern because minorities are concentrated in the big cities. In a time of declining enrollments, the suburban districts now are encouraged with fiscal advantage to fully utilize their facilities to promote integration.

- **Budgetary assistance is given to fiscally deprived Milwaukee.** We know that Milwaukee, as most big cities, has been losing ground with the exodus of some of its higher income families and some of its economic base. The Milwaukee Public Schools, and therefore also the Milwaukee citizen and taxpayer, gain financially from the legislation.

- **Transportation aid is provided** for all transfers that promote integration, both inside the district and to other districts. In the past, transportation sometimes has been considered a seemingly insurmountable cost problem.

- **Joint planning will take place between the city and the suburbs.** The plans that are finally decided upon by the respective boards will be voluntary, but the planning process itself is compulsory. Thus the city and the suburbs must sit down to think through and work out possible new kinds of cooperation. In the long run, this could be one of the most important aspects of the legislation.

This bill that has just been passed by our State Legislature is not going to solve the integration problems of Wisconsin or Milwaukee. It is relatively small scale and it relies upon voluntary support.

Significantly, this new metropolitan framework was *not* imposed by a court. It was developed through legislation and the support of public opinion.

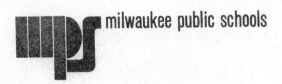

milwaukee public schools

RIVERSIDE HIGH SCHOOL

1615 east locust street
milwaukee, wisconsin 53211
area 414:964-5900

Proposal of the Riverside Educational Improvement Project

Years before the desegregation order, many minority students had been enrolling in the Milwaukee Public Schools. Since some parents we knew already had concluded that school quality was deteriorating, they were either moving into the suburbs or switching to private schools. Our son Eric had just entered Riverside High School, and his brother would be joining him in two years. While we and other interested parents decided to stay with the public schools, we committed to invest energy toward elevating quality. Here is the Project's story.

Background and Organization of the Project

At the last meeting of the Student-Teacher-Parent (STP) group of Riverside High School held in May 1971, it was decided in view of urgent and widespread interest in conditions at Riverside to endorse a proposal; it was titled: To Prepare a Plan of Action for Developing a High Quality Riverside High School. The proposal called for a comprehensive analysis of Riverside High School and preparation of recommendations for action. Upon completion, this plan of action would be submitted to the Superintendent of Schools for review and also to the Board of School Directors as a basis for decisions regarding school improvements. This would include new construction to be funded by a portion of the $60 million bond issue approved by citizens of Milwaukee in 1970.

It was recognized that the quality of Riverside is closely related to the quality of the five elementary public schools of the so-called Riverside Cluster, which fed most of their students into the high school. It was considered essential that the Plan of Action be district-wide and should include representation from each of the Cluster schools, plus two public schools on the periphery of the Riverside District. The feeder schools and the high school should have equal representation in a district-wide Policy Committee, constituted of 21 from Riverside and 21 from the feeders.

Along with the students, parents, teachers, and administrators directly involved in the Project, there was interest also in maintaining regular communication with the School Board members residing in the Riverside District, the aldermen whose jurisdiction extends into the Cluster area, officials in the central administration of the Milwaukee Public Schools with special responsibilities relevant to the Riverside Cluster, and the Milwaukee Teachers Education Association. All have been ex-officio members of the General Policy Committee.

> The quality of Riverside is closely related to the quality of the five elementary public schools of the so-called Riverside Cluster, which fed most of their students into the high school.

All meetings of the General Policy Committee—ten of which have been held to date—are open to the community. Dr. Belden Paulson, co-chairman of the General Policy Committee, chaired the meetings. Some 165 pages of materials were assembled from investigations of the Project's four task forces. In addition, a fifth task force, with representatives from the other four, organized a comprehensive random survey of Cluster students from the sixth grade through high school, and a sample of parents of these students.

The task forces focused on these five themes: demographic and related data on district; educational innovations; what kind of schools do we have?; what kind of schools do we want?; and a comprehensive survey of the student body and student and parent interests.

The first draft was written in 1972, and there were a total of four drafts. The fourth draft was discussed with Superintendent Gousha and his staff.

Various curriculum specialists of the Milwaukee Public Schools (MPS) central office met on October 23, 1972, with several of the Project's members. It was agreed to establish six small task forces, with parents or teachers serving as co-chairs. MPS curriculum specialists from the central office were assigned to work with each task force. Each group also included at least one Riverside High School teacher and one from a Cluster elementary school, as well as at least one high school student. They dealt with these subjects: science; media communication; music, art, and drama; industrial education; home economics, physical education/recreation; supportive services.

This was perhaps the first time, at least in recent memory, when a significant number of community people met in the community with MPS curriculum specialists, teachers, students, and administrators to plan an educational program for a group of schools such as the Riverside Cluster.

From the outset, it had been agreed that not only would all meetings of the Riverside Educational Improvement Project's Policy Committee be open, but that the proposal would be discussed in public community meetings. A series of evening programs was therefore arranged.

Announcements were made in the schools. News sheets were sent home to each parent, along with a copy of an article in *The Milwaukee Journal.* These open sessions indicated support for the proposal.

The overall statement includes a set of assumptions based on the perceived realities of people in the Riverside Cluster, and includes a practical proposal that is submitted as a basis for policy-making.

The Assumptions

This proposal is based on the premises and assumptions that follow:

- There is increasing recognition of the interrelatedness of the schools that constitute the Riverside Cluster. It is believed that the quality of the high school is closely related to the quality of the schools feeding into it. There is little value in emphasizing innovative educational approaches on the high school level unless a massive effort is undertaken to assure quality education in the earlier grades. It is felt that the Cluster must be viewed as a *learning system.*

- There is a high priority on reduced student/teacher ratios, especially in the feeder schools. This would permit the teachers more time to emphasize teaching of basic skills (reading, writing, language, arithmetic), facilitate more individualized attention for students needing special help, and give teachers opportunity for class planning and preparation.

- Mastery of the basic skills before entry into high school is given such high priority that a monitoring effort is needed at each grade level to identify reading and other skill problems. In addition, special monitoring will take place at the end of the fifth grade prior to entering the upper intermediate level. This monitoring should analyze individual teacher as well as student results. A concentrated attack then should be made, with a *results* emphasis rather than merely time employed.

- As a part of quality education, prime importance is given to vocational-technical training, not only as a skill base for employment but also as preparation for adult life and self-help in the home. Included courses would be basic home maintenance, simple plumbing, carpentry and furniture repair, electricity and electrical repair, cooking, sewing, metalwork, auto mechanics, etc. Coursework would be offered beginning in the sixth grade and become increasingly specialized as the student moves through high school. It has been suggested that every student graduating from high school should have at least rudimentary knowledge of one of the above skills.

- Much importance is given to a quality physical education facility. This would include ample gym space properly equipped, a swimming pool, tennis courts, and other areas.

- The kind of specialized facilities now being recommended for the staff and students enrolled in the upper intermediate grades (grades 6-7-8) of all Cluster schools and in high school are not adequately available at present.

- There is broad, if not universal, interest in the "open approach to education" so as to maximize learning related to the child's abilities and interests. *Stimulus*-oriented settings and work opportunities should be offered to students so they can develop and pursue their interests and needs. *Goal*-oriented experiences should than be offered so that students can pursue in depth those interests and needs that have been identified. Teachers need to be prepared as stimulators and resource leaders rather than exclusively oriented as transmitters of information.

- The emphasis must be upon learning rather than teaching. The single most important factor is the teacher and the interaction between the teacher and the learner. Thus major interest is required in teacher selection, in-service training, providing the teacher access to new ideas and approaches through visits to alternative learning situations and workshops and seminars, and giving the teacher enough flexibility to be creative.

- While the first obligation of the school is to serve the children who are students, these public facilities, which are financed by the whole community, should be open to wide community use as part of a comprehensive educational program for the total community.

- Recognition is given to salient demographic trends in the Cluster area that have been carefully studied:

  a) The District seems to subdivide naturally into three areas that have some homogeneity internally. Populations east of the Milwaukee River have been and probably will continue to be predominantly white; the number of school-age children here has decreased, and the percentage of those children attending MPS has been decreasing. Children attending feeder schools west of the Milwaukee River have been predominantly white, but this is likely to change radically within the next 10 years because of an increasingly black and Spanish-speaking population and an increased number of school-age children. Farther south and west is a demographic area that is predominantly black and has the highest density per block of school-age children.

  b) Of particular interest is the number of children in the Cluster feeder schools enrolled in the first grade, for this can be a useful indicator of predicting future student population in the Cluster.

SCHOOL	TOTAL ENROLLMENT		FIRST GRADE		GRADUATING CLASS	
	Fall 1971	Fall 1972	Fall 1971	Fall 1972	Fall 1971	Fall 1972
Hartford (K-8)	775	746	64	83	115	75
Maryland (K-8)	467	447	41	41	53	61
Bartlett (K-8)	468	440	50	42	61	66
Fratney (K-8)	557	523	66	52	44	47
Pierce (K-6)	851	833	112	121	90	128
Holmes [1]	1,053	980	141	131	112	120

c)   The trend in the Cluster during recent years has been the increase of nonwhite student population.

d)   It is believed that a major, even *dramatic,* effort to promote quality education in the District, both in the feeders and the high school, could reverse the current trend of people seeking alternatives to public schools. It is also believed that effective teaching of basic skills, approaches at open education, more individualized attention, a variety of educational innovations in the schools, and more teacher time for planning and study of new approaches would combine to require a redefinition of school-size capacity. This would mean that children would no longer automatically be transferred into the District's schools whenever enrollment is slightly reduced. Instead, as space becomes available, it could be used to improve the quality of education.

- The population living in the Cluster has a commitment, first and foremost, to *quality* education. Good education is considered possible and a necessity in any school, whatever the social or racial makeup. At the same time, the Cluster population is committed to maintaining an *integrated* school district. Maximum effort should be made when developing educational strategies for the District, including the construction of new facilities, to take into account the fact that residential neighborhoods are segregated to a considerable degree by race, and that segregation should be avoided.

> The population living in the Cluster has a commitment, first and foremost, to *quality* education. Good education is considered possible and a necessity in any school, whatever the social or racial makeup. At the same time, the Cluster population is committed to maintaining an *integrated* school district.

In order to maximize the productive use of the funds provided the District under the Capital Improvements Program, as well as the expenditures of the operating budget, it is proposed that a Cluster Center be established for the Riverside District.

This proposal outlines a pilot pattern of urban public education that has dimensions as a *model* for interrelating high school and feeder schools. It combines the neighborhood school concept with a Cluster Center that involves some cross-neighborhood integration along with specialized facilities and staff.

The Cluster Center would be centrally located to serve the whole district. It would serve as a focal point where various interests of the Cluster as a whole can be identified. It would create an image of innovation in the community, of quality based on specialized staff and first-rate facilities. It would involve the community in its governance.

The Cluster Center would serve as an administrative center for the Cluster, interrelating the individual schools into a learning system while simultaneously respecting the individuality of each school and its neighborhood. Each school presumably would continue to have its own principal, but there would be co-leaders representing the high school and the feeder schools and exercising some Cluster-wide responsibilities. In order that each principal in the Cluster could make substantive input into the management of the Center as well as have maximum motivation to utilize the Center for the mutual benefit of all participating schools, a Council would be developed that involves all of the principals in the Cluster. It would also be desirable to have a Cluster-wide group representing teachers from the different schools.

> We can expect reduced social tensions and more viable relationships between ethnic and racial groupings, both as a result of upgraded achievement and of social contact at an earlier age.

There would be three Cluster-wide groupings: 1) principals, 2) teachers, and 3) parents, students, and community people. They would meet together regularly to discuss matters that affect the educational health of the Cluster. This combined council of all three groupings would be involved in decision-making.

Structure of the Cluster Center

The first component would be a Media Center. It would be the hub of the whole cluster center, serving both students and teachers. It would offer materials from specialized maps, films and videotapes, graphics books, and simulation games and artifacts to resources produced or reproduced within the Media Center. This would also serve the science laboratories; and a music-art-drama-crafts center.

A second component of the Cluster Center is the *Industrial and Home Economics Education Facility.* This would provide well-laid-out facilities with first-rate equipment and staff for such learning opportunities in industrial arts as the use of hand tools and in attaining basic skills in wood, metal, plastics, graphic arts, electricity, and some power machinery. Home economics learning would be enhanced through the use of multipurpose instructional areas and specialized staff.

The Cluster Center's third component would be the *Physical Education Complex* for both the high school and the feeder schools. A field house and swimming pool complex should be built. This would include gyms and some adjacent outdoor multipurpose facilities for football, baseball, track, tennis, field hockey, and other intramural activity. The primary purpose of these activities would be for personal physical development with emphasis on individual or lifetime sports, but an interscholastic program is recognized to be desirable to the degree that it would not conflict with this primary purpose.

A need continually brought to the attention of the Project's task forces: the inadequacy of counseling services in the district. These *Supportive Services* have been described as fragmented and ineffective, with counselors, social workers, psychologists, and related personnel seemingly being unable to serve student needs well. Teachers lack suitable training for "counseling situations" brought to their attention. It is recommended that all counseling services in the district be centralized at the Cluster Center.

> Good schools take more than money; they must have community support and teacher commitment, but they also need leadership at the top.

This proposal could be implemented without any redistricting. It is desirable for each of the elementary schools having a K-8 grade range to minimize the number of transfer students from outside the Cluster system so that the constructive efforts for planning for K-12 system-wide could take hold.

Perhaps the most significant, if most intangible, aspect of this proposal in terms of benefits accruing to all of the schools is the new image that will be projected in the Riverside Cluster area. There will be high-quality facilities, teaching innovations, and new emphasis on teacher training and retraining. The student-centered curriculum in the upper intermediate grades will emphasize an open approach that capitalizes on student interest and demand. We can expect reduced social tensions and more viable relationships between ethnic and racial groupings, both as a result of upgraded achievement and of social contact at an earlier age.

All of this will combine to place the Riverside Cluster in the forefront of educational innovation and quality in the city and the state. This in turn can have an effect in stabilizing the population in the area, which has tended to seek alternatives to public education, whether through change of residence or transfer away from the city schools.

In the final analysis, the real fruition of this total effort will be the degree to which students and parents and teachers and administrators of different orientations, lifestyles, and racial and ethnic backgrounds are capable of drawing out and building upon the potential of each other in a mutually reinforcing learning experience. It is doable.

THE RIVERSIDE EDUCATIONAL IMPROVEMENT PROJECT

To Seek School Board Approval

1975

Since the Riverside proposal had been approved in principle, it now required final School Board action and disbursement of the money already allocated to the school in a city bond issue. At this critical Board meeting, I was the first speaker. This was a difficult time, because the desegregation issue and racial quotas now absorbed the Board, while our parent-formulated Riverside Project proposal meshed quality learning into an overall desegregation policy.

Every once in a while a crucial decision comes up that affects the health and vitality of a community. Your School Board Committee faces such a decision tonight.

In the spring of 1971, there was a racial incident at Riverside High School that threatened to get out of hand. Subsequently a number of meetings were held in the community to discuss conditions at Riverside. In the course of these discussions, a community proposal was given to the elected Student-Teacher-Parent body at Riverside. The group declared that instead of dealing only with a particular incident, a more fundamental question should be addressed: What is needed to develop quality education in the Riverside area?

An organization was formed called the Riverside Educational Improvement Project. It has involved over 100 parents, teachers, and students who for four years have been working closely with the school administration.

Because the questions of concern tied directly into construction plans, the studies and recommendations of the Riverside Educational Improvement Project became those that would be submitted by Riverside High School and its feeders for the capital improvement dollars allocated.

The task forces that were established did their homework. They analyzed the present situation of the schools. They checked out relevant educational innovations in Milwaukee and nationally. They conducted a survey of students at Riverside High School and the upper grades in the feeders to find out what students wanted. They utilized professional educators and others in the area who had children in the schools.

While the original administrative recommendation had called for a new junior high school in the Riverside area to serve the poorly met needs of the upper intermediate grades, the task forces learned that the community did not want a junior high school. Instead, a new concept was developed: a Cluster Center, which would provide specialized facilities and staff for sixth, seventh, and eighth grades. The proposal recognized that the only way to promote quality was to view the whole Cluster as one learning system, K-12. It recommended a way to facilitate social and racial integration at an earlier age than high school. It emphasized basic skills in the lower grades, but also development of more specialized skills beginning in the sixth grade. It requested closer links between school decision-makers and the community. It asked, among other things, for decent physical education, industrial arts, and home economics facilities in the Riverside area, while at the same time maintaining good balance between academic-college preparatory coursework and vocational training.

> A new concept was developed: a Cluster Center, which would provide specialized facilities and staff for sixth, seventh, and eighth grades. The proposal recognized that the only way to promote quality was to view the whole Cluster as one learning system, K-12.

Superintendent Richard Gousha told members of the Riverside Educational Improvement Project that the Cluster Center proposal was the most carefully thought-out, innovative, and responsible educational effort to emerge from any Milwaukee school cluster in years.

By spring 1974, when the MPS administration began to seriously consider the whole Riverside proposal, a new environment was facing MPS: everyone was concerned with inflation and the cost squeeze. It was clear that citywide enrollments were declining, which implied budgetary constraints on new ideas. There was a developing "wait-and-see" attitude regarding the court decision expected from Federal Judge Reynolds regarding school integration.

So the Riverside Project pushed for certain program and instructional improvements that could be implemented without bricks and mortar. Curriculum specialists of the central office worked with the Cluster in developing plans, and these were initially approved by the School Board during the summer of 1974.

Representatives of the community and the Cluster administration met with Acting Superintendent Dwight Teel and his staff in 1975, at which time they indicated their reluctant willingness to make major compromises in their original proposal. This was on the assumption that the administration would make every effort to speed up actual implementation.

The final educational specifications document is before you now, also approved by the school administrations in the Riverside district.

When we began the Riverside project in the fall of 1971, there were 943 white students at Riverside High School, 655 black students, and 59 with Spanish surnames. Today there are 579 black students, 475 white, and 38 with Spanish surnames. This relative balance has been maintained only because of the control of transfers proposed by the Riverside Parent Teacher Student Association (PTSA) in spring 1974, approved by the School Board and carried through to this date. Whether or not there is to be a court order for Milwaukee schools to integrate, we in the Riverside district *are* already integrated.

When we began this effort, we were able to enlist over 100 people who invested enormous amounts of time and creativity in a cause they believed in—to promote quality, integrated education in their schools. Today there is much disillusionment in our community because the proposals became bogged down in administrative delays. During these delays, many families and schoolchildren have continued to seek alternatives to the Milwaukee Public Schools.

We see the ominous trend of public education in our big cities—and this includes Milwaukee—to become educational systems for lower-income families, but we think that solid, imaginative efforts in our city public schools can moderate this trend.

Also, the value of the dollars originally designated for Riverside has been drastically reduced. At a number of junctures, it was apparent that the Milwaukee Public Schools could not relate to the innovative approach to quality integrated education that had been introduced in the Riverside community, even though we were continually reminded of the excellence of our proposals and were given no substantive criticism or objections.

Some people in our community have turned to other solutions. In these four years, several of our most effective families in the community have withdrawn their children from our schools and their energies from further participation. I personally have seen one of my sons—a freshman at Riverside High School when we began to work—graduate; my other son will also finish before most of the Riverside program will have been realized. As a concerned parent, I have invested considerable energy as chair of this community effort.

I must publicly state that many of us continue to believe that quality, integrated education *can* be achieved in the city public schools. We see the ominous trend of public education in our big cities—and this includes Milwaukee—to become educational systems for lower-income families, but we think that solid, imaginative efforts in our city public schools can moderate this trend. We note the trend toward segregation by race as well as by income, and the tensions that often result when court action is required to rectify inequities that community and school action could not deal with on their own. We are aware that good schools take more than money; they must have community support and teacher commitment, but they also need leadership at the top.

> …the stage of proposal writing, discussion, and delay is in the past. Now we need School Board authorization to move forward.

The Riverside Cluster effort is perhaps unique in the city, not only because of the content of the proposals, but because of the significant investment of human resources from the community, and of teachers who came to meetings and served on task forces outside their regular hours and not for pay.

Time is critical now. People are continuing to leave our area or threatening to leave. Families with children who would like to live in the area are hesitant because of the schools. We believe, as we believed four years ago, that a *dramatic effort to promote quality education in the Riverside Cluster is still possible.* It can maintain enrollment, it can attract new families, it can bring about schools that have both quality and integration.

But the stage of proposal writing, discussion, and delay is in the past. Now we need School Board authorization to move forward. We trust that Board action tonight will be the first step in this direction. The Riverside Cluster may still offer our city the best chance for quality integrated schools.

Education's Radical Role

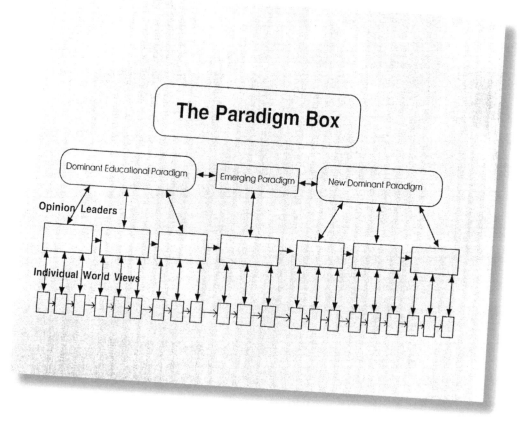

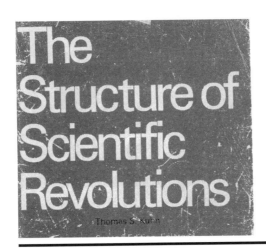

The Structure of Scientific Revolutions

Thomas S. Kuhn

Exploring Paradigm Questions to Enhance Learning

Presented at Explorations, 1997

After Howard Fuller resigned as superintendent of the Milwaukee Public Schools in the mid-1990s, he met with a small group of us to plan several sessions with 100 civic leaders to rethink urban schools. A main theme of these Explorations was the need for new paradigm thinking. I helped to inaugurate these sessions with this talk.

These explorations in very large degree are about paradigms and paradigm shifts. If the best happens, we'll be getting beyond marginal change questions and working on paradigm questions. At the same time, we recognize that there is much in our experience about learning that works, on which we can build. We are not starting from zero.

We are all familiar with paradigms in a general way, but let's return to the source. You undoubtedly know that Thomas Kuhn popularized the term when he was a professor at the University of Chicago and his book came out in 1962, *The Structure of Scientific Revolutions.*

He was interested in analyzing why great scientific breakthroughs have taken place through the ages by asking the question: what happens when scientific theories, once well-established and accepted, become out of date when they no longer fit the realities they are supposed to explain. He was primarily interested in such fields as astronomy, physics, chemistry, and biology, but his thinking has been applied to societal issues.

You recall that one of his famous examples was Nicolaus Copernicus, a Polish astronomer and leading scholar around 1500 AD. Up until that time, the prevailing assumption was that the Earth is the center of the universe, and the sun, all the planets—everything out there—circles the Earth. It took a while to convince leading scholars that the Earth is one small planet circling one sun, all of which are part of a much vaster reality. Kuhn talked about the "Copernican Revolution," which in essence describes the need for new perceptions when time-honored models no longer fit. He argued that new paradigms—paradigm shifts—can lead to transforming the world.

Fritjof Capra, a physicist at the University of California-Berkeley and one of today's trenchant thinkers about paradigms, organized a symposium to rediscover the ideas of Kuhn and place Kuhn's thinking into broad societal issues that go way beyond the physical sciences. Capra rephrased Kuhn and came up with one of the best definitions I have found. He broadened the term and defined a social paradigm as follows:

> A constellation of concepts, values, perceptions and practices shared by a community, which forms a particular vision of reality that is the basis of the way the community organizes itself.

Keep in mind three key ideas: perceptions and values, vision of reality, and the use of these for the community organizing itself in terms of behavior and action. Values, vision, action. When we deal with paradigm and paradigm shift questions, we must reemphasize that we're concerning ourselves with something far more complex than the usual changes we work with daily, be it in education or any other field. We're really dealing with how we see the world, which in turn is the basis of how we organize ourselves.

In Chapter Eight of Kuhn's book, he addresses the problem of paradigm crisis. What happens when people lose faith in an established paradigm because it is more or less irrelevant to contemporary reality? Incidentally, he notes that paradigm shifts don't happen easily or often.

All paradigm crises begin with a kind of blurring condition: people know there's something wrong, things don't work, but they have a hard time explaining why. People begin with simple solutions until they find that something more is needed. Kuhn then argues that all paradigm crises close in one of three ways:

- Changes are made that at least over the short term seem able to handle the crisis. These may take the form of reforms that will satisfy enough people to forego further action.
- The problems that underlie the paradigm crisis don't go away, but for whatever reason, people at this given time seem unable to find the tools for solutions. So the matter is postponed for a future generation.
- The crisis leads to the emergence of alternative ideas that over time become emerging paradigms and eventually a new dominant paradigm. Normally there are major ensuing battles and numerous false starts during this transition period. Of course, at some future date, this new paradigm will itself become outdated as realities change.

Let's quickly apply these ideas to education and to the proposition that we may be in the middle of a paradigm crisis about learning. This is the basis for these Explorations sessions. We know that each of us lives in a "paradigm box" that contains our perceptions and values and visions about the main themes of our lives, including education. These values and visions, in turn, determine our behavior, such as how we organize our schools, train our teachers, write the textbooks, define intelligence. In effect, it's how we put together the whole educational enterprise that influences how our children learn.

Do we need to break out of our boxes, which in public education were largely formed in the 19th century when America was organizing a factory culture to become a great industrial power? This culture emphasized monolithic buildings, hierarchical control, standardization, and discouragement of creativity as a deviation from efficiency. We know that today we live in a different historical period when new paradigm thinking could bring radically different models. What preparation is needed for today's learners who will spend most of their lives in the 21st century, probably with unprecedented changes in many walks of life? The emerging global economy, the technological revolutions, world diversity, and environmental concerns pose exciting new opportunities, but they also challenge us to be able to anticipate change and adapt to new realities. We also know that a great deal of research

> **Kuhn talked about the "Copernican Revolution," which in essence describes the need for new perceptions when time-honored models no longer fit.**

has taken place in recent years about the whole process of learning, including the multiple functions of the brain. How can we incorporate these findings into our everyday learning processes in order to nurture each individual's talents?

Dominant paradigms are heavily influenced by opinion leaders. These people communicate both with the people with whom they closely associate and with the machinery of decision-making that over time maintains or changes paradigms. If an emerging new paradigm in education, in learning, is going to take place, these opinion leaders will play crucial roles. Presumably the people participating in Explorations are some of these opinion leaders.

As Kuhn discussed and we all know, there is considerable turbulence, even chaos, in periods when paradigm shifts are taking place. These periods are times of great frustration but also great opportunity. Today many ideas and theories are circulating that challenge the dominant ones in process of being replaced. Some prevailing ideas, moreover, "work" and do not need to be replaced. This is a time of exploration, thus the importance of this Explorations series. It is an opportunity to reexamine established paradigms and to bring new thinking that may produce the result we all seek: to maximize the learning environment of our children.

Breaking New Ground: Creating the First Public Waldorf School in the United States

Taken from Odyssey of a Practical Visionary, *2009*

Milwaukee Public School Superintendent Robert Peterkin had become interested in Waldorf education, a learning model operated with great success in Europe and in selected private American schools. This is the story of the Urban Waldorf School in Milwaukee, the first *public* Waldorf school in America, also the first one located in the inner city.

R udolf Steiner is one of those names that surfaces again and again when the conversation veers away from ordinary topics toward seminal thinkers associated with great ideas.

Born in Austria in 1861, Steiner left a legacy as a radical social thinker a century ago that seems surprisingly contemporary. He talked about the relationship of our inner human landscape to our outer world. The social sciences and humanities, he said, seek to comprehend man's inner experience as expressed in history and culture, while the natural sciences seek to explain the causal laws of the physical world. He was always interpreting the interplay between the individual and the larger community.

In 1919, five months after the end of World War I, Steiner visited the Waldorf-Astoria cigarette factory in Stuttgart, Germany. Defeated in war, Germany was facing economic, social, and political chaos. Steiner shared his ideas about social renewal with the workers. The time was ripe, he said, to reorganize society. After his lecture, he met with Emil Molt, a friend and owner of the factory, and other plant staff. Molt asked Steiner if he would establish a school for the children of company employees.

All present were enthusiastic about the proposal, but Steiner would agree only if they accepted his four conditions: 1) The school must be open to all children; 2) It must be coeducational; 3) It must be a unified, 12-year school; and 4) The teachers would have primary control of the school with minimal interference from the state. At that time in Germany (as in most of Europe), these were radical ideas.

The school opened in September with a curriculum of three fundamental pedagogical courses. Steiner incorporated a new understanding of the human being and of child development, and new methods of instruction.

When Hitler came to power in 1933, there were seven Waldorf schools in Germany, as well as seven in four other countries. While Hitler closed all the schools in Germany, the Netherlands, and Hungary, the seed had been planted. Waldorf education came to the United States in October 1928 with the Rudolf Steiner School of New York.

By the 1990s, there were about 100 Waldorf schools in North America and more than 500 worldwide. Connected to the movement were adult education and training centers.

Steiner's threefold image of the human being relates to the psychological faculties of *thinking* (brain and nervous system), *feeling* (rhythmic system of heart and lungs), and *willing* (limbs and metabolic system),

> Steiner emphasized that thinking, feeling, and willing don't develop at identical rates.

all of which together serve or make up the total person. They also relate to three realms of social life: cultural, where the dominant value is freedom; political-legal, where the key emphasis is equality; and economic, which requires cooperation.

These ideas have direct implications for education. Steiner emphasized that thinking, feeling, and willing don't develop at identical rates. For example, in the first seven years of life, the child is mainly focused on *will*, learning almost everything through physical activity. Imitation of adults and older children is crucial. The child's *feeling* life becomes especially strong between the ages of seven and 14. At the high school level, human relationships take on central importance; much of what is taught is through imagination and the arts.

Thinking, with cognitive and intellectual development, becomes the next learning focus, especially in the sciences. Independent judgment is fostered here, as is approaching questions with diverse points of view.

I had known vaguely about Steiner and the Waldorf movement. Then I learned much more from Mark Stamm when he participated in one of my UWM seminars. Mark decided to train in Detroit to become a Waldorf teacher. He worked with Werner Glas, founder of the Waldorf Institute of America and a beloved teacher.

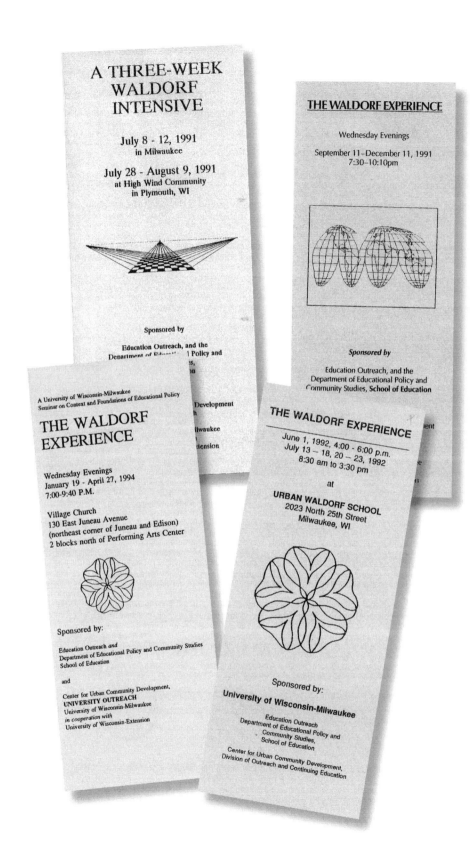

A THREE-WEEK
WALDORF
INTENSIVE

July 8 - 12, 1991
in Milwaukee

July 28 - August 9, 1991
at High Wind Community
in Plymouth, WI

Sponsored by

Education Outreach, and the
Department of Educational Policy and
...

THE WALDORF EXPERIENCE

Wednesday Evenings

September 11–December 11, 1991
7:30–10:10pm

Sponsored by

Education Outreach, and the
Department of Educational Policy and
Community Studies, **School of Education**

A University of Wisconsin-Milwaukee
Seminar on Context and Foundations of Educational Policy

THE WALDORF
EXPERIENCE

Wednesday Evenings
January 19 - April 27, 1994
7:00-9:40 P.M.

Village Church
130 East Juneau Avenue
(northeast corner of Juneau and Edison)
2 blocks north of Performing Arts Center

Sponsored by:

Education Outreach *and*
Department of Educational Policy and Community Studies
School of Education

and

Center for Urban Community Development,
UNIVERSITY OUTREACH
University of Wisconsin-Milwaukee
in cooperation with
University of Wisconsin-Extension

THE WALDORF EXPERIENCE

June 1, 1992, 4:00 - 6:00 p.m.
July 13 – 18, 20 – 23, 1992
8:30 am to 3:30 pm

at

URBAN WALDORF SCHOOL
2023 North 25th Street
Milwaukee, WI

Sponsored by:
University of Wisconsin-Milwaukee

Education Outreach
Department of Educational Policy and
Community Studies,
School of Education

Center for Urban Community Development,
Division of Outreach and Continuing Education

Mark knew that Dr. Peterkin, then superintendent of the Milwaukee Public Schools, had been in contact with the Waldorf School in Detroit and apparently had been impressed by the Waldorf approach to learning. Mark approached Peterkin and encouraged him to consider establishing such a school in Wisconsin. This idea caught on immediately.

The Association of Waldorf Schools of North America was intrigued, because if the MPS Board could be convinced to approve and fund this project, it would be the first *public* Waldorf school in the United States. All others were privately operated and financed.

An additional incentive to obtain MPS support was the intention to place this new school in the heart of Milwaukee's inner city, which would be another innovation. Waldorf schools generally were located in middle-class environments where families had the ability to pay tuition and parents were committed to get heavily involved with the school—one of Steiner's original preconditions. Since in Milwaukee, the children of the lower income and minority populations usually ended up in inferior schools, any credible innovative effort to enhance learning was welcome.

In June 1990, Peterkin got the school board to establish a task force to explore all the issues; this included interested teachers and community people as well as national Waldorf representatives.

I'd been in contact with Mark occasionally since the latter 1970s and had followed his career as he became a Waldorf teacher and developed close contact with the national movement. By the latter 1980s, he had begun telling me of his great interest in shaking up public education in Milwaukee, at least a little, with a Waldorf school. There were already fledgling private Waldorf schools in the area, but he recognized that this would not be easy, as there was no precedent for public Waldorf schools in the entire country.

I was surprised when Mark contacted me in fall 1990, describing Peterkin's intense interest, formation of the task force, and the expectation that the board would approve the school.

Preparing the Teachers

Mark told me that one of the biggest bottlenecks, which could kill the whole project, was the complete lack of qualified teachers to run such a school. He wanted me to get the university to organize a fast-track program to train a cadre of teachers, should the school open in September 1991.

In December 1990, the school board did approve establishing the Urban Waldorf School. It would open in the fall of 1991 with 325 students from kindergarten through grade five. The board also appropriated money for staff training and tuition reimbursement. At the outset, half of the teachers were to be MPS-certified and half were to be certified Waldorf teachers, or would gain certification within three years. Eventually all teachers would be both MPS and Waldorf-certified.

MPS agreed to contract UWM to develop a Waldorf training program under my supervision, to begin in summer 1991.

People in the national Waldorf movement seemed excited about this turn of events, quickly including Milwaukee's Urban Waldorf School in their publicity and mentioning the

UWM training program I was organizing. MPS began looking for trained Waldorf teachers anywhere in the country, but initially made only a halfhearted effort.

Luckily, one key person was recruited. Ann Pratt, a veteran Waldorf teacher-administrator, agreed to temporarily leave her position at Antioch College in New Hampshire. She was hired as implementer in the school, a key position second in importance to the school principal.

Ann became my indispensable ally for several years and one of the major forces bringing early successes to the new school. Dorothy St. Charles, the principal, was extremely efficient in troubleshooting all the inevitable problems of the fledgling venture. She pushed the central administration bureaucracy to an unaccustomed level of support. The three of us constituted a kind of *troika*: Ann provided the Waldorf knowledge base and linkage to the national leadership; Dorothy knew the MPS system and how to run a school (although not a school like this); and I contributed to organizing the training component, meeting the academic requirements that were laid on us and relating this public school to higher education.

I had never had responsibility for offering courses where I knew so little about the content and had to depend so much on others. Yet I was responsible to the university for quality control and presenting an acceptable learning format, even though Waldorf had its own distinctive traditions. Notwithstanding all of this, most of what we did worked, confirmed by the affirmations of the constant stream of visitors who showed up from around the country.

While I couldn't get the university to commit to a comprehensive, ongoing program to create a major to train Waldorf teachers, I was able to develop a series of courses that were approved, one by one, by the School of Education. We had no inkling when we began that we were embarking on a three-year program involving 27 credits, from 1991 through spring 1994. This led to a certificate issued by the national Waldorf Association, and also helped enrollees accumulate credits toward an advanced degree if they so desired.

While I provided the overall program framework, Ann supplied the content. I must say that our product was a first-class curriculum, covering all the essential readings of Steiner and other Waldorf educators, with detailed materials and procedures to be used for each class, from kindergarten through fifth grade.

Since the Waldorf model is very different from what teachers normally use in a mainstream school, the effectiveness of the Urban Waldorf School depended very heavily on what they were learning in our classes. It was a little like the military: what you learned in boot camp and other specialized experiences could save your life later in combat.

Each semester we invited numerous Waldorf teachers and leaders from around the country to Wisconsin. Apart from offering specific content, they placed this school into the worldwide framework of the Waldorf movement.

In spring 1991, MPS Superintendent Peterkin and his associate superintendent resigned and left MPS. With a leadership vacuum at the top, the bureaucracy moved in. Although the school board had approved the new school, planning had barely begun. Mark and other strong Waldorf supporters heard rumblings about certain members of the central administration having serious doubts about the whole Waldorf approach to education. Perhaps it was too radical, too far out of mainstream teaching. And why did Milwaukee have to be a guinea pig for this public school experiment? Now that Peterkin had left, there was still time to reallocate the monies. Different bureaucrats raised different questions.

For example, why were there no textbooks in the early grades? (The teacher takes responsibility for creating the lessons, pulling in a wide array of material.) Early on, why is there so much focus on the arts? (Nurturing imagination is critical.) Does it make sense to begin teaching a foreign language in first grade? Will teacher competence be compromised because the same teacher accompanies the same class of children through all the elementary years, responsible for all the main subjects? (While Waldorf has specialized teachers for such areas as foreign language, crafts, and physical education, the teacher gets to know each child deeply to help him/her to develop.)

Is the two-hour main lesson every morning a good idea instead of many short periods?

> # The essence of Waldorf is to educate the heart as well as the mind and, as Steiner said, serve the healing of society.

(The primary academic substance of the day is presented in a block of time when the child is most alert and then is built onto.) Is it effective to teach science experimentally? (The teacher sets up experiments and guides the discovery of the underlying law or formula.) What's the point of eurythmy (a system of rhythmical bodily movements) in the curriculum? (Movement art nurtures harmony between consciousness of the mind and activity of the limbs.)

Speaking of consciousness, the essence of Waldorf is to educate the heart as well as the mind and, as Steiner said, serve the healing of society. This is a scary mission for traditional school officials. Mark and I worked with Mary Bills, school board president and a strong Waldorf advocate, who canvassed some board members and top-level bureaucrats to get absolute assurances that the board's decision to establish and fund the school would be implemented.

In May 1994, almost three years after our training began, a ceremony was held at the school to award graduation certificates for this first wave of teachers (who had already been teaching at Urban Waldorf for three years). The ceremony was sponsored by the Association of Waldorf Schools of North America in cooperation with MPS. After Ann introduced the program, I summarized the three-year training experience from the early fears of the teacher recruits to their current success in operating the first public Waldorf school. National representatives of the Association extended congratulations.

Henry Barnes, now one of Waldorf's top national leaders whom we had brought in to lecture, urged me to document the first year's activity. We agreed that people were especially interested in the start-up process: the school board agreeing to authorize the project and use public money, the teacher training, the broad ramifications for public policy. While Barnes had misgivings about Waldorf becoming part of a public system where there were prescribed procedures, he also knew the financial struggles of private Waldorf schools and the urgent need for new models.

As a beginning effort, I agreed to interview all the teachers and staff after completion of their first year. I ended up interviewing 14 classroom teachers and specialists, the school principal and implementer, seven staff, and two parents—25 people in all. The principal and eight of the teachers were African American, as was one parent.

The majority of teachers were white, while most of the students were minority. This brought out the recognition that most Waldorf schools in America had not thought through the implications of Waldorf's origins; Steiner's experiences and concepts came out of his European background. Our inner-city, lower-income culture required significant adaptations: different stories and heroic figures and myths, different teaching/learning styles.

With parents less involved than in middle-class neighborhoods, more responsibility was placed on the school itself. The children's homes were often full of stress and anger, forcing the school to become a kind of oasis where the kids felt safe and cared for and where their talents could flower.

The teachers realized that the whole experience was creating a powerful spiritual environment. Some of them sensed that to become a Waldorf teacher is really a life's work, not a job. Because the school had only a small handful of experienced Waldorf teachers, it had the advantage of being a work in progress; it could make mistakes.

> ...most Waldorf schools in America had not thought through the implications of Waldorf's origins; Steiner's experiences and concepts came out of his European background. Our inner-city, lower-income culture required significant adaptations: different stories and heroic figures and myths, different teaching/learning styles.

The one point that continually emerged in the interviews was the emotional involvement of the teachers in this school in contrast to their past experiences. The staff had to become a kind of family. There was a sense of responsibility for the whole school as well as for their individual assignments. The empathy and caring, even a sense of love, made the job a moral, spiritual experience—all fodder for building a more compassionate world.

Although it would seem that Milwaukee's Urban Waldorf School had some influence on national Waldorf policy-making—noted in references in the literature of the movement—after two decades the school was defunded. Nevertheless, when other big-city public systems considered establishing Waldorf Schools, it was likely that their research included the Milwaukee experience.

Global Learning Center: A Valiant Effort

Taken from Odyssey of a Practical Visionary, *2009*

This is the story of an adventure in innovative learning in the inner city. The goal: to prepare middle school students to become global citizens.

I have described my four trips to China in the years 1989–1992. Since China was in the early stages of its economic modernization and contact with the outside world, there was a ravenous appetite for all things American. This included learning the English language and something about our culture. We were asked to remain in China to teach, or to send others.

On my return home, I discussed China with Reuben Harpole, my university colleague who knew everyone in the inner city. He got me on his radio program, where we received an enthusiastic response from call-ins when I proposed selecting 100 youth from the community to be prepared as global citizens. When I visited MPS Deputy Superintendent Bob Jasna to urge development of school curricula that focused on the emerging global economy, he was receptive.

I drafted a paper, "A 'School' for Global Citizenship—Working and Living in the 21st Century, The First 100 Project." The goal: "To prepare 100 students to work in the global marketplace and to live sustainably with appropriate mental set, technical skills, and personal qualities."

The plan stimulated a good bit of discussion.

Seminars Lay the Groundwork

After exploring the global learning center idea with several colleagues, we decided to offer a two-part seminar in fall 1995. One part would be a class led by my colleague Bob Pavlik. This would focus on brain-mind research and multiple intelligences, his area of expertise.

My teaching partner, Wil Kraegel, and I would offer the other part in our UWM series on global sustainable futures.

While the overall purpose of the seminars focused on systemic change in the learning process, the narrower emphasis had the goal of designing a draft for a Global Learning Center (GLC). Students from both classes presented their findings in the last session, attended by school board president Mary Bills.

The seminars proved most productive. A student team wrote a GLC vision statement that began: "We believe that the children of today need to be prepared to meet fundamentally different challenges in the coming age. As the nations of the planet become more politically and economically intertwined, globally educated citizens are essential."

The final document included the teaching and learning goals and guiding philosophy of the Milwaukee Public Schools and curricula notes on global education and a sustainable culture. There were organizational and operational suggestions.

The next semester, winter-spring of 1996, Wil and I taught another futures seminar, which attracted three bright teachers from the inner city Jackie Robinson Middle School. They were drawn to the class because they had heard about this Global Citizen project; one of them, Jewell Riano, was assistant principal at Robinson. We encouraged the women to function as a team, investing creative energy to link their acumen to the evolution of the GLC.

We Conceptualize the Model

Bob Jasna had been appointed to replace Howard Fuller, who had resigned as superintendent in latter 1995. Since previously I had discussed global education with Jasna after returning from China in the early 1990s, it was logical that I now update him. He asked me to convene a group, where he would participate fully.

We met first in June 1996. Included were Tom McGinnity, another innovative educator; Bob Pavlik, and I; the three teachers and half a dozen other creative educators, along with Jasna. At the first meeting Jasna surprised us by urging that we think *radically*; make end runs around the bureaucracy, go way beyond what now exists. There is no point in investing a lot of energy just to establish one more school, he said. "Be creative. Shake us up!"

The planning committee met eight times with Jasna, its last session with him in December 1996. We agreed that should this project ever be approved by the school board, we would nominate Jewell Riano to serve as GLC principal.

During the year following the UWM seminar, we completed a draft of the GLC model. Here are the key points of the proposal we agreed on to submit to Jasna and the school board:

The GLC mission is to provide a learning system that produces citizens who understand the world as an interconnecting set of human and natural systems, and who possess the knowledge, skills, and mindset needed to prepare them to fit into the global marketplace and build a sustainable future.

Further, GLC is an innovative school as part of the new MPS policy; the imperative is to get away from school in favor of learning. This learning system is decentralized, not based in a traditional school building but in a number of interconnected learning stations where teaching and knowledge can interface with real-life experience. The100 middle school students in sixth and seventh grades (eighth grade to be added the next year) will be assigned to one of six learning stations called Cluster Centers—16 to 17 per center. These stations are to be carefully selected to represent different facets of the city's culture.

The clusters will include space at the Milwaukee Art Center; the Schooner Project (a classroom attached to the port facility where a tall ship is being constructed that will sail the Great Lakes); initially the downtown UWM campus; and other places being negotiated. Each learning cluster has a learning facilitator and one or two learning mentors. There are four certified teachers who move around as needed among the six centers. The mentors, while not certified teachers, have college degrees and are adept at working with children. There is strong parent support, each student family signing a learning agreement as a GLC stakeholder, and parents are encouraged to participate in the program.

There is no principal as usually defined but an administrator, with governance provided by a staff council, parent council, and community advisory council. While the adult-student ratio is exceptionally high compared to traditional schools, substantial monies are saved because there are no school buildings to maintain, and there are fewer certified teachers because of the use of learning facilitators and parents. GLC leases the cluster facilities at minimal rent. At the outset, the GLC has a cooperative arrangement with Jackie Robinson Middle School for fiscal administration and other logistical supports. The administrative hub is initially at UWM's Center for Urban Community Development, where Professor Paulson provides technical assistance as unpaid consultant. Technology connects the six learning centers, as well as linking them to the broader community.

> Jasna surprised us by urging that we think radically; make end runs around the bureaucracy, go way beyond what now exists. There is no point in investing a lot of energy just to establish one more school, he said. "Be creative. Shake us up!"

In the fall, we submitted the GLC proposal to the Innovation School Reform Committee of the school board. A number of us showed up and testified at the public meeting, summarizing the proposal and requesting approval. The superintendent only asked them to approve the *concept* of the proposal, since this was not yet the final document. The committee didn't ask hard questions and complimented us on our hard work and the innovative quality of the GLC. They voted approval five to zero. Afterward, several of us adjourned to the Irish pub nearby to celebrate this initial success.

For the next round at the December 2 meeting of this same committee, the MPS administration submitted the full proposal for approval, with a first-year operating budget of $508,000, plus $103,000 for startup and transportation expenses. The administration noted that some costs would be raised by the GLC from outside sources for rental of the cluster sites and for technology that went beyond usual classroom use. I led off the hearing, recapitulating the proposal and asking for support, followed by a number of other speakers, including folks from the community.

This time the committee had plenty of questions.

The most radical aspect of our model was to discard the school building in favor of six decentralized learning sites in the community. Perhaps they envisaged what could happen if many others followed our example? What about all those school buildings that had been constructed and had to be maintained, and all those service jobs for janitors, utilities, and security? What would happen to the centralized control of the school system that emanated from the superintendent's office and flowed down into each school building? Our model dispersed power into six relatively independent sites, each with considerable flexibility, with governance shared with teachers and parents. How could creativity in each Cluster Center be controlled; was there too much flexibility?

To garner political support, Riano and I met at the home of one school board committee member who favored anything to shake up the system. I also met with the most skeptical board member, who once had worked with us at CUCD on the Harambee project. We got through the Innovation School Reform Committee, and, finally, the full school board approved the GLC in February 1998.

Coping with "It Can't Be Done!"

Since the decentralized Cluster Center sites were at the very heart of the GLC, we still had to get them officially approved by MPS and the City of Milwaukee—no simple task.

The Division of Facilities and Maintenance Service at the MPS central office had responsibility for assuring that our classrooms met state codes for occupancy. Each of our sites was visited, and we were told most did not meet requirements comparable to regular school buildings. Although these premises were regularly used by the public— the university space, the Milwaukee Art Museum, and so on—we were surprised that this problem even existed.

More and more, we heard the same words from the school bureaucrats: "Can't." "Impossible." Most of them were good people, but they were unable to imagine a teaching situation that could take place outside the hallowed structures and routines of the past. There were the usual supportive responses, as if to say the schools needed this kind of thinking. But the bottom line was the same: "This is the way the system works and we have no choice but to follow the rules." The system simply didn't have the flexibility for innovation.

I wrote two Milwaukee aldermen I knew, one a former student of mine, explaining the project and the need to get the spaces approved quickly. The result was that the Board of Zoning Appeal gave us variances for 10 years, which resolved the issue.

So it went for each aspect of the project. The MPS Insurance and Risk Management Department was at a loss as to how to handle liability for non-MPS spaces. Finally we contacted the city attorney, and the issue took three meetings to resolve. With the Department of Transportation, we had to work out a plan to get the students to the six Cluster center sites without the chartered buses used for the regular schools. We finalized a system for each student to get tickets to ride city buses in situations where parents didn't drive them.

Regarding food service, since our kids and staff didn't eat in school dining halls, we arranged with the director of food services to prepare bag lunches at school kitchens nearest the particular Cluster location. A designated staff person or parent picked up the food and delivered it to the students.

Since technology was a salient dimension of the GLC, meetings were held with the MPS director of technology to wire each Cluster Center.

Most controversial was developing the Memo of Understanding (MOU) with the Milwaukee Teachers Education Association (MTEA). From day one, the teachers union made clear they did not like the whole concept of the GLC: decentralized classrooms instead of a traditional school building, use of teaching assistants (mentors) along with certified teachers to run the program, a curriculum that incorporated the global dimension into the standardized course structure, and student-centered learning that could vary somewhat in each center depending on the capabilities and interests of the students and staff instead of the rigid, 50-minute course routine with prescribed ways of operating.

> Global Learning Center: decentralized classrooms instead of a traditional school building, use of teaching assistants (mentors) along with certified teachers to run the program, a curriculum that incorporated the global dimension into the standardized course structure, and student-centered learning that could vary somewhat in each center depending on the capabilities and interests of the students and staff instead of the rigid, 50-minute course routine with prescribed ways of operating.

The New School Opens

On August 26, 1998, when the GLC opened, Riano wrote:

> A memorable moment! A reality long anticipated in the process of creating an innovative model for a small urban middle school.

The first year turned out to be surprisingly successful. In contrast to many schools in the system, attendance was nearly perfect, and there were few disciplinary problems. With the small classes (16 to 17 students per center) and more adults per student, bonds developed between staff and students altogether different from many conventional school settings. Parents were more involved, although they did push for more structure. They were not used to such flexibility and creativity.

More and more effort was invested in curriculum development, trying to incorporate global thinking into the basics required for MPS testing: global-oriented programs, skits, lunches, exhibits related to different countries. On May 4, 1999, Mayor John Norquist issued a GLC Proclamation Day for Hispanics,

Much effort was invested in assessing student learning: we used the multiple intelligences concepts instead of tests alone, as well as portfolios of work completed during the year. The model and experience of home schooling was also valued.

> A number of teachers, tops in their fields but conditioned by years in the traditional system, experienced the GLC as an impossible assignment.

Since one learning site was based at the university, it was easy to enlist cooperation of the Jason Project, a nationally known Internet classroom founded by Robert Ballard, the oceanographer who discovered the underwater wreck of the *Titanic*. This popular scientific learning tool drew in students to explore ecological systems in different areas of the world.

The GLC also had access to the university's technology computer center. We designed a partnership whereby the student families could buy used computers cheaply and be trained to use them. The GLC created a Community Advisory Committee that brought in interesting ideas, such as students getting involved in a nationally organized stock market game and contact with Milwaukee's international businesses.

The spring 1999 election for Milwaukee's school board resulted in one of the periodic turnovers of its members, a near-disastrous blow for the GLC. Now we had to face the labyrinth of the traditional school bureaucracy, cooperating as mandated, but the world was different.

Riano soon found that a number of the teachers, tops in their fields but conditioned by years in the traditional system, experienced the GLC as an impossible assignment. This resulted in considerable turnover. Because each Cluster Center was more or less self-contained, although there was considerable interaction among the six, the teachers had to be creative in utilizing the freedom they'd been given.

They had to enlarge their view of "school." Instead of teaching one or more subjects in a large school building as in the past, the GLC was now one big learning family, with six stations and 100 students and homes—all interacting. We found that even teachers with excellent resumes found this arrangement baffling. In contrast, the learning assistants in most instances found the GLC an easier fit because they often had better rapport with the students, and they loved the increased responsibility in helping to run the centers.

Riano was questioned more and more by MPS administrators about different aspects of the GLC. Why didn't it operate like regular schools? We learned from a friendly budget analyst that MPS spent approximately $100 million per year on building-related costs (construction, debt amortization, repairs, utilities, personnel services) for some 100,000 students, or $1,000 per student per year. Since the GLC used no MPS building facilities, and it was financing the cost of the Clusters from its instructional budget, Riano requested some additional dollars to cover Center expenditures (e.g. rentals, furnishings, etc.), but MPS made clear that these costs were not in the original budget and could not be covered.

Ahead of Its Time

I participated in several staff meetings to explore the GLC becoming a charter school. The State of Wisconsin had approved legislation to authorize charter schools, and in Milwaukee, numerous charters were in process of development independent of most school authority, including the MTEA. Originally the city had approached us to consider the GLC as one of its first charters. At the time, we were encouraged not to take this route but to stay in the system—there was potential to maximize a GLC role as a force for change.

At the very time that MPS decided to defund the GLC, some experienced outside observers were so impressed with the GLC model that they urged us to copyright and market it, and to move forward with the charter school initiative. Later when we participated in a big conference in Detroit sponsored by the President's Council on Sustainable Development, we presented models of sustainability-oriented education. Some in the audience urged us to use our experience for national application.

> The learning assistants found the GLC an easier fit because they often had better rapport with the students, and they loved the increased responsibility in helping to run the centers.

Relating University Resources to Urban Needs

UWEX UNIVERSITY OF WISCONSIN—EXTENSION

600 WEST KILBOURN AVENUE   MILWAUKEE, WISCONSIN 53203   (414) 224-4143

CENTER FOR COMMUNITY LEADERSHIP DEVELOPMENT

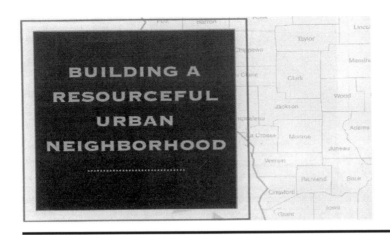

Status of Extension's Urban Programming

In Journal of Extension, *Spring 1973*

As a joint appointment of University of Wisconsin-Extension and University of Wisconsin-Milwaukee, I participated in a small group to develop strategies to bring new emphasis in urban extension programming. This focus would build on the long, successful history of university rural Extension. The *Journal of Extension* invited me to be guest editor of this special issue to explore the subject.

To learn about Extension's efforts in urban programming, I sent a questionnaire to the top Extension administrator at each land-grant university in connection with this special urban issue. We pointed out that while considerable information is available about ongoing Extension activities at the various universities, we know relatively little about specifically urban-focused Extension programs. The questionnaire data would serve as a beginning effort to fill the gap.

We are happy to report that 39 of the 50 institutions responded in some way. As the responses came in, a number of problems quickly became apparent. Four universities replied that they wouldn't or couldn't be delineated according to place of residence—such as rural and urban—or that much of the high priority need is rural-based, not urban, or that information on primarily urban programs simply isn't available.

We can conclude that urban Extension is still too new to have become effectively integrated into the Extension apparatus.

A number of respondents noted that their information sources weren't structured to provide specific data on urban-type programs, but that they'd searched for material through less regularized channels. This point is made by one administrator:

We know we have numerous urban programs and many different staff members devoting a great deal of time. A great deal of financial support is devoted as well. The only way I know we could more accurately get this information is to conduct a survey.

Paraphrasing another administrator: Until urban Extension has a development period comparable to agricultural Extension, with significant federal legislation and with a track record of universities extending their resources into the urban community, we can hardly expect urban Extension to match agricultural Extension's current level of effectiveness.

What "urban Extension models" will emerge on this new landscape?

Many comments indicate a growing interest in building an Extension capability and outreach that effectively deals with urban needs. In the process, new alliances undoubtedly will be forged between urban and rural community interests. New administrative arrangements can be expected to evolve both in universities and government, which may intermix the resources of such federal departments as Housing and Urban Development and Agriculture. New models will be created with as much appropriateness to urban as rural problems.

What "urban Extension models" will emerge on this new landscape? Can the agricultural Extension model be transplanted into the cities without major modifications?

In trying to assess the applicability of agricultural Extension models to urban problems, it is essential that there be some agreement on the nature of the agricultural model itself. Essential points that were reported include the following:

- The problems of local people are identified by an elected or other group from throughout the county.
- A core of subject-matter specialists provide program leadership and technical support.
- One of the aims of programs is to develop local leadership.
- University knowledge is an essential backup for programs.
- Learning often is best accomplished through practice demonstrations.
- Educational methods have infinite variety—university resources must be adaptable and sensitive to the needs.
- The university has a constant obligation to extend the results of research.
- The use of volunteers both involves the people and multiplies resources.
- Program results must be evaluated to determine their degree of success and the changes needed.

To the question "What are the limitations, if any, of the 'agricultural Extension model' in facing urban needs?", there was a surprisingly candid outpouring of comment. Responses fit into six general categories:

- *Personnel:* Several times this type of comment was made: "Our professional staff do not recognize the differences in people resulting from various environments, cultures, and social conditions."

- *Organization and administration of delivery systems:* "Extension's history is in agriculture, and even today a majority of staff and clientele are related to agriculture. There is inertia to suddenly turn to urban. The delivery system needs major adjustments to reach the urban audience."

- *Research base:* "Our research base for building urban models is very fragmented. Urban research is altogether lacking."

- *The urban milieu:* "Large numbers of people create problems. Our geographic boundaries are not realistic in terms of looking at the urban area. Leadership is less defined; how do we identify relevant key leaders for a large population? The clientele is more mobile. An individualized approach is not as possible with mass audiences. . . . Urban people may expect more programs handed down instead of self-help. The Extension agricultural model was designed for a rather scattered population that has similar values and cultural backgrounds and is highly production-oriented." Reference was made to "Extension's output of things as against development of people and behavioral change."

- *Public Image:* "The public's image of Extension is that it is strictly agricultural." Several statements were made that people assume Extension has no relevance to urban problems.

- *Commitment:* A number of statements were made depicting the awesome proportions of urban problems: "there is the sheer volume of the audience, and the funding required to make a measurable impact."

A Statement and Perspective on the Mission of Effectively Relating University of Wisconsin Resources to the Urban Community in Metropolitan Milwaukee and Wisconsin

1973

The dean of the newly established Division of Urban Outreach—DUO—formed an Urban Extension Organization Task Force. One of its first efforts, which I chaired, was to develop a mission statement. We coalesced ad hoc faculty groups drawn from the UWM campus and UW-Extension. Our Extension department also surveyed faculty and administrators to determine their interests and capabilities. With my colleagues I wrote this report that was used for formulating policy.

The term "University outreach" is not easy to define. There are at least three meanings:
- **University activities that by their very nature reach beyond the campus into the community.**
  The whole field of art, for example, reaches out beyond the confines of the campus and classroom: dance, drama, music, and the visual arts engage in a comprehensive dialogue with the public. The university sponsors a multitude of activities in the arts, extending from the Summer Arts Festival, which is

enriched by visiting artists, to plays and dance performances and concerts throughout the year. It works with community groups in developing new organizations such as the Milwaukee Ballet Company, the People's Theater, and the Community Theater Institute.

- **University degree-oriented credit courses or lab work, which traditionally have been carried out on campus but in recent years have begun moving off-campus into the community.**

These courses are off-campus for the convenience of particular population groups. Students and/or faculty may enrich their own learning and/or teaching experiences and simultaneously contribute to community needs through degree-oriented study and combination work/study arrangements off-campus; in inner city libraries, as practice teachers in the Milwaukee Public Schools; or as student social workers assigned to social agencies.

- **University problem-solving activities whose function is clearly determined by the needs of a given population.**

University resources are marshaled to solve a problem or category of problems that have community, regional, and/or national significance and that utilize University interest and capability. The activity may or may not be for-credit and degree-oriented. It may be off- or on-campus. It may take a variety of forms, ranging from teaching and research to consulting and demonstration projects. It may require "repackaging" of the knowledge so that it is usable by those needing and seeking it, or it may require the generation of new knowledge through pilot efforts and demonstration projects or applied research.

Historically speaking, university outreach activity was first systematically articulated by university extension efforts around the country that were primarily organized for agricultural and rural development. This process was greatly assisted by a body of federal and state legislation beginning with the Morrill Act of 1862, which provided a land endowment to each state for establishment of colleges of agriculture and mechanical arts. The Hatch Act of 1887 provided federal appropriations to support agricultural experimental stations. The Extension Division of the University of Wisconsin was established in 1906–1907 when President Charles Van Hise asked the state legislature for a grant of $20,000 for general extension work "under which the university goes out to the people." The model initiated at the University of Wisconsin was later emulated throughout the country.

No comparable university *urban extension model* has been developed for analyzing urban needs and conducting relevant urban research with the kind of close interrelationship between campus-based and field resources that evolved between colleges of agriculture and county extension offices. As yet there has been no massive university investment to develop instructional programs and to design demonstration projects in order to help solve urban problems. University work in urban communities has not led to the organization of strong interest groups as a base for political and financial support in any way comparable to the Farm Bureau and cooperatives and other support groups in agricultural extension.

These deficiencies have begun to be recognized. For example, a broad range of top university extension administrators set forth their views in a national questionnaire survey published by the *Journal of Extension* in spring 1973.

Successes in university extension in agriculture and rural development over the last 50 years point up the important role of federal legislation in bringing to bear the authority and financial support of the federal government. We should not underestimate the federal resources that have also been brought to bear on urban problems, especially since the early 1960s. But these efforts have been highly fragmented and short term, without any central thrust. No viable relationship has yet been created between the federal government and universities for specifically focused urban extension activity, a relationship that would:

- Provide a flow of substantial resources from the federal government to universities for urban activity on a continuing basis;
- Create an apparatus in cooperation also with state and local government for long-term planning and programming; and
- Facilitate development of a delivery system that relates the knowledge base of the university to the points of need in the cities and their urban surroundings.

University work in urban communities has not led to the organization of strong interest groups as a base for political and financial support.

The University of Wisconsin System is one of the relatively small number of state university systems that at present has certain inherent strengths as a base for building an urban extension program—a program that has potential for accomplishing the kind of pioneer work in relating university resources to problems of the cities that the university did earlier in responding to agricultural and rural needs.

The University of Wisconsin-Milwaukee is located in the state's major metropolitan area and urbanizing region. It has an expanding urban research base. It has several professional schools already with substantial community outreach and a number of faculty members who are both community oriented and interdisciplinary in their range of urban interests. Its administration has stated its firm commitment to its urban mission.

A major portion of the statewide Extension faculty based in the Greater Milwaukee area is an *urban extension faculty* dedicated to problem-solving in an urban, primarily metropolitan context.

University of Wisconsin-Extension has a core mission that was developed over many years. Its mission was succinctly stated in the UW System document recently presented to the Board of Regents:

To coordinate and, jointly with University of Wisconsin campuses and centers, provide a program of outreach designed to bring University of Wisconsin System resources to bear upon problems confronting the people and institutions of the state.

Now the issue is to forge these strengths into a combined university urban outreach effort that has the vision, can mobilize the resources, and can develop an appropriate apparatus to usher in a new phase of university involvement in confronting urban problems. It would appear that there are few such opportunities anywhere in the country for developing university structures to deal with urban problems that involve a campus and an extension program of the stature of UWM and UWEX.

> The secret of the early county agent's success was a state of mind combined with practical knowledge for solving problems.

University urban outreach, in its present modest proportions, is referred to in terms of a limited number of individual faculty members in consulting assignments, and a few units with specialized expertise for particular kinds of programs. "The University," referring in particular to the University of Wisconsin because of its predominant size and resources (although the same problem probably exists in academia generally), conjures up no image of significant urban problem-solving.

A major reason for this could be that the university has only begun "to get its hands dirty" in urban problem-solving. We who are interested in urban outreach might recall the role of the early county agents who helped to pioneer development of what has been called "the most creative invention of continuing informal education, the Cooperative Agricultural Extension Service." One of the reports gave this description:

> They were, essentially, itinerant rural philosophers. They were men who were at home with the efforts and thoughts of rural families….The demonstration of new ideas became the chief educational technique of the early county agent: showing how calves grow better without their horns, placing a strip of fertilized pasture at the bend in the road for all to see, helping a boy to grow hardier corn than his father had using the fabric of sugar sacks for draperies, and staking out a sample of plowing that would reduce the sudden damage of thunderstorms. Showing people how to do an old task in a new way and encouraging them to observe the outcome of the experiment formed the educational basis of the rural revolution in America.

The secret of the early county agent's success was a state of mind combined with practical knowledge for solving problems. He knew his clientele and he could develop their trust. He believed that change was possible, he implemented change through a series of manageable educational steps, and in working with farmers, he actually produced results. Much of the technical knowledge that the county agent brought to the countryside was the result of agricultural research carried out in the College of Agriculture and its field stations. Over time, curricula were developed for training students in the College based on that special combination of university-based research and practical field experience. These students in turn were to serve the farmers in appropriate ways.

The critical question is: what is relevant education in the context of contributing to the extremely complex setting of today's urban environment? Do the theories, concepts, and alternative solutions that are regularly lectured about, discussed, and debated in the classroom and lab provide any answers? One approach to dealing with this query is for the university to borrow from the early county agent and itself become directly involved in working on solutions for certain problems. This would be to demonstrate approaches that take the form of developing models for interrelating theory and practice to bring actual results. Because of the complexity of most urban problems and the likely need to formulate and test hypotheses, the "demonstration" would take the form of an experimental research design to determine "what works."

It can be argued that carefully designed, managed, and evaluated demonstration projects should be a major area of effort for DUO. They provide large opportunities for mobilizing clusters of university resources on an interdisciplinary basis. Being task oriented rather than structured according to conventional departmental lines, demonstration projects might suggest new types of organizational arrangements of inter-unit communication that would outlive the particular project. Through offering students new kinds of linkages between campus-based theoretical coursework and practical problem-solving in the field, some innovative methodologies for teaching and applied research could result.

> **Through offering students new kinds of linkages between campus-based theoretical coursework and practical problem-solving in the field, some innovative methodologies for teaching and applied research could result.**

Over time, they could have substantial repercussions for the University. DUO could use demonstration projects as a main vehicle for investing in particular units and faculty of UWM or Extension, in the process setting standards of quality and strengthening or redirecting energies toward high-priority needs and goals. Perhaps most importantly, genuine excitement could be brought back into education—the frame of mind characterized above by the early county agents who regularly experienced the drama of generating and harnessing knowledge to cope with some of society's significant problems.

There are at least three glaring deficiencies to keep in mind regarding the present financing of University Urban Outreach activities:

- Most urban efforts of universities, including the University of Wisconsin, are underfinanced, which in itself virtually precludes major results in problem-solving. This traces to the relatively recent arrival of universities into urban outreach, and the lack of substantial institutional commitments by the university as well as by government for utilization of universities for this purpose.

- Most efforts lack long-term planning and programming. In depending on income generated from the activity itself or on short-term government, foundation, or other types of grants, urban work has not been institutionalized into a framework of personnel and resources, as historically was the case in rural extension.

- Linkages have been lacking between campus-based urban research and training and extension-type activities. It is not often that broad strategies and interdisciplinary proposals for urban problem-solving are developed and submitted for funding. Given the complex interrelatedness characterizing many urban needs, this greatly weakens university capacity for preparing strong proposals.

DUO could serve an extremely useful role in beginning to overcome these deficiencies. It could work closely with the various urban outreach units, be they in Extension or UWM, in formulating proposals that assemble in a maximum way the strengths of the University for urban outreach.

Traditional research proposals without a clear urban problem-solving focus, or extension projects without a well-articulated tie-in to research and/or training activity, would be unacceptable.

DUO should occupy itself in a major way in pushing for urban federal funding designed to draw substantial resources on a long-term, continuing basis. The eventual result could be the structuring of an apparatus involving federal resources collaborating with those from the levels of city, county, and state government, for providing universities the substance for long-term institutional commitments for services in our country's urban areas.

TEN REFLECTIONS ON URBAN POLICY DRAWN FROM PRACTICAL EXPERIENCE IN LOW-INCOME AREAS OF WISCONSIN AND ELSEWHERE

April 2012

—READING ABILITY with youth is a crucial break-through for positive behavior and achievement (experience: 65-block community survey, reading demonstration, tutorial centers)

—EFFECTIVE SCHOOLS require linkage to the surrounding community infrastructure, not only school attendance (experience: Central City Teacher Project)

—COMMUNITY DETERIORATION is unlikely to be significantly improved only through single-focused initiatives; comprehensive strategies keyed to multiple variables are required (experience: Harambee Revitalization Project)

—COMMUNITY HEALTH relates not only to physical health but cultural change tied to interrelated facets of community life (Community Health Project)

Ten Reflections on Urban Policy:

Drawn from Practical Experience in Low-Income Areas of Wisconsin and Elsewhere

April 2012

Years ago a number of us organized the Greater Milwaukee local chapter of the World Future Society, America's main body for futures studies. Occasionally I also made presentations such as this recent talk. It is a brief summation that outlines some of my thinking on urban policy, drawing from a wide range of personal experiences over many years. Several of the points that follow were discussed in the earlier International section; most are referred to in this Urban section; and several are detailed in subsequent chapters. In aggregate, this listing of discrete experiences constitutes a kind of skeleton for elaborating a number of key components for a rather comprehensive urban policy.

- **Reading Ability** with youth is a crucial breakthrough for positive behavior and achievement (experience: 65-block community survey, reading demonstration, tutorial centers).

- **Effective Schools** require linkages to the surrounding community infrastructure, not only what happens inside the school (experience: Central City Teacher Project).

- **Community Deterioration** is unlikely to be significantly improved only through single-focused initiatives; comprehensive strategies keyed to multiple variables are required (experience: Harambee Revitalization Project).

- **Community Health** relates not only to physical health but to cultural change tied to interrelated facets of community life (experience: Community Health Project).

- **Powerlessness and Anger** can be overcome through residents learning to understand and effectively utilize the political system (experience: Harambee Ombudsman Project).

- **Use of Community Volunteers** brings ownership of improvement initiatives; money and jobs are likely to be required, but a personal stake in outcomes nurtures positive results (experience: neighborhood block work, role of "small intellectuals").

- **Confronting Institutional Racism** is complex and subtle and demands sophisticated strategies and willing leadership (experience: Milwaukee-mandated school desegregation, Riverside Project, seminars on jobs with business, urban training with churches and civic organizations).

- **City-Suburban Connections** greatly facilitate placing inner city isolation and resource poverty into broader interactions, which bring new resources and political support (experience: Chapter 220 of Wisconsin Statutes, Greater Milwaukee Goals 2000 Project).

- **Sustainable Development** is an essential futures policy that interrelates environmental initiatives to economic development, providing jobs, improving housing conditions, and enhancing overall community betterment with ecological significance (experience: Department of Energy contract, Changing Role of Work conference, seminars on sustainable futures).

- **Implementing a Creative University Role**, where experimentation is linked with traditional learning and service, relationships are developed between indigenous leaders and outside resources, bottlenecks are identified to break open the status quo (experience: all of this described in application of the nine-cell matrix model).

Urban: Postscript

Local communities in today's America seem to be where the action is. With the national government paralyzed with partisan dysfunctionality, leadership has gravitated to the states, cities, towns, and villages. Although each community is different, they all have problems to be solved, whatever the political party or ideology. Concerns are debated—more or less government, passing a bond issue or not for essential infrastructure, selecting a school superintendent or police or fire chief. The quality of the decision may be high or low, but decisions cannot be postponed indefinitely, as is what often happens in Washington.

Even traumatic situations like the bankruptcy of Detroit, after years of incompetent government combined with historic economic dislocations, are stimulating new revitalization paths. *The New York Times* columnist David Brooks recently wrote: "The happiest people these days are those who leave Washington and get elected mayor or governor. The most frustrated people are people who were mayor and governor and get elected to the Senate. They end each day knowing they were busy. They're just not sure they accomplished anything."

When I joined the University of Wisconsin in the early 1960s, I was soon immersed in sessions dealing with the urban environment. Parts of the city of Milwaukee were deteriorating; the minority community was up in arms for being left out of the country's growing prosperity; public institutions, from schools to certain city services, were labeled insensitive to needs. The business community admitted it was at a loss in dealing with racism and the widening gap between the inner city and the broader community. Some observers warned that we could be approaching a new civil war in America, which in the latter '60s did ravage some cities, including, to some degree, Milwaukee. I was part of a small group mandated to figure out how Wisconsin's major university could creatively reallocate resources to make a difference in this potentially explosive situation.

Since I was a joint appointment between UW-Extension and the UW-Milwaukee campus, I served on two fronts. The university's Extension historic program focus, and where its leadership was nationally recognized, was rural and small town populations. The Milwaukee campus was heavily oriented toward teaching and research. The challenge now was to pull in some of these resources to impact the urban community. When I helped the university establish its first department to address urban poverty and racism, we brought Extension into the heart of the inner city, and linked up with campus departments. Top university administrators were soon calling on our department to help upgrade their effectiveness.

I felt the key to drawing in Extension was to translate its historic expertise in community development and preparation of leaders in rural communities to comparable responsibilities in the urban community. I knew that University Extension administrators nationally were searching for ways to become more relevant to urban problems.

The key to drawing in the academic campus was to offer professors and staff professional development opportunities that transcended their usual departmental work. We found that magnets for enlisting campus academics who typically resisted getting involved in "urban service projects" included: conducting surveys in unexplored inner city terrain, building power models for the powerless, defining the meaning of a healthy community, breaking new ground in school innovation, and stimulating graduate students to come up with novel solutions to problems.

Since I had only recently returned from Europe, where for years I worked with people in desperate straits, I now faced the challenge of functioning in the very different American setting. While our inner city conditions were often considered inhumane, they were not comparable to the overseas homeless and refugees living on the margin of life. American "poverty" would often qualify as middle class or better in much of the world. Nevertheless, our affluent country continues to face a maze of stark, complex problems that have defied ready solutions. Today they appear even more urgent and intractable then when my university urban work began. I briefly mention three:

- There is growing inequality of income and opportunity—a long-term downward spiral of the middle class. The 2010 census reported 43.6 million people under the poverty line—the largest since records began in the 1950s. At the same time, our country's wealthy has prospered as never before. From the end of World War II to 1976, the top 10 percent of our population took in less than one-third of pre-tax income; now it gets almost 50 percent. The top 1 percent receives 23 percent. The American dream of upward mobility was more prevalent then than today.

- Our economy can now produce all the goods and services our society needs without its total labor force. Modern technology has brought spectacular benefits, and total wealth has dramatically increased. Yet fewer people are needed for full-time jobs, accentuating the inequality. For 40 postwar years, people moved from manufacturing into services and new jobs opened up. Now computers and robots and globalization are ushering in a new, very different era.

- Our education is falling behind. A 2011 international survey reported that the United States was now 21st, 23rd, and 25th, respectively, in science, reading, and math among 30 developed nations. Not only science and technology, but the capacity to think creatively and problem solve are sorely needed. Breaking through the bureaucratic labyrinth for a paradigm shift in learning institutions is a priority challenge.

As a final word, the university department, Center for Urban Community Development, that I helped to found almost half a century ago, continues its strong work in Milwaukee, Wisconsin, and nationally. After I chaired it for 22 years, my successor from the staff, Dan Folkman, served almost as long. Our new chair, Kalyani Rai, also rising from the staff, represents the exceptional continuity and contributions that the university affirms. As needs change, we adapt in order to remain on the cutting edge. Some years ago we helped the university enhance its effectiveness by merging Milwaukee-based Extension with the UWM campus. Notable community projects such as Harambee continue.

Creative learning initiatives remain CUCD's central priority, notwithstanding extreme frustration with the public schools. The department's innovative inner city efforts—such as the Central City Teacher Project, Summer Prep (which redirected some gang leaders), the Riverside Educational Improvement Project, and the two pilot schools (Urban Waldorf and Global Learning Center)—all have provided exceptional models. But they were forced to accept goals below their potential due to shortsighted bureaucratic leadership in the system.

Since CUCD has always focused heavily on improving life in the minority community, it faces big, negative odds. Milwaukee remains one of America's most racist cities, with segregated housing and inner city schools that are almost all minority. Poverty in the black and Hispanic communities is elevated. August 2013 signifies 50 years since the famous 1963 March on Washington for Jobs and Freedom, remembered with Martin Luther King Jr.'s "I have a dream" speech. Like our department, much has happened since then, but much remains to do.

PART III
Sharing Lifestyles and Values in Community

Belden and Lisa Paulson, co-founders of High Wind eco-intentional community and their passive solar house near Plymouth, Wisconsin

Community: Introduction

This section begins in a remote corner of northern Scotland. In fall 1976, my wife Lisa lived in an unusual enclave there for three weeks. This experience had a decisive impact on her life and mine and on that of many others.

Located near a Scottish fishing village on the North Sea, Findhorn is a spiritual/ecological community founded in 1962 by Peter Caddy, a former RAF officer; his wife Eileen, who "received detailed guidance through meditation"; and Dorothy Maclean, who through meditation connected with the patterning forces in nature. Over a number of years, the three of them drew people from across the globe to create a community committed to cultural transformation. Their immediate, practical commitment was to rebuild the connection between people and nature.

In 1970, a young mystic and teacher, David Spangler, joined the emerging community and helped design educational programs that focused on creating a "planetary consciousness." Spangler, through his books that contributed to the community's practical models for "the good life," also originated the term "New Age."

The Findhorn Foundation recently celebrated its 50th birthday. Its 300 members come from around the world; thousands are drawn each year for conferences and workshops and deep-level experiences. With a strong commitment to ecological practice and demonstration, reportedly the Findhorn community has one of the lowest carbon footprints in the United Kingdom. Its buildings are powered by solar and wind, and its sewage is biologically treated by a "Living Machine." Findhorn is listed as a Non-Governmental Organization with the United Nations, and its ecological training is carried out in Scotland and other locations around the world.

On returning home, Lisa gave many talks and her missionary zeal impressed everyone. When people asked her how Findhorn differed from other idealists who extol "the good life," including members of major religions, she replied, "They are actually living it." Although an attentive listener, I harbored skepticism until I met Peter Caddy and went to live for a week at Findhorn. Over the years, Lisa has been to Findhorn nine times and I seven times, including arranging for five university seminars there. Most of the students came away with transformative personal life experiences.

When in 1977 we invited Peter and Eileen Caddy to speak at UWM, we had standing room only in the biggest meeting space on campus; 1,200 people showed up. Subsequently we invited David Spangler and others of his group from Findhorn to teach with me. Our seminars became a kind of new "curriculum" on a range of subjects that focused on thinking about what a new culture would look like as we examined the dysfunctionalities of contemporary life. One of our early offerings with high impact was an oversubscribed course we entitled "New Dimensions of Governance."

A group of 50 people from all walks of life who attended many of these offerings bonded together, with a commitment not only to attend classes but excitement about initiating "something practical." We created a nonprofit organization, the High Wind Association, "to develop a sharing community where people live together in cooperation with one another and nature," to construct buildings using renewable energy and conserve the ecosystem, and to educate through demonstration and dialogue.

In 1980, the US Department of Energy gave High Wind a small grant to build a bioshelter: "a structure inspired by biological systems, capable of providing its own energy and climate, treating its own wastes, and growing food for the residents." Since Lisa and I owned a 46-acre farm near Plymouth, 50 miles north of Milwaukee, we were happy

> We created a nonprofit organization, the High Wind Association.

to dedicate it to High Wind use. A group of volunteers gave up their jobs to become the construction crew to build the bioshelter, and in due course, several stayed on. The construction crew became an "intentional community"—defined as a group that comes to live together with the *intention* of embracing certain shared values and purposes. We agreed on a credo; although often reviewed, it has survived for decades unaltered.

With no road map and no community models we knew about in the Midwest, we simply put one foot in front of the other, learning through trial and error. Our very intense, close-knit intentional community lasted for 12 years, from the early 1980s into the nineties, with an average of 20-plus residents. Counting the board of directors and the High Wind bookstore in Milwaukee and various committees and projects, hundreds of volunteers became involved, and thousands of people, drawn nationally and even from overseas, participated in planned events.

In the nineties, our High Wind board made the decision to shift from the intense lifestyle of the intentional community—where we all worked and ate together and decided everything by consensus—to the looser format of a Learning Center. High Wind's focus now was increasingly to share its experience as a community, while placing this into the larger conceptual framework of envisaging an alternative culture.

In 2001, the High Wind board made another important shift: it sold the property owned by the community to two Buddhist groups that had come to know the community well and shared its values. Over time, High Wind has consulted closely with one of them, the Shambhala Buddhists, which is creating a Midwest center they call Windhorse. Windhorse plans to mesh Buddhist values with the High Wind tradition of conscious, sustainable living. A number of High Wind members who had built homes continue to live on the land, now viewing their relationship with each other and the Buddhists as an "eco-neighborhood." The High Wind board continues intact, now serving as a small foundation that provides grants to compatible groups and engages in outreach. A tract of contiguous farmland once owned by the community is now a successful, privately run model of sustainable agriculture; Springdale Farm, operated by two former community members, provides naturally grown vegetables to hundreds of families.

When people asked me to describe High Wind I used the image of a three-legged stool. There was the Spiritual Dimension, building on the Findhorn experience, the teachings of David Spangler and others, and spurred by the impulse of contributing to creating a new "consciousness."

There was the Technological Dimension, of practicing conservation and sustainable living, using renewable energy, and growing food naturally. At High Wind, we built the bioshelter and incorporated the latest ideas about energy efficiency in our everyday living. Some of us also engaged in a major entrepreneurial project on a contiguous tract of 144 acres, an ecological treasure called Silver Springs. When the property was about to be subdivided for commercial development, a small group connected with High Wind bought it. We created an entity that we called Plymouth Institute to conduct R&D, and we designed a state-of-the-art ecovillage—SpringLedge—a plan that attracted national interest. This proved too radical, however, for the conservative local authorities and was rejected.

Finally, there was the Educational Dimension, which focused on conceptualizing what we were doing and communicating our experience in many ways. This included regular collaboration with the University of Wisconsin-Milwaukee and University of Wisconsin-Extension in co-sponsoring courses and conferences, and contracting the Milwaukee Public Schools to provide onsite learning for inner city teachers and students.

One notable effort with the university was the "three-community-seminar," where students drawn nationally lived at High Wind, Findhorn, and another intentional community, receiving academic credit for the full semester. Because I played the dual role of a university professor and also a High Wind leader, the university's legal department had to be assured there was no personal financial conflict of interest. Since Lisa and I made substantial contributions to support this enterprise, with zero personal monetary gain, I passed muster.

High Wind required an intense effort for all involved, especially for those of us who co-founded the project and stayed with it. When we began this initiative in the latter 1970s, some of the group were pushing for fundamental, radical shifts; it seemed clear that the existing culture could no longer be repaired through marginal, band-aid kinds of change. It was a time for a new start. The term "transformation" came up in every discussion.

Years later, when a questionnaire study assessed the High Wind influence and challenge, I responded this way:

The commitment to live in an alternative community such as Findhorn or High Wind is, in essence, to grapple in a very concrete way with the search for a new vision of society. It's committing to a vision of sustainable living in your daily life. . . . It requires patterns of human relationships that favor cooperation over competition, sharing of resources in contrast to seeking all you can get for yourself, listening to people whose ideas you don't accept and making decisions based on consensus instead of majority-minority rule. This paradigm comes face-to-face with the prevailing mainstream culture that is not sustainable, is organized around political/social/economic hierarchy, and is driven by short-run goals and achievements rather than the long-run building of a new culture.

I'm convinced that fundamentally we're talking about raising the level of consciousness of each of us as individuals and through this process, of society generally. . . . Living in an alternative community is very hard, because it involves commitment to a paradigm that challenges most of the values of our dominant culture. We quickly find that while the vision is extra-ordinary, the people in the community are themselves ordinary. Thus there is the gap of expectations not realized. . . . It's easy to get frustrated and angry.

There was another personal challenge that Lisa and I and our early compatriots faced—the so-called "founders' syndrome." At a conference at Findhorn in the 1980s, a panel of founders of intentional communities from different areas of the world addressed this topic. They had all begun with a central vision focused on cultural change and living sustainably, they all had a strong eclectic spiritual dimension, they all practiced non-hierarchical consensual decision-making, and they all contributed disproportionately to their community's money problems. And they all recognized that apart from the difficulties of starting the community, they found it a complex undertaking not only for themselves to practice the values of the emerging culture, but to convey this same commitment to newer community residents.

> Living in an alternative community is very hard, because it involves commitment to a paradigm that challenges most of the values of our dominant culture.

Over High Wind's history, people arrived in four waves. Our first wave had been involved in the early seminars and contact with Findhorn and David Spangler and others. Successive waves also gave up remunerative jobs and arrived with high idealism. Since they were basically volunteers, their reward system depended not on material gain but the intangible conviction that they were contributing to something very important—that they would contribute to changing the world in some small way.

Resident staff at High Wind community in mid-1980s

Obviously this kind of idealism would not last very long because life is full of conflicts. Decisions had to be made about construction and lifestyle and how a very heterogeneous group of people would get along together. Sometimes people would get bitter and leave, even penniless. Sometimes they would blame the founders about the gap between their expectations and the realities of daily living. As the distance increased from the early, formative years, the understanding of goals and values often became more murky. Since High Wind had its own needs and problems, in essence, how was it really different from mainstream society?

High Wind produced a periodic newsletter, *Windwatch*, which evolved into a small newspaper edited by Lisa. Anyone could write articles or news items. Its purpose was to chronicle what was happening, while regularly re-emphasizing the community's original goals and values as well as reporting on related High Wind activities, such as its bookstore in Milwaukee, educational events, and compatible efforts elsewhere. Sometimes Lisa's editorials were criticized by community members because they felt there was little relationship between the ideals being expressed and the community's nitty-gritty, real world. Since High Wind had developed a broad mailing of several thousand, *Windwatch* generated remarkable interest in its experiment nationally and even beyond.

The Spiritual Dimension

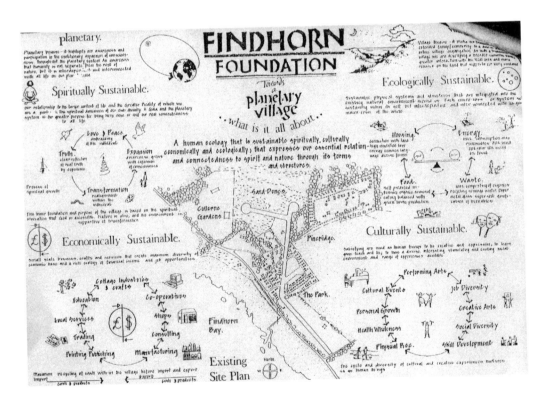

REVELATION
THE BIRTH OF A NEW AGE

by David Spangler

INTRODUCTION BY WILLIAM IRWIN THOMPSON

The New Age

Notes taken from "An Ecological Community," in Odyssey of a Practical Visionary, *2009*

After Lisa returned from Findhorn in fall 1976, we quickly engaged in a whirlwind round of intense conversations. More than only her Scotland experience, we explored influences that could affect the next steps in our lives. A term that surfaced regularly was "New Age." This was a concept more than a term. Historically speaking, I was familiar with the term "age" to categorize the evolution of cultures and civilizations: Dark Age, Age of Reason, Industrial Age, Atomic Age, Information Age. Now, what was the New Age?

Lisa pulled out her Findhorn notes:

Basically the New Age means recognizing that mutual cooperation and respect and love are essential if our planet is to survive at all. All living things but humans operate naturally within this system. Greed and selfishness and lust for power have gotten in the way of a larger awareness. David Spangler says in *Revelation* that "the New Age is fundamentally a change of consciousness from one of isolation and separation to one of communion, attunement and wholeness."

She continued with further thoughts of Spangler and others:

A person must love without limit, be limitless love before he can begin to be entrusted with New Age energies. One of the prime Laws of Manifestation—on which Findhorn was founded and through which it has operated successfully for 15 years—is that every need is met perfectly through faith. These energies and gifts have to be cycled back to the source. If you receive you must return the gifts; nothing must stop with you. You own nothing, not even land, but are simply given stewardship of it for a time. This love energy must be kept flowing. . . .

Lisa shuffled more notes. Her ideas tended to come in the middle of the night, or on buses or atop barren moorland. One of these came through at 5:30 one morning and she had to write it down:

Practice looking into the soul of another and see the great good, beauty and perfection that is in each one, which is the stuff of the soul. With the strength of this vision you can actually transform that person into that image. Projection. Thoughts, images becoming reality. This is how the world will be transformed, how humankind will be saved from itself, how groups and nations will be brought to the new consciousness.

They will be loved and lifted by the few to the higher planes where there is no longer a need to prove power and position. There won't be the unloved condition of insecurity and self-hate that makes one person have to hurt another. This must be the task of everyone, each working in his own small personal way. To find the greatness in every human being we touch and help him to see and own it too. Not to judge. It has to start one to one.

Later on when I began teaching with David Spangler I recorded these words from one of his talks:

The New Age is a myth, a metaphor of the Golden Age, of Utopia, of Progress and the creation of a more Perfect and Just Society. It is a metaphor for our creative ability to learn, to gain new insights, to change, to imagine, to be open to the unpredictable and the new, and thereby to build a future different from what we already know or expect. . . . The New Age is rooted generally in all those mythos of humanity that speak of unfoldment and the birth of a better world. . . .

It is also rooted in what Aldous Huxley called "The Perennial Philosophy," a collection of ideas about the interrelationships of humanity, God and nature that together form humanity's most pervasive and ancient spiritual insights....The agenda of the New Age is to use available, familiar strategies (economic, political, medical, artistic, educational, and technological) at every effective level of action (personal, institutional, municipal, regional, national and global) to secure and promote the well-being of every person creature on Earth, as well as of Earth itself. . . .

The future is not determined; we can be co-creative with each other, with nature and with God and thereby open doors to wonders and unfoldments we can just begin to imagine. In so doing we must honor communion, build community, empower individuals and keep the process going in playful and creative ways.

I felt the door was opening on how to link my university urban work with New Age themes. I participated in a meeting at UW-Madison where I saw Professor Ted Shannon. He was one of the deans of University Extension who had asked me to join the university in 1962; he belonged to that small nucleus of administrators who stuck their necks out as creative risk-takers. When he asked me what I was up to these days, and I recited an inventory of my activities, including my interest in what was happening at Findhorn, he was immediately curious and wanted to know more about the community and its ramifications. By the time we finished the conversation, he was urging me to figure out ways to bring this whole subject into the university's educational process. "There's nothing more important," he said.

The hour-and-a-half drive home from Madison unfolded as a prolonged meditation sparking a thousand questions for me. Was my university focus being radically reshuffled to bring in a whole new dimension (without much clarity as to what this new dimension might be)? How to interrelate my years of work in urban community development and political science with the world of alternative thinking? Would I be throwing out all that had been built up in my department for an unknown field of endeavor? How to convince my deans and other university powers-that-be of the need to invest time and resources in this fledgling field, especially in a day of tight budgets and demand for tangible results? Given that the essence of the New Age had a strong spiritual dimension, how to deal with the absolute requirement of a public university that church and state be kept separate? In that the heart and soul of this new area of activity was for now centered in Lisa's experience and her zeal, what new relationship would unfold for us personally if we were to engage in a common work? And as there were few if any faculty in the university with a knowledge base for offering learning related to this New Age, where were the collegial resources to work with me? As one question led to the next, my only respite was the finiteness of the 80-mile trip home.

> The New Age is a myth, a metaphor of the Golden Age, of Utopia, of Progress and the creation of a more Perfect and Just Society.

Two of the people I valued most in my urban work were my former dean, Glen Pulver, and Marie Arnot, an innovative professor at the University of Nebraska-Lincoln, who had invited me to serve as a judge to select the most outstanding community development projects in Nebraska. When both of them presented talks at an annual Community Development Society conference at about this time, I was delighted to hear this salient theme in Pulver's words:

> There is a need to reexamine our way of life. . . . For many years society as a whole accepted the premise that big was better, growth was great, and technology was terrific. There seemed to be an almost universal belief that all problems could be solved if somehow we produced more. . . . There was little or no public concern about fossil fuel reserves, clean air, or how the benefits of growth could be dispersed. In the last quarter of this century, there will be increased recognition of the limits of growth.

And Arnot talked about "Values for the Years Ahead," stressing these same themes, even quoting E.F. Schumacher and his classic book *Small Is Beautiful*.

With this kind of thinking in relatively high places, I decided to communicate what was on my mind with one of the top administrators in the UW System, senior Vice President Donald Smith, whom I knew when chairing the Extension Chancellor Search Committee. Because I'd found him to be one of the more enlightened among the university's higher echelons, I was curious as to whether he was on the same wave length as people like Pulver and Arnot. I sent him a packet of material from our classes, conferences, the Findhorn visit and recent talks. He replied:

> I was particularly interested in your talk in Sheboygan. The theme is one I have examined in some of my own speaking, and it seems to me to hit at one of the major transitions facing the profile of our efforts in research and instruction, including our continuing education and public service activities. . . . Can we, in fact, help society prepare itself to understand and cope with a future which may require, for survival, some fundamental changes in preferred values and goals?

I was becoming convinced that new thinking was no longer merely associated with an isolated enclave in northern Scotland or those of us at High Wind. Mainstream culture recognized a pressing need for a fundamental new direction in values, visions, and action. At least on the surface, the time had begun to translate the vision into action.

Findhorn's "Hobbit house" sanctuary for meditation and Taize a cappella singing

The Coming Transformation and Educational Change

Presentation at Findhorn Community, Scotland, 1979

On my second trip to Findhorn, with a group from Wisconsin associated with our fledgling efforts to establish High Wind, I made this presentation to the community.

This morning our Wisconsin group began the third week of its one-month stay at Findhorn. It is focusing on the subject: "Strategizing for reentry after Findhorn." Obviously caution is needed about what we mean by "reentry" in that four weeks hardly gives time for entering and absorbing fully the Findhorn experience. We mean reenter not in the physical sense of our particular group going home, but rather in the context of the fundamental question: How does a person who has entered a "new culture" cope with his/her surrounding world? How does one reenter the environment one had left and strategize to change it?

The premise is that change is integral to the planetary mission of those who have begun to experience a new culture. Reentry in this sense refers to all of us who are striving to change the "old," not just our Wisconsin group, not only Findhorn members, but indeed everyone who has joined in this quest.

A few days before our group left for Findhorn, two colleagues with whom I was teaching, David Spangler and Milenko Matanovic, met with us. I jotted down a few notes from their comments :

> There are small numbers of people going out into the world who have passed beyond the limitations of personality and ego to unfold new perspectives of life. They seek the emergence of the spiritual domain in the world. They are a kind of spiritual board of directors who enter government, business, academia, and so forth. They seek to build a New Culture. They are guided by an energy that contends that

the New Age is not just an individual experience; it is collective experience, responsive to a higher field of energy.

In describing Findhorn, David noted that two kinds of energy always seem to be moving through Findhorn, often in tension:

- The School: the esoteric training center to bring about a New Age
- The Community: a village to explore human relationships

The School concept refers to the many aspects of teaching and training; the center as a showplace, the willingness to set aside personal desire for service to the world. The Community concept implies fewer visitors, less interest in and contact with the outside, emphasis on the internal building of the community.

While the two concepts may be in friendly conflict as the focus of Findhorn, both are essential and interrelated. Findhorn can be seen as a certain kind of "university." It is creating a distinctive spiritual community, which is a demonstration. Then the vision and attributes of this distinctive community are conceptualized, and through teaching and publishing, they are brought into the larger environment. I should add that universities, too, have demonstration projects, although certainly not like Findhorn's, and they, of course, have research, teaching and publishing functions.

The Coming Transformation

This morning the Wisconsin group saw a visual presentation prepared by the community on major dimensions of the planetary crisis. A mass of data was displayed. Frequent references were made to one of the most astute current thinkers on the global crisis, Willis Harman of the Stanford Research Institute. I have brought him to Wisconsin to speak and to teach with me in conferences.

In two recent articles on "The Coming Transformation" (in *The Futurist* magazine), Harman succinctly outlined and related the formal outline of the crisis to its underlying spiritual dimensions. His basic theme is that the dominant paradigm, or way of looking at the world, of the modern industrial state is heading for collapse. Here, in Harman's words, is a summary of the vision of reality that has influenced Western culture for at least 200 years:

- Development and application of the scientific method and technology;
- Industrialization through organization and division of labor, and replacement of human labor by machines;

- Acquisitive materialism, unlimited material progress and economic/technological growth as the dominant value;
- Manipulative rationality, a search to control nature;
- Pragmatic values, with individuals pursuing their own interest as the way to produce the "good society."

Harman affirms that industrial societies—both capitalist and socialist—have been extraordinarily successful at achieving their goals. They have achieved high material standards, optimal nutrition, university education, longer lives, efficient productive systems, and generalized affluence for most people in the Western world.

We should add that while many people associated with New Age thinking criticize these achievements, they usually participate fully in the advantages. For much of the world population, achieving minimum material and social levels of life are still the great driving force in their lives. It is not by accident that Findhorn and counterpart communities elsewhere attract few people from the developing countries or from pockets of the richer countries still plagued by the culture of poverty.

Harman discusses four great dilemmas that have been generated by the successes of 200 years of industrial progress:

- *The growth dilemma:* We need continued economic growth, but we can't live with the ecological and environmental consequences of that growth;
- *The control dilemma:* As resources become scarcer and the impact of technology on nature more ominous, we need more centralized control, but this would jeopardize the private market system and democratic government, which we value so much;
- *The distribution dilemma:* We need to narrow what has become an ever-widening and explosive gap between the richer and the poorer nations in the world and also between the haves and have-nots at home, but we lack the will and perhaps the resources to do it;
- *The work roles dilemma:* Advanced industrial systems have demonstrated their inability to provide employment for all their people (except in wartime), and in particular they lack capacity for providing meaningful work.

These dilemmas, argues Harman, are inherent in the very successes of modern industrial systems. In overcoming the "old scarcities" related to food, clothing, shelter, and so on, by means of economic and technological progress, these systems have brought a "new scarcity" as we approach the impassable barriers of a finite planet. Obvious limits are on the horizon as regards such essentials as fossil fuels and minerals, natural fresh water, food-productive land, waste-absorptive capacity, and life support ecosystems.

There are still many optimists, however, who believe that:

- Technological breakthroughs will solve the energy, waste, and resource problems;
- New measures will control population growth and increase food production to adequate levels;
- New products and services will solve world unemployment;

- Arms treaties will preserve world peace, and international controls will prevent the use of biological and nuclear weapons; and
- Capital and know-how channeled into the less developed countries will close the gap, and the intense interest of these areas to industrialize will not unduly pollute the world.

The measures listed above are undoubtedly very important for incremental improvements. But Harman, after amassing data, lays out this conclusion: the basic system that has dominated the industrial era has begun to counteract human ends. The result is a massive and growing challenge to the legitimacy of the basic goals and institutions. Above all, this is a *value crisis*, a challenge to the underlying culture of the modern industrial state. Lewis Mumford has written that there have been only a limited number of profound transformations in Western society since primitive man. The transformation we are undergoing is therefore a rare event.

In recent years, we have seen much literature about various dimensions of the outlines of a new era—the New Age to come. Findhorn has made its contributions to this new vision. Whatever the details, this coming period, again in Harman's words, can be expected to have two fundamental dimensions:

- *An ecological ethic*, which relates to holism, the interdependence of the total planet, and constraints on individual egos in favor of the whole;
- *A self-realization ethic*, which affirms the proper end of all individual experience to be development of the higher self and the human species.

The coming transformation we have been discussing is, fundamentally, a *cultural crisis.*

Findhorn above all knows how hard it is to be a Center of Light (its term), which tries to apply a spirit of love, knowledge, and vision of alternatives, and a will that grounds the love and knowledge into nuts-and-bolts action. To the degree that Findhorn is a Center of Light, it is in a sense also a certain kind of university. It is:

- A place of inquiry, inspiration, and experimentation;
- A seeker of the truth;
- A challenger of traditions, no matter how respectable, when "old baggage" gets in the way of the truth;
- A builder of awareness in people about the fundamentals of life and survival, of the planetary crisis and possible alternative visions to confront it; and
- A center committed to growth, to fulfillment, to self and community realization of the highest values.

These are or should be among the qualities of any university worthy of its name.

It is difficult to see an institution like the University of Wisconsin as a Center of Light in the sense that Findhorn is. But our traditional universities are ready for change. They only need people with the will to change them.

Afrofest:
A Slice of Culture
by Ruthe Ann Bowen and Tim Forkes

On the weekend of August 2, a major cultural event took place in our city, but the city, by and large, didn't notice. Afrofest, held at the easily accessible Summerfest grounds, attracted only about 7500 people.

Even on Saturday, a day filled with sunshine and warm temperatures, the Summerfest grounds were ominously empty. And that's a pity, considering the impressive array of displays and events, the comfortable atmosphere, and the homespun products of community spirit.

Among the attractions was the health tent, a free clinic staffed by trained hospital personnel and community workers. They checked people's weight and diet, accessed diabetes risk, dental prob-

A Revolution of Consciousness
UWM's Professor Paulson Sees a New Age Rising

by Bill Conroy

The death of the industrial era is upon us.

We are living in the dawn of a new society.

At least that is what Belden Paulson says. Paulson, a professor of political science at UWM since the early 1960s, is a social scientist who advocates a spiritual rebirth in the modern age.

"There aren't very many times in history when you have really fundamental

out practical lifestyles and values that translate deep kinds of spiritual values into life," Paulson says. "I'd call it a spiritual growth center."

When Lisa returned with news about the Findhorn community, Paulson was at first skeptical: "I said this stuff's okay, but I'm a social scientist. This was kind of a lot of hot air as far as I was concerned."

But Paulson was drawn into the movement nonetheless. A series of events brought him into contact with many of the leaders in the New Age movement. Grad-

that the community is part of a much broader social phenomenon that transcends labels and mainstream conceptions.

"There is an unfolding going on throughout the planet that we have an opportunity to tune into," Lagerman says. "It's a revolution that could change the world."

And that, he believes, is imperative. "We know the world is in unprecedented danger. We're living in an age where we have tremendous technological leverage, but we may not have the wisdom to

A Revolution of Consciousness: UWM's Professor Paulson Sees a New Age Rising

By Bill Conroy in The Shepherd, 1985

The Shepherd has been and is Milwaukee's main alternative newspaper. This interview was conducted by one of the paper's regular writers, Bill Conroy.

The death of the industrial era is upon us. We are living in the dawn of a new society. At least that is what Belden Paulson says. Paulson, a professor of political science at UWM since the early 1960s, is a social scientist who advocates a spiritual rebirth in the modern age.

"There aren't very many times in history when you have moments of really fundamental change," he says. "But we're probably in one of those unique points in history now. We're moving from the Industrial Age to a new cycle of history. The Industrial Age, to a certain degree, has become obsolete."

Paulson is not an ivory-tower scholar who ponders the world through the pages of dusty books. Rather, his background is that of a man who has toiled to mold the future out of the dust of the earth.

During the early 1950s he helped organize a social assistance center in the bombed-out slums of Naples, Italy. In the latter part of the decade, he returned to Italy to set up a community for Eastern European refugees on the island of Sardinia.

Because of the success of the project, which still exists today, the United Nations asked Paulson to join its Rome-based High Commission on Refugees. By the time he returned to the United States in the early 1960s to accept a teaching post at UWM, Paulson had experienced first-hand the fallout of the industrial revolution.

Community   **211**

In the America of the 1960s, however, some of that fallout was beginning to stir up anger in the streets.

"During the 1960s, the urban chaos began, and, like other cities, Milwaukee began to rumble a little bit," Paulson recalls. "The blacks were getting restless, and hell was starting to break loose."

Paulson is not an ivory-tower scholar who ponders the world through the pages of dusty books. Rather, his background is that of a man who has toiled to mold the future out of the dust of the earth.

It was in response to that unrest that Paulson, in cooperation with local black leaders, helped develop various projects dealing with low-income people in the inner city.

The success of those projects led to the creation of a new department in the UW-Extension called the Center for Urban Community Development, which Paulson has chaired ever since.

But the new age that Paulson now talks about was not part of his thinking during the turbulent '60s. In fact, it was not until 1976, when his wife Lisa, visited an intentional community in Scotland called Findhorn that Paulson's philosophical revolution began.

"Findhorn is basically a spiritual community, and its main purpose is to work out practical lifestyles and values that translate deep kinds of spiritual values into life," Paulson says. "I'd call it a spiritual growth center."

When Lisa returned with news about the Findhorn community, Paulson was at first skeptical: "I said this stuff's okay, but I'm a social scientist. This was kind of a lot of hot air as far as I was concerned."

But Paulson was drawn into the movement nonetheless. A series of events brought him into contact with many of the leaders in the New Age movement. Gradually, he became convinced that there was a lot more to it than hot air.

Together with his wife and a number of interested students and speakers, Paulson launched a series of seminars at the university on such New Age topics as planetary survival, new dimensions in governance, and global peace/alternative futures. The seminar series is still part of the university's curriculum.

"The central focus in all these courses," Paulson explains, "is that the world is in peril and old solutions are not adequate."

The seminars were a success, and by 1980 some of the participants began to look for practical applications. From this commitment sprang a New Age bioshelter created under the aegis of the High Wind Association, a nonprofit group.

The Paulsons donated 45 acres of land near Plymouth, and the US Department of Energy chipped in $25,000 startup money. The bioshelter, which is nearly complete, is an experiment in using appropriate technology.

"The bioshelter is a micro ecosystem where you're using renewable energy—solar heat and thermal storage—and you're growing protein and vegetables," Paulson says. "All of the elements of the system help to sustain each other. It's working *with* nature, not taking from her."

The High Wind community outside Plymouth, which now has about 11 full-time and part-time residents, is only one in a network of alternative communities throughout the world, Paulson explains. The New Age communities, although different in their individual approaches, are all working toward the same goal of developing appropriate lifestyles for a changing world.

"There's a lot of potential here," says Etienne (Steven) Schuh, 26, a former student at UW-Madison who is now a part of the High Wind community. "The people here are committed to creating a certain relationship with the planet and each other in a sensitive way. They are developing a value system that will be sustained a long time."

Another resident of the High Wind community, 44-year-old David Lagerman, sees the project as an offshoot of some of the philosophies developed by the hippies of the '60s. He stresses, however, that the community is part of a much broader social

> We're living in an age where we have tremendous technological leverage, but we may not have the wisdom to use it appropriately.

phenomenon that transcends labels and mainstream conceptions.

"There is an unfolding going on throughout the planet that we have an opportunity to tune into," Lagerman says. "It's a revolution that could change the world."

And that, he believes, is imperative. "We know the world is in unprecedented danger. We're living in an age where we have tremendous technological leverage, but we may not have the wisdom to use it appropriately.

"We can't take a Band-Aid approach. A fundamental moral awakening is needed because fear and greed propel so many things that are happening.

"Those things may be traditional in human history, but in the context of the high-tech era, they have to be stopped, or they will be stopped for us through nuclear war or some other disaster."

Lagerman is convinced the solutions can be found in the spiritual realm if we are willing to believe in those powers.

"There may very well be forces afoot on the planet that can help us through the crunch," he says. "That is in the realm of belief, but there are non-material beings here to help us.

"If we choose to align with those forces and become part of them, they can help [the New Age] to unfold. There is a spiritual thread that runs through High Wind and the New Age, even though it is also a very practical movement."

Part of the practicality of the High Wind Association includes recognizing the need to attain some economic clout in order to survive in mainstream society.

The association operates a bookstore on Oakland Avenue called High Wind Books and Records that not only serves a networking function by tuning people to alternative movements but also is a potential source of income for the High Wind community.

In addition, a land company has been formed through High Wind that has put together a group of investors; it is located on 20 acres of land adjacent to High Wind's Plymouth community.

The New Age movement is committed to providing a viable alternative to the philosophy of mainstream society, which, its members believe, is dangerously short-sighted. "We have lost our consciousness, our capacity to understand that we're parts of history," says Paulson. "Living in the present, we're using up our historical resources, which means someone else has got to pay for them in the future."

The alternative communities, he adds, are an attempt to grapple with the dichotomies and conflicts in society, which our mainstream culture is not doing.

"So when I talk about New Age, I'm talking about a whole context. It's a value context; it's a behavioral context. It has to do with harmony and balance. It's the way we think and live, and it has rippling implications for all aspects of life on the planet."

The High Wind Association Credo

In 1977, a small, dedicated group of us established the High Wind Association, a not-for-profit organization. At that time, we formulated the High Wind mission. Our credo was authored by Lisa Paulson and others of the group. Although it has been reviewed many times over three decades, these words have stood the test of time.

To walk gently on the Earth

Practices: Respect and cooperate with nature; protect the environment; reflect on the gifts in nature; become sensitive to the strengths and vulnerabilities of the Earth.

To know the spirit within

Practices: Engage in self-reflection; nourish personal sensibilities; imagine; make transpersonal connections; recognize, honor, and take responsibility for our role in the larger scheme of things.

To hear our fellow beings

Practices: Work for social justice; become increasingly compassionate; listen deeply; engage in interpersonal dialogue; build bridges of understanding among people with different worldviews; stand in the shoes of others; build sources of hope for others.

To invoke the light of wisdom

Practices: Develop our intellect; expand our knowledge; articulate values; develop new perspectives; think critically and use good judgment; engage with others in promoting societal movement in these directions.

To build the future now

Practices: Engage in practical actions; develop an orientation to future needs; envision possibilities and their outcomes; translate metaphor and myth into "real world" situations and opportunities; engage in the arts and unfolding sciences; cultivate new skills.

The Educational Dimension

Peter at his Springdale farm with visiting inner city students

New Dimensions in Governance:Images of Holistic Community

From a brochure describing a new UWM seminar, 1978

This seminar was probably the most influential class we offered in helping to lay the groundwork for the High Wind community. Initially I had difficulty in getting university approval, and my proposal ended up in the vice-chancellor's office for approval. The class met two nights a week for 15 weeks. Participants drawn from around Wisconsin and the region could enroll for graduate or undergraduate credit or non-credit. To prepare, my fellow instructors David Spangler and Milenko Matanovic of the Lorian Association met with me to figure out how to address politics and governance from a holistic perspective.

Purpose
- To explore social and political concepts related to the idea of people becoming more sensitive to resource scarcities and preservation of the Earth, more aware of the possibilities for new forms of human interaction and connectedness— on the premise that changed individual priorities can lead to changed ways of ordering society.

- To form a "support group" or community of people able to communicate with one another about new values and their practical ramifications in daily life.

- To learn about alternative communities in the United States and to make one or more in-depth visits to them.

- To relate concepts to practice, which includes participation in the designing of a concrete experience or project and interacting with outside discussants drawn from government and related fields.

"Holocracy"

Included among the sacred ideas of the modern Western tradition are individual self-sufficiency, the balance of power, political process fueled by the conflict of individuals and groups pursuing selfish interests, and the role of government as arbiter in the struggle for scarce resources, which in the future will be still scarcer.

Recently the "universal community" of the ancient and medieval periods is being rediscovered and placed in a contemporary setting. People are experimenting with its principles in alternative communities. A vision of governance is emerging based on "wholeness." Holism is a view of reality that sees everything as interrelated, that sees the universe as a wholeness in which nothing is ultimately separated or isolated from anything else.

"Holocracy"—a term coined by the Lorians—means rule by the whole, which begins on the level of consciousness and then is translated into forms of varying complexity on the levels of the individual, local community, nation, and planet. Wholeness is more a *quality* of a community than a form; it is the consciousness that creates the form.

What are the implications in a holocracy for the meaning of power, authority, decision-making, freedom, and responsibility? How do these work in the New Age? How do individuals and groups use them in relationship to each other? Can a system based on wholeness lead to new dimensions of governance without ending in new forms of totalitarianism?

The Class as Community

The keynote of the seminar will be a balance between information and experience. The class will be asked to see itself as a "mini-community." Games, exercises, and imagination will play a part in the self- and group-discovery process. A substantial part of the course will be carried out in small groups based on individual interests and centered on the practice of sensing the connection with each other. Wholeness will be viewed from various perspectives, using ideas and models drawn not only from existing alternative communities but also from holistic medicine, humanistic and transpersonal psychology, comparative religion, and esoteric traditions.

> "Holocracy" . . . means rule by the whole, which begins on the level of consciousness and then is translated into forms of varying complexity on the levels of the individual, local community, nation, and planet. Wholeness is more a quality of a community than a form; it is the consciousness that creates the form.

The class is designed as an interface between ideas and action. It can provide a support structure for those already involved individually in establishing New Age lifestyles and livelihoods or who might be ready to make fundamental changes. With each member a co-creator, the class can be exactly what its participants want and need. The instructors will reinforce whatever projects the small groups create, offering the depth and experience of their own backgrounds. It is probable that the concrete projects and associations initiated here will be the beginning of some ongoing life patterns.

> The class is designed as an interface between ideas and action. It can provide a support structure for those already involved individually in establishing New Age lifestyles and livelihoods or who might be ready to make fundamental changes. With each member a co-creator, the class can be exactly what its participants want and need.

Small Interest Groups

These groups will have three goals:

- To design a project using theory primarily as a springboard for more experiential components: cooperative relationships and testing of ideas through practical endeavors such as becoming actively involved in environmental issues, building an ecological bioshelter, working with self-sufficient lifestyles, experimenting with new politics, formulating new education, practicing holistic health and nutrition, developing a business enterprise, designing a community on the land, creating an artistic performance, and so forth.

- To be aware of the process by which group members are working together within a holistic framework.

- To put together a paper and/or another type of creative product interrelating the project experience with the group's interpretation of holocracy.

Community Visits

During a two-week period in the middle of the semester, each participant will visit one or more alternative communities that are attempting to practice various aspects of holistic governance. Background study plus in-depth onsite experience will offer opportunity for intensive community contact. A pool of communities in different areas of the United States and Canada will be made available, and assistance will be provided through key resource persons in each community. The class will compile a publication presenting the findings from these visits.

Outside Discussants

Toward the end of the course, selected representatives from government and other areas will meet with the class to react to the formulations about "New Dimensions in Governance" made by the class. Preparatory to these "real-world dialogues," course participants will work out their own understanding of holistic concepts drawn from classwork, experiences in the small groups, and community visits.

Trip to Findhorn

A maximum of 30 students from the seminar will be offered the opportunity to spend four to six weeks at Findhorn in Scotland during the period March 10-April 21, 1979. Findhorn is considered one of the most successful examples of a community attempting to practice "holistic governance." Students will live as part of the community among its 260 resident members, taking part in its work program as well as a seminar format.

Arrangements have been made with the Findhorn community to make this a unique experiential and learning situation.

David Spangler

A Working Paper for a Proposed UWM Class on New Dimensions in Governance

1978

One of our discussions, led by David Spangler

A vision of new possibilities in the arts of governance, conflict resolutions, group interactions, and personal development and creativity is emerging in the last quarter of the 20th century. Nurtured by a convergence of discoveries, new theories, insights, practices, and research from such diverse fields as science, business management, ecological studies, comparative religions, philosophy, education, and psychology, this vision is summed up by the words *Holism* (or *Wholeness*) and *Synergy*.

Holism is a view of reality, increasingly supported and elaborated by research in ecology and quantum physics, that sees everything as interrelated: the universe is a wholeness in which nothing is ultimately separated or isolated from anything else. Synergy describes a process by which different elements combine to create a wholeness that is more than the sum of its parts and that is not maintained at the expense of those parts; in a synergic relationship, both the parts and the whole are mutually advantaged by each other.

Western political systems are largely based on the integrity and independence of the individual; the person is considered the "atom" of the political and social universe, a concept greatly enhanced by the Newtonian image of the universe as being made up of interacting but ultimately separate particles relating according to the rigid laws of gravity. This is an important and useful concept, but how will it adapt to the new image of reality arising from modern nuclear physics: that the atom is only a "cloud of probabilities" and that the ultimate particle is the universe itself? If Western political theory, especially in America, was influenced and to an extent justified by older scientific theories, how will it be influenced by newer ones? What styles of governance should or will emerge to reflect theories of wholeness?

Also, Western politics, particularly in the United States, are influenced by images of "rugged individualism" and self-sufficiency in which the state becomes an adversary to the freedom and growth of the individual. Governing is seen as the art of maintaining and balancing a condition of tension between the individual and the state, in which each seeks advantages at the expense of the other. How will this condition respond to new images of wholeness? What are the possibilities for a synergic style of governance in which state and individual citizen are each partners in a joint enterprise of creating a wholeness in which both are advantaged? What are the strategies for developing non-adversarial approaches to politics, social relations, and conflict resolutions?

These questions and possible answers are being explored in a variety of ways today, from classes in self-development to new styles of business management. Perhaps the most interesting new approaches are being explored in small, intentional communities being developed in various parts of the world where holistic and synergic strategies of governance are being tested and applied.

> Western politics, particularly in the United States, are influenced by images of "rugged individualism" and self-sufficiency in which the state becomes an adversary to the freedom and growth of the individual. Governing is seen as the art of maintaining and balancing a condition of tension between the individual and the state, in which each seeks advantages at the expense of the other. How will this condition respond to new images of wholeness?

Governance at Findhorn

background paper by Jim Maynard, 1978

This discussion was used as background for a paper written by Jim Maynard, whom I met at Findhorn in 1978. I asked Jim, an attorney, as a community member, to summarize his experience regarding Findhorn governance. He attended one of our class sessions, and this model generated considerable controversy—why it worked at Findhorn but would offer a huge challenge when applied in the larger society. I've greatly edited his paper.

At Findhorn, the process of government in the context of an emerging New Age is seen to be based not on the will of the majority, as in democracies, or on the will of a ruling elite or individual, as in oligarchies or totalitarian structures, but on the will of the whole. The basic operative principle is not one of reconciling competing interests, as in traditional political processes, but of determining what is in the interests of all by means of an intuitive attunement to what is seeking to emerge. Such emergence is considered in the light of the growth and unfoldment of all of the evolving life in a given situation.

During Findhorn's unfoldment as a community, the greatest authority and decision-making responsibility has been entrusted to those who have successfully demonstrated a capacity for attuning to that level of awareness whereby correct intuitions would be proven by experience or confirmation by others to be responsive to the needs of the entire community. For example, in the early years of the community's development, authority for the unfoldment of the community was entrusted in the spiritual guidance received by Eileen Caddy; this was carried out through the executive leadership of Peter Caddy, because such guidance proved over and over again to be correct and responsive to the needs of the community.

At the center, at the core of decision-making for the community, is what is called a "Core Group." This consists of those who have demonstrated a high capacity for tuning into and expressing the central vision for the community. This group has final authority for community policy-making. Yet members at the grassroots level of the community also have the opportunity to consider and discuss major issues that are before the community. Any member may do this in meetings for the full community, in meetings of that person's departmental working group, and, if necessary, in meetings of the Core Group. Thus there is a certain circulation of shared visions, insights, and viewpoints between the center and the periphery of the organism.

As this organism has grown larger and more complex, increasingly specialized organs within the body of Findhorn have come into being to handle particular areas of responsibility. A threefold pattern of responsibility now flows from the Core Group through three groups that are responsible for three broad areas of the community's organization. These are considered to correspond to three types of consciousness energy: Will, Love-Wisdom, and Intelligent Action. The energy of Will expresses through the Administrative Branch headed by the Management Committee. This committee is responsible for administering policies of the Core Group and is carrying out the will of the Whole. The

> **Keep in mind that Findhorn does not have "directors," "managers," or "coordinators." Focaliser is a Findhorn synonym for "leader."**

Administrative Branch makes decisions and takes action with regard to the flow and circulation of resources within the community—financial, material, and human.

An Education Branch, headed by the Education Core Group, is responsible for the Love-Wisdom function of nurturing the growth and unfoldment of consciousness within the community. This is done through educational programs, classes, workshops, and conferences, and also through ideas about education and growth processes shared in the working life of the community—in departments, community meetings, and meetings of department focalisers (the persons who focus or coalesce group energies). Keep in mind that Findhorn does not have "directors," "managers," or "coordinators." Focaliser is a Findhorn synonym for "leader."

The energy of Intelligent Action (or active intelligence) is seen as flowing through the work departments—the Action Branch of the community, the central group of which is the Focalisers' Group. This is comprised of the focalisers of each department who meet every week to discuss affairs of their departments and the community and to make decisions concerning the day-to-day functioning of the community.

The functions of these groups are very different, yet the process that each group seeks to utilize for its decision-making is the same: to attune to a higher level of understanding whereby one obviously right course of action can be discerned and the group can move together in consensus. Sometimes it is necessary for the group to cease discussion and have a silent time to turn within to find the answer. This procedure has been found to work amazingly well for resolving differences and swinging the group from polarities of viewpoints to consensus. Sometimes it is necessary to do this more than once until a right course of action emerges in most people's minds, and the group can move in unanimity.

Findhorn's smallest unit of governance is, of course, the individual. Each person has the challenge of meeting his or her needs while, at the same time, contributing to meeting the needs of the community. Ideally there is mutual fulfillment in this process so that the needs of the whole are met, as are the needs of the parts.

The "focaliser" of a group is not a "boss" in the conventional sense. He or she is a person who acts as a point of focus for the group, who holds the vision for what the group has come together to do and who provides as much direction—or "indirection"—as is necessary to enable the group members to take responsibility for accomplishing what they have come together to do. The focaliser focuses awareness not only on the work needs but also on the growth needs within the group. The consciousness with which one does a job is considered to be at least as important, if not more important, as the work actually done.

> The focaliser focuses awareness not only on the work needs but also on the growth needs within the group. The consciousness with which one does a job is considered to be at least as important as the work actually done.

Thus, the focaliser is there to help nourish the growth and unfoldment of consciousness as much as to facilitate the group's getting the work done properly. Also, the more successful a focaliser is in releasing responsibility to others and not exerting leadership that is too strongly directive, the more opportunity there is for all in the group to exercise their own urges for creative self-expression and to exercise responsibility on behalf of the group as a whole. In this way, authority is generally shared in proportion to the willingness of people to take responsibility.

In the working groups at Findhorn, there are frequent opportunities for members to share in the group any observations or feelings concerning their individual process, the group process, or the community process or issues.

Conflicts are generally resolved at the level of authority that has responsibility for the matter. Within a department, a focaliser has authority for the resolution of conflicts. Each of the branch groups has responsibility for the resolution of conflicts or issues within their branch areas. The Core Group has final responsibility or jurisdiction for the resolution of conflicts or issues.

The Personnel department is also an important organ within the community for mediating and resolving different interests, wants, desires, and needs. This department is responsible for the coordination of work needs within and between departments, of accommodation needs of members, and of membership status: determining who will be allowed to become members of the community and who will be required to leave the community. If a member wants to change from one work department to another, or from one accommodation situation to another, or leave the community for a time, then that person will usually interview with one or more members of Personnel. Expulsion from the community is the ultimate sanction of Findhorn for those who act contrary to what the community is trying to do. Short of this sanction, there may be considerable time and attention given to the individual to resolve any difficulties before this sanction is resorted to.

The Findhorn model of governance differs radically from most models in that there are very few laws or rules for governing behavior. In fact there are only two: 1) Use of illegal drugs is not allowed, and 2) No smoking is allowed in rooms or buildings that are used by the community as a whole.

The process for removal of people in leadership positions is largely an intuitive group process. If it is apparent to enough people that a focaliser is no longer the appropriate person for a particular function, he or she may be asked to release that role. The focaliser's group may do this, or the Personnel or Core Group. A focaliser may come to such a realization with or without prompting from others. Changes in leadership at all levels of Findhorn have happened in this way. For example, Core Group managers have withdrawn from that group when they or a consensus of others in the group have noted that it was time to withdraw. Peter Caddy, the co-founder and dominant executive force in the unfoldment of the community, relinquished focalisation responsibilities when it became apparent to him and others that he was carrying too much authority. Similarly, focalisers of departments and branch groups have released their roles in this way.

Premises on Which the Findhorn System of Governance Is Based: Summary

1. Shared vision and values. All are committed to spiritual growth and following the guidance of the "Spirit within." There is a common commitment to mutual support, group cooperation, love, and sharing, and, above all, to living the spiritual life, subordinating one's personal desires to this.

2. A high level of evolvement and commitment on the part of members. Rules are not necessary to assure a minimum standard of behavior.

3. Small-scale of community unit size. As Findhorn expands, no single population grouping is larger than 25 people, thereby allowing a high degree of contact and inter-relatedness among the members.

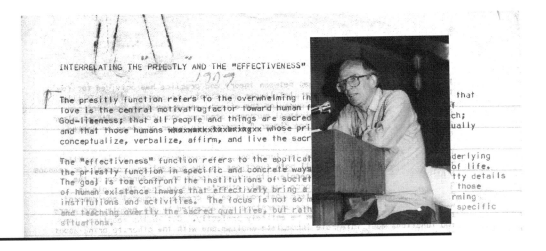

INTERRELATING THE PRIESTLY AND THE "EFFECTIVENESS"

The presitly function refers to the overwhelming in
love is the central motivatingfactor toward human f
God-likeness; that all people and things are sacred
and that those humans whxxwxrkxxxxbxingxx whose pri
conceptualize, verbalize, affirm, and live the sacr

The "effectiveness" function refers to the applicat
the priestly function in specific and concrete ways
The goal is tox confront the institutions of societ
of human existence inways that effectively bring a
institutions and activities. The focus is not so m
and teaching overtly the sacred qualities, but rath
situations.

Interrelating the "Priestly" and the "Effectiveness" Function

Background paper from UWM seminars, 1979

I wrote this paper for one of our High Wind-University seminars. It turned out that the argument was widely discussed in subsequent programs. Since the essence of the "New Dimensions" seminar related to the question of how can people exercising governance responsibilities operate in a new way, the concept here is that the "priest" will strive to become more "real-world practical," and the "effective" practitioner will become more priestly. Examples used were Gandhi and Mandela.

The "priestly" function refers to the overwhelming influence of God in the world; that love is the central motivating factor toward human fulfillment in the direction of being Godlike; that all people and things are sacred and should be treated as such; and that those humans whose primary overt work is to continually conceptualize, verbalize, affirm, and live the sacred qualities are priests.

The "effectiveness" function refers to the application of the consciousness underlying the priestly function in specific and concrete ways in the general environment of life. The goal is to confront the institutions of society and the everyday nitty-gritty details of human existence in ways that effectively bring a new consciousness to bear in those institutions and activities. The focus is not so much on conceptualizing, affirming, and teaching overtly the sacred qualities, but rather to apply the qualities in specific situations.

The underlying condition of both functions is the existence of a certain consciousness about bringing God into the world and the sacredness of certain qualities. But the priestly function stresses purity, while the effectiveness function stresses "getting things done" on the practical level. The priestly function requires constant reaffirmation and discussion and recommitment in order to withstand the pressures from the surrounding environment. The effectiveness function requires action and interest in strategy that enhances effectiveness. To maintain its spiritual purity, the priestly function demands caution so that the priest is not co-opted by other forces and the attributes are not sullied, which can easily occur when concepts are applied and values are placed into the cross-currents of choice.

In an environment that is basically ego-centered, materialistic, and short-run oriented, the priestly function is unlikely to be understood and accepted by the multitude. It will be recognized and followed by the more spiritually evolved people. But the pressures and energies of established institutions in an environment that is very distinctly not God-like, can overwhelm the priest in certain circumstances. For example, a priest who enters the political world of prevailing values must either adapt in certain ways to accommodate that world and be understood by it, or become an outcast, misunderstood and stigmatized. It could be said that the priest may risk much and gain little in the circumstance of entering a political environment when that environment is diametrically opposed to the qualities of the priest. The priest, instead, may better utilize his or her energies through other means.

A major and appropriate task for priests is to interrelate with people whose commitment and work is the effectiveness function. Their underlying consciousness may be the same, but effectiveness practitioners are prepared to face the "impure" pressures of dealing with the nitty-gritty, of making political decisions, and of being recognized by the culture not as priests but as businessmen or university employees or elected officials or bureaucrats, and so forth. By dealing with specifics, they are forced to take stands. And in a heterogeneous society where people may have very different needs and interests, by definition any stand creates its counter-stand, and one's role is countered by someone else's role with different values and maybe a different substantive orientation on specifics.

> A major and appropriate task for priests is to interrelate with people whose commitment and work is the effectiveness function.

People performing the effectiveness function can hardly perform the priestly function, at least not until the surrounding environment is more hospitable. But the priest can give clarity of vision, reaffirmation of faith, and insights about values and choices—which for the person dealing with effectiveness may be difficult or impossible. Likewise, the effectiveness person can collaborate closely with the priest in helping to provide outlets for the sacred qualities. He can assist in applied and practical ways to implement the priestly qualities in specific settings of the surrounding environment.

It is clear that these two need each other. The priest, without practical effectiveness, can become a recluse or a person only of vision and words and rhetoric. Eventually he may not be taken seriously, because the gap between theory and practice has provided too few tests. He is an expounder of platitudes and empty phrases, which may have little effect on others.

On the other hand, the person pursing the effectiveness function can fall into activism without purpose—programs and projects without clear discrimination to identify quality that separates "higher" from "lower." He may become immersed in power or money or vested interests for their own sake.

> The person pursuing the effectiveness function may become immersed in power or money or vested interests for their own sake.

The two sets of qualities, the two functions, are complementary. It is doubtful that, for reasons stated above, the same person could fulfill both functions in the present environment. But different people with primary focus on one function or the other can work together, can reinforce the other's role so that the whole is realized. The eventual, long-term goal would be to create a general environment where the priestly qualities are understood and accepted by all people, and where the effectiveness function can be entirely priestly. But in the meantime, the two functions must seek to integrate one with the other, to bring about the greater whole.

A LIVING/LEARNING
EXPERIENCE
IN
ALTERNATIVE COMMUNITIES

Spring Semester 1986

March 26 - June 14, 1986

Sponsored by Department of Culture Foundations of
Education of University of Wisconsin-Milwaukee, and
Center for Urban Community Development of Division of
Outreach and Continuing Education

A Learning Adventure: The Three-Community Seminar

From Odyssey of a Practical Visionary, *2009*

In September 1984, we inaugurated a completely new educational experience; it was not new only for High Wind, but I don't believe there had been anything quite like it elsewhere. Given our interest in models that could enhance learning, and given our critique of much that transpired in formal education on all levels from public schools to universities, we found the idea of a Living/Learning Seminar in Alternative Communities (which we came to call the Three-Community Seminar) extraordinarily intriguing.

For a number of years, the idea for this program had been percolating. I'd seen the enthusiastic response of participants in our one-week seminars at High Wind each summer when we brought in various members of the Lorian group, usually David Spangler and

> While we knew that this seminar would build on our previous learning efforts at High Wind, we were also interested in using it to expand our knowledge base and to muster new creative thinking about alternative communities . . . and to contribute to the essence of the larger societal role of the intentional community.

Milenko Matanovic, sometimes others. The subject matter meshed with spiritual values of community life, along with practical community living. The seminars always seemed too short, and there was not enough substance to get university credit approval. Folks would have found it easier to invest a longer time if there were an academic payoff.

Since the groups we previously had taken to Findhorn invariably had very positive experiences and our colleagues in Scotland were very receptive to our proposal, Findhorn's involvement was a natural. We also had contacts with various other communities, such as Sirius in Massachusetts and the small, innovative Eourres group located at a spectacular site in the French Alps. One month in each location would offer a substantive experience of community living. At each site, a rigorous program was offered that introduced students to the theory and practice of community while they temporarily became working members of these communities.

A key dimension was that the participants created their own mini-community, so they were challenged and had to grapple with many of the same issues that existed in the surrounding communities they joined. This also gave them some continuity and internal support as they moved among the three established communities.

While in the eyes of UWM, I served as academic director, each community designated a key person to coordinate its own program and to work with us to develop a plan to maximize the learning experience. We also selected a sensitive resident from our community or the board to accompany the group for the entire program as a kind of administrative coordinator, handling logistical details and helping with internal needs. There were no tests, but everyone was expected to participate fully, keep a daily log, and write a final, comprehensive paper incorporating what he or she had learned.

For the first seminar, in 1984, we enrolled 12 extraordinary folks. Three came from California, two from the East Coast, two from Canada, one from Kansas, and four from Wisconsin. We had one married couple and two people who had grown up not far from Lisa and me in Sheboygan and were already a couple of sorts. There were seven women and five men. All were in their 20s except for the married pair (30s and 40s). One New Yorker was in his 30s. Everyone registered for credit—five for graduate credit, the rest undergraduate.

For the first month at High Wind, we brought in some heavy hitters. For Week One, David Spangler held forth on the nature and role of the sacred in the value systems of alternative communities. Week Two introduced Lee Olsen, one of Wisconsin's most respected ethno-botanists who speaks several Native American Languages and demonstrates how forests and meadows and wetlands can supply most household needs and medicines without relying on stores and pharmacies. Week Three focused on the arts with Milenko: the role of art and celebration in promoting transformation. In the evenings, he and community resident Betsy Abert took up their guitars, joined by our New Yorker with his tub bass. In Week Four, I pulled together all the themes while addressing the topics of new politics and new economics.

The 12 then traveled to the Sirius community for the next four weeks where the founders, Gordon Davidson and Corinne McLaughlin, led an equally ambitious program. In fact, it was so full that several mischievous students produced a hilarious short film satirizing their very full schedule.

The third month at Findhorn included the intensive "Experience Week"—the basic introduction to the community. There were talks about creating community and on the pitfalls of the inevitable issues of power, money, sex, relationships, and conflict, as well as speculations about Findhorn's role as a "center of light" in making a contribution toward changing the world. Participants joined some of Findhorn's 26 work departments, laboring side by side with members. For the final week, the students played Findhorn's famous Game of Life (variously called The Transformation Game), where they identified their own significant challenges and turning points that could involve life-changing decisions.

In introducing themselves and their expectations of the experience, the 12 participants wrote a few words. Here are brief descriptions:

Bob: From California, age 24, just graduated from university with bachelor's degree in English. Has worked a lot with emotionally disturbed children, tutored English as a second language. As a child despised religion, regarded science as key to the future. As adolescent discovered drugs, which opened him up to spirituality for the first time. No longer condones drugs.

Elizabeth: From Ontario, Canada, age 23, trained as a teacher, recently left a master of social work program and now trying to make it as a writer and creative artist. Worked with children in the classroom, at day camps, and as a drama teacher. Since leaving grad school has been pursuing a career as a freelance writer and delving into other creative endeavors such as carving rubber stamps, weaving, drawing, dance, and painting.

Susan: In mid-20s, a professional photographer from Connecticut. Also loves cooking, eating, and growing food. Been member of two meal cooperatives the past two summers. Also enjoys meditating, dancing, swimming, traveling. Exposed to alternative living in an alternative college in Massachusetts. Sampled both mainstream and alternative lifestyles but unable to achieve balance between the two. Became restless in an unchallenging job.

Ingrid: Age 22, from Vancouver, British Columbia. Been saving money as a waitress, searching for an alternative education avenue to discover the best way to help alleviate the pain of the world. Spent time in Africa, interested in how New Age thought applies to non-Western society. Drawn to horticulture; also loves children and singing and dancing. Is aware of the nuclear threat, ailing governments, and wealth imbalances and wants to contribute.

Tom: Mid-30s. A carpenter and builder by trade. With wife Lori, is one of two couples in the program. In recent months, they gave over their home to close-knit group of eight people where individual spiritual growth held primary importance, but this has not jelled at the level of collective consciousness. Interested in conflict resolution, alternative economics, land-use management, and redefining male-female relationships. Wants to experience living together in these three communities.

Lori: In mid-40s, married to Tom. Has dream of living and working harmoniously with others in community but it has been difficult to find comfortable community situation—one with no religious leader or guru. Wants to learn nitty-gritty ins and outs of community living. Believes eventual cultural transformation will happen through a decentralized society of communities. Likes organic gardening, yoga, folk dancing, new models of man-woman relationships, solar technology, and herbology. Is full of questions about these communities, their economics, leadership, money issues, spiritual practices, how conflict is resolved, and role of children, arts, and celebration.

Sheila: Naturalist and outdoor educator; age 29, from Kansas. Has dream of finding a way to educate the whole child. Her own schooling stifled her creativity and curiosity. Had been looking for graduate program focusing on new forms of education, communication, and spirituality. Finally discovered a graduate program and was accepted, then felt it uncanny when she saw that this seminar seemed to incorporate everything she wanted.

Paul: In mid-20s, from Milwaukee, he makes recreational medieval armor for a living. His two great dreams in life are to be a creative writer and to help create a better Earth. For the first, he intends to use the seminar's experiences in connecting with like-minded people to enrich his knowledge of human behavior. He envisions the seminar as greatly aiding his second dream of living in and working with these Earth-conscious places. He loves work, even laboring to exhaustion, in a good cause, and believes that by working with his hands directly with people who have a practical knowledge of the Earth, bioshelters, education, etc., he will further his own growth.

Kesha: Age 24, a student at UWM in comparative religions. Especially interested in North American Indian and Goddess spirituality. Has worked as a psychiatric aide and would like to become a Unitarian minister. Is deeply connected to the Earth and all its creatures who have been exploited. Was attracted to the seminar to get involved with people who work toward positive change on the planet, who have a vision of creating a world of peace; also to be involved with communities having an overall spiritual emphasis while maintaining practical, workable approaches. She sees this as a chance to strengthen the web of world community by interconnecting with individuals practicing alternative lifestyles in various pockets of light.

John: A cab driver from New York City, also a musician, 34 years old. Interested in exploring the connection of humor and music with healing. Envisages that he will gain insight into himself through the seminar and interaction with the communities —discovering what it really is to be a human being, how we are connected, what dimensions of ourselves are unexplored, what actions he can take that will contribute most to world unity.

Jane: Partner with Etienne (Steve), 25, currently milking cows and gathering maple syrup at a farm near High Wind. Her relationship with Etienne is relatively new, and she sees it as posing some big challenges while living in community for three months. Senses this experience will help get a handle on the direction of her life and using her own unique talents to serve.

Etienne: Age 25, Jane's partner, grew up in Sheboygan, not far from High Wind. Recently left UW-Madison, where he was studying philosophy and found the search for "The Truth" to be singularly unenlightening and not leading in the direction he wanted to go. Tending to be cynical and relying too much on his mind, he wants to rediscover his spontaneity, creativity, and openness. Dreams of writing but has difficulty with the words flowing as he wants. Like Jane, is aware of the challenge for a young relationship when living in community, constantly surrounded by other people, but is receptive to this seminar.

The participants decided to work with me to write up the whole experience. We received requests from around the country for information about this learning model, and other educational institutions picked up our example. While we knew that this seminar would build on our previous learning efforts at High Wind, we were also interested in using it to expand our knowledge base and to muster new creative thinking about alternative communities. With the significant added resources of the other two communities, plus the inputs of our smart and questioning student participants, we had opportunity to contribute to the essence of the larger societal role of the intentional community.

> Students must be prepared to become global citizens; curricula must break out of narrow departmental confines to cross disciplines; learning must have experiential, real-world value beyond the traditional classroom; values and societal concerns must be integrated into the cut-and-dried process of transmitting knowledge.

As I thought back to the various university efforts I'd participated in to reform higher education, certain planks had surfaced regularly in every commission or task force: Students must be prepared to become global citizens; curricula must break out of narrow departmental confines to cross disciplines; learning must have experiential, real-world value beyond the traditional classroom; values and societal concerns must be integrated into the cut-and-dried process of transmitting knowledge.

The final papers and evaluations indicated that most participants had one of the more profound experiences of their lives. They kept using the word *transformation*, not just to describe the culture but what happened to them personally. We've stayed in contact with most of them.

Here are a few comments:

"Though we did not realize it, we had formed a learning group whose research took place in the laboratories of three different communities. . . . Our relationships to one another were nurtured as we taught each other about love, support and trust."

"The alternative community focus is definitely the starting point in learning how to change one's cultural perspective from a competitive, individualistic point of view to one of living in cooperation and peace."

"I feel more responsible in what I'm doing with my life in connection with my relationships with others. . . . I now know how to pursue many things in my life. I became clear on how I want to live."

"There is something special happening within these communities. Things can happen there that can't necessarily take place within the mainstream. Most of all, drastically different energies are present."

"Being in this group through this time has made me look at how I listen and how I speak. The way I interact with the group is a microcosm of my interaction with the world. I feel I have opened in the last three months to see that each of us is struggling to move to that [place of] centeredness, to that heart and that spirit in order to bring it into our lives, affecting the planet in a healing and loving way through the choices we make—to realize our own potentials through our individuality and our inseparability from each other and the earth. The choices we make and the actions we take create the world."

My own conclusion about this learning adventure was that apart from the positive impact on the lives of the 12 participants and the receptivity of the three communities to the initiative, plus the expressed intent of the university to sponsor more such programs, once more I became convinced that even though the focus had been studying alternative communities, what really took place was the creation of a *community of consciousness*. Since that 1984 seminar, Lisa and I have had periodic contact with many of these folks over the years. As far as I know none of them is currently a resident in an intentional community. Nevertheless, they are all lifetime members of this other parallel community of consciousness.

The High Wind Association and Its Relationship to the University of Wisconsin

Taken from an informational document provided to the UW legal counsel, 1981

Since High Wind has been using a property owned by Lisa and me—some of it soon to be donated to High Wind—the question arose as to a possible conflict of interest. I had begun organizing High Wind educational programs jointly sponsored with my university department, so my dean and I agreed that we should consult the university's legal counsel. After careful analysis, it was decided there was no conflict of interest, but a scenario was opened where High Wind might serve as a kind of university "field station." This, however, did not materialize, in part because the High Wind community itself was not interested.

Background Overview

The High Wind Association is a small nonprofit corporation established in Wisconsin on November 23, 1977, "to help restore the balance between people and the Earth."

High Wind was accorded tax-exempt status under section 503 (c) (3) of the Internal Revenue Service code as a public foundation on February 27, 1979. High Wind has no paid employees.

In August 1980, High Wind received notification of being awarded a grant by the US Department of Energy Small Grants Appropriate Technology Program for $25,000. Seven projects in Wisconsin were funded. The High Wind funded project is to design and build a "bioshelter" patterned after the models developed by the New Alchemy Institute on Prince Edward Island, Canada, and Cape Cod. A bioshelter is described as a non-consuming micro-farm with a passive solar greenhouse that heats an attached living space with no fossil fuel backup. In the greenhouse are indoor vegetable gardens and translucent tanks that double as thermal storage and "ponds" for fish production.

The bioshelter will have approximately 2,500 square feet of living area for the solar residence, research greenhouse, and educational space. Calculated at $40 per square foot, the building cost is estimated at $100,000. In that most of the labor is voluntary and suppliers are offering discounted materials, the actual cash outlay is expected to be approximately $50,000. In order to provide the balance needed to match the $25,000 government grant, former UWM Chancellor J. Martin Klotsche is assisting High Wind in approaching various corporate and civic donors.

Belden and Lisa Paulson with several others from the Greater Milwaukee and Sheboygan County areas initiated the founding of High Wind. In January 1970, the Paulsons had bought a 46-acre farm in the Northern Kettle Moraine area in Sheboygan County, 55 miles north of Milwaukee. They had used this property as a weekend and vacation retreat for their family and friends and also raised vegetables. In 1977 and 1978, a number of people who shared the pur-

> A bioshelter is described as a non-consuming micro-farm with a passive solar greenhouse that heats an attached living space with no fossil fuel backup.

poses of High Wind began coming to the farm on weekends. The Paulsons and this group decided to remodel the chicken coop, which could then serve as a hostel and rustic meeting facility and living space for the group. The Paulsons paid the cost of materials, and the total group provided labor. It was this group that played the key role in establishing High Wind. They invited David Bergmark, the designer and builder of the New Alchemy Institute Ark projects on the East Coast, to help design a grant proposal for the Wisconsin bioshelter project. This proposal led to the Department of Energy grant.

In the fall of 1980 and the first half of 1981, High Wind activities accelerated. Considerable grassroots support appeared, manifested by the people who became High Wind Associates. A number of people from a variety of professional backgrounds decided to move to the Paulson farm, in effect creating a small "community." They work on the bioshelter's construction, which began in summer 1981, in organic gardening, in various small alternative energy experiments, and in educational activities. Sizable numbers of people visit the farm.

The bioshelter and all land related to it is the property of High Wind. In order to improve the buildings, to be used for community living space and for educational and experimental purposes, the Paulsons invested more than $25,000 of their personal savings—and later on, far more.

The total facility available for High Wind activities, experimentation, and education now includes an extension of some 107 acres and two sets of farm buildings.

The Educational Framework

The fundamental purpose of High Wind is educational. It is for the people who at present live at the farm full or part time, for the Associates who belong to High Wind and participate in its activities in various ways, and for all others who are touched by or whose activities in one way or another relate to the endeavor. This is a voluntary project and has many volunteers.

If one accepts the proposition that limits on material consumption heretofore unknown in our lifetime may be imposed (either voluntarily or through centralized coercion) due to declining nonrenewable natural resources and ecological and environmental factors, then sweeping changes will be required. The most significant level of change may concern basic assumptions, values, and attitudes that presently underlie much of our economic, social, and political life. In a sense, this is a cultural crisis. Education therefore will be a chief means of identifying the new knowledge and values needed to confront the future creatively and effectively.

High Wind has been working educationally most closely with the University of Wisconsin and particularly with the Center for Urban Community Development (CUCD), which for some time Belden Paulson has chaired.

Over the years, CUCD has been recognized as a "cutting-edge" department in the university, specifically in University Extension. A number of its urban programs have gained national recognition as pilots in their fields of competence. By the second half of the 1970s, CUCD became increasingly sensitive to new needs posed by crises related to energy and other natural resource scarcities. The department assumed responsibility for the energy conservation program funded in Wisconsin by the Energy Extension Service for dealing with low- and moderate-income urban people.

Several years ago CUCD began working with a number of other groups both locally and nationally in developing educational programs in the subject area of futures studies. Paulson in particular has been active in these fields, giving a number of talks at national and international meetings and working with

> "We can only talk and study so long. We need to get our hands dirty, get personally involved, put our commitment where our mouth is."—Belden Paulson

various groups in Wisconsin and nationally on formulation of new educational models.

He had become increasingly conscious of comments made regularly by students enrolled in courses and seminars in recent years: "We can only talk and study so long. We need to get our hands dirty, get personally involved, put our commitment where our mouth is." Lisa and Belden Paulson decided to make their farm available for educational purposes.

The Paulsons received no financial gain whatsoever from allowing this use of their farm.

Policy Questions and Options Concerning the High Wind/UWEX Relationship

Apparently questions have come up as to a possible "conflict of interest" for Belden Paulson, given that he has used his position in the university to steer this educational work to the High Wind Association and the High Wind farm, a property that he and his wife own and an organization in which he holds a leadership position.

The Paulsons received no compensation for the use of the property. It is difficult to allocate any increase of value to this property that serves as an educational facility.

There is the larger question of the relationship between High Wind, with its farm base, and the university. Several options appear. One view would be that even though there appears to be no identifiable financial conflict of interest for Paulson, the fact that Paulson plays a decision-making role in both CUCD and High Wind has overtones that are undesirable and could lead, if repeated in the future, to abuses. In the event that Paulson's personal commitment induces him to want to continue developing educational activities that involve High Wind's facility, then he should be asked to work on a part-time basis with UWEX and develop his High Wind-related activities with other educational institutions.

A second way to proceed would be to continue with the status quo, with an understanding that future programs be considered on a case-by-case basis but that adequate consultation should take place to determine their feasibility, with special attention given to university conflict of interest rules.

A third option would be the development of a more carefully planned and systematic type of linkage between the university and High Wind with its facility—recognizing the opportunities for joint research projects, student internships, possible relations with university departments for interdisciplinary programs, and so forth. In this context, some aspects of the "experimental farm" model might be worth exploring. High Wind, while maintaining its autonomy, would work with the university in joint educational undertakings. It would offer an experimental and community facility in return for certain university resources and assistances. The "experimental farm" could deal with energy, small-farm organic food production, aquaculture, ecological systems, social science-related disciplines and activities, and so on. Over time, this "field station" could become an integral part of an explicitly focused futures studies program where the university would begin to focus more attention on a set of issues now perceived to be inadequately addressed.

The Technological Dimension

Cartoon in local newspaper after Town board rejected ecovillage project

Simply Solar

From Harrowsmith Country Life, *April 1995*

This illustrated interview article describes our solar house at High Wind, which we designed and had built. Thousands of visitors have come to the community for classes, workshops, and tours, and viewed the buildings that used renewable energy and the contiguous farm practicing sustainable agriculture.

The Review, Thursday, August 15, 1996

Town of Mitchell Rejects Ecovillage Proposal

In The Review, *Plymouth, Wisconsin*

A number of us associated with High Wind established a parallel, not-for-profit organization we called Plymouth Institute. One of its activities was to design a sustainable ecological village, SpringLedge. This innovative project was rejected by our conservative town board. Here is one of 47 recent columns that I wrote for the Plymouth newspaper (a few of these were authored by Lisa).

Only the fickle hand of fate prevented a state-of-the-art ecovillage from being established just outside of Plymouth less than 20 years ago. From the start, High Wind had been committed to protect the hills and valleys in its Kettle Moraine sub-region of Sheboygan County from conventional subdivisions and development. Three times when surrounding lands had come up for sale and developers were hungry to move in, High Wind had arranged for compatible groups to buy the land. This happened on two different adjacent 20-acre tracts, and also on a large 62-acre parcel.

Thus, when a part of the contiguous 144-acre ecological treasure known as Silver Springs was plotted out for a subdivision, we were concerned. This property was a natural gem, with abundant spring water, forested ridges and wildlife. In earlier years it had one of the noted trout farms in the state. It included a lodge with restaurant, and four chalets that could be used by visitors who came to fish or enjoy the rural ambience. We searched across the county for a sensitive buyer who would protect the property while utilizing the existing facilities. At the last minute, in lieu of any alternative, a small group of High Wind-related associates risked their limited personal resources to buy this unique property themselves.

Our goal was not land investment but to expand High Wind's contribution to sustainable living. After discussion of many plans, including the possibility of using this special setting for a model conference center, we reached the decision to design a state-of-the-art ecovillage. The three purposes: 1) to demonstrate a high-quality example of land use, keeping in mind the ecology of the property; 2) to implement the sustainable living ethic with advanced use of renewable energy practices; 3) to generate income to pay off the mortgage so that the land would not once again be opened to conventional developers.

> Our goal was not land investment but to expand High Wind's contribution to sustainable living.

Since this was a complex undertaking requiring specialized knowledge across several fields, a think tank approach was needed. Bil Becker of our small High Wind core group (himself a professor of ecological design at University of Illinois-Chicago who at one time worked with the eminent Buckminster Fuller), enlisted an experienced architect from Chicago, Mike Gelick. He also brought in an inventive water expert from Illinois, John Hinde. Lisa and I recruited Michael Ogden from Santa Fe, a national specialist who designed biological waste treatment systems using controlled wetlands to eliminate the need for conventional septic systems. Bob Pavlik, also of our core group, (professor of education at Marquette and Cardinal Stritch Universities) worked with Becker and me to develop an education advisory group to use the ecovillage experience for tangible learning demonstrations. Tom Scott, telecommunications design expert, drew in talent to create a state-of-the-art telecommunications center so that some village residents' work could be home-based. Mel Blanke, Plymouth-based attorney and High Wind board member, formulated an ecological covenant and structured the project as a land condominium where individual and joint ownership are combined.

The ecovillage enterprise evolved through the exciting interactions of this talented group over a couple of years. We allocated 70 of the total 144 acres of Silver Springs for the ecovillage. There would be 25 units aesthetically clustered on the high ridge with spectacular views and surrounded by hardwood and pine forests. Homes would be solar with several designs offered by Gelick, or members could create their own. All homes would link into the "Living Machine" wetlands technology with human waste converted into clean water passing through an array of plants and living organisms. All buyers would own a share of the substantial common land—a wilderness to which they would all have access. During a naming process Lisa ended up with the agreed-upon "SpringLedge." As soon as word leaked out—that we were seeking people looking for "the good life" who wanted to become land stewards respecting the earth while creating their own nest of extraordinary beauty in a quality environment—a line of folks showed up as potential buyers.

The Midwest Renewable Energy Association recruited Becker and me for their annual big gathering to lead a discussion on ecovillages using our example. Plymouth Institute hosted a national conference, "Ecovillages and Neighborhoods." This drew academics and practitioners who told us that our project was one of the most carefully thought-out models they had ever encountered. A luncheon, cosponsored with *The Review*, brought in John Todd, one of America's foremost innovators in ecological design and a colleague of Ogden in creating biological waste treatment systems.

On June 5, 1996, Mel Blanke submitted our plan to the Mitchell Town Board for approval. According to local ordinances, a sketch plan had to be provided for final approval. There were architectural sketches for proposed solar homes and a draft for the condominium declaration. There was detailed material on the waste disposal system, which had been discussed and approved by the state and county officials; they supported this model with low environmental impact compared to conventional septic systems. The project would contribute significantly to the local tax base, and with the condo association taking responsibility for the plowing and driveway maintenance, there would be minimal demands placed on local authorities.

Usually Mitchell Town Board meetings were sparsely attended, but at this one there was standing room only. The people who spoke were all virulently against the plan. They opposed a number of new people moving into the area—they said this might create a voting bloc that would take local control. They said the waste system would never work, and they agreed that commonly owned land rather than individual ownership was alien to the local culture. One vocal person complained that High Wind itself did not pay property taxes (the town treasurer refuted this).

The board made no decision to approve our sketches, postponing action until the next monthly meeting. In the

> Plymouth Institute hosted a national conference, 'Ecovillages and Neighborhoods.' This drew academics and practitioners who told us that our project was one of the most carefully thought-out models they had ever encountered

interval several of us met with five residents in the town, all opposed to the project. It turned out that they themselves had moved to Mitchell in recent years. At the next Town Board meeting the crowd was even bigger. One of the most adamant neighbors stood up to read a petition he said 80 people had signed to oppose SpringLedge. He asked who in the room approved the petition; almost everyone stood up except for our small group and a few others. Someone in the meeting pointed a finger at me and suggested that I move to Russia. Obviously anyone who advocated holding land in common must be communist. Another person voiced a concern that our proposed low-cost buildings would draw "undesirables" from the city who might bring vandalism and crime to our bucolic neighborhood. At this point Mel asked to table any decision until the next board meeting.

Early pioneer founders of Plymouth Institute, 1993. top row from left: Kathy Kennard, Bil Becker, Lisa; front: Jim Kennard, Bethe Hagens, and Bel

We were urged to talk to *The Review* and the *Sheboygan Press*—there had been no coverage yet on what was happening. The newspapers attempted to summarize the arguments of both Plymouth Institute and the opposition, and they also discussed the concepts of the ecovillage and sustainability, as well as the environmental and educational work of High Wind and Plymouth Institute. There was even a description of our own solar house. While the press criticized Plymouth Institute for not having invested more energy in educational work with the public (most effort had gone into working out the complex details of the project), the articles and editorials were, by and large, supportive of the ecovillage. They also liked the contributions of new thinking and models and resources that this initiative would bring to Sheboygan County and the Plymouth area.

Before the next Town Board meeting our Plymouth Institute group, at the suggestion of several neighbors, reserved the town hall for an informational meeting. A number of us made presentations about project details, including one Sheboygan business leader who was so enthusiastic about the project that he had already made a deposit on one of the building sites for his family. The atmosphere with 50 people in attendance was more civil than the hostile environments of the previous meetings, although I doubt that many opinions changed.

At the next Town Board meeting, again with standing room only, there was no opportunity for discussion. The three board members rejected the ecovillage, and a one-year moratorium was imposed on any new development in Mitchell.

In the next days, a plethora of articles was published on how our work had stimulated the area to think about smart growth and enlightened zoning policy. Editorials in both newspapers emphasized that this whole process served as a wakeup call for new thinking.

The Sheboygan Press, Sunday, March 12, 2000

Buy. Sell. Trade. Call Classified at 457-7711 Toll Free: 1-800-686-3900

Ecological development : A vision that could become reality

By Belden Paulson

When my wife and I bought our small farm southwest of Plymouth in Sheboygan County in 1970, there was little development in Mitchell Township.

There was a handful of farms along County U going west from Highway 57. We could bathe there out of buckets of water on the front porch of our turn-of-the-century farmhouse (we had no indoor plumbing then), because passing cars were a rarity.

With our two small sons we hiked and picnicked in the surrounding, still wild, landscape. At the time this was our second home, as I was teaching in Milwaukee.

In these intervening 30 years we've watched farmland and woodland turn into lots and septic fields.

What's happening in Mitchell Township and Sheboygan County is happening in much of Wisconsin and the United States.

City life for many people has become dysfunctional, so they're moving out. In Southeast Wisconsin first they often move to the inner sub-

The bottom line is that many well-intentioned individual decisions, with little or no planning, are threatening the very quality of life that first drew the people here.

Various public opinion polls note that more and more people would like to live in the country rather than large cities. Yet the polls also indicate that people want less growth in rural areas, and, further, they feel that land use decisions should be left primarily to the marketplace.

Government involvement and planning are considered "interference." These contradictions are emphasized even more when people say that urban density needs to be encouraged in order to preserve the countryside, noting that this refers to other people. They themselves would choose to live in the country.

Last fall the Wisconsin State Government agreed on a Smart Growth Law requiring every community to have a comprehensive land plan by 2010. A few financial incentives will be offered. In the meantime, this inexorable helter-skelter development process can be expected to continue and accelerate. More farms will be chewed up, and the ecology of the natural world will keep becoming more

est, and protecting wildlife.

Another question: Could we handle the human waste from each home with a more intelligent waste treatment system, without the necessity of putting individual septics that rise so much land and threaten the water table in effect, flushing toilets into the drinking water?

BELDON PAULSON

It is connected to each home by an underground pipe.

This process, used successfully in many parts of the nation, converts liquid sewage into clean water using natural, biological processes. Clusters of homes share wells. Roads and driveways are minimized. A legal instrument (be it a home owners association, planned unit development, land condominium, community land trust, etc.) would lay out ownership details for the 10 participating households, including joint ownership of the 45 acres of green space. This entity would take responsibility for maintenance of the shared interior road and waste system, just as individual lot holders in conventional developments take responsibility for their own interior driveways and septic systems.

While voluntary, the participating households could encourage one another to design and build their homes using methods of conservation and renewable energy, such as low-E windows facing south for passive solar gain, super-insulation, earth berming, and other energy efficient features.

While photovoltaic (PV) systems, which feed electric power composed by the sun back into the

---

Ecological Development: A Vision that Could Become a Reality

In The Sheboygan Press, *March 2000*

After the town board rejected our SpringLedge ecological village, I was asked by *The Sheboygan Press* to give an example of what eco development meant.

When my wife Lisa and I bought our small farm southwest of Plymouth in Sheboygan County in 1970, there was little development in Mitchell Township.

There was a handful of farms along County U going west from Highway 57. Because passing cars were a rarity, we could bathe there out of buckets of water on the front porch of our turn-of-the-century farmhouse (we had no indoor plumbing then).

With our two small sons we hiked and picnicked in the surrounding, still wild, landscape. At the time this was our second home as I was teaching in Milwaukee.

In these intervening 30 years we've watched farmland and woodland turn into lots and septic fields. What is happening in Mitchell Township and Sheboygan County is happening in much of Wisconsin and the United States.

City life for many people has become dysfunctional so they're moving out. In Southeast Wisconsin first they often move to the inner suburbs around Milwaukee, then to the "exurbs" a little farther out.

In recent years they've been attracted to small towns and rural areas in places like Sheboygan County. They are looking for quality of life: low density, few social problems, safety, good drinking water, wildlife and quiet, beautiful scenery.

Most of this development has been haphazard. Typically someone with some capital buys up a farm or sizable tract of land and becomes a developer. He breaks up the land into lots to sell. If necessary, he cuts down trees and levels odd configurations in the terrain to put in roads and utilities. The new buyers then build houses, drill individual wells, and put in septic systems.

Often the buyers will reestablish some of their urban lifestyle, with architecture and construction technologies that are heavy consumers of energy and with lawns not unlike those they had in the city.

Forests have been eliminated or thinned to the point that wildlife is endangered. Septic fields (never meant for rural density) begin to threaten the purity of the water table. The result is rural sprawl.

> Many well-intentioned individual decisions with little or no planning are threatening the very quality of life that first drew the people here.

The bottom line is that many well-intentioned individual decisions with little or no planning are threatening the very quality of life that first drew the people here.

Various public opinion polls note that more and more people would like to live in the country rather than in large cities. Yet the polls also indicate that people want less growth in rural areas and, further, they feel that land use decisions should be left primarily to the marketplace.

Government involvement and planning are considered "interference." These contradictions are emphasized even more when people say that urban density needs to be encouraged in order to preserve the countryside, noting that this refers to *other* people. They themselves would choose to live in the country.

Last fall the Wisconsin State Government agreed on a Smart Growth Law requiring every community to have a comprehensive land use plan by 2010. A few financial incentives will be offered. In the meantime this inexorable helter-skelter development process can be expected to continue and accelerate. More farms will be chewed up, and the ecology of the natural world will face increasing stress.

Imagine If . . .

Let's create an imaginary scenario. What would happen if small groups of people were to take leadership into their own hands by proposing a completely different approach to development? Let's start with a given. Like it or not, there are going to be more and more people flocking to the towns and rural areas of attractive places like Sheboygan County.

First of all, these "new leaders" might agree among themselves that experimenting with another kind of development is sufficiently important that they would forego any personal profit for themselves.

They would borrow or put up money only repaying themselves for actual costs. Far different from many developers who "profit and run," they are local people who expect to stay and be part of the new scheme.

Their next step would be to engage in a careful planning process. They would deal with questions like these: Is it possible to allow a number of people to construct homes and live here, but with minimal impact on the land? This means preserving the maximum amount of open space and forests and protecting wildlife.

Another question: Could we handle the human waste from each home with a more intelligent waste treatment system, without the necessity of building individual septics that take up much land and threaten the water table—in effect, flushing toilets into the drinking water?

Another question: Could homes be designed and built so as to conserve energy and use valuable resources more efficiently? Finally, could we work with residents and local authorities in the surrounding areas so that this project could influence the development process itself?

To keep it simple, let's imagine that this experiment includes 10 homes on 50 acres. Our study would compare what we call "conventional development" with "ecological development."

The conventional development model is based on lots, individual septics and roads and driveways that infringe on and endanger open space, wildlife, agricultural land and the water table.

The ecological development approach clusters the 10 homes on half-acre building sites, which occupy a total of five acres. (These numbers are arbitrary for this illustration.) The rest of the land is preserved, be it woodland, wetland, wildlife conservancy or food production or recreation area.

Instead of individual septics, the waste treatment system would be a "constructed wetland." This is a marsh (not wet at ground surface level) created with a lined bottom that separates it from the water table, under gravel, in which natural organisms and self-generating vegetation flourish. It is connected to each home by an underground pipe.

This process, used successfully in many parts of the nation, converts liquid sewage into clean water using natural biological processes. Clusters of homes share wells. Roads and driveways are minimized. A legal instrument (be it a home owners association, planned unit development, land condominium, community land trust, etc.) would lay out ownership details for the 10 participating households, including joint ownership of the 45 acres of green space. The entity would take responsibility for maintenance of the shared interior road and waste system just as individual lot holders in

> The ecological development approach clusters the homes. . . . The rest of the land is preserved, be it woodland, wetland, wildlife conservancy or food production or recreation area.

conventional developments take responsibility for their own interior driveways and septic systems.

While voluntary, the participating households could encourage one another to design and build their homes using methods of conservation and renewable energy—such as low-e windows facing south for passive solar gain, super-insulation, earth-berming and other energy efficient features.

While photovoltaic (PV) systems, which feed electric power generated by the sun back into the grid, are not cost-effective in traditional economic terms at this time, they are going to be seen more and more as the fuel situation changes. They become, therefore, an option to be considered on a pilot basis.

The total cost of this eco-development model is estimated to be no more and maybe less than the conventional model due to savings on road/driveway construction, smaller distances for utility infrastructure, shared wells, a common waste treatment system and operational savings from use of renewable energy. The design encourages foot travel within the whole 50 acres rather than relying on cars. Some people may also appreciate the enhanced sense of community and security of the clustered housing.

This is only Imagination. But it is doable. This kind of model, multiplied many times, could enhance the quality of life in Sheboygan County.

MILWAUKEE PUBLIC SCHOOLS			
in Levels of Partnership with			
PLYMOUTH INSTITUTE/HIGH WIND LEARNING CENTER			
FOR SUSTAINABLE FUTURES			

Level I	Level II	Level III	Level IV
Purposes: Make initial contact with PI/HW; introduce ideas about future-oriented careers, and identify participants for subsequent activities. **Time:** One day during September and early October '94 **Program:** Tour PI/HW facilities with practitioners in organic food production, aqua-	**Purpose:** Introduce students to hands-on applications and futures-oriented careers. **Time:** 2-3 days **Program:** Hands-on activities working with practitioners: • Aquaculture • Organic food production • Solar energy and construction	**Purpose:** Develop sustainable futures mind-set and involve students in community-building experiences, project-oriented and skills development for emerging work options. **Time:** 9 1-week modules **Program:** Hands-on field studies with follow-up home	**Purpose:** Prepare secondary students for global marketplace. (planned during 94-95 school year) **Time:** Four years **Program:** Interdisciplinary projects leading to Global Education Certification; annual "threshold" experiences with international travel for the

Field Experience Campus

1992

During the six years that Plymouth Institute owned Silver Springs, we conducted sustainability-related R&D, and with High Wind, sponsored an array of educational programs. These included a contract with the Milwaukee Public Schools to create a field station for inner city youth, especially from the Grand Avenue Middle School through leadership of its principal, Tom McGinnity. They came to live in the countryside for a few days for nature study, to learn about solar energy, aquaculture, and sustainable agriculture. Here is an outline of the agenda—the ideas and activities we wanted to introduce through this program.

- Introduce students to the "mindset" of global-oriented sustainable futures: futures orientation, concept of sustainability (protecting the environment while meeting needs of today), global interdependence (economic and political), whole-system thinking, environmental careers

- Give students access to the natural environment of Plymouth Institute/High Wind

- Provide contact with technologies and practitioners of those technologies, as related to sustainable futures

- Give opportunity for personally living in a community setting and taking individual responsibility for making the community function

- Adapt and refine the approach of Multiple Intelligences in this program's context, which recognizes and builds on the uniqueness of individuals' abilities and talents

- Integrate this field experience into the daily learning environment of Grand Avenue School

Living in Intentional Community:
Some Larger Perspectives

*High Wind
residents in 1991*

COMMUNITIES journal of cooperation

no. 67 $3.00

Community Dilemmas

In Communities *magazine, Summer 1985*

This was a talk I presented at a global conference at the Findhorn Foundation in Scotland. It is based on experiences in our High Wind community.

Alternative communities present in fairly exaggerated ways some of the dilemmas and paradoxes of a changing culture. The mysteries therein provide tension, but they also unleash creative energy as they explore useful approaches in dealing with daily personal issues as well as planetary concerns. Here, by way of illustration, are six such dichotomies drawn from High Wind experience; they find a new integration as they work out their own balance.

Elitism and diversity

Alternative communities get their internal cohesion and strength through shared visions and values and "sounding a note" in defining their purpose. This opens them up to being called elitist—an elitism not in terms of socio-economic factors but in their values. Yet their ultimate importance and relevance is in their relationship to the diversity of the larger society.

Public learning center or place for personal growth

Alternative communities potentially have a special role to play in creating and testing new models, and communicating and sharing their findings and process. The members, however, have their own individual needs for growth, family nurturing, and private space free from any public involvement.

Outside and inside the system

By their very nature, alternative communities challenge the status quo on many fronts. They embody alternatives to various aspects of mainstream culture: methods of growing food, building shelter, planning for land use, making decisions, and so forth. At the same time, there is need for a certain degree of credibility that comes from working with and participating in existing institutional systems and their values.

Economic insecurity and market economy jobs

Many participants in alternative communities have dropped out or would like to drop out of models for earning a living as practiced in the existing, market-oriented economy. Nevertheless, this economy controls most of the wealth, sources of money, and welfare and social benefit systems that affect one's material well-being.

Transformational leadership and pragmatic leadership

Participants in alternative communities make conscious efforts to redefine the ways that power is used. Honest attempts are made to move away from adversarial relationships and to resolve conflicts without cementing rigid majority and minority positions. Nevertheless, particular individuals and sub-groups may wield special influence, and there is sometimes a thin line between effective governance and paralysis from complete dependence on consensus.

Playfulness and crisis orientation

Alternative communities tend to be unusually sensitive to the precariousness and manifold crises facing humanity and the planet at this historic moment. Yet having fun, being able to laugh at one's foibles and efforts, being adventurous, taking time for appreciating nature and beauty, and celebrating are intrinsic to communities that work.

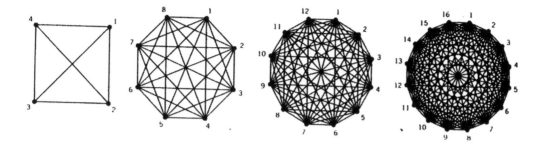

On Being an Orchestra—
of Many Unique Instruments

In Windwatch, *April 1987*

Since *Windwatch* was the journal periodically published by High Wind, I was among the regular contributors on issues currently facing the community. This one focused on the role of individuality in the community.

D oes one lose one's individual identity in intentional community?
Simple question, profound implications.
By way of illustration, take anyone at High Wind—me for example. I am a person full of ideas, one who tends to dangle several complex projects in the air and work on them more or less simultaneously. I am a futurist who likes to peer fairly far ahead, a risk taker who is not afraid to tackle "the impossible," someone who likes adventure and constantly getting into new things, an avid reader of seemingly disparate information. I also have a relatively thick skin and sometimes am insensitive to the individual pain of others around me.

Often I find it hard to understand people who live only "in the now," and I wonder how people can relate to the world when they don't read the daily newspaper. I get into trouble with those who feel tremendous pressure if they take on more than one project at a time. I tend to get impatient in meetings that focus mainly on "process" as opposed to "getting something done." This description exaggerates a little, but you get the gist of my "personality DNA."

In the High Wind community, as in every community I know (not to mention society at large), each person has unique attributes, many of which are essential to make the community "work." If carried too far, however, they have inherent tendencies to create cleavages in relationships and all sorts of community tension.

It could be said that the art of community living includes sanding down the rough edges just enough so that members can live together happily in a fairly tight synergistic association. In the best of circumstances, each individual's talents and special characteristics are integrated into the larger whole, like an orchestra, which creates glorious harmony with many distinct instrumental voices. The danger of community comes when we try to sand down the rough points so that they are as smooth as a wall that has no blemishes instead of building an interesting fireplace hearth made of hundreds of stones of different shapes and colors, mortared together.

In these circumstances, one may feel that one's identity is being sacrificed to the "larger good" of getting along with everyone else, which can result in frustration and unhappiness.

After living for six-plus years in the High Wind community, full or part time, I have become convinced that when the community is "working," we have created a "chemistry" where all the different parts recognize, respect, and have come to terms with the uniqueness of each other, and at the same time are bound together by common purpose. When the community is "not working," this sense of acceptance and even encouragement of diversity breaks down.

Some people then try to sand down the rough edges of others so that they will correspond to a certain image of correctness. The binding glue then dissolves, leaving in its wake disgruntled people and a community lacking in clear purpose and high energy.

The particular orientation of a community at any point in its history seems to have much to do with its propensity to encourage diversity or to restrain it. In High Wind's early years, the major thrust was construction of the bioshelter, which brought the community together in the first place.

The national energy crisis was at its peak, and many of us agreed that renewable energy served as a viable alternative. We attracted many volunteers, some of them strong willed and with richly varied backgrounds, to design and put up this solar building, along with other energy-efficient structures. Believing in what we were doing, we brought in the public, which resulted in considerable educational and outreach activity.

In time, various residents felt their own needs were being neglected and that High Wind should turn inward to focus more on its spiritual side and interpersonal relationships. For a couple of years now, this has been a primary focus. There has been a strong effort to build connections on deeper personal levels, an activity that living in community accentuates.

By way of illustration, in the diagram at the top of the previous page (page 255), English writer C.P. Snow noted that the number of possible "connections" grows exponentially when the number of people increases arithmetically. This was brought home last year when the number of full- or part-time people in the community increased to 16 (including two children), and the connections suddenly expanded.

If the connections are all straight lines as in the diagram, the complexity is already considerable. But when each dot and line represents an individual personality "DNA," with all its sharp points and rough edges, then we are dealing with the full weight of human diversity.

As mentioned, this diversity can be tremendously enriching if there is consensus to accept the differences, but in turn, there needs to be general agreement on overall purpose. For a while, during High Wind's bioshelter construction period, there was broad agreement on purpose, and this facilitated acceptances of big differences among the human beings within the community.

In recent years, our general acceptance about focusing on getting along and relating created a similar situation. During the changeover from one period to another, however, there was considerable tension. Now, it seems, High Wind is once again in a changeover period, with much debate about purpose and direction of the organization. Resurfacing are tendencies to "sand down" individual differences to fit the "correct images," whatever they are.

The impetus for the present change point has been High Wind's actual physical expansion (acquiring more land and fixing up buildings), along with a projected increase in public programs and community population. While all this activity and planning generated high levels of energy and excitement, in the aggregate, it also created a sense of pressure that induced some people to leave or consider leaving.

Out of this ferment will emerge, I expect, structural and organizational changes, which will create new effectiveness and sustainability. I think the viability of these emerging models will depend on our understanding of what has been happening in the community in recent years.

My "photograph" of the prevailing realities suggests that five distinct though interrelated groups of people are forming in the community—each with its own peculiar as well as complementary needs and interests.

- *Long-term residents.* A number of us have made a more-or-less permanent commitment to live at High Wind evidenced by our building homes. We are unlikely to pack our bags and leave even when things get difficult or we feel burned out. It also happens that at least one member of each of these family units has a job outside the community. This provides income for long-term sustainability, but it also limits the time and energy available for community work.

  Obviously we residents, along with the board of directors, have a long-term interest in anchoring the High Wind vision and in assuring that High Wind's fundamental purposes, as described in the original papers of incorporation and the recently prepared Purpose Statement—the so-called "constitutional issues"— are respected. I believe that each unit in this grouping (and I expect the number of units will increase in the near future) should tithe a monthly donation.

- *Paid staff.* We've become clear that there are essential tasks that must be carried out to maintain the physical infrastructure of our property, which in the last year has doubled in size—as well as to create an environment conducive to receiving guests and operating educational programs. These activities require several full-time people. The "pay" would be modest by market standards but quite attractive in the existing voluntary environment.

  Staff would be selected for a strong attunement to what High Wind is about and be willing to commit one year at a time. This would be an excellent opportunity for those people, including mature students, who would like to live for a period in community. At various times, paid staff could include members of the other groupings described here. Funds would come from education and guest program revenue, rents from use of facilities, and tithing by long-term residents.

- *Working volunteers.* Each of us here has been and will continue to be a working volunteer because this is basic to our shared commitment. However, as the community evolves into long-term residents and paid staff, this particular role becomes clearer.

  I trust that we will continue to attract people to join the community and volunteer their energy for limited periods of time. Also, as our Associate Program, these folks who come for limited periods, is strengthened, we will look to a number of our extended High Wind family to spend time with us. Working volunteers will continue to be the "breeding pool" for people who subsequently assume the other roles.

- *Participants in special projects.* While one never knows how the community will unfold, a decentralization process seems to be emerging. In addition to general interest in community, individuals may be attracted to High Wind who have fairly specifically directed energies and talents that fit within the overall High Wind purpose framework: for example, to focalize a sustainable agriculture project, or to create a small business around woodcraft, or to develop a guest house/bed and breakfast, or to create a study center as part of the New Synthesis Think Tank now under discussion, or to establish an alternative school, or to work on programs for youth, or to set up an outlet in the local area for High Wind Books & Records—not to mention to help with general focalizing of education and guest programs along with existing residents.

- *Community members at large.* Some people are drawn to High Wind not necessarily as long-term residents or paid staff or even as working members in the community. They may choose to participate in deep-level relationships, or retreat for a time, or enjoy uninterrupted time for artistic pursuits, and so on.

  In a sense, this is the true "intentional community," where clearly defined individual intentions are the motivation, as opposed to the purposes of High Wind as an institutional entity. These people (paying rent) would be expected to participate in occasional community functions, but their main contribution would be the important energy that their presence represents.

*Sunrise Indian balance
dance at High Wind*

Gaian Politics

In Windwatch, *Fall-Winter 1988*

This issue of *Windwatch* relates to a global conference held at Findhorn. While the Cold War was ongoing, Gorbachev was opening up new thinking about world relationships. Our seminars at High Wind were focusing on the outlines of creating fundamental societal change.

"Gaia" Is in the Air.

Since 1979, when British scientist James Lovelock published his groundbreaking book, *Gaia—A New Look At Life On Earth,* the hypothesis that the Earth is a living organism has entered more and more into ordinary conversation. This hypothesis is no longer limited to the perennial wisdom of religions and philosophies or to the explorations of research scientists.

I was greatly impressed by the wisdom embodied in the responses to the "matrix of concern" study organized by the International Center for Integrative Studies (ICIS), published earlier this year. The study sought comment on three questions: What are the five most crucial issues facing humankind today? What are the root causes of these problems? What are the existing seeds of change for transformation that offer potential for advancing the human and world condition? Replies came from more than 100 people—some of the world's top thinkers—published in the March issue of ICIS's *Forum.* While 27 different categories emerged from the responses, my interpretation would be that most of them have something to do with Gaia.

In the recently available 1987 edition of *Future Survey Annual,* the unrivaled publication of recent literature on trends, forecasts and policy proposals published by the World Future Society, a central theme is the ever-increasing intertwining of national and global concerns, which ties into Gaia.

Gaia at Findhorn

In October, Lisa and I joined more than 200 people from different areas of the world at the annual conference held at the Findhorn community in Scotland. It was titled "The Individual and the Collective: Politics As If the Whole Earth Mattered." The openness of the speakers from the Soviet Union, Poland, and Hungary was especially impressive. Joseph Goldin, one of the major Soviet speakers, said, "The resolution of East-West tension and world transformation will start here at Findhorn. This is the role of the Findhorns of the world. It's also time now to have centers like Findhorn in the USSR for citizen diplomacy. It is time for a quantum jump there, because there is no longer any risk. It is the Findhorns that are the places where real world change will happen; you have a great responsibility."

> Gaia is one of the beginning attempts to look at whole systems, to reverse our tendency to look at reality in simple and piecemeal terms rather than as a whole, which is complex.

What was even more interesting than the conference lectures and discussions was the intense dialogue that took place among the Findhorn Fellows during their two-day meeting just after the conference. Much of this centered on the changing relationship at Findhorn itself between the people living in the 25-year-old community and the many people who were previously in the community but now have moved into the surrounding area. This was the Individual and the Collective in real action—the underlying challenge was how to place this new dynamic into a Gaian perspective. Which raises the question: What do we mean by Gaia?

The Meaning of Gaia

Obviously there are many interpretations. The scientific one is referred to in Lovelock's book. I'd like to draw on the discussion we had at our one-week seminar at High Wind the last week in June; it was titled "The Gaia in You—An Exploration of our Role in a Holistic Universe." David Spangler shared the following thoughts, among others:

- Gaia is one of the beginning attempts to look at whole systems, to reverse our tendency to look at reality in simple and piecemeal terms rather than as a whole, which is complex. We somehow assume that the "invisible hand" will take care of the whole, and we have no individual accountability.

- The Gaia experience is to extend our boundaries in order to comprehend larger and larger systems, to see ourselves as a part but not in domination over the whole, to recognize the connectedness of everything.

- Gaia requires that we use our imagination, because these boundaries go far beyond our direct experience and maybe our intellect. This stretching of perception becomes vision as opposed to fact. Science extends our boundaries—building on what we "know" exists—while poetry can transcend boundaries. Our task is to synthesize the two.

- Organisms that survive through time have learned how to cooperate. Gaia promotes and sustains life. It is womb-like, constantly offering new possibilities of unfoldment while building on "what is."

- Gaia means not only the Whole, but also all of the constituent parts—the unique, individualized, differentiated cells that fit together into their larger systemic interdependence. Thus the essence of Gaia is *relationship*.

- The meaning of Gaia for each of us as individuals is that we seek to express fully the richness of our individuality while always relating to the larger whole. The Gaia in me is manifested through my discovering in my own special way my contribution to the whole.

- The meaning of Gaia for group behavior and organizational structure is that we participate in the process of nurturing co-creativity, of utilizing and blending different individual contributions, which then relate our decentralized individualism to the center.

Katherine Collis, a fellow Lorian, built on David's comments at the seminar to discuss Cycles of Incarnation—change, the bringing of new forms, transformation. The first step is initiation, a new level of consciousness that breaks the inertia and initiates one's passage from one state to another. As old perceptions and old paradigms break down, there may be need for healing as new relationships evolve. The key is *synthesis:* to be part of a process of transcending polarization and separation, to build on the old while going beyond it, to recognize the importance of all the parts as they seem to interrelate into the ever-more complex synthesis. Gaia in its truest sense is *community*.

> Gaia in its truest sense is *community*.

Speaking Politically

At the seminar and again at Findhorn, I built on these remarks to give an interpretation of Gaian Politics, which in essence could mean the application of whole-systems thinking to political life. To some people, holistic thinking and politics are a contradiction in terms because politics—using the formulation of Harold Lasswell's classic book *Who Gets What, When, How* (written in 1930)—usually refers to short-run, narrow, material self-interest. Whole-systems thinking, however, implies a redefinition of politics. It would take into account characteristics that students from my graduate class and I formulated together:

- *Cooperation*: interrelationships where the parts of the whole work together for the common good;

- *Sustainability*: each part uses what it needs but contributes to and enhances rather than infringes on the whole;

- *Empowerment*: each part gives strength to the others, all thus benefiting with a "win-win" result;

- *Compassion*: each part extends open arms to the others, giving without expectation of a particular return, thereby creating an underlying trust in the viability of the overall system even though some participants may be perceived as contributing more than others; and

- *Long-term perspective:* each part places its needs of the moment into a time continuum that far transcends its own existence.

Living in the Future:
___ The Complex Choices of Right Livelihood ___

During a seminar sponsored by the Midwest Greens two summers ago, the leaders laughingly suggested I not bother with an activity visualizing the future because, they said, I was already living there.

The High Wind lifestyle might well be an image of a possible future for the world. What's it like? A few characteristics stand out.

Networking

I was driving back from Wellspring, a community near Newberg, Wisconsin, where I had been

although I loved her, I had a living to earn, and my priorities didn't include volunteer work just then. The only message she would receive from that was that she lived in a world where her needs were never met, a world that contained only adversity. So I chose to drop whatever I was doing when she cried, and meet her needs first. That way, I reasoned, she would get the message that the world includes both misery and comfort, both problems and solutions. And I would have to listen to a lot less crying.

This kind of selflessness cannot be sustained

to buy a hamburger and fries. But there were lots of potatoes in the basement.

I let my mind work around this concept as I finished my supper and cleaned up. Is there a way we could all eat potatoes and carrots and onions, instead of hamburgers and fries, and all of us be healthier, and none of us be hungry? Maybe, but a lot of things have to change. Many lessons must be learned.

Becoming Indigenous People

Perhaps the most important lesson to be

Looking Back from the Future

From Windwatch, *Fall/Winter 1989–90*

The following two articles address the intense ferment in the world: the end of the Cold War and other great contemporary issues. It was important to keep in mind our small-scale, local efforts in the context of the big picture. These *Windwatch* articles, although 25 years old, show surprising contemporary relevance to what we were thinking.

This seems to be one of those rare moments in history when the world is very fluid. As a high-ranking US official recently said, "The world is changing in very big ways, hour by hour. It keeps you humble when someone says, 'Please draw me up three scenarios for the future . . .' "

I cannot recall a comparable time since the end of World War II. At that time, leaders in our country and elsewhere were trying to figure out the kind of world to construct out of the ashes of the war. Very quickly major elements of the postwar period, the next 40 years, fell into place: the United Nations and its agencies, the Cold War and nuclear stalemate, international assistance beginning with the Marshall Plan, and rapid economic growth in the industrialized world.

I was a teenager at the end of WW II, and people of my age were vitally interested in knowing where we were heading—toward peace or more war, to what kind of job, in what kind of world.

Looking back from the perspective of a Monday morning (or 40 years later) quarterback, I am surprised by the relatively conservative nature of the answers that the leadership of that day provided, if we take into account what we know now. Naturally this is a slightly ludicrous exercise, because the leaders then were dealing with the fast-moving situation of the end of a shooting war and the beginning of a political/ideological war. Today's leaders will undoubtedly appear as shortsighted when reviewed 40 years hence.

A truly wise leader with a futures perspective might have envisaged in 1949 the need for such transitions as the following:

- **From economic growth to sustainable development**

  The great theme of the last 40 years, unlimited material growth—the heart of our culture—has become obsolete.

  The world's industrial production has increased more than one hundredfold in the last 100 years (much of it since WW II), and we are running out of certain essential raw materials. Energy use has grown by a factor of 80 in this same period, and the resulting increases of carbon, sulfur, and nitrogen in our atmosphere have created ominous environmental consequences. (Figures from William Clark, "Managing Planet Earth," *Scientific American*, September 1989.)

  The issue is not *whether* there should be growth but *what kind* of growth. An enlightened approach is *sustainable development.* According to the World Commission on Environment and Development, sustainable development means that economic and social progress must "meet the needs of the present without compromising the ability of future generations to meet their own needs."

- **From national states to a global community**

  When the Allied leaders were designing the United Nations, they considered a new kind of world order, which would limit sovereignty. But this was considered far too radical a step, and the United Nations is today an organization of national sovereign states.

  We have paid dearly for this decision. Over $17 trillion of the world's resources (1986 US dollars) have been consumed in arms production in the last three decades. The world stockpile of nuclear weapons totaled 57,000 in 1989, 98 percent of them held by the United States and the USSR with an explosive force equal to 1.2 million Hiroshima bombs. (Figures from Ruth Leger Sivard, *World Military and Social Expenditures,* 1989.) Other nations are developing nuclear capability, and the threat of nuclear terrorism is real.

  We are living in a global community—a single marketplace and an ecological system that has nothing to do with national borders—but we are still saddled with nationalistic institutions that are increasingly dysfunctional.

- **From Western investment to Third World strategy**

  The great issue directly after WW II was to rebuild Western Europe, which led to the Marshall Plan. Today a salient concern is to rebuild Eastern Europe. Most of the world, however, lives elsewhere, in poverty.

> The issue is not *whether* there should be growth but *what kind* of growth. An enlightened approach is *sustainable development.*

A World Bank map shows that 42 countries have "low income" economies (per capita income of $480 or less) and 53 countries are "middle income" (per capita income of $481 to $5,999). Most of these areas are on the continents of Asia, Africa, and Latin America, with a population of 3,861 million. This is compared to the 25 high-income countries with a population of 777.2 million (Figures from *World Development Report,* 1987.) The world's population growth is concentrated in these areas, in countries also weighed down with international debt totaling more than $1 trillion. In their struggle to survive, the people in these lesser developed countries are exhausting the natural resource base with deforestation, destruction of topsoil, reduction of the water table, and desertification. This can lead to disaster for themselves and for the planet. The whole complex of poverty and ecological stress may be the world's greatest source of instability today. A global strategy with massive resources is required.

- **From technological expansion to innovation with a human face**
    New technology was spurred by WW II, but in retrospect, that period appears modest compared with today's rampant technological change. Business analysts suggest that 60 percent of productivity growth is now linked to technological know-how, and that an engineer's training becomes outmoded in three to seven years. Information technology—computers, microelectronics, telecommunications, software engineering, systems analysis—is transforming the "feeling, sensibilities, perceptions, expectations, assumptions and, above all, the possibilities that define a community. The changes being wrought are as great as those brought about by the medieval castle, the printed book, and the automobile." (Shoshana Zuboff, *In the Age of the Smart Machine.*)
    Along with all of their exciting new possibilities, these new technologies also present problems. Potential for corporate or governmental control of communication channels, the emergence of a new underclass based in technological illiteracy, the invasion of privacy from computer banks, the redefinition or even elimination of work as we have known it—these are a few of the negative symptoms of new technology.

These trends were barely discussed in 1949. Only now are they beginning to be considered seriously.

Reconceptualizing the World

The other day I was reviewing what we had been doing over the past several months. I knew we had been on the run, but what, exactly were these activities?

- A conference we helped organize on "Education in the 21st Century," which involved 125 University of Wisconsin administrators and faculty, presumably some of "the best and the brightest."
- My 14-week fall seminar, "Innovation in Education," essentially addressing the need for restructuring education at its roots.

- A talk focusing on paradigm shifts and their meaning for education, presented to 75 administrators and academics who work most closely with students on the UW-Madison campus.
- Helping to plan a conference on "New Realities: Doing Business in the Emerging Global Economy" to involve 75 business leaders.
- Meetings and writing of the first papers for a whole-systems think tank.
- Preparations for participating in a "Citizens Summit" in Moscow in January 1990, to involve 180 Americans and several hundred Soviets, focusing on "Restoring the Global Environment—Sustainable Development for the New Millennium.
- Planning for a study delegation to China in April 1990, to include a global conference in Shanghai titled "New Trends in Science, Technology, Economy and Society in the Pacific Basin."

What could I make of these activities in the aggregate? They involve national and international thinkers and doers breaking new ground in their fields: futurists, educators, government officials, businessmen, economists, biotechnology and information-processing experts, and leaders in the Soviet Union and China. The basic theme is that we are rethinking the way we see the world.

Relationships among the superpowers are shifting in fundamental ways unimagined a few months ago, and we are just beginning to feel the tremors. Technological changes are restructuring the global economy into a single marketplace, creating tremendous opportunities and tremendous problems. Multiple environmental crises are generating growing pressure to reassess lifestyle patterns: how we use energy, grow food, and price products to include the real costs of raw materials and the environmental effects of production.

All this is tied to the underlying hypothesis that the world is not a machine made up of separate pieces, but an indivisible whole where all the parts, including people, are in dynamic relationship. We must extend our mental perimeters to comprehend larger and larger systems, eventually including the whole Earth and all of humanity. As we redefine our parochial boundaries, we are moving toward community in its truest sense—where everyone and everything is connected.

Living in Intentional Community: Some Personal Observations on Governance and Shared Consciousness

On Community Governance

From Windwatch, *Spring/Summer 1990*

Community members were often frustrated with "governance issues": Too much power or not enough; too much processing of personal issues or not enough; too much philosophizing on ideals on why High Wind exists or not enough, and so on. Perhaps it's easier to understand governance issues in a small community than in the larger world.

A recent Sunday *New York Times* article concluded: "As America's democratic visions and values seem to triumph around the world, an unhappy consensus has emerged at home that domestic politics has become so shallow, mean and even meaningless that it is failing to produce the ideas and leadership needed to guide the United States in a rapidly changing world" (18 March 1990). Moreover, the excitement of people working on the new frontiers of science and technology is starkly contrasted with the gloom of people observing modern government. "Governance" has almost become a dirty word.

None of us is immune to strong opinions on the subject. We may bail out of the political process altogether, or simply not bother to vote. Some of us get into the thick of it and do what we can. Most of us criticize.

A very few join intentional communities, which attempt, in various ways, to "start over," building more or less from scratch whatever "alternative" governance structures and behaviors seem important and doable.

As I look over High Wind's decade of experience, including its current reality, I find that "governance" at High Wind usually has had something to do with three general themes:

- The ongoing discovery of High Wind's inner essence—its original core;
- The desire for decentralized, non-hierarchical authority and power; and
- The struggle to interrelate the core values to efficiency.

The Discovery of High Wind's Inner Essence

It seems that at almost every one of our meetings, the question arises: What really *is* High Wind? Why do we exist? Of course, one could ask the same question about America: What really *is* America? I venture that a serious investigation of this question could elevate significantly the quality of politics and governance.

As to the first question: at one level we could say that High Wind is 17 residents living on 128 acres in a cluster of relatively energy-efficient buildings 55 miles north of Milwaukee. These people have an interest in ecology, a global outlook, they are caring individuals (most of the time), and they are part of a national/world network of like-minded people.

On another level, we could look at our Articles of Incorporation—the legal document we drafted to establish the nonprofit organization. It states the goal of High Wind:

- To develop a sharing community where people live together in cooperation with one another and with nature;
- To design and build shelters and power systems and small enterprises, which rely on renewable energy sources and which utilize ecological and technological systems appropriate to the conservation of resources and the preservation of the environment and the production of food;
- To utilize the land in a way that gives full recognition to the soil as an ecosystem, which views agriculture as the activity of a natural human community, and which respects variety and balance;
- To serve as a demonstration project in the sense of demonstrating the above through the actual example of people who live and/or work in the sharing community; and
- To serve an educational role by means of generating and disseminating knowledge and information on learnings from the above experiences using the written and spoken word and a variety of communication media.

Several years later High Wind amplified that document with a Purpose Statement. At the time, there was considerable conflict among certain residents, but after intense discussions, agreement was reached on our purposes and values. The first article reads:

"The purpose of the High Wind residential community is to develop a sharing ambience where people live in honesty and harmony with one another and with nature, acknowledging and celebrating the divine interconnectedness of all life. At the same time, along with similar groups around the world, we are affecting the healing and transformation of the planet."

Article II discusses High Wind's educational role, Article III its commitments to holistic thinking and living (which are spelled out), and Article IV the residential community's relationship to other parts of the Association.

In all the discussions, in my view, it has become clear that High Wind's fundamental purpose, its inner essence, has to do with spiritual deepening based on belief in an inner divinity and the connection this makes among each of us here, to the world and to Mother Earth. Sometimes the search for the inner essence is a very personal effort by High Wind members. At other times, it takes group forms through meditations, retreats, celebrations and rituals, and study and educational programs.

Sometimes the inner essence shines clearly, even radiantly, in the community and beyond. At other times, it is submerged by more "practical" activities, personality conflicts, and so on. At any given moment, the quality of the community, including its governance, is directly linked to how well we are working with our purpose and vision.

Decentralized, Non-Hierarchical Power

There is an aversion to bureaucracy at High Wind. Rules, and regulations are thought to stimulate equal counter-efforts to get around them. Most of the time we can eliminate them by filtering who joins the community as well as through ongoing consciousness-raising. We believe that people who are committed to High Wind's purposes and values—implying a tight relationship of individual behavior to the larger interests of the whole—need few formal rules. We followed Findhorn's model where there are only two explicitly stated rules: no illegal drugs and no smoking in public places.

This open, fluid environment places maximum responsibility on each individual to fit into the rhythms of the community. These rhythms are not preordained; they have evolved organically and can change as community membership changes. The original Articles and Purpose Statement can also be changed (as can any basic documents, including the US Constitution). Presumably any changes would be deliberated carefully.

> There is an aversion to bureaucracy at High Wind. . . . People who are committed to High Wind's purposes and values— implying a tight relationship of individual behavior to the larger interests of the whole— need few formal rules.

Authority at High Wind is vested in the Board of Directors— nine members—the majority of whom are community residents but several of whom are long-time High Wind Associates living elsewhere. While High Wind has "officers" who sign their names to documents required by the state, it has no single "leader." Original board members were self-appointed; replacements are appointed by the board. Board members rotate in serving as facilitator at the monthly meeting, in alphabetical sequence. The recorder taking minutes at a given meeting chairs the subsequent one. All community residents are urged to participate in board meetings; their input is welcomed.

Much actual decision-making takes place in committees appointed by the board. For example, the Personnel Committee plays a key role in determining who joins the community and in addressing personal issues. The Education Committee deals with learning activities sponsored by High Wind. The Guest Committee is in charge of food and lodging for those visiting High Wind or participating in programs. The Bookstore Committee advises the board on policy for the HW Books business located in Milwaukee. Ad hoc committees are established as needs arise, such as for long-range strategy, land use, or new construction.

Each committee has one or more "focalizers." This person is not a "boss" or director in the conventional sense but serves as a point of focus for the group, taking special responsibility for relating the larger High Wind purpose to the given activity. Focalizers normally emerge as volunteers from the group and are endorsed by the board. High Wind has a Finance Coordinator and an Administrator who takes responsibility for coordinating daily administrative matters.

In community meetings, there is a strong effort to listen to all points of view and to resolve issues without a majority or minority view monopolizing the discussion or crystallizing. Sheer power does not dominate decisions. While petty bickering sometimes overwhelms higher purposes, there generally tends to be a lack of arrogance and greed in decision-making and a caring kind of discussion and negotiation.

The above is not to suggest that there is no "power structure" at High Wind. While formal authority is dispersed among the board, committees, focalizers, coordinators, administrators, and managers, there are all sorts of subtle informal relationships. The people who have founding roles, the individuals with disproportionate material resources, people with special expertise, and also people with time to invest in a particular activity all exercise distinctive kinds of power.

All in all, this system of decentralized, non-hierarchical governance is sometimes seen as downright dysfunctional. Board meetings can become tediously long when "value" questions go far beyond the particular item requiring decision. Someone may blurt out, "What this community needs is a strong leader," or "What are we doing here if we can't even resolve this particular question?" or "If we can't improve our efficiency, we're not an alternative to anybody."

The Struggle to Interrelate Inner Essence and Efficiency

We cannot overlook the fact that there can be an inherent conflict between "doing what is right" and "doing what works." For example, at what point do you stop a discussion when there is need for certain people still to be heard, or to what degree are important needs and sensitivities of individuals to be subordinated to actions desired by the larger whole? The person who describes one meeting as tediously long because no feeling-level matters come up may be chagrined at the next meeting when a personal matter is placed on the docket and others complain that the discussion is tedious or inappropriate. In governance terms, there is always the test between adhering to the larger value context, which is fundamentally why High Wind exists, and the need to function with task-oriented efficiency, which is essential for survival.

As High Wind has grown in size and complexity, we have found that the key is to separate policy decision-making, which intrinsically is linked to the purpose/value context, from the implementation function, which is linked to efficiency. In High Wind's early years, there was little if any distinction between the two. There was no Board of Directors; community residents were both the policy and operating group. Everyone was involved in everything.

The first major project was to design and build the bioshelter. Virtually everyone participated in discussing the function and design of the building (an experience in itself), and then they went out and built it. Naturally there were designated skilled individuals who "ran the show" when there was a need for technical expertise. Likewise, the whole community dealt with education and guests on the policy level, and then pitched in to do the work. Several years later the board was established and committees came into being.

In recent years, both High Wind residents individually and the community as an organization have committed to full economic sustainability. Small businesses have begun to flourish, including a producing farm, desktop publishing, woodcraft production, the bookstore, and now the initiative to convert guest and educational activities into businesses that pay for themselves.

Several residents work full time outside to cover their economic needs while participating actively in community life and contributing financially to High Wind. It is important to note that the community is financially separate from the High Wind Association. While the community nears financial autonomy, the Association still relies on donations from the public and annual memberships to continue the larger outreach and educational work.

We are in the process of trying to sort out how much latitude the managers of private businesses are given, and where their areas of responsibility leave off and those of High Wind begin. Often the manager of an activity may be fully engrossed in the operational details of the work, and there needs to be an advisory mechanism to hold the larger purposes of the Association in view.

One model includes advisory committees to bridge the gap between the internal essence of High Wind and the day-to-day work of the community. Ideally most issues and conflicts can be discussed and processed in these filter mechanisms, with the committees bringing informational reports and questions of policy to the board.

A diagram of how this might look appears below.

The High Wind Essence portrayed in the diagram is the fundamental reason for our existence as an Association and the community. The small inner circles are the committees, or filter mechanisms, that serve as consultative/advisory bodies both to an operation activity and to the High Wind Board of Directors. The outer boxes are the operational activities themselves.

Identification of particular circles and boxes is for illustration only. The board might come up with a different model. The intent is to develop an organizational model that maximizes the decentralization and autonomy of operational activities while at the same time interrelating them with the inner essence of the Association and the community.

The inner circle committees can be thought of as allies/support/assistance for both the operational activities and the board, although at times they can ply the role of "brokers" when conflicts must be dealt with. All High Wind board members and residents serve on one or more filter committees so that they are integrally involved in the overall governance as well as protecting and promoting the activities in which they are most interested.

This "structure" of governance is more complex than that of mainstream organizations because it is decentralized. Power is dispersed. All the energy invested at the levels of the board and the inner circle is voluntary and is carried out as an embodiment of the commitment of members to the larger purposes. At present, the outer boxes are implemented by business activities or volunteer labor. An important goal of the Association and the community should be to make all of our activities self-sufficient. This is the essence of sustainability.

Granted, the chart looks formidable. However, there are several considerations to keep in mind. First, some of these activities are required of everyone whether they are members of the community or not. They simply relate to daily living, and this system can bring support and assistance in return for an investment of energy. Second, some activities require concentrated time and energy only for startup of the system, and others only at certain times of the year. Finally, High Wind has access to many like-minded people outside the community whose help can be solicited when additional energy is needed.

In the final analysis, this type of non-hierarchical system of governance depends on a high level of commitment and trust rather than on hierarchical discipline and material motivation—the usual incentives of the market economy. Thus its real efficiency depends on the power of the fundamental essence as it radiates out into the various levels of the effort.

This article began by noting the malaise of modern government, whose most serious defect may be its low moral quality. The higher purposes of America seem to have been lost in selfishness, cynicism, and trivialization.

Governance in alternative communities like High Wind may have little that is practical to offer the complex workings of modern government, given our small-scale size, minuscule resources and power, and considerable social homogeneity. Nevertheless, every now and then a political leader visits the community and comments, "It would be a great idea to bring small groups of politicians and government leaders to spend a weekend or two at High Wind. They would have to return to their own 'Monday morning agendas,' but they might take with them a quality, a spirit that is almost non-existent today in some organizations and political transactions." This quote was from a state legislator after a weekend where the conversation was quite "idealistic," but then he had to return to his "Monday morning agenda" in the real world.

20th Anniversary Reunion Group— returnees come from across the United States, 1998

Birthing the Village: Evolutionary Steps

From Windwatch, *Summer/Fall 1991*

I trace the story of High Wind from its beginnings to the decision to change from an intentional community to an ecological village and learning center.

"The good is the enemy of the best." So said David Spangler in his nationwide computer course, Manifestation—The Inner Art, which six of us at High Wind participated in last winter.

I understand this to mean that at a certain point we come to accept "what is," recognizing our limitations in achieving "what could be." At the same time, we remain sensitive to the deeper issues holding us back from the best. The ideas that motivate us to expend tremendous energy seeking "the best" run into all the usual stumbling blocks of the human condition.

There is a fascinating dichotomy: on one hand, I am awestruck that people continue to invest their hearts and souls and money in the grandly elusive goal of building "the good community," while on the other hand, they know or should know as "realists" that "the good community" in its ultimate sense may be as much a mirage as water in the desert.

Today at High Wind, we are receiving more letters than ever before about joining community from people around the country and even farther away. I assume that other intentional communities are experiencing the same.

What Is the Magnet?

What are these folks looking for? Why do they want to come here? Every situation is unique, but I'll give a few obvious answers:

- Today's world is in some ways frightening. Change is so rapid and often so incomprehensible that people have lost their internal anchors. They are looking for a safe refuge that an intentional community may provide.

- The job market is increasingly complex. In the emerging global economy, where one's skills and human energy are competing not only with fellow Americans but with millions of others who hunger for a better life, a community may seem to offer security where one can live with few resources in a relatively noncompetitive environment.

- Family structures have broken down. In former times, families seemed to stick together through thick and thin, and relationships were for life. In today's fast-moving culture, where almost nothing lasts and people want quick gratification, where families break up through separation and divorce, and often kids have poor relationships with their families, community becomes a kind of substitute family or even substitute parent.

- People are genuinely searching for alternatives. Community projects an image of love and kindness and caring, a new model of living, a microcosm of what society could become. Community is seen as a kind of oasis away from materialism and careerism, from runaway consumption, from the exploitative workplace, from disempowering government, from the spiritual desert of mainstream culture.

Great expectations! As I reread passages from the seminal book on intentional communities, *Builders of the Dawn* by Corinne McLaughlin and Gordon Davidson, and the excellent recent issue of *In Context* magazine about living together in sustainable communities, my images of what is expected in community are in some ways confirmed.

I offer these introductory comments as a context for describing in some detail the evolution of our High Wind community and projecting some significant changes in our immediate future. I write as a cofounder of High Wind, one who has been very close to the community through its ups and downs in 10 years of existence. I have invested considerable time and resources in its development and continue to love what it stands for. I expect to remain living here.

Perceived Need for Fundamental Change

During the last year, there has been much discussion among High Wind residents about the dysfunctional aspects of this community. Here are some of the elements of "malaise" that have been mentioned:

- High Wind is in reality a "pseudo community" and is therefore not viable;
- There is a gap between the rhetoric of the community as it is described to outsiders and the actuality;
- There are too many meetings, and many of them are too long and unproductive;
- There is a sizable monetary debt with little expectation of its being paid off;
- High Wind does not give enough "support" to community members;

- There is no commonly held vision and set of shared values to motivate the community;
- Instead of finding serenity and simplicity in the life here, people have found tension and frustration;
- There is a class structure, especially between the people who have built homes and the "renters," with the latter doing much of the "grunt work" without adequate compensation;
- The community's founders exercise too much (or too little) power;
- And so on . . .

These criticisms are not new. Since High Wind's founding in 1980–81, there have been such recurring comments and perceptions; they go in cycles.

Typically a person is drawn to High Wind with certain expectations (as described earlier). After arrival she/he tends to work hard and enthusiastically for High Wind, usually as a volunteer, and then gradually realizes that High Wind community members are very much like people on "the outside." They have the same baggage of ego-tripping, drive for power, laziness, abdication of responsibility, erratic temperament, difficulty in navigating thorny relationships, and so forth.

However, the High Wind "transformational rhetoric" is ever present. At some point, "burnout" occurs from the work and from frustration. Eventually the individual leaves the community, often in disillusionment, or remains and demands "fundamental change."

The people making these judgments for the most part are not malicious but are among those in our larger society who are earnestly seeking a better world. They looked to High Wind as one avenue. I believe some of these comments are also symptoms of some profound ills in contemporary Western society—a complex subject that the world's sages and scholars are grappling with without great success. For this discussion I focus on just three topics with reference to High Wind: vision/consciousness/spirituality (used here interchangeably), power and decision-making, and economics/livelihood.

The High Wind Vision

What has become known as "High Wind" evolved from a number of personal experiences, a few of which are mentioned here.

In the summer of 1976, I led a seminar at the United Nations that pointed up ominous world trends and convinced me to refocus some of my intellectual energies. In the fall of 1976, Lisa spent a month at Findhorn in Scotland and found a level of consciousness and a community model she felt had great significance. In the years 1977–80, we arranged for Peter and Eileen Caddy, cofounders of Findhorn, to come to Wisconsin, and for David Spangler and Milenko Matanovic of the Lorian Association to become "ad hoc professors" at the University of Wisconsin-Milwaukee.

During these years, we offered many seminars and workshops, which characteristically had a philosophical/spiritual base and suggested that a "new kind of energy" was beginning to turn society upside down. It was an energy that needed to be converted into practical forms through basic changes in politics, economics, education, health care, the arts, lifestyle patterns, and so forth. We drew on a broad body of trans-disciplinary, cutting-edge transformational literature. Such wide-scale shifts, we felt, could lead to a wholly new culture.

During this period, one of the critical issues facing society was the energy crisis and the need to evolve a fresh approach toward use of resources—an "eco-view" of life. This led a group of us to create the nonprofit corporation we called High Wind. It pushed David Lagerman to leave his job as editorial librarian at the *Milwaukee Journal* and to become the first resident on the rundown farm Lisa and I owned. It propelled us into a close relationship with the New Alchemy Institute in Massachusetts and its pioneering work in appropriate technology and renewable energy. And it led us to obtain a seed-money grant from the United States Department of Energy to build an energy-efficient "bioshelter." A group of volunteers arrived at the farm to build this new structure, and although at the time we didn't realize it, the High Wind community had come into being.

> The vision we all felt we were tapping into, like all spiritual energy, was nebulous, but it was strong.

The vision we all felt we were tapping into, like all spiritual energy, was nebulous, but it was strong. This same energy led us to organize onsite educational programs, begin organic food production, establish the High Wind bookstore in Milwaukee, and develop the other activities, which in aggregate became "High Wind."

Governance Issues

One dimension of this new vision had to do with redefining power. Ideas that were discussed:

- A broadened base for citizen involvement, in contrast to representative government, where most people become dependent on a small, elected elite;
- Consensus-based decision-making instead of majority rule, which habitually results in decisions based on the lowest common denominator;
- Minimal bureaucracy and hierarchical structure, which meant more informal leadership, and organizational effectiveness based more on intuitive wisdom and consciousness than coercion.

There were lively debates on the relationship between the "priestly function" and the "effectiveness function"—that is, between behavior based on a high level of purity and consciousness and that based on the compromises believed necessary to be effective.

We tried to express these ideas in a number of operational ways at High Wind, including the design of our board meetings and working committees.

Economic Issues

We felt that people should not be excluded from involvement in this micro-experiment in societal "transformation" because of economic factors.

Thus in the early years of High Wind, there was relatively little discussion of money other than to fund completion of the bioshelter, to buy seed for the garden, and other basics. People lived simply, using the farm buildings on the property. Lisa and I paid the taxes and covered most of the retrofitting costs. Everyone contributed to food and utilities.

There was a kind of "pressure cooker" existence of many people crowded into small spaces. All work was volunteer, although monies received from seminars and guests were divided among the people who did the work. The residents often bartered, providing services for each other in a largely non-monetized environment.

The land itself, besides being an economic resource, took on a kind of mystical quality; many visitors, including our American Indian friends, found a power in the land. The ecological ethic at High Wind was very important—evident in our organic gardening, woodland stewardship, composting garbage, conservation practices, and our strong interest in solar heating and super-insulation when we began to construct other buildings.

The "Founders' Malaise"

During those first years at High Wind, some patterns evolved, which brought consequences with which we are now trying to cope. Here I'll cite three: the founders' role, the efficiency factor, and peoples' expectations.

Lisa and I developed a kind of "visceral" response: whenever a financial or organization need came up, we would try to "take care of it." This was not because we had a lot of money or because we wanted to "control" everything, but because we sensed that "we must make this experiment work."

Lisa developed a kind of overprotectiveness about the visionary facets and I with the more practical organizational and financial aspects. Like many of the early people associated with High Wind, we were strongly committed to believing that this kind of community could contribute to a society in process of major shifts.

What happened, however, was a perception by some community members that "ownership" of the vision—some of the "important things"—were in the hands of Lisa and me.

There was also the belief among residents that "If I leave out of frustration, the Paulsons will always be there to pick up the pieces." This latter psychology began to change once others started to build homes.

Although the two of us had little formal power over the lives of anyone else, an informal power structure developed, not unlike that of most churches or other organizations where several "pillars" keep the operation going. Then other members of the group give deference to the pillars in order not to displease them or out of fear they may withdraw.

The "Efficiency Malaise"

The High Wind community adopted in practice various "New Age" or "transformational" ideas about governance and economics, which gradually took on a life of their own, having little to do with actual results. The consensual style of decision-making sometimes brought a high level of cohesion and feeling of participation, but at other times it blocked action.

There were many meetings, but frequently "processing" became more important than "results." People drawn to live at High Wind often had evolved a fairly advanced level of new consciousness, but were not necessarily "mainstream," high achiever types accustomed to producing practical results. Significant energy was invested in criticizing society and High Wind as the residents processed their own inner-life needs—their "stuff."

A kind of poverty consciousness took hold in the early years, and there was a revulsion toward the idea that High Wind should operate any money-making business. Efficiency had a fairly low position on the totem pole of priorities.

The "Expectation Malaise"

The community that evolved over these 10 years at times generated sparks suggesting "we are really onto something"—that maybe High Wind and Findhorn and all the other communities truly do have significant insights to offer the emerging culture.

But the downside was the high level of frustration. Much of the time, High Wind didn't seem to work very well—because of the decision-making process, the meetings, the lack of money, the modest living conditions, the rifts developing between homeowners and renters, and concern about the debt incurred with the purchase of Springdale Farm (an adjacent property acquired from a former member).

There were perpetual conflicts. There was friction between the "vision-holders" and others who didn't understand the original visions or didn't want to buy into them. There were problems between people playing key roles on committees and getting work done, and others more on the sidelines. Underlying it all was the "founder factor" described above, and the unmet personal needs of residents, which had brought them to High Wind in the first place.

> A kind of poverty consciousness took hold in the early years, and there was a revulsion toward the idea that High Wind should operate any money-making business.

Virtually everyone had an image of "what a community should be like," but their expectations (often wildly divergent) led to frustration as they observed High Wind in practice not fulfilling those ideals. This, in turn, was exacerbated by the High Wind outreach efforts, since visitors tended to see the visible, positive dimensions rather than residents' frustrations. Even though *Windwatch* has gone out of its way to detail the trials and tribulations of living in community, somehow residents have felt that it promoted the "glamour of community" rather than "the facts."

The one obvious exception to all of this related to our education programs, which brought hundreds of people into the orbit of "new thinking," often stimulating life changes and sometimes attracting national and international interest. However, education also had its downside, because it often led to burnout of those responsible for the kitchen and housekeeping chores, with little material compensation.

From Intentional Community to Ecological Village

The above discussion is background for the very significant turning point that has been reached as the community enters its second decade.

In Chapter 8 of *The Structure of Scientific Revolutions*, the classic book on paradigms and paradigm shifts, Thomas Kuhn states that science is always in a state of small crisis. This is because the world and nature are in constant flux, and thus our comprehension of reality is always changing.

But sometimes the discrepancies between existing theories and the evidence at hand are so deep and pervasive that the theories can no longer accommodate the new realities. The paradigm—the values and practices, which form a particular current vision of reality as the basis for organizing life—must change fundamentally.

Today in the larger world, we see paradigm shifts in many areas such as science and technology and the political arena. The Soviet Union, for example, is undergoing at present a monumental paradigm shift as old models are increasingly found inadequate to explain the new situation there.

Communities, too, are in constant flux. Certainly this has been the High Wind experience. But in the past, each change has been more or less absorbed without radical alterations.

Now, however, there is broad agreement among the residents and the Board of Directors that we will best maintain our essential integrity through fundamental restructuring that could be described as a genuine "paradigm shift." In essence, the shift centers on the following points:

- On May 11, 1991, the High Wind Board agreed to identify the community as an ecological village, changing its identity from an "intentional community."

  This may seem only a subtle difference, but it has significant corollaries. It lowers the expectation of new arrivals as well as ongoing residents. Villages are more "normal" human settlements, and are generally better understood.

  Organized community functions that formerly were more or less "community obligations" now will be minimized. At the same time, when residents themselves organize activities such as spiritual gatherings, potlucks, work projects, and so on, people will be coming together because they really want to.

- High Wind will recognize and reaffirm that its main reason for existing as a nonprofit, tax-exempt organization is to carry out educational activities. This is clearly stated in its original charter.

  The High Wind Learning Center now forming will give renewed focus to this education function, but it will only involve those residents living in the ecovillage who wish to participate. The land and buildings in the community known as the "public sector," which encompasses roughly five acres at present and includes the community center, bioshelter, barn, coop, and domes will be the physical hub of the Learning Center.

- Parts of the 62-acre (Springdale Farm) property are being put up for sale—some for sustainable agriculture and some for building sites to new residents. Everyone buying land will sign a covenant that commits them to supporting sustainable land practices and respect for their neighbors.

  One enduring, generally agreed-upon commitment of High Wind is to its ecological ethic. This means caring for the land and specifically designing land usage that serves human needs while preserving the natural resource base for future generations. Along with High Wind's woods, the wetland fen area will be placed into conservancy and preserved as a wildlife refuge—some 40 acres in all.

  Funds received from the sale of this property are paying off in full the debt assumed when the land purchase was made in 1986. The process of selling land to carefully selected future residents has been approved by the High Wind board and is being implemented.

- People who now own land here and have built homes, along with new residents who buy and build, comprise the ecovillage. In addition, the learning center is represented as an institutional entity within the village. A village council is being established and discussions are in process to define what it will look like. No individual has "power" over the lives of the villagers any more than in a mainstream town because everyone controls their own lives and property.

- The High Wind Board of Directors, which is the legally established entity responsible for the High Wind Association, continues. It is the ultimate decision-making body for the learning center, although the center is developing its own governing structure.

  The High Wind board has no direct authority over residents of the ecovillage except to oversee observance of the legally binding restrictions in the covenant.

High Wind Books in Milwaukee, which as of July 1, 1991, was incorporated as a separate nonprofit corporation with its own board, continues to be owned by the High Wind Association and also is ultimately responsible to the High Wind board.

The Learning Center

From the outset, education has been at the heart of the High Wind community.

The nonprofit High Wind Association was formed by a group of people who had participated in some formative learning experiences. The bioshelter building project was funded, we were told by the Department of Energy, because of our strong commitment to education, including the close relationship High Wind had to the University of Wisconsin-Milwaukee.

Every summer since 1981, High Wind has offered educational programs, which have been a major source of ongoing income to support the community. High Wind seminars, workshops, and conferences go well beyond the traditional classroom format: they involve "living/learning" approaches that utilize the unique experience of living in community (however the community is defined), on the land, and close to nature.

Programs seek to draw in top thinkers and practitioners who are breaking out of old patterns of belief and behavior, just as we as a society broaden our horizons in the direction of the interdependent, sustainable world that we are all attempting to bring into being.

As it develops, the learning center in the countryside will cooperate closely with the bookstore in Milwaukee to carry out High Wind educational activities. High Wind outreach, including its Open Days (periodic tours and times to communicate with visitors) and its journal, *Windwatch*, will continue as a function of the educational work of the nonprofit.

As the "community" moves toward a "village," there will be an interesting process to document, in that a number of intentional communities in different areas of the world appear to be undergoing the same change. This relates to the educational and research work of the learning center.

As discussed above, people living in the village who desire to participate in the learning center, including sharing their knowledge, expertise, ideas, and insights (which is "learning" in the broadest sense) continue to have opportunity to do so, but there is no obligation.

> As the "community" moves toward a "village," there will be an interesting process to document, in that a number of intentional communities in different areas of the world appear to be undergoing the same change.

A goal of the learning center is economic self-sufficiency. Income generated from its activities will be used to cover most expenses of the land and buildings (taxes, insurance, maintenance, and so forth), plus paying staff to run the programs. Staff members will be housed in the buildings administered by the learning center.

Association members who do not work directly with the learning center and who do not live in the ecovillage will, we hope, continue to contribute to the nonprofit High Wind Association, investing in its ongoing education program, its vision, and its outreach.

With a more clearly articulated educational focus, the High Wind Learning Center can build on the relationships it has developed with the University of Wisconsin and other higher educational institutions, the public schools, and national and international contacts. Through the learning center, the High Wind Association will continue to maintain close contact with intentional communities around the world as they process their own transitions.

With a planet experiencing incredibly rapid change, and with the former chasm between "mainstream thinking and behavior" and "new paradigm thinking" lessening by the day, enormous new opportunities are emerging for cooperative learning experiences with the corporate sector and public and civic organizations of all kinds.

HIGH WIND:
A Retrospective

Belden Paulson, University of Wisconsin professor for 35 years, cofounded (with his wife Lisa) the High Wind Association in 1977 and the High Wind community in Plymouth, Wisconsin in 1981. The following interview-style article gler, one of the conference speakers, who wrote in his *Revelation—The Birth of A New Age:* "the New Age is fundamentally a change of consciousness from one of isolation and separation to one of communion, attunement, wholeness."

High Wind:
A Retrospective

In Communities *magazine, Winter 2009*

Taken from an interview I wrote with Geoff Kozeny, which never took place. A well-known observer of intentional communities and ecovillages in America, he had visited High Wind several times. As he was interested in my assessment of communities looking back over many years, he planned to meet with me. Geoff died before we could get together, but I imagined his questions and created the interview.

How did you get involved with intentional communities?
In October 1976, Lisa went to a conference at Findhorn, the spiritual community in Scotland, for three weeks. She'd already had a traumatic encounter in northeast Brazil with Macumba (a voodoo-type experience that almost paralyzed her). Recently she had helped found Psy-Bionics, an organization in Wisconsin teaching altered states of consciousness.

In those days, the latter 1970s, the term "New Age" had not yet become an overused cliché. Her scraps of notes included this: "The New Age means recognizing that mutual cooperation and respect and love are essential if our planet is to survive."

How did you take to all this New Age stuff?
I was very perplexed. We'd been married for more than 20 years, and I'd never seen her so fired up. I wasn't even sure of the best questions to ask to draw out the Findhorn experience. Lisa obviously felt she would soon be dragged back from the heights of the New Age into the mainstream culture.

I myself was at a point of some openness to alternative thinking. I had joined the University of Wisconsin-Milwaukee and University Extension in the early 1960s, teaching political science, and was heavily involved dealing with inner city poverty and racism. Lisa and I had met in the waterfront slums of Naples, Italy, soon after college and worked for years overseas. After our immersion on the front lines of great world needs, both of us were concerned with a culture in trouble.

Several months after Lisa's return from Scotland, she talked me into driving to Chicago to attend a lecture by Peter Caddy—who, along with Eileen Caddy and Dorothy Maclean, had cofounded Findhorn. I was impressed by Peter's down-to-earth talk on the community's successes and challenges and his idealism about serving the planet with a new consciousness.

How could you relate any of this to your position at the university?

A professor in the university's school of engineering had just received a grant to explore advanced thinking on the interrelationship between technology and culture. I introduced him to the "Findhorn story," with its emphasis on lifestyle changes and the ideas of E.F. Schumacher, one of the Findhorn conference speakers, whose book *Small Is Beautiful* advocated simple living. He was intrigued and asked me to represent the university on a planning committee for a major Chicago conference in spring 1977, to be keynoted by Schumacher.

With Schumacher the magnet for the 2,300 attendees, along with 60 lectures and workshops, we reserved a room for 15 people where Lisa could talk about Findhorn. To our astonishment, 400 folks lined the corridor, demanding a larger space. Next to Schumacher, "Lisa's Findhorn" was the big event of the conference. I had invited one of my deans, who was so enthusiastic about her workshop that he urged me to organize New Age education through the university.

Since people were thirsty for information, in June 1977, we got the university to sponsor talks by Peter and Eileen Caddy. In the largest available space on campus, they wowed the 1,200 attending, drawing in people we never imagined were interested.

In short order, I got approvals from university officials to begin lining up a series of seminars. Over the next two years, we offered cutting-edge programs including "Planetary Survival and the Role of Alternative Communities," and "New Dimensions in Governance—Images of Holistic Community" (with David Spangler and Milenko Matanovic, co-organizers of the Lorian Association). We drew people from business, government, and academia as well as traditional students and people who had attended our previous talks and were questioning conventional trends and belief systems.

During all this activity, what was happening with you—with your initial skepticism about intentional communities like Findhorn and the New Age?

By the end of 1978, I was realizing that I was no longer the same person I'd been. In spring 1978, when Lisa returned to Findhorn, I went along and participated in a weeklong intensive experience of the community. My contact with the leaders and residents convinced me of the significance of this kind of model for rethinking the future of our culture. My intimate collaboration with David and Milenko, along with many others we had brought in for classes and consultations, had deepened my perceptions of reality far beyond anything I had learned at Oberlin College and the University of Chicago.

As increasing numbers were drawn to our seminars and presentations, we began hearing the comment: "We're seminared out. Let's do something practical." That's when we established the High Wind Association to develop a sharing community, relying largely on renewable energy, working with the land as an ecosystem, serving as a demonstration, and taking on an education role. Lisa and I made available our run-down, 46-acre farm 55 miles north of Milwaukee.

With two colleagues, we accepted the invitation of John Todd and his associates to visit the New Alchemy Institute on Cape Cod and in Nova Scotia to see their experimental bioshelters. The New Alchemy experimenters were pioneers in solar energy, energy-efficient construction, and sustainable agriculture. They convinced us to try something comparable in Wisconsin. They helped us design a bioshelter that we could build at the farm, and we submitted the project to the US Department of Energy in its small grants program for appropriate technology.

When we convened a meeting on a blustery evening in February 1981 to announce the new grant and recruit volunteers, we thought 15 would be a good turnout. Two hundred showed up, and immediately an experienced carpenter agreed to be lead builder for bioshelter construction. A teacher/gardener said she would come to grow food to support the workers. Soon a PhD psychologist signed on; she would manage the household, including the kitchen operation. We already had an idealistic technical genius onsite who worked at the *Milwaukee Journal* as editorial librarian. Suddenly the farm was humming with activity, the farmhouse had become a "pressure cooker" with 10 residents and two dogs, and a construction gang was on the ground. Soon we had evolved into an intentional community.

> I was undergoing my own personal revolution. Maybe a better word would be "transformation." I fully endorsed the *vision*. The test now was whether we could find the will and resources to move beyond the talk and rhetoric and actually *do* it.

I was undergoing my own personal revolution. Maybe a better word would be "transformation." I fully endorsed the *vision*. The test now was whether we could find the will and resources to move beyond the talk and rhetoric and actually *do* it.

What was your first big conflict, when the community could have blown apart?
We all knew the bioshelter was a complex building with no examples except New Alchemy's "Ark" out east. The construction engineer who'd been advising our lead builder wanted to use wood construction in the greenhouse, while our well-known solar architect, who had volunteered her services, favored Spancrete flooring. I won't get into details other than to say her model was strongly preferred by several at High Wind—who happened to be women.

Since our builder and his mostly male crew had already gone ahead, they would have to tear down what had been done. Winter was coming on and the building had to be closed in. Our builder was feeling the criticism and tremendous frustration; it would be a disaster if he quit. Likewise, it would be most undesirable if our architect pulled out with her professional oversight. The building inspector had approved her design. Underlying it all there was resentment against the macho energy—"the men know best."

We told our builder to hold up the work. This was our first internal crisis, which threatened to break apart our fledgling community. We held numerous meetings and contacted outside experts who had differing opinions, but mostly they sided with the architect. I felt some personal responsibility because I had recruited both the engineer and architect. I personally was open to either solution. We finally agreed to continue along the lines our builder and his allies laid out. Our architect resigned, and no other architect would touch the situation. While Lisa was one of the builder's biggest critics on this, she wrote him a heartfelt letter of appreciation of him as a person. One of the guys wrote the community: "We at High Wind represent an ideal that we must uphold. This means not getting trapped in tactical-level controversies that afterward will seem like tempests in a teapot."

As High Wind evolved, what were the biggest personal challenges you felt?

When a host of sticky community issues surfaced, especially in the earlier years, they often ended up with Lisa and me. After all, we had started the whole enterprise, we had owned the property even though most of it was now in High Wind hands, and some we had donated, and when serious financial bottlenecks occurred, we usually stepped in. Often it came down to an issue of perception: who held the power?

"Founders' Syndrome." This was the title of a panel with founders of six communities from around the world, brought together at a Findhorn conference. The panel articulated a universal issue all the founders faced: the tension between the originators who articulated the vision and purposes and community members who rightly wanted to make the experience their own. This might mean seeking to reframe community goals and challenging the initial leadership. High Wind, like all the panel's communities, emphasized its commitment to non-hierarchical leadership and governance by consensus. I cannot recall a single High Wind community decision reached by consensus that Lisa and I overturned, even if we had had the power to do so.

But there were many intense debates during interminable meetings to reach consensus. On several occasions, when we felt the community might be falling apart with factions developing and we were unsure of our proper role, we sought counsel from experienced Findhorn or Lorian friends. Their response was always the same: founders hold responsibility to sound a clear note about the vision. If there are members with other visions, they should be respected but asked to leave and create their own community. Though we respected these advisors, we found their counsel impractical, as visions do evolve, co-authored by others in the community. In fact, Peter Caddy was asked to give up his role due to his authoritarian leadership. The Lorians, although often indicating interest, never founded a residential community.

Another personal issue?

Processors and Doers. As residents at the farm evolved from the original construction gang to an intentional community, some people were very production/goal-oriented. Others were more concerned with the process of getting there. While both obviously were essential, at times one or the other approach took over and, in my view, became extreme. Sometimes Lisa leaned toward process: slow down, take care of the ever-present human dimensions. Often I was so concerned about all the challenges before us, holding a lot of responsibility for "results," that I could go too far toward "getting it done."

I could become impatient, for example, when evening sessions were convened where everyone was required to "share your pain," even if at the time there were those who didn't feel any pain or didn't want to share it. I was labeled as someone with "thick skin," insensitive to those with "thin skins" who were easily hurt by life's experiences. (My "thick skin" was also nurtured by having worked for years in areas of dire need with poverty and refugees, and also as a teenager caring for an invalid mother who could die at any moment.)

I welcomed our periodic "internal conferences," sometimes with an outside resource person, when each of us could express our needs and wishes and gripes. Lisa and I, as much or more than other community members, got a healthy share of criticism: she for her lofty visions—shared in editorials in *Windwatch*, the community newsletter, meant to lift the residents out of their daily nitty-gritty grind. I received even more censure, in part because I was often introducing ideas and plans for educational programs that scared the community and that they thought too hard to carry out. Also, when someone else came up with a project and I said, "Great idea, you do it," it was interpreted as code for "I don't think it will work and I don't want to get involved."

The most significant issue I had to confront was the realization that as the years passed, I was not very good at intentional community group dynamics. At High Wind, I learned that while visionary thinking was what we were all about, it could be scary, even oppressive. Everyone agreed that while the community's mission was imperative, the process was at least as important as the results. The qualities that were optimally required for my approach did not fit too well with how the conventional intentional community worked and made decisions as a group.

What about the high points of your High Wind experience?

Notwithstanding the challenges, our community was an exciting place. Dedicated folks were converging at the farm to give their all, the bioshelter was moving toward completion, and the media had made High Wind its darling. Residents were very aware of the dysfunctionalities of modern life and were seeking a new way to approach the world. For me, this endeavor merited every ounce of my energy (although I couldn't give it my all because I also had a full-time university job). This was one place to *take a stand*. What we were attempting to create had more potential than anything else I was aware of.

I learned that when the community really "worked," there was a special "glue" that held together the vision and the practical daily operations. (Sometimes the vision became too starry-eyed, or in the crush of daily demands we forgot its purpose.) It seemed only certain people had that unique gift of integrating the larger High Wind vision with implementing the essential daily tasks. They embodied an unusual spiritual capacity that cemented our community life into a functioning whole. It was only later when some of us looked back on High Wind's peak periods that we could identify those particular individuals.

As a learning center, we had many successes. We brought in "new thinking" from around the country and world, combining "the spiritual" with "the practical."

What happened to High Wind?

In 1991, the High Wind board decided to end High Wind as an intentional community. We now considered ourselves an "eco-neighborhood." This was a searing decision, but the old idealism had lost its intensity. Four different waves of residents had shared their lives in the community for shorter or longer periods. After a dozen years, most of us were burned out. We felt we could no longer serve the lofty mission in the same way as at the time of our creation. High Wind continued for another decade as a learning center with a full educational program and receiving some substantial funding. Then in 2001, the board decided to sell its "public campus": the bioshelter, farmhouse complex and other buildings, and some adjoining lands. Those of us who continue to live at High Wind still have substantial lands, share the same values as initially, run tours, meet with visitors, and consult, but the tempo is free and easy compared to the past. The organic farm, now owned and managed by two former residents, is a major CSA in the region, feeding over 500 families.

The High Wind Board now operates as a foundation, using funds from the sale of the property, added to by sensitive investing. It provides small grants to sustainability-related organizations in the region. The new owners of the public buildings are two Buddhist groups that for years had been sponsoring retreats at High Wind.

Ultimately, no matter what form it takes, High Wind's work goes on. A certain creative spiritual power always had its role to play in both the residential and non-residential communities because it didn't deal with place but with vision and spirit. In this circle of consciousness, life actually is hard, because it involves commitment to a paradigm that challenges most of the values of our dominant culture. The vision itself is extraordinary, while we ourselves are ordinary. Yet I believe that the intentional communities movement—I refer to all the actual residents of communities and to all those who are not residents but have embraced the idea—is truly on the cutting edge of the emerging culture.

When I went to the Findhorn community the first time, the highlight was participating in Experience Week. In one week, the community gives an in-depth overview of what Findhorn is. I met key leaders who discussed the history, the values and philosophy, the challenges, and the ups and downs over the years. Since part of each day was actually in a work department, we selected a couple where we'd spend time during the week. I picked Gardening and Publications. In the circle dancing and at mealtimes and tea breaks and intensive conversations, we got to know the others in our group as well as Findhorn residents. Among the 15 in my group, of all ages and many backgrounds (although little racial/ethnic diversity), I latched onto a fellow roughly my age with a comparable professional background—a doctor in a major New York hospital.

As the week wound down, we began asking each other: What would happen when, back home at our jobs—he at the hospital and I at the university—if we were to try to function the way folks live their lives at Findhorn?

Our colleagues might ask if we'd taken to drink or if something had happened that required immediate help. While idealism as well as curiosity had drawn my medical colleague and me to Findhorn, we were practical observers looking for real-world models that might have something to offer. Since both of us were skeptical enough to spot empty rhetoric and big-promise, world-savior types, we were nevertheless somewhat blown away by what we found. We discovered people hard at work striving to create a new culture. Human relationships focused on cooperation, not competition. We sensed no money-making greed or lust for power. Governance was by consensus decisions. Leaders, called "focalisers," used their positions to sharply focus the energy of their group on the project at hand and serve the growth of everyone involved. People exercising responsibility were selected on the basis of their "evolved consciousness," as acknowledged by general agreement. When solving problems, there was much listening, including extended periods of silence, and "listening" to one's own intuition and inner promptings. An overriding community mission was for members to set aside personal desires in order to serve the world—the larger whole.

My medical colleague and I agreed that it would be an interesting experiment to talk this kind of language and try, at least to some degree, to walk the talk at our place of work. However, we guessed that career-wise, we might not last very long.

Findhorn sees itself as an alternative to mainstream society. There are many alternative groups, hundreds or thousands worldwide, that each in its own unique way attempts to grapple with cultural patterns it considers dysfunctional. Whatever the perils, something happens within the groups that impels adherents to give up something in order to invest a small or big part of themselves in an alternative model they are convinced will make life better.

They experience an intellectual shift of some sort. They encounter a body of knowledge that confirms the need to go beyond what is currently in practice or known. There's an inner push of commitment to values that prompt them to refashion what they are doing in some new way. And then there's the decision to translate what they know and are feeling into some concrete, problem-solving policy alternative. Finally, they make the huge jump to mobilize this knowledge and commitment and policymaking into taking action that may change the course of their lives—where they will use their energy, talent, and resources in new ways.

The more radical the alternative, the more important becomes a surrounding support group. Findhorn residents, and the folks who joined our High Wind community, for example, became attuned to a commonly agreed upon body of knowledge, a commitment to a set of values, and a shared consciousness. Holding on to this alternative model through thick and thin depended on our inner strength, individually and as a group, and a sense of mission in offering the alternative. This depended on our own inner clarity and on the cohesion and intensity of the commitment of the group around us. Generally alternative organizations with lofty goals committed to significant societal change face huge ongoing pressures.

Over its 50-year history, Findhorn has faced enormous trials. For example, in the earlier decades, its eclectic approach to spirituality frightened and alienated its straitlaced neighbors. At one point, the community was dangerously drawn in by the wiles of a visiting psychic who persuaded members to buy a property they couldn't afford—throwing Findhorn into an economic nightmare.

Take also the experience of our High Wind community. We were fairly ordinary people with an extraordinary mission—that of birthing cultural change. Sometimes some of us were ready to give up. How could we continue to stand up to a sometimes hostile surrounding environment? What made us think we really had something vital to offer? Sometimes with no regular income, some of our group were almost penniless, having given up jobs in the mainstream economy. Now and then disagreeing among ourselves on how to proceed, and also facing difficulties in living together in close quarters, how could we present a credible alternative to the larger world?

Or take several examples of others who had close contact with us, who felt they were part of the High Wind alternative although they did not actually reside in the community. Judy was a kind of prodigy. She took all our seminars from the time she was a high school senior. She went to Findhorn, wrote books and composed music, subsequently married, earned a PhD, and landed a university teaching job. Later, even though she admitted her life had changed completely, she wondered if the High Winds and Findhorns were more or less useless because they were isolated in their own little worlds. Any committed person really concerned in bettering society, she said, had to plunge into the bigger world of social injustice, not remain in this micro-enclave.

Or take Ernst, who was in charge of the foundry at the local technical college. He was working class, a strong labor union member, patriotic, but convinced the culture was completely off course. He took my seminars, read the books, and visited High Wind with his family. In the college forge, he made an iron plaque for us, inscribed with the High Wind credo. His regular admonishment: "No bullshit." In a final, 27-page class paper, he wrote: "I keep thinking about Professor Paulson's statement: 'The future does not exist, it exists only in our minds.' I'm a steel foundry journeyman by trade and have only dealt with things I can see, touch, smell. I have, however, come to recognize that a new consciousness is all that will save us."

Or take George, a hard-working, idealistic young man in his twenties, leader with church youth, who spent much time at High Wind although never as a full-time resident. Later, after more intimacy with politics and the church and also thwarted in idealistic efforts, he wrote to us: "My advice to High Wind, to anyone who thinks they can make a positive contribution to this world at this time, GIVE IT UP. RESISTANCE IS FUTILE. IF YOU HAVE HOPE, IT IS ILLUSION." In subsequent years, he moderated his frustrations, was elected a local official, and is now a pillar in his rural Wisconsin community.

Or take comments of many people who responded to a lengthy questionnaire we sent to 180 people who over the years had close experiences with High Wind. Typical among both the laudatory and critical responses: "IT'S IMPORTANT THAT HIGH WIND EXISTS. America needs you. With the failings all around us, High Wind stands for *something*. Not that it's always so great, but there's a visible idealism the world desperately needs, which you are helping to provide."

As a final word, there are hundreds of people who have been engaged with High Wind who now work creatively in every imaginable kind of project. Some pioneering endeavors, such as the Plymouth Institute think tank, or the Springledge ecovillage, did not materialize as planned. Whether or not the projects succeed fully, the underlying commitments have been for the "long haul."

PART IV
Conscious Sustainable Community

To build a sustainable world requires us to experience inner individual development along with mastering the requisite knowledge and skills, and to create a sustainable culture of beliefs and understandings locked into enduring institutions which produce appropriate technologies and actions. In effect, this model is a four-quadrant strategy

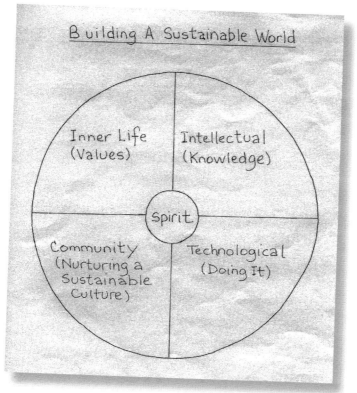

Sustainability: Introduction

Creative people in many walks of life in the 1970s and 1980s were challenging the seeming dead-end of conventional politics. Whether dealing with the ominous policy of the mutually assured destruction of the Cold War or the country's high-consumption, materialist life style, there had to be a better way to organize civic life. Terms like "new politics" or "New Age" brought forth new thinkers even in America's remote corners.

We were long overdue to go beyond the polarity of left versus right by integrating the highest values in our nation's conservative and liberal heritage. Public policy is only one face of politics. Political work takes place all the time in community life—in the workplace, in personal relationships. Problem-solving also requires going beyond politics and economics. In a world of swiftly moving change, one of our greatest challenges is to rethink how we see the world. A change of consciousness may be essential as we cross the threshold of transformation to a sustainable world.

I felt alternative thinking would probably not find a home in the university's department of political science. At this time, I was in contact with colleagues at other colleges and universities who shared my concern. They, too, were offering new, academically rigorous courses that didn't fit the traditional curricula. All of us had begun to participate and present papers in national and international conferences organized by the World Future Society. The time had come to use the label "Futures Studies," which seemed to be acceptable all around. It heralded new thinking about the future that transcended narrow disciplines and departments.

Located in our little patch of the world in Midwest America, we were aware that our efforts would not significantly impact national policy. But we could carve out specific areas where we could make a difference. I recalled the famous 18th century conservative Edmund Burke: "All that is necessary for the triumph of evil is that good men do nothing."

Over the years, a group of us—my university department (CUCD) or High Wind, or both—pulled together some of the most experienced thinkers and practitioners in a series of conferences on critical issues. We wanted to find answers to the seemingly intractable problems of improving conditions in low-income neighborhoods; dealing with the future of work in an economy where modern technology is producing all the goods and services society needs without need for the total labor force; and recognizing that nothing less than societal transformation may be required to cope with the historic issues of climate change and dwindling resources in a finite world.

The organizing premise of each of these conferences was to work on two tracks: seek solutions using the best models now available, and at the same time recognize that even today's best are inadequate, pointing to the urgent need to come up with new models.

This poses a gigantic challenge for higher education if we accept what was conceptualized years ago by the University of Wisconsin as its primary purpose: "To provide an environment in which faculty and students can discover, examine critically, preserve, and transmit the knowledge, wisdom, and values that will help ensure the survival of the present and future generations with improvement in the quality of life."

Many of us accept that there may be no other entity out there with the non-partisan goal of generating and transmitting knowledge to build a better world. Apart from our teaching, research, and all our other activities, this ideal pushed me and others to serve on university commissions established to figure out how to rethink the university, even in a radical way, so that it can best serve today's needs. For me, this included joining an international study group in Japan to explore what a university of the future might look like.

> Next to war and peace, we recognized that the most critical need facing us is how to build a sustainable world.

Next to war and peace, we recognized that the most critical need facing us is how to build a sustainable world. We're aware of the background that the UN Secretary General set up in 1983—the Commission on Environment and Development—to develop strategies to cope with both the global environmental and the have/have-not crises. We've seen its path-breaking book in 1987, *Our Common Future,* popularizing the sustainability idea: that we must work to fulfill today's needs without compromising the needs of future generations. The Earth Summit in Rio de Janeiro in 1992 assembled thousands of people, including heads of government, to flesh out an agenda.

President Bill Clinton then established the President's Commission on Sustainable Development to organize initiatives in the United States. I served on its task group focused on education. In its various meetings, one theme was stressed regularly: the UN and governments can pass resolutions, but the real action will take place on the state and local level. It's also there that constituencies will have to be mobilized to push government and business to move. A number of us organized a citywide town meeting and the statewide "Sustainable Wisconsin" policy group to enlist people from all sectors to formulate strategies.

For more than two decades, I, like many others, operated on multiple fronts. This included teaching university seminars on sustainable futures, which included hundreds of public school teachers and principals. Their tuition was subsidized by the school system, and their assignment was to adapt what they learned to their own classrooms. Another effort has been offering presentations in colleges and at international conferences. In one graduate seminar, half a dozen students stayed together for a extra month to come up with a well-thought-out values statement for sustainable living. With colleagues in the university and High Wind, we constantly endeavored to "connect the dots"—to integrate the sustainability ideas across the board with educational institutions, churches, businesses, and other civic organizations.

While serving on the commissions, we recognized the significance of the think tank approach—task groups that not only collect and digest information but explore creative alternatives to solve complex problems. Since policymakers themselves rarely have the time and expertise, they depend on lobbyists and, above all, think tanks. Leaders in government on both national and local levels said they would welcome policy recommendations based on the experience and values of alternative groups, in contrast to the flood of paper crossing their desk from mainstream interest groups.

After much consulting around, several colleagues and I assembled 40 leaders in Milwaukee open to "new thinking" for a series of meetings over two weeks to imagine what a new think tank would look like. The goal was to synthesize the best policy ideas being articulated on a range of issues facing the mainstream culture, with the best alternative thinking. Since this proved to be a fertile exercise, our next initiative was to sponsor a national "Invitational Dialogue" in 1987 at the United Nations Plaza in New York. We brought together 60 leaders of alternative organizations, along with people from government, business, and the media.

This generated so much enthusiasm that a group was formed to seriously consider establishing the New Synthesis Think Tank, later changing its name to Plymouth Institute. A range of observers, including a high UN official, endorsed the idea, and encouraged us to form a planning contingent. Since I was associated with a major university, where many think tanks were based, I was chosen as the lead person. Over the next couple of years, we attracted many interested participants and began collecting materials for policy papers.

At an international summit on sustainable development held in Moscow in January 1990, I was invited to co-chair a US-USSR Think Tank Task Force on Global Perestroika. We concluded several days of intense deliberations to propose the establishment of a global think tank. Its council would begin with five country members: the USA, the USSR, India, the UK and China. It would focus on policy formation, publications, and education/consulting.

Soon thereafter, in April 1990, Roger Collis of Pacifica Foundation and I co-organized a global conference in Shanghai, China, on the interrelationship of the environment and economic development. The Chinese delegation eagerly endorsed the think tank and pushed for early implementation. Unhappily, the plans that were evolving came to a screeching halt with the collapse of the Soviet Union and the chaos that ensued.

As the initial plans evolved, these varied efforts generated surprising national and international interest and queries for more information, but establishment of this or a comparable think tank awaits new actors in another day.

While our efforts toward building a sustainable world focused on the physical, economic, and political dimensions, of equal emphasis was the deeper realm of values. Nurturing a culture that encompassed a new world view and willingness to reassess our lifestyle was an essential part of our teaching and all of our efforts. Since our goal was to encourage people to be conscious as participants in shifting from today's unsustainable culture to a culture embracing sustainable living, we needed to deepen our understanding of the meaning of "consciousness." This led us to the seminal thoughts of philosopher Ken Wilber. We held gatherings to discuss his books about the evolution of consciousness as we ourselves evolve from childhood to adults, and as we strive to elevate our consciousness from insensitive acceptance of contemporary mainstream values to holistic beings. Central to Wilber's approach is comprehension of the interrelationship between one's inner life and outer behavior, and between functioning as an individual and as a member of the larger society—the so-called four quadrants.

Many of us recognize that what exists is not the best that can happen, but it's the most likely. In a world of complexity, which sometimes ends up in the chaos of wars, disasters (natural or man-made), and very inadequate problem-solving on issues great and small, we tend to grudgingly accept what is. Perhaps it's because we feel relatively powerless to do much about it beyond the orbit of taking care of our own personal lives. We may be good at criticizing and complaining, but we've learned to live with existing institutions and lifestyles and values, notwithstanding their recognizable limitations. At the same time, there are a number of us who are really committed to investing time and resources beyond our own personal situations to improve conditions.

We are regularly searching for more fundamental alternatives. Although we often can't precisely put our finger on the fundamental cause(s) of the cluster of problems before us, in our more intuitive moments we sense that the boundaries of "business as usual" are obsolete, that we need a new mindset to go beyond where we are. Even though we may not see readily visible answers, some of us have an inner drive to utilize whatever experience and creative energy we can muster to plunge in.

If the best happens, we CAN make a difference.

What Role Higher Education in a Changing World?

The statement adopted on February 26, 1969 was as follows:

> The purposes of a university are: (1) to provide students with optimum opportunity for learning from the heritage of the past, for gaining experience in use of their intellectual and creative capacities, and for developing themselves as concerned, responsible, humane citizens; (2) to extend the frontiers of knowledge through research; (3) to provide society with objective information and with imaginative approaches to the solutions of problems which can serve as a basis for sound decision-making in all areas.

from a University of Wisconsin–Madison faculty document,
The Purpose and Function of the University, *May 1969.*

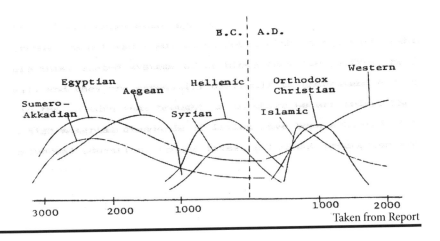

B.C. | A.D.

Western

Egyptian   Aegean   Hellenic   Orthodox
                                   Christian

Sumero—
Akkadian   Syrian   Islamic

3000   2000   1000   1000   2000

Taken from Report

The Educational Implications of New Perspectives for an Interdependent, Shrinking World

1986

In the early 1980s, the University of Wisconsin established a statewide commission on "The Wisconsin Idea in the Twenty-first Century." Its 20 members—faculty and administrators—worked for two years and formed several task forces, including this one that I chaired. I wrote its report, submitted to the commission.

According to Arnold Toynbee in his classic *A Study of History,* civilizations follow patterns of growth and disintegration. When a civilization finds itself on a plateau in a relatively static condition and then is challenged by the natural or the social environment, it must respond in some way. The success of this response determines whether there will be a new period of growth or whether a process of disintegration will set in that may lead to eventual collapse.

The critical qualities that condition the response include creativity, flexibility, and the role of prophetic minorities. When social structures and behavior patterns become overly rigid and conformist, and when the dominant social forces and institutions hang on to their prerogatives without opening the culture to new energies and ideas, then the natural processes for creative change and growth are obstructed. No civilization can automatically take for granted its survival. This is well illustrated by the rise and fall of the major civilizations around the Mediterranean area over the last 5,000 years.

Today as we move through the last years of the 20th century, there is ample evidence that our Western industrial culture is being challenged as it has not been for a long time. Ironically, these challenges arise from the extraordinary successes of 200 years of technological, economic and social development.

These trends are not isolated. They cannot be dealt with in a linear fashion one by one. They are interrelated systems of problems that emerge from the dominant culture itself, and they are especially difficult to understand and resist because they belong to the culture that brought us to where we are today. No one can dispute that high material standards of living have been achieved: better nutrition, universal education, longer lives, efficient production systems, and generalized affluence for the majority, if not all the people.

In Toynbee's challenge-response formulation, the interactions are very complex. Identification of the causative challenges that set the process in motion is a hazardous undertaking. For different civilizations, Toynbee nevertheless pinpoints particular natural or human pressures or sudden blows that serve as triggering events, forcing responses. In reviewing the recent history of our own Western industrial culture, one such event might be the oil crisis of the early 1970s. During the period from roughly the end of World War II to the oil embargo of 1973, much of the world experienced dramatic economic growth. Lester Brown in his *State of the World* sets the scene:

> For most of humanity the century's third quarter was a period of unprecedented prosperity.
>
> World output of goods and services expanded five percent annually, tripling in less than a generation. Rapid growth had become commonplace, built into the aspirations of consumers, the earnings projections of corporations, and the expectations of governments. Few stopped to calculate that even a four percent rate of economic growth, if continued, would lead to a fiftyfold expansion in a century. And even fewer considered the pressures this would put on the earth's resources, both renewable and nonrenewable.
>
> Cheap energy, specifically cheap oil, quite literally fueled this record economic expansion. At less than $2.00 a barrel, oil was so cheap that, from the perspective of the late twentieth century, it appears to have been almost a free good.

Suddenly, in 1973, a powerful blow struck us, which first of all influenced the direct users of oil but in time was symptomatic of a whole range of other resources. It gradually forced us to begin to reassess our lifestyle and, more fundamentally, certain assumptions and values. By 1983, the price of oil had increased more than 15-fold to more than $30 per barrel, with massive rippling effects on the economies of most countries. Although the oil price has recently dropped by about one-half, at least temporarily, a point was made. The time had come to begin to take seriously the proposition that for some years we had been living beyond our means. We had been going more and more into debt, living off our capital and borrowing resources from future generations that can probably never be repaid.

Due to declining nonrenewable resources, ecological and environmental factors, and the restructuring of the world economy, we may face limits on continued economic growth unknown to us in recent years. If we accept this premise, we may be entering a new era where the legitimacy of the basic goals and institutions of the present industrial system will be questioned.

In fairness, we must observe that many articulate voices in contemporary culture argue that there is going to be an ever-continuing, upward spiral of income, production and consumption, discovery or invention of new resources, declining pollution and disease, and a very bright future ahead. This is probably the generally accepted majority viewpoint.

Whatever one's scenario for the future, it is difficult to escape the proposition that by becoming more interdependent, the world is "shrinking." In 1980, there were some 4.75 billion people on Earth. The World Bank projects 8.3 billion in 2025, with most of the increase in the Third World. The proportion of the world's population living in Western industrial societies is getting smaller and smaller. At the same time, the world order of the last four centuries, based in sovereign national states—each committed to maximizing its own narrow interest—has become increasingly obsolete. Cooperation and communication, both between richer and poorer countries and among nations in political and ideological conflict, has become imperative. The likely alternative is terrorism and violence with unprecedented consequences.

The prevailing paradigm—our way of perceiving reality and acting out that particular worldview—is being profoundly challenged. The ideas that have dominated our culture for several hundred years are questioned: for example, our belief in unlimited material progress, society viewed as a mechanical system based on competitive struggle, the rational and linear and quantitative characteristics of the scientific method as the only respectable approach to knowledge, and the power of patriarchy in controlling institutions and decision-making.

Implications for Education

Education is one of the chief means for identifying the new knowledge and approaches that will be required as we relate to the rapidly changing world. Educational institutions at all levels can serve as places of inquiry, inspiration, and experimentation to seek the truths about an interdependent world. They can provide a fresh context for what, in effect, may be a new historical period. In this sense, education means not only leading people from ignorance to knowledge and enlightenment in the classic sense but also helping people prepare to move from past and contemporary times to a new period. This gives education a uniquely radical thrust needed for a period of radical change.

> Education is one of the chief means for identifying the new knowledge and approaches that will be required as we relate to the rapidly changing world.

Seen in this light, this means not only new courses, new approaches for training students and teachers and the use of advanced technologies, but also innovative ways of looking at the world and our own society and our individual roles.

The educational establishment, like many of our basic institutions, is a conservative operation. Often it is ill prepared to take on educational programming that accepts and responds to the challenges of a new environment. This points up the need for educational risk-takers, innovators, advocates, and opinion leaders who do not fear the controversy that inevitably emerges in a time of change. Because the new realities transcend narrow, specialized disciplines and fields of knowledge, the new educators must be able to think holistically, building on the strengths of individual disciplines but transcending their limitations.

Moreover, changing values and new worldviews have policy implications; there is an issue as to the roles educators should play in arenas of public policy. They have unique responsibilities in helping society identify what is happening and recognize the changing realities that characterize a shrinking world. They can help interpret available knowledge and experience in delineating future trends. They can propose potential alternatives and practical models that will require rigorous experimentation and testing.

The new context for education is the framework for designing a new curriculum. While utilizing what we know in the physical and social sciences and the arts and humanities, the new curriculum would encompass fresh content, giving many existing offerings a new conceptual framework. While courses must be developed for credit-oriented degree programs, there must also be significant attention given to noncredit, continuing education in all forms, including providing for the general mass of the population access to essential new knowledge and information. Advanced technological methodologies for program delivery, such as teleconferencing and computer-video systems, can multiply impact.

The key to all of this is the availability and commitment of people in education who are prepared to stake out new paths, who do not fear experimentation and controversy to challenge the thought patterns of much of the surrounding mainstream culture, not to mention of our educational institutions. The new educators must be willing to take the consequences of working as a minority group. Development of a cohesive core group of people from various campuses and educational agencies to serve in a lead role for moving ahead is an essential first step. This group would sponsor the actual development of curriculum ideas and models and delivery systems that would then be tested out in classes, both on the campuses and through extension programs.

In that the boundaries of the university and other educational institutions are now the world, ever-broadening interrelationships must be developed with counterpart groups across the nation and in other countries. Given the holistic nature of the new curriculum that must bring together material from various fields of knowledge, and where factual information must be meshed with values studies and intuitive learning, other learning sites, along with conventional classes and laboratories, are needed.

New thinking and new models are easily buried. We need, then, to establish with a clear policy statement and modest material backup a task group to take responsibility for beginning to design an experimental curriculum that reflects the new realities of our world. The task group needs a specific time frame, and its members need to commit themselves to the actual testing of curricula in a number of settings through agreement with various campuses and extension programs, public schools, the vocational and technical colleges, and citizen bodies.

Toward Global Sustainable Community: A View from Wisconsin

From Sustainable Global Communities in the Information Age

A small group drawn from around the world gathered on Awaji Island in Japan for several days in August 1993. Discussion topic: "Renewing community as sustainable global village." The meeting was co-sponsored by UNESCO and The World Future Studies Federation, along with several Japanese organizations. It was coordinated by Professor Kaoru Yamaguchi, who edited the 20 papers in this book. The group was interested in conceptualizing a University of the Future. Since most of my presentation focused on material covered elsewhere in this book, my comments here are limited to a statement on higher education.

Universities are the prominent and accepted institutions of the knowledge/information infrastructure of modern society, and they play such a crucial role in defining the realities upon which we shape our future. It is therefore rather amazing that a number of global thinkers like ourselves should have to assemble here to ponder the creation of a future-oriented university. Every country should already have at least one. Despite the tremendous strengths of our universities, there is a dinosaur mentality that seems to have prevented them from seriously taking on futures studies. Let me simply cite three reasons, among others:

1. Universities are fragmented. They are classic examples of the Cartesian model of subdividing wholes into small compartments. Academic disciplines and narrow specializations certainly have their place in understanding the complexities of the world, but

today there is a crying need to comprehend larger wholes and how the disparate variables of reality fit together—economic, political, ecological, cultural, psychological, and spiritual. One of the achievements of some scientists in the last 20 years has been a healthy humility about how little they really know and the recognition of the need to create more holistic models. Your new university here will need to create processes to transcend not only boundaries between nations and cultures, but also the fragmentation of knowledge.

2. Universities have great difficulty in dealing with values and larger visions. For almost 50 years, the Western democratic world focused its most creative energies (and material resources) on containing communist expansionism. Now we are in need of new visions that will focus and mobilize our creative energies as we move into the new century. It is interesting to note that an international, interdisciplinary, multicultural study now underway, organized by the American Academy of Arts and Sciences, is focusing on "fundamentalisms" on seven continents. In identifying 14 different fundamentalist movements, most of which are surging in membership and influence, the study notes that despite their differences, the fundamentalisms share certain strongly held underlying values—for example, fighting back against modern secular society. These values have their ramifications in politics, economics, education, family and sexual relationships, and so on. We too need to be able to deal with value concerns on the deepest level while maintaining an openness to dialogue as we search for truth and promote the larger common good. The new, unifying vision for the years ahead may well be the recognition that we live in an *interdependent global community where the future consequences of our present actions have taken on great importance.* I assume that this is an essential premise of the new university under discussion.

3. Universities lack imagination. The future does not exist; it is an image in our minds. However, it is the limits of the limitlessness of our own imaginations that will determine the possibilities of whichever frame of reference we choose to focus on. In the 20th century, imaginations have been fertile in certain fields of science and technology, but there has been a compelling dearth of imagination in reshaping institutions such as education. Our American colleague Michael Marien, editor of *Future Survey,* in 1989 pronounced the university a "trivia factory" with the academic penchant to think small. "Academics are locked into a pattern of trivial pursuit and are even rewarded for it," he wrote. In the context of seeing the world as a whole, the University of the Future needs to identify trends, visualize and estimate future possibilities, prepare students to be discriminating in identifying preferred futures, and give stimulus and energy to "go for it."

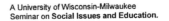

SUSTAINABLE
FUTURES LEARNING

Tuesday Late Afternoons
Sept. 8 to Dec. 8, 1998
4:30 – 7:10 p.m.

Sustainable Futures Learning

Fall 1998

From the latter 1980s to the end of the 1990s, I offered a university seminar each semester on Sustainable Futures, usually with my prominent local futurist colleague Wil Kraegel. Hundreds of teachers and administrators from local educational institutions enrolled, among others. Most classes were off campus to facilitate community participation. Kraegel and I also produced a *Futures Reader*.

Here is a sample course brochure, and the Introduction to the *Futures Reader*.

Introduction to Futures Reader, 1991

This *Futures Studies Reader* is a supplement to assigned books for our seminar, Creating Interdependent Sustainable Futures.

The literature in this general subject area, which may attract such diverse people as futurists, policy analysts, environmental scanners, trends analysts, futures researchers, and so on, has proliferated in recent years. Book publishers, research institutes, general interest magazines, major newspapers, and scholarly journals, as well as a number of publications exclusively described as "futurist," offer an enormous diversity of material from which to select. Not only the multiple sources of material but conflicting viewpoints create large challenges for making selections for a *Reader*.

These seminars, as defined by the title, have a distinct point of view and purpose. They relate not only to a longer-term perspective on today's concerns—the usual characteristic of futurists—but also recognize three highly significant developments. These are the global interdependent community that is emerging; the need to focus on sustainability, given threats to the Earth's natural resources and environment from human intervention; and our need to act responsibly in that today's actions or inactions condition tomorrow's events. The materials in the *Reader*, by and large, reflect this set of viewpoints.

While this *Reader's* subject matter should appeal to many sectors of the community, it emphasizes in particular the relationship of futures thinking to education. In various ways, we are all educators, whether in a formal learning institution or in our other roles as citizen, parent, professional, or social activist. Most of us recognize that education is a principal means for identifying new knowledge and approaches in order to help us understand the world that is and to prepare for the world that is to be. We believe that one of our great challenges today is to learn to rethink the way we see the world and to play our respective roles in the communication and integration of these new insights.

> In various ways, we are all educators, whether in a formal learning institution or in our other roles as citizen, parent, professional, or social activist.

There are hundreds of selections that could be included in the *Reader*. This is merely a sampling of items on a range of topics; many important topics are excluded altogether. The material is organized so as to follow in a general way the unfolding of the seminars.

We emphasize that this material has been prepared and reproduced for the university courses and is being distributed to class participants at cost. It is not available commercially.

AN INVITATION TO RETHINK THE WAY WE SEE THE WORLD

In this day of tumultuous change, people continually ask: How can we think about and prepare for the future? Whether a teacher, a business or government or civic leader, a parent, or a student planning a career, we need to develop the capacity to look ahead. Moreover, the future doesn't just happen. Our actions or inaction today condition tomorrow's events. In a real sense, we do create the future.

During most of the past 50 years, much of the creative energy of America and the West went to responding to the challenges of the "Cold War." During the next 50 years, our most critical challenge may well be figuring out how to create a sustainable world. This will require our learning to rethink much of what we know and to cultivate values conducive to sustainable living. We will become ecologically literate, globally sensitive, technologically competent, and prepared to live in a diverse local and world community.

This is a core course in sustainable futures thinking. While we recognize that education is a chief means for identifying the knowledge and skills that we need, we're also aware that the whole educational enterprise itself is undergoing transformative changes. Thus this seminar focuses on helping us to rethink the future in the direction of creating sustainable lives and communities, while also fitting into and contributing to a context of ferment on how best to learn.

The course will culminate with class members building on the knowledge base of sustainable futures and transformative learning, to design a final project that is related in a practical way to their life or work.

SEMINAR SESSIONS

I. RETHINKING THE FUTURE

Sept. 8   Concept of seminar: relationship of futures studies to education and sustainable living.
Sept. 15   Understanding the future: core ideas, scenarios, forecasting.
Sept. 22   Paradigm shifts: changing thought patterns, whole-system thinking.

II. WORLDS OF THE FUTURE

Sept. 29   Demography: relating population to the Earth's carrying capacity.
Oct. 6   Ecology: interdependence of human and nature.
Oct. 10   Field trip to Plymouth Institute (10:00 a.m. – 4:00 p.m.)
Oct. 13   Gender: women's movements – how they are emerging and connecting.
Oct. 20   Technology: driving force of change.
Oct. 27   Governance and Economy: keys to global sustainable futures.
Nov. 3   Review of readings.

III. SUSTAINABLE FUTURES LEARNING

Nov. 10   Preparing for transformative changes in learning systems.
Nov. 17   Utilizing advanced brain-mind research. (Speaker: Robert Pavlik)
Nov. 24   Values for sustainable futures.

IV. SUSTAINABLE LIVING AND US

Dec. 1   Summary and class projects.
Dec. 8   Class projects

Important Values of "The Good Life"

1987

After one futures seminar ended, half a dozen bright students decided to meet with me for several more weeks. They articulated values they considered to be the most fundamental in designing a learning system for living in and promoting a "good society." After weeks of probing they came up with five **fundamental values**. Of these, their top priority was *compassion*.

- **Compassion:** concern for others, being emotionally present and understand, "gifting" (giving without expectations)
- **Respect:** acceptance of diversity, holding sacred the Earth/society/self
- **Responsibility:** commitment to whatever one chooses to become engaged in, obligation to appropriate action
- **Comprehension of Reality:** intellectually understanding what is and what ought to be, recognizing change/flux and what is known (permanence/impermanence)
- **Joy:** viewing obligations positively; celebration, transcending obligation, spontaneity, fun, play, humor

These qualities, in turn, could all be aggregated into an all-encompassing value, the **perennial wisdom**, which is an awareness of the highest state of being and reflects the essence of different religions through the ages.

They also identified **significant related values:**

- **Fair Exchange of Energy:** equity, TANSTAAFL (there ain't no such thing as a free lunch), energy input produces energy output (law of manifestation); energy includes Effort, related to Responsibility and Compassion

- **Cooperation:** co-creative participation toward a common goal, related to Responsibility, Respect

- **Honesty:** dealing in truth fully and straightforwardly with others and oneself

- **Trust:** consciously giving oneself to the unknown, the willingness to release to another's power

- **Balance:** equilibrium between diversity and commonality, between highest vision and immediate circumstances, between past/present/future, appropriate scale of action

- **Adaptability:** dealing truthfully, adjusting to change, survivability, versatility, willingness to alter one's belief

- **Creativity:** expression of insights/energy/motivation, distinct interpretations of reality, may come from overall/universal energy, (M-fields—i.e., morphogenetic fields); related to Comprehension

- **Intuition/Inspiration:** tapping into realities that transcend one's past conditioning and conscious senses

Using Future Studies as an Over-Arching Theme for Alternative Thinking

FUTURES

READER

Several years ago I participated in a big conference in Detroit sponsored by the President's Council on Sustainable Development (the Clinton era); at the time I was a member of the Council's Education Task Force. One of the keynoters was Ray Anderson, CEO of the largest company manufacturing carpets, a high pollution industry. He gave a standard talk on the environment challenges. Afterward I saw him briefly and mentioned that what the people most wanted to hear from him was the personal transformation he had experienced— moving from a conventional businessman to one of the business community's most committed statesmen to sustainable development. He said it would be too embarrassing to tell his own personal emotional epiphany before thousands of people. In any event, I'm going to share something of my personal story—how I ended up in futures studies and how living sustainably has become a top agenda of my life.

Futures Studies: Sustainable Living and Alternative Communities

2004

I gave this talk at Oberlin College when on campus to receive an award for Distinguished Achievement. As most of the details about my life have been discussed previously in this book, here are simply a few items related to futures studies.

One of my special interests in recent years has been to urge young people, such as you students here, to become pioneers, to take risks and become innovators out on the farther frontiers. Today I'll cite personal experiences as I tried to confront old problems in new ways during the last half of the twentieth century since I graduated, just as you will with today's multiple challenges after leaving Oberlin.

By the end of the 1970s and early 1980s, I was offering a sequence of new courses with strange titles such as "Planetary Survival and the Role of Alternative Communities," "New Dimensions in Governance," "A Meta-Curriculum for the Future," "Framing a Peace Culture," "Transformation-oriented Politics," and "Ancient Visions—Modern Futures." Most of these seminars had large attendance in a time of declining university enrollments.

Although I used catalog numbers from political science or education, my two teaching bases, these courses did not really fit the traditional curricula. At this time, I was in contact with colleagues at other colleges and universities with the same experience. They also were offering academically rigorous new courses that were drawing large attendances, but they didn't fit. All of us had begun to participate in national and international conferences organized by the World Future Society and were presenting papers. The time had come to use the label "Futures Studies." In some instances, new departments or majors were created. Notwithstanding its broad focus, there are some common concepts. Here we mention six core ideas of futures studies, and then apply them to thinking about building a sustainable world.

Imaging. Since the future does not exist, it's an image in our minds—possible futures, probable futures, preferred futures. I'm often surprised at how few people have invested time and energy in imaging their own future or that of their country or the world.

Use of Scenarios. To identify alternative futures, a meaningful approach is to construct different futures based on different assumptions and values. Some years ago James Robertson in *The Sane Alternative* identified five scenarios that are illustrative as a simple starting point:

- Business as usual;
- Disaster (catastrophe looms);
- Totalitarianism (the best way to prevent disaster is to give full power to an authoritarian government);
- Hyper-Expansionist Future (science and technology are assumed to be our unique contribution to history, along with rapid economic growth); and
- Sane, Humane, Ecological Future (the key to the future is not continued expansion but a fundamental change of direction).

Identification of Long-term Trends: Each of us may have our list of projected trends.

Transcending Narrow Disciplines: By definition, futures thinking is holistic, encompassing all reality. It deals with "wholes" in terms of subject matter, in transcending nations and cultures, and in spanning time to include the past and present and future.

Understanding Paradigms, Paradigm Shifts, Paradigm Crises: Thomas Kuhn in *The Structure of Scientific Revolutions* notes that when people lose faith in an accepted paradigm, there is a paradigm crisis that ends in one of three ways: short-term reforms, postponement of action to a future generation, or emergence of alternative ideas that over time become a dominant new paradigm.

Applying the Concept of Transformation: Simply put, "transformation" means moving from one state of being to another. For example, in the physical world, it means from liquid to solid, from tadpole to frog, from caterpillar to butterfly. In the social world, it has been used to describe fundamental shifts in personality or culture.

Let's apply for a moment these core ideas used in futures studies to building a sustainable world.

Regarding **imaging**, if we imagine what a sustainable world would look like, as a first step, we must learn to rethink how we see the world, which involves a shift in perception because the culture we live in is not sustainable.

If we construct **scenarios** of the probable futures following our current path, the available evidence points to a disastrous destination. However, with imagination, we can design alternative scenarios with more positive, preferred futures.

If we analyze long-term **trends**, we can make data-based projections. For example, there are a number of recent authoritative studies that project the finality of the petroleum age. While one must account for likely discontinuities such as wars, instability of oil sources, and inexact estimates of reserves, there is still the long-term trend that the petroleum age in the foreseeable future will end, which will force new interest in a more sustainable world.

If we transcend the narrow subject matter **disciplines** of our educational institutions, it is conceivable that we will better comprehend the interdependence of all reality and overcome the fragmentation of knowledge that obstructs our understanding of the concept of sustainable living.

If we describe the **paradigm** of today's culture, we will recognize that our lifestyle and institutions are using up nature's capital that is basic to our livelihood—water, minerals, trees, soil, air, and the living systems such as grasslands, wetlands, rain forests, wildlife, and species diversity. Sooner or later we will break out of this paradigm box.

If we describe the paradigm of today's culture, we will recognize that our lifestyle and institutions are using up nature's capital that is basic to our livelihood—water, minerals, trees, soil, air, and the living systems such as grasslands, wetlands, rain forests, wildlife, and species diversity. Sooner or later we will break out of this paradigm box.

If we learn that our very survival will require **transformation**—fundamental shifts—then we will have arrived at the starting point of reassessing where we are and what we must do to build a world that is sustainable.

I began this talk with my personal story. Now it's your turn—I'll be watching as you play your roles in building a sustainable future.

WORLD FUTURE SOCIETY
BULLETIN

Scenarios for Greater Milwaukee: Citizen Participation

In Projecting Futures in World Future Society Bulletin, *May-June 1983*

I prepared this article for the Goals for Greater Milwaukee 2000 project in consultation with the project's Futures subcommittee, and a city of Milwaukee planner. After the Goals program ended, a fledgling effort emerged to create a citywide Futures Institute with broad community support. Although this did not materialize, futures-oriented programs continued in our university department. It should be added that the Goals project, begun in 1980, projected 20 years into the future. Today the same analysis could easily continue to 2030.

One of the great challenges of futurist programs such as goals projects is to translate futures thinking into the thought processes and lifestyle of the ordinary citizen. An individual in the local community might ask: How do the sweeping projections of people like Alvin Toffler, Willis Harman, and Herman Kahn relate to my life? What do they have to do with me and my needs?

One approach is being tried in the nation's heartland, Milwaukee, Wisconsin. Since 1980, citizens of the four-county metropolitan area have been developing Goals for Greater Milwaukee 2000. The project has involved more than 600 people working through committees and task forces to preserve the positive elements of today's community while developing new responses to tomorrow's needs. The hardest task is identifying what those needs are.

Even the more sophisticated leaders of Goals for Greater Milwaukee 2000 tend to be entrenched in the assumptions and paradigms of the present and recent past. For the business person, the balance sheet of the next quarter, or at best the next year or two, has overwhelming importance. For the educator, the great current struggles have dealt with the crisis of educational relevance and leave little creativity to envisage emerging trends that could make today's thinking obsolete.

It is in this context that the Futures Subcommittee has been working with the board of directors and nine task forces to develop alternative scenarios to illustrate factors that are likely to influence the future of Milwaukee. The scenarios help illuminate one's assumptions about the future of issues that have central personal importance. They force one to make choices: What do I really want to have happen, and what price—in terms of policies and resource commitments—am I prepared to pay to facilitate my preferred future?

Our Futures Subcommittee has also developed a simple "game" that a large number of citizens can play. It takes the form of a short questionnaire where respondents take a stand on key assumptions underlying the scenarios. By stating what they think will happen and what they would like to have happen, they are in effect opting for particular scenarios. These data, along with other citizen input and task force materials, bring the views of many citizens into the formulations of the central thrust of this future-oriented community planning project.

For simplicity's sake, we have identified four main variables:

- Economic growth
- Natural resource availability and use
- Policy and activity of major institutions
- Lifestyle attitudes and values

We posed two questions for each.

Alternative Scenarios

Utilizing sharply contrasting perspectives on the future and discounting the disaster scenario of nuclear war or other catastrophic possibilities (which may be quite realistic but is even less predictable than the other alternatives), we hypothesized four broad scenarios for Greater Milwaukee toward the year 2000.

Scenario 1—Shrinkage

This scenario holds that the economy is experiencing a long-term downturn, and that people should accept this trend and prepare to cope with the consequences. Much of the Midwest economy has been based on heavy industry and oriented to high resource and energy consumption. The most obvious example is the automotive industry. To reverse the current downturn would require massive recapitalization in new technologies as well as imaginative leadership, entrepreneurship, and broad-scale work retraining. This view believes that economic opportunities for such a large investment do not favor the Midwest relative to some other regions. No national government policies are likely to draw in large subsidies from other areas of the United States to assist redevelopment of the Midwest economy in the way that the Midwest once subsidized the economic growth of the South and the West. Already there is a significant shift in the Midwest from manufacturing to service industries. Average incomes are decreasing because the only available service jobs pay at lower wage scales. The population in the city of Milwaukee and the county has been static or in decline for some time. The proportion of lower income population is likely to increase in the city as more mobile and higher skilled people leave, further decreasing the city's attractiveness.

Scenario 2—Stabilization

This scenario holds that the quality of life will remain approximately as it has been in the good years of the recent past. At the same time, it is believed that little significant growth can be anticipated in the economy, in jobs, and in population. Undoubtedly there will be cyclical ups and downs but no significant trend in either direction. The skilled labor force and the solid local businesses that bring incremental technological change to keep a degree of modernization will preserve this area's relative ranking in the national spectrum. The reputation of Wisconsin and Greater Milwaukee for honest government, the natural environment, the cultural amenities, and the rich ethnic pluralism of this metropolitan area will continue to serve as attractions. Future scarcities of resources will not take place to any significant degree, or if they do, they will not dramatically influence local life. Prevailing values and lifestyles will continue.

> Goals for Greater Milwaukee 2000 has aimed to enlist maximum citizen involvement in thinking about the future.

Scenario 3—Growth

The future in this scenario will be characterized by growth. New technologies will modify or completely replace what now exists. New job opportunities will open up in a whole range of areas, from microelectronics and robots to genetics and space applications. Jobs in service industries will expand. With the need for new discoveries and new skills, the education and information industries will draw in new resources and provide opportunities as knowledge and innovation burst forward. Science and technology will overcome the limitations of natural resource scarcities through new discoveries of raw materials and more productive and efficient ways to utilize what is available. Government will reduce regulations and taxation so that private enterprise can take full advantage of emerging opportunities. This view believes that industrialism, rather than nearing the end of an age of cheap abundant natural resources, will enter into a new period of rapid and sustained growth because of technological breakthroughs. Incomes, consumption, and the standard of living will increase.

Scenario 4—Change of Direction

This scenario holds that the conceptual model we use to view the future is itself outdated. As we formulate new criteria for looking realistically at the future, we must alter some of our basic assumptions and values, which will result in significant changes in the ways we approach the economy, technology, the use of natural resources, and our lifestyles. This scenario takes the view that limits hitherto unrecognized may force us to change our world-view. It will include the need to drastically increase our sensitivity to ecological and environmental factors. It sees the coming years as a possible "historic turning point" in our culture, a time when we begin to recognize that there is an impassable barrier to the onward and upward progression of the production and consumption of the past. Values will slowly change, with people taking more interest in cooperation and working together for the large common good of survival and fulfillment, in contrast to mainly emphasizing the pursuit of self-interest and immediate material gain. One of the likely burgeoning new areas of jobs will be the "natural economy," where people do more for themselves. People will reduce their heating costs with strategies that use energy conservation and renewable energy. They will take more interest in either raising some of their own food or developing cooperative arrangements with other people for food production and distribution.

It should be repeated that these are polarized models, although the real-life versions would undoubtedly integrate shades of various scenarios and their underlying assumptions.

Conclusions

Goals for Greater Milwaukee 2000 has aimed to enlist maximum citizen involvement in thinking about the future. At least 600 people have been serving on the board of directors, the four standing committees, the nine task forces, and several ad hoc committees. A 12-page supplement to the *Milwaukee Journal*, Wisconsin's major newspaper, summarized the preliminary recommendations of the task forces. More than 10,500 citizens completed and returned a lengthy and detailed newspaper ballot that indicated their opinions on many key issues.

In all this involvement, however, there is still the tendency to think in "the present" rather than project the future. The scenario approach, which to date has been used with the executive committee, task forces, and some citizen groups (although not with the broad public), provides some structure in helping people think through their expectations about the future. It relates the "big picture" of Kahn's "growth model" and Harman's "coming transformation" to the context of metropolitan Milwaukee. It helps people to pin down their assumptions and see the relationship of their beliefs and premises to the alternative futures that are likely to result.

Our experience to date indicates that many people think that **Shrinkage** or **Stabilization** is most probable but that **Growth** and/or **Change of Direction** represent the preferred future. People in business/industrial/labor/political groupings tend to favor growth, according to our findings, while members of "alternative" organizations that relate to ecology, energy, politics, education, and "new economics" emphasize change of direction. Whatever the combination selected, we have found that playing the "scenario game" invariably generates much discussion and debate, even among people little disposed to think about the future.

The Future Is Coming

Leave Your Impression.

Goals 2000

Report of the Ad Hoc Committee on Inter-Local Relationships

In Goals for Greater Milwaukee 2000 Special Committee Reports, *1985*

As the Goals 2000 project concluded after more than two years of work and with hundreds of citizens participating, it recognized that there were four problem areas requiring further attention. These were minority issues, leadership and planning, taxation, and inter-local relationships. I chaired the last group and wrote this introduction to its report.

A s we approach the year 2000, one of the significant themes emerging in the 1980s is the trend toward increasing interdependence. There is the interrelatedness of the world economy, the ecological interweaving of the natural and human worlds, the importance of inter-nation understanding to prevent a nuclear disaster, inter-cultural/inter-racial understanding to preclude domestic chaos, and the sharing between haves and have-nots, both in the world and domestically, as impending scarcities urge the need for cooperation. Each local region and community is also a complex of interdependent relationships.

Goals for Greater Milwaukee 2000 is well aware that the reality of our community must be seen as a whole. At the same time, Goals has made its work manageable by focusing on fairly specialized subject areas, which led to the establishment of nine task forces and a number of standing committees. Several issues emerged, however, that transcended the specific focus of these bodies. Ad hoc committees were formed to address these "all-pervasive issues" that were important to the overall project but could not be dealt with adequately by each task force.

One such key issue was local/regional relationships. While a number of task forces discussed this particular issue and made recommendations that were regional in nature, there was a felt need for a more systematic effort to look at local/regional relationships in the four-county area. A small ad hoc committee was therefore established.

From the outset, the Goals project has been a metropolitan endeavor, including Milwaukee Country, Ozaukee County, Washington County, and Waukesha County, although major emphasis was given to Milwaukee County. We know that metropolitan areas cannot function exclusively in the compartmentalized isolation of the many political jurisdictions into which they happen to be subdivided. The 19 municipalities in Milwaukee County, for example, are interdependent in a number of ways.

Many people living in the suburbs are employed in the city and vice versa; therefore, they are financed in various ways by property taxpayers in jurisdictions other than those that they themselves sustain. The infrastructure of roads and public utilities recognizes no political boundaries, nor do the "people problems" related to the effectiveness or ineffectiveness of police and fire protection, primary and secondary and higher education, welfare, the arts, and the like. The future of employment and income levels in this whole Greater Milwaukee area is going to be closely related to the sustenance and revitalization of the economy as seen from a regional perspective.

To provide some leadership and structure that reflects these underlying facts, as well as to prevent waste and duplication in a period of strained resources, a certain amount of common planning and working together is essential. At times, this may involve the whole metropolitan area—at other times various parts thereof.

Despite this need for common planning and coordination, which can increase efficiency and reduce waste, we also want responsive government. And we often believe that government is more likely to be responsive when decisions are made in the local community and public officials are accountable locally. We want government that is flexible to change according to the requirements of particular communities or neighborhoods. Thus we value small size and closeness between citizens and officials.

In essence, then, we face a basic contradiction: on the one hand, the need for planning for needs and problems that can best be cared for at metropolitan or county or other inter-municipal levels, and on the other hand, the need for local community control and accountability. Ideally these should be complementary, not contradictory. Each problem or issue should be dealt with at the most appropriate level of decision-making.

We also know that many community issues can best be handled outside of government altogether by efforts in the private sector and voluntary organizations. Some decentralization seems to be taking place in the United States, whereby power and responsibility move from the federal government to state and local government, and from governmental intervention to spheres of activity outside of government.

It is in this large and complex context of regional interdependence and desire for local autonomy that this paper on inter-local relationships has been prepared.

A New Kind of Think Tank

> We would invite you to participate in creating a major new think tank with a select group of influential thinkers and doers in business, government, academia, and the media, and representatives of innovative projects based on a holistic view.
>
> from letter "An Invitational Dialogue"
> sent to Think Tank consultation participants

Envisioning an Alternative Think Tank

From Odyssey of a Practical Visionary, 2009

This is background information for discussions and planning to consider establishing a new kind of think tank.

My mind kept returning to the university initiatives of recent years, such as the Wisconsin Idea Commission and the other efforts that looked at the future of higher education. This included also the Goals 2000 Project, with its scenarios about the future, and the new politics agendas of various groups. All of these had the common characteristic of using a kind of think tank approach. This meant involving the participants in task force settings to go beyond the mere digestion of information. They would utilize their knowledge and experience to explore creative alternatives in dysfunctional problem areas.

I decided to learn more about think tanks as a problem-solving technique. On a business trip to Washington in the mid-1980s, I visited three prominent think tanks: Brookings Institution, an influential group founded in the 1920s with a fairly liberal point of view on major issues; the Cato Institute, a market-oriented, libertarian entity believing that the less government the better; and the Heritage Foundation, a well-funded conservative operation very interested in influencing national policy.

Heritage was so impressive that I became convinced that we needed to consider establishing a think tank in Wisconsin with similar, far-reaching clout.

While in Washington, I spent most of my time at Heritage, observing their method of operation. Months before the 1980 presidential election, a group of conservatives had advised the Heritage Foundation to draw up a plan of action for a possible conservative administration in January 1981 to challenge the past liberal bias of the federal government. Should a conservative win the election, the 10 weeks between the election and the presidential inauguration would provide little time to prepare a new governing philosophy and a radical redirection of policy. Their premise was to offer a well-thought-through platform of conservative ideas that could reshape the intellectual and political landscape of a new administration.

Heritage organized 20 project teams involving 300 participants to develop comprehensive policy recommendations for all the Cabinet departments and several federal agencies. Each team had a chair and included academics, congressional staff, and conservatives who had been in the Nixon and Ford administrations. The result of this operation was a 1,000-page-plus document, *Mandate for Leadership: Policy Management in a Conservative Administration.*

This was published just as President-elect Reagan was putting in place his transition team at the end of 1980. Reportedly by the end of Reagan's first year in office, nearly two-thirds of *Mandate's* more than 2,000 recommendations had been or were being turned into policy. The two large volumes became best sellers in Washington. For the 1984 election, Heritage went to work again, publishing *Mandate II.*

Heritage distributed its ideas to every member of Congress and aides regardless of party. In the early Reagan years, many of the ideas were considered far out and controversial, but through continual education, a deluge of publications, and heavy marketing, it was amazing what happened to change the political climate.

As I thought about this Heritage model, I envisaged what might be accomplished were a similar methodology to be implemented with different values. Could we establish a new kind of think tank that approached each societal problem using a context of holistic values? What about breaking out of obsolete paradigms, as in miniature we were attempting to do with High Wind?

I mentioned this idea to a former university colleague, now a member of Congress from my East Side Milwaukee district. He was enthusiastic; he said he regularly received Heritage's hard-hitting, well-researched papers on every conceivable issue. They arrived at the ideal moment before the debate and voting. Nothing comparable had ever crossed his desk with other values.

Several weeks later, Francois Duquesne showed up in Wisconsin for a few days. The Frenchman, who had succeeded Peter Caddy as the focalizer of Findhorn, was astute and very interested in policy questions and in the relationship of the alternative community movement to mainstream culture. When our conversation hit on the idea of organizing a conference with values and models that were emerging from alternative groups in different parts of the world, we agreed that there were two interesting questions: Was something really being learned in the alternative communities—the Findhorns and High Winds and hundreds more—of importance to the larger society? If so, how could better bridges be built between today's alternative movement and the outside world, including with decision-makers?

Soon thereafter, Gordon Davidson and Corinne McLaughlin spent a couple of days with us during a national lecture tour for their new book, *Builders of the Dawn: Community Lifestyles in a Changing World.* As cofounders of the Sirius community in 1978 in western

Massachusetts, and having previously lived at Findhorn, they were among the most knowledgeable students of communities in America.

They had visited or researched 100 intentional communities (including High Wind) and consulted with governmental agencies and corporations as well as alternative groups. They were familiar with Heritage and the other think tanks in Washington. They grasped the Alternative Think Tank idea. One of the key themes in their book was that intentional communities are "laboratories for researching and testing . . . components of a new cultural vision . . . training places for creative participation in the unfoldment of the future. They are schools for change, for transformation."

A Consultation at the UN Annex

We all agreed that before planning a conference or considering the more grandiose venture of creating an alternative think tank, we needed a preliminary gathering to examine in depth what we were trying to do. Gordon and Corinne urged us to include leaders of the International Center for Integrative Studies (ICIS) in New York—a rich trove of experience and wisdom. We also had with us Mary Inglis, an astute member of the Findhorn community.

We gathered in Milwaukee for two weeks in February 1986. I organized a university noncredit seminar for four nights and a Saturday, "Toward an Alternative Think Tank," to which we invited 40 of the city's real thinkers to dialogue with us. They included a number from our past classes and also elected officials, business executives, and civic leaders.

> Intentional communities are "laboratories for researching and testing . . . components of a new cultural vision . . . training places for creative participation in the unfoldment of the future. They are schools for change, for transformation."

In these rigorous discussions, one prominent theme kept emerging: the need for a multiplicity of intermediate structures that bring together in a new synthesis the best of the mainstream paradigm of contemporary culture with the best of the new alternative paradigm. The discussion opened up a fascinating dialogue where we were able to transcend old assumptions and models that no longer worked, while at the same time recognizing that there was an abundance of knowledge and skills and resources available in today's society. We started playing with the hard-to-pronounce term "New Synthesis Think Tank."

Gordon and Corinne went ahead to secure ideal conference space at the United Nations Plaza across from the UN headquarters in New York. They also marshaled an incredible list of people—a veritable who's who cross section of alternative organizations of the 1970s and 1980s, spread across the landscape of cutting-edge thinking and action in American life. The 60 participants also included representatives from the media, government, and business.

A Timely Idea

Prior to the conference, ICIS, one of our conference co-sponsors, had published several of our papers in their magazine, *The Forum*, circulated among its distinguished leadership. These included an introductory overview of the project by Gordon, my think tank paper, several other articles, and a request for comments/reactions to the think tank project. We were startled—because we didn't expect a top UN official to read and get excited about the think tank idea—to read the next *Forum* issue, just before the October conference. The responses included the following:

Robert Mueller (assistant secretary-general of the UN): "I wish these articles would be read by all chief delegates to the UN. . . . Regarding a New Synthesis Think Tank, I would certainly welcome a powerful counter-lobbying group matching the new conservative thank tanks described in Belden Paulson's article. Such a think tank in Washington seems imperative. . . .)"

Riane Eisler (author of *The Chalice and the Blade: Our History, Our Future*, co-editor of Institute for Futures Forecasting): "I see the New Synthesis Think Tank . . . as a very important and exciting project. I am particularly interested in the construction of 'intermediate structures.' . . . The excellent papers by Davidson and Paulson bring out the necessity for a clear understanding of the systems relationship between values (content) and structure (form)."

Neil Riemer (author of *The Future of the Democratic Revolution: Toward a More Prophetic Politics*, professor of political science at Drew University, and my former colleague at UWM): "I like the idea of a new think tank between a liberal Brookings and a conservative Heritage Foundation. I share Belden Paulson's judgment that to be effective it would need the capability to make its 'new thoughts' available to policy shapers and makers in the right format at the opportune time. I would hope that a new think tank would concentrate, in the tradition of prophetic politics, on . . . 'creative breakthroughs in politics' . . . on problems that the conventional wisdom says cannot be solved."

Frances Vaughn (psychotherapist, formerly president of the Association for Transpersonal Psychology): "I must say I was very favorably impressed by the proposal for a New Synthesis Think Tank. It is certainly an idea whose time has come. . . . I would add my own bias in favor of emphasizing attention to consciousness itself as a central agent, instrument and object of change. Without a change in consciousness, reforms and programs are notoriously ineffective."

The dialogue in *The Forum*, plus the two intense days at the United Nations Plaza, convinced us we had entered into an endeavor that could have far-reaching potential. It went way beyond anything any of us had bargained for.

Toward a New Kind of Think Tank

In New Synthesis Think Tank Papers, *1987*

I presented this paper at the Consultation at the UN Plaza in New York City in October 1987.

While the term "think tank" only entered our vocabulary about 25 years ago, it reflects a long tradition in our young country of marshalling and applying expertise to solve problems of public importance. In our highly pragmatic society, we have always had a certain respect for experts who somehow will use knowledge and technology to overcome whatever ills beset us. At the same time, in our type of democracy, which has offered more access to achievement and upward mobility than probably anywhere else, we are suspicious of eggheads and people who believe they "know it all." From the earliest days, Americans have often transcended this dichotomy between the expert and the common person by banding together in an infinite variety of organizations to define problems facing society, getting "the facts," and proposing solutions.

Today, however, the speed of change, the complexity of problems, and the high stakes of failure may have made us more conscious than in the past of differences between information and wisdom, between facts and values. Most of us are aware that we have at our fingertips more information than ever before, but we may also feel more powerless to solve our problems.

Broadly defined here, think tanks are concentrated intellectual energies focusing on practical problems in order to influence public policy decisions. It is, therefore, not by accident that they have proliferated during the last couple of decades A recent study indicates that there are upwards of 1,200 private nonprofit research institutes concerned with public policy questions in the United States. They vary from diverse centers and institutes in universities—where most are located—to contract research organizations, consulting firms, and policy advocating entities. About 150 of them are located in Washington. All are small compared to the vast research operations that take place in government, but they seem to have taken on increasing importance as problems outrun solutions, and as more and more people believe that they may have something to contribute to solutions.

One of the most influential early think tanks, the Brookings Institution in Washington, was formed in the 1920s, and for decades it played a leading role in articulating liberal positions. It produced innumerable carefully prepared studies on major issues facing the nation, with accompanying educational and outreach efforts. Then in the 1970s, the conservative think tanks began moving to center stage, and during the Reagan years, these have helped to define the agenda of the federal government. Since 1980, one or another of such think tanks as the American Enterprise Institute, the Heritage Foundation, the Center for Strategic and International Studies, and the Cato Institute have developed detailed plans and recommendations for virtually every federal agency and on most major policy issues facing the national government.

While the viewpoints of liberal think tanks like Brookings and the above-cited conservative counterparts have varied widely on such issues as the government role in the economy, it could be argued that they have shared a common inability to stand outside the maelstrom of specific contemporary policy issues in order to address the challenges facing our culture—environmental degradation, fiscal and opportunity inequalities, future of work, the obsolete, self-serving national sovereign state system—in fundamentally new ways.

Effective responses are probably going to require us to break out of both the mindset of the industrial culture, which brought us 200 years of successful technological and economic development, and the international order based in the nation state system, which emerged out of the bloody Thirty Years War in 1648 and brought us several centuries of national social and political development. The systems that generated the problems also brought high material levels of living for most people. Moreover, the systems are not discrete, isolated phenomena to be dealt with in a linear fashion, one by one, but are intricately woven together both in terms of their underlying values and their institutions.

One of our most baffling dilemmas today is that we are living in a global political community and a global economy, but we are still saddled with a maze of narrowly parochial nation states and an array of economic entities constrained by national rules and regulations. The global community and the natural systems of the planet are crying out for a transformation of thinking that will lead to the creation of new political and economic structures reflecting a world altogether different from the times in history when these structures were created.

What is increasingly obvious is the need to look at the world in fundamentally different ways, with a new value context that will enable us to participate in creating a long-term future for all people of the planet. We need to bring new clarity to defining the problems we face. We need processes for translating broad, macro-level thinking based on new values into practical policy options that decision-makers can utilize as they search for solutions. We need to break out of our rigid conceptual conformism so we can reshape the intellectual and political landscape with questions heretofore seldom posed on the national agenda.

The time is ripe for a new kind of think tank.

The Context of Values

The images we have of the present and future are shaped by our assumptions and values—our views of the world, our paradigms. Our paradigms in turn influence our behavior, our individual actions. Cultural paradigms have major impact on the development of national and local policies. They provide the overall context within which policy-makers work.

This new think tank would seek to approach each societal problem from the perspective of a set of values that, taken together, constitute a radically new paradigm from that recognized conventionally in most contemporary decision-making. Much creative effort has been invested in recent years by many wise thinkers in articulating a holistic value context that stresses cooperation, empowerment, and sustainability, as applied to all levels of social organization—globally, nationally, locally and individually. As the New Synthesis Think Tank evolves, much energy would be needed to translate its ideas into concrete, policy-level work.

> Cultural paradigms have major impact on the development of national and local policies. They provide the overall context within which policy-makers work.

To be holistic, this value context would need to mesh long-run, futures thinking with short-run, immediately applicable policy-making. It would also need to use a systems approach in comprehending the interdependence of different aspects of reality—that disparate policies and seemingly unrelated subject area disciplines and factual data are different facets of reality that must be brought together when policy is formulated. Keeping in mind this kind of framework, the New Synthesis Think Tank would not be "liberal" or "conservative" but would represent a beginning attempt to offer a new kind of conceptual model where conventionally used approaches for viewing the future and developing here-and-now policy have become increasingly obsolete. The premise is that if we can alter some of our basic assumptions and values about key issues, significant policy changes would result.

What follows are only illustrative statements and reference points to be included in the dialogue. One set of values is drawn from the insights and experiences of intentional communities. For years, these social microcosms have been serving as living examples of a more holistic way of life. Some of these values are summarized in a recent book of communities, *Builders of the Dawn* by Corinne McLaughlin and Gordon Davidson:

- An awareness of the oneness of humanity and all life, with a corresponding conscious response to the global crisis;
- A commitment to personal change *and* social change, to psychological/spiritual growth and to service in society where individual needs are balanced with group needs;
- An emphasis on cooperation and some form of sharing of resources and skills;
- A dedication to healing the earth and working in harmony with the forces of nature rather than exploiting the land and its resources;
- An emphasis on "living lightly on the earth," embracing appropriate-scale technology (including tractors and computers) while reducing our consumption, recycling resources, and using renewable sources of energy such as wood, solar and wind;
- Development of some degree of self-sufficiency in food and energy, but also developing interdependence with others through barter and business;
- A commitment to non-violence, world peace, and racial and sexual equality;
- A commitment to *process*, to facing up to interpersonal conflicts and working them out through some agreed-upon method;
- A respect for the wholeness of the individual—body/emotions/mind/spirit;
- A dedication to 'thinking globally, acting locally'—working to create solutions to universal social problems in a chosen local field of focus;
- A commitment to the primacy of an individual's relationship to God, to the Universe (or to 'The Common Good', if the community is more secular in orientation), and a corresponding reverence for the Divine within all life—God immanent (or Life itself)."

Values related to feminism have a crucial role to play. In a new book, *The Chalice and the Blade*, author Riane Eisler traced a holistic view of our cultural evolution. She concludes:

When social systems past and present are reexamined using a data base that includes women as well as men, it becomes apparent that there is a significant correlation between rigid male dominance, a generally hierarchic and authoritarian social structure and a high degree of institutionalized social violence ranging from child beating, wife battering, rape, and the institutionalized male violence we call war. Conversely, there is a strong systems correlation between the elevation of 'feminine' values such as caring, empathy, and non-violence to social governance and equal partnership between women and men. This also seems to go along with a more egalitarian, socially responsible and peaceful way of living on this earth.

Another approach to formulating a new value context is to compare three of the most basic political functions to be found in all political systems using the existing prevailing "conventional model" and an "alternative model" that is more aligned to the value context under discussion.

POLITICAL FUNCTION	CONVENTIONAL MODEL	ALTERNATIVE MODEL
Definition of interest	Self-interest	Interdependence
Organizing principle	Competition for scarce resources	Cooperation to overcome scarcity
Educating/socializing for participation in our culture	Assumes unlimited resources, pollution can be absorbed	Embraces resource stewardship, ecological ethic

Giving the Values Policy Content

Questions are often raised about the "utopian" or "unrealistic" nature of values such as those discussed here. The fact is that there are innumerable individuals and groups of people working in very practical ways and living out their lives in a value context that is sensitive to global needs and creates harmony, promotes human growth, and offers a service to the culture at large. There may be an openness today toward creating a "new synthesis" of the best mainstream approaches of values and models with those that may be "alternative" to the more conventional ones used by major institutions and communicated by the mass media.

The Values and Lifestyles Studies (VALS) conducted by Stanford Research International conclude that more than 20 percent of the population in the United States is receptive to the kind of values discussed here. Leaders in business, politics, and education who are interested in new thinking and seeking new models often see *themselves* as a "minority," out of step with the mainstream institution to which they belong, which suggests increasing institutional malleability. People are moving from discussion of holistic values to operational implementation, from talking and writing to doing. Ideas and programs that not long ago were considered "way out" are being taken more seriously.

These ideas and programs take many forms. Insurance companies and businesses are beginning to emphasize "wellness" and holistic health. In some sectors of the population, there are notable efforts to create socially conscious money market and investment funds, in using methods of food production based in sustainable or regenerative agriculture, in designing and maintaining buildings in ways that use renewable energy and emphasize conservation. Businesses and other large organizations are finding that decentralization into human-scale units and group decision-making that uses consensus improves morale and increases productivity.

Further, innovative educational approaches abound that stress self-directed and experiential learning, which includes synthesizing information and values. Many groups are experimenting with political processes that substitute more truly democratic approaches for selecting qualified leaders rather than simply "electoral politics." On the international level of diplomacy, creative initiatives are multiplying that focus on new models of negotiation emphasizing "common ground" and broadening areas of shared values even while respecting divergences of interest and ideology.

A high-level bureaucrat in county government who participated in a seminar with other leaders on changing values said he was responsible for making a cutback of $30 to $35 million in his personnel budget and would like to utilize the above values in his decision-making. However, the discussion group recognized that for public policy-makers to revamp in a serious way the process for making decisions, they would need to explore in-depth the value context they use in defining problems, establishing priorities, and generally organizing their operation.

In this particular instance, for example, the official might want to explore a new approach to personnel policy. This would require attention to some redefinition of work tasks, rethinking labor-management relationships (leading to a new kind of relationship with the powerful union with which he must deal), and so on. While his institutional goal might remain the same—to provide the best quality services at the least cost—a new value context might improve his agency's effectiveness and at the same time enhance the well-being of the actors involved.

> For public policy-makers to revamp in a serious way the process for making decisions, they would need to explore in-depth the value context they use in defining problems, establishing priorities, and generally organizing their operation.

These illustrations are merely the tip of the iceberg, but they reflect the fact that growing numbers of people are beginning to recognize that certain conventional values and institutions in our culture are creating massive dysfunctionalities.

Imagine a group of people coming together who had developed a coherent value context along the broad lines of the ideas outlined in the above pages. Imagine them seeking to apply this value agenda in a carefully thought-out, well-researched manner to a series of concrete issue areas such as, for example, issues facing the government official mentioned above. Or much more expansively, they might take on a very formidable task, as the Heritage Foundation did in the summer of 1980, focusing on the cabinet departments of the federal government and other key agencies. This group would invite the assistance of key people from varied walks of life—government, business, labor, academia, the professions, nonprofit innovative groups, and intentional communities—to develop specific policy options.

The key qualification of all participants, apart from their professional competence, would be their general empathy with the agreed-upon value agenda. They would reflect, of course, many differences in terms of how to apply the values in given situations and, therefore, would normally present policy alternatives within the given broad value context. This group and its advisers, recognizing the merits of much that has gone before, would build on and utilize the excellent work of the many policy-oriented think tanks in public universities and notable private ones. They would seek to mesh, where possible, its values, proposed policies, and resulting structures with those that already exist. Very likely a multiplicity of "intermediate structures" would be proposed: that is, structures in business and political life and education and social services and so on, which are a synthesis of what is already there and need to remain because they really work, and what is new that will transcend old assumptions and models that have become obsolete.

The distinguishing characteristic of this group would be its value context providing the framework, its worldview, from which all of its policy formation stems. The group would be known as the **New Synthesis Think Tank**.

We cannot overemphasize that the first essential characteristic of this group would be its underlying philosophic commitments. The noted social analyst Yehezkel Dror, in his exhaustively researched study on "Required Breakthroughs in Think Tanks," notes that a common weakness of think tanks in different areas of the world is their lack of an "underlying philosophy of knowledge," their inadequate handling of values, and the lack of explicating the professional biases of their members. He stresses the need for "ideal models as guides," prescriptive models, and the importance of "sensitivity testing to alternative value systems." A major contribution that think tanks could make, he states, is the "exploration of deeper roots of critical predicaments, macro-diagnosis of the state of societies," and to "question the accepted and debunk the habitual, in clear contradiction to the traditionalism and conservatism built into most bureaucratic behavior." He believes that think tanks are, instead, "oriented to the explicit goal of governments and policies, ignoring the hidden agendas dominating the latter."

A second essential aspect would be the development of an "infrastructure" of research, knowledge, operational models, and alternative solutions and approaches that would become a kind of resource bank for translating this value context into usable policy recommendations. In that we assume there is a rich reservoir of broad-gauge, transdisciplinary experience available for this effort, the resource bank would identify this body of talent and facilitate the flow of information. A computerized, online, bibliographic database covering key publications and other sources could be put in place. During the last two decades in particular, a wealth of practical experience as well as conceptual work has become available, but in most instances, it is dispersed, unorganized, and lacking access to a policy-relevant organism that could help in translating this body of material into a public policy format. The New Synthesis Think Tank proposes to do this.

An obvious critical aspect of this process would be initial agreement regarding priorities about problem areas that would serve as focal points for think tank attention and that would demand thorough analysis. The "problem definition" process, in many instances, might be "problem redefinition." Seen from a different value/paradigm context, "problems" might be characterized very differently than in conventional usage. For example, a fundamental redirection of Cold War policies toward the Soviet Union that have been cemented into place during the last 40 years, if responding to "openings" made by Mikhail Gorbachev and others, might have set into motion a vast creative effort in international relations and alternative uses of resources. Or let us presuppose a view of a restructured American economy, anticipating that up to one-third of the labor force might no longer be needed to produce all goods and services for the marketplace as presently defined. It would then require a new elaboration of the meaning of "employment" and "work" as well as significant changes in government policy and the functioning of education.

Marketing the Policies

Many or most think tanks produce materials that have important intrinsic worth, but they never see the light of day other than in the most restricted circles, and their influence is minimal. If the overall goal of the New Synthesis Think Tank is to apply a broad set of values considered essential to living and prospering in a more interdependent world, then the test is whether anyone will consider seriously the practical policy proposals it produces. A maximum result would be for its work to contribute to reshaping the national agenda so that the kinds of fundamental challenges discussed above are effectively addressed.

It is a quantum jump to develop a process for converting data that hitherto has been concentrated in small-scale, dispersed pockets of activity, usually limited to relatively exclusive audiences, into a broad policy framework that could have societal significance. This operational model would have much to learn from the experience of various leading think tanks and others in assembling knowledge and experience and converting it into policy recommendations. A carefully thought-out and comprehensive marketing effort would be essential in order to process the products of the New Synthesis Think Tank in usable form and to distribute them in the arenas where public policy dialogue and decision-making take place.

> Marketing strategy and overall educational effort is as important to overall effectiveness as the policy formulation process itself.

If the real product is not only policy papers but also new cultural norms that may at times be fundamentally different from those conventionally accepted, then the marketing strategy and overall educational effort is as important to overall effectiveness as the policy formulation process itself.

We do not need to look far to identify models that in recent years have been extraordinarily effective in inserting ideas into the policy arena and actually influencing public decisions at the highest level. The last annual report of the Heritage Foundation and an address delivered by its founder and president, Edwin Feulner, "Ideas, Think Tanks and Governments," read like clinical case studies. The fundamental purpose of Heritage is to "produce the conservative ideas that would change the terms of public debate and reshape the intellectual and political landscape."

The point of this inventory survey is to illustrate the massive marketing effort that Heritage organized and funded to make known its ideas, which in 1980 were considered "way out" and highly controversial.

In its "battle of ideas" to bring changes in policy, a few "operating principles" have been used, as stated by the Heritage president. "First and foremost the product must be available in a timely fashion. It does no good to publish an incisive report the day after the debate and vote...." The second principle is the "briefcase test," which means that arguments should be concise and clearly presented: "We try to limit our *Backgrounders* to 10 pages—a document that stands a much greater chance of being put into a briefcase and read before the debate than a book that generally ends up on a bookshelf."

A third principle: "The product must reach the right people. We spend quite a bit of time updating and refining our list of congressional and administration aides. We try to ensure that the assistant handling welfare reform does not receive a paper on military reform." The final operating principle: "Of course the product must be credible. Because we are a tax-exempt educational research entity, not a lobbying group, we are free to express our views as outspokenly as we want."

In discussing marketing methodology, we cannot overemphasize that the process to be used by the New Synthesis Think Tank, as well as the content communicated, must reflect holistic values. Also important, after much energy is invested in the content area, it would be unfortunate if the material were to reach few people because of poor marketing. At the same time, the goal is to contribute to enlightened public judgment on crucial issues facing us, not merely influencing public opinion that remains confused, ill informed, and full of bias and emotion.

The social analyst and pollster Daniel Yankelovich has noted that issues of public importance go through three phases. The first is when the public becomes aware of the problem—consciousness raising. The second is the time of "working through," which involves much dialogue, identification of both the "values" being used and the "facts" as they can be discerned on the issue, as well as the preparation of alternative choices around which public judgment may coalesce. The third involves political compromise when some resolution is hammered out. The mass media, he observes, are proficient at getting people excited over an issue—the first step—but then are woefully inadequate at "working through" issues. Thus they produce public awareness, but also public ignorance at the same time. The New Synthesis Think Tank could make a notable contribution in this area.

The New Synthesis Think Tank is a formidable undertaking. It could have significant implications if it can be organized, funded, and developed into an effective organism that brings a new context to major policy issues facing us. But its bottom-line impact will depend on marketing capability. It should be recalled that the Heritage Foundation was begun only a little more than 10 years ago by a few individuals with small initial resources. It made its mark through its marketing excellence. The final test of the New Synthesis Think Tank thus will lie not only in the intrinsic merits of its values and in the capabilities of think tank staff to develop enlightened, far-reaching policy proposals. It will also rest on the genius that is given to the marketing and education function.

**THE PROMISE OF THE LAST YEARS
OF THE TWENTIETH CENTURY**

BY WILLIS HARMAN, PhD

Coalescing Around the Think Tank Idea: The October Conference in New York

In Windwatch, *January 1988*

The New York Consultation generated an enthusiastic response. The next step was to explore possible solutions for implementation. Many small meetings identified personal commitments for involvement. In this edition of High Wind's newsletter I commented on the Consultation.

QUESTION: *What would it take to translate holistic and planetary ideas into public policy— ideas that clearly reflect sustainability, cooperation, empowerment, interdependence? What would be needed to give the federal government a comprehensive operational set of policy recommendations that would challenge the obsolete framework now used?*

ANSWER: *It would take some clear thinkers looking at the world in new ways, some hard-headed, holistic-minded government insiders working on the front line, a well thought-out communications/marketing strategy for bringing new models into the public domain, some money, and a nucleus of committed, energetic people crazy enough to believe that the time is ripe to begin to bring a new value context into government and who are courageous enough risk-takers to help make it happen.*

These were the kinds of questions and answers in the back of our minds when we went to the Dag Hammersjkold Room at the United Nations complex in New York City this past October. Some 60 people had gathered from around the country and abroad to discuss the feasibility of creating a New Synthesis Think Tank. This was a hand-picked group of leaders who are professionally involved with politics, energy and ecology, psychology, holistic health, socially responsible economics, education, human services, and the media who came together for two intense, high-energy days. They were invited because they were thought to reflect the kind of synthesis being advocated: alternative *and* main-stream approaches to solving social problems; liberal concerns such as human rights and equality *and* conservative concerns for security and self-reliance; and interest in science and technology *and* the transcendental reality of spiritual values.

Turning Different Values into Fresh Politics

While bringing fresh politics into the federal government would be a political operation, the attendees were not interested only or even primarily in politics but in values. This helps to explain the difficulty that people at the conference—many of us—have had with the presidential campaign already begun. The real problem is that the candidates have not identified what's really important. It's the same old stuff. What's "really important" is radical stuff, and most politicians assume there is no constituency for such matters. If they want to stay in office, they stay with the "tried and true."

So what is *really* important? At the conference, various people made presentations and summarized their views. Some illustrative projects were described. In my remarks, I stressed the importance of our standing for a moment outside the ferment of specific contemporary issues in order to address the comprehensive interrelationships of such fundamental challenges facing our culture.

New Mindset Necessary

We must figure out how to transcend the old industrial culture and the narrowly parochial nationalism that we have known in our lifetime. We need a new value context that will enable us to participate in creating a long-term future for all people on the planet. We need processes for translating broad, new, macro-level thinking into practical policy options that decision-makers can utilize as they search for solutions.

But there was no consensus at the conference on how to proceed. In my various conversations with people around the country since October, there has been unanimous agreement on the pressing need for a process to begin to introduce holistic ideas into the government—whether via a "think tank" or some other vehicle. The test is whether the organizers of the conference—Gordon Davidson and Corinne McLaughlin of the Sirius community, Lorraine Mai and Lamar Carter of the International Center for Integrative Studies, Mary Inglis and Roger Doudna of the Findhorn Foundation in Scotland, and we from High Wind and the University of Wisconsin—with all the other people who are equally committed to the idea, can design a workable strategy to take the next action steps.

USSR
USA INDIA
CHINA COUNCIL UK
OF
MEMBERS

Toward a Global Think Tank

In Global Conference on New Trends in Science, Technology, Economy and Society, Shanghai, China, April 1990

The think tank initiative stimulated significant interest in converting our focus from the American government to the international stage. After all, most of the big problems are global. In January 1990, through the interest of futurist Barbara Marx Hubbard, Lisa and I participated in a Citizens Summit held in Moscow. I co-chaired a task force whose major recommendation was to establish a global think tank. Over four years, my university department, with Roger Collis of the Pacifica Foundation organized futures studies trips to China. These included co-sponsoring three global conferences held in Shanghai in cooperation with Chinese scientific and policy institutes. In April 1990, one major focus was the global think tank proposed in Moscow. Among the numerous papers presented, my talk introduced this project. As one of the proposed think tank members, the Chinese were eager to begin immediately.

We are rapidly moving toward living in a global community—a single marketplace and an ecological system that have little to do with national borders—but we are still trying to "make do" with institutions developed in another historical period. This challenge, of creating new institutions that are able to function in the context of today's objective realities, will be the magnet that draws forth much of the world's creative energy during the decade of the 1990s and later.

Two of the great issues that we must grapple with and find answers for are 1) working out a process for achieving sustainable development on a world scale and 2) designing institutions for a transnational world order.

Sustainable Development

For most people during this century, another word for "progress" is economic growth. It doesn't matter where we fit in the political spectrum—maximum control by government in the economy or maximum freedom for the private sector—the idea of unlimited material growth is critical. Notwithstanding much poverty in the world, industrial societies in particular, both capitalist and socialist, have gained great benefits in terms of increasing material standards of living.

Obviously the person who argues that there are absolute limits to growth will find few supporters. The people who have benefited the most from growth can hardly be expected to slow down suddenly when they see opportunities abound for continued economic development. Far more importantly, during the next century, there will be a doubling of the five billion people now living on the planet, most of whom will live in the lower income areas of Asia, Africa, and Latin America. Simple equity requires that they participate in rapid economic growth using modern science and technology to eliminate their mass poverty.

> There are large pockets of lower income people within the industrial world who will never accept remaining in poverty "to protect the environment."

The countries in the Pacific Basin can be expected to experience extraordinary economic growth during the 1990s. There are also large pockets of lower income people within the industrial world who will never accept remaining in poverty "to protect the environment." The World Commission on Environment and Development predicts that a five- to tenfold increase in world economic activity will be required during the next 50 years to meet the basic needs and aspirations of the future population.

In order to cope with the implications of this kind of growth, a fundamental shift in perception is mandatory. The issue is not whether or not there should be growth, but whether there should be an altogether new kind of growth, known as "sustainable development."

Sustainable development cannot be implemented by a few feeble efforts. It will require that we begin to look at the world in fundamentally different ways. It will require basic shifts in production processes and in our prevailing lifestyles.

Transnational World Order

We will have to face an equally fundamental shift in how we relate to the nation state. Like economic growth, the primacy of the nation state is part of our modern cultural heritage. The sacred duty of every national leader is to promote the "national interest." The great question is: what do we mean by national interest?

The prevailing assumption in international relations textbooks on the subject is that it is defined in terms of national security, which above all means to preserve the integrity of the national territory and its institutions. The traditional premise of international politics was zero-sum competition: my win equals your loss. Each nation pursued its own narrow self-interest to maximize its own advantage.

The advent of the atomic age made this approach obsolete. In April 1987, a group of five retired American and Soviet generals and admirals, with years of combined active military service, met to discuss the continued arms buildup. Their unanimous conclusion: "nuclear arms cannot be used for any rational military or political purpose."

The environmental crisis has also forced a radical redefinition of national security. When dealing with such concerns as climate change and global warming, security defined in terms of national territory is as archaic as was the castle in the age of gunpowder. The Earth has certain natural thresholds that, if crossed, impair its capacity to sustain life. We now know that the Earth's natural systems are at risk on a global scale. In an interdependent world, ecological security has an entirely different meaning from the narrowly conceived nation-centered perspective of the past. Most of the great issues now facing the world, such as stabilizing the growth of population, preventing nuclear war and terrorism, improving the material level of living in the poorer countries, and coping with the multiple environmental crises, are planetary problems. Individual countries can exercise important leadership, but the issues are beyond the capacity of even the most powerful.

A transnational world order is beginning to emerge that will gradually take on responsibility for certain problems of the global commons through transnational structures and measures. Regional groupings, such as the 11-nation European community and developing regional affiliations in the Pacific region, are pushing toward larger configurations than the nation state. Joint economic ventures that involve businesses crossing national boundaries are becoming increasingly important. When it comes to investment and technology, one analyst wrote, "The key decisions . . . will be made in boardrooms, not cabinet rooms."

Toward a Global Think Tank

More and more of us today recognize the need for a global strategy to deal with change. There are wise thinkers in each of our countries aware that solid planning must mesh a long-run futures perspective with short-run, immediately applicable policy-making. They know that a systems approach is required in order to comprehend the interdependence of different aspects of reality. Disparate policies and seemingly unrelated subject area disciplines and factual data are different facts of reality that must be brought together when policy is formulated.

For example, the now-obvious interrelationship between economic and environmental issues was not understood until recently. Wise thinkers know that the enlightened application of technological change is one of the great needs of the day. They know that decision-makers are becoming overwhelmed by the glut of information, and given the speed of change, the complexity of problems, and the high stakes of failure, political leaders need all the help they can get in formulating wise policies.

It is not by accident, therefore, that "think tanks" have proliferated during the last couple of decades.

The challenge of moving toward the establishment of a global think tank received strong impetus during a non-governmental Summit held in Moscow in January 1990, which brought together 300 Soviets and 200 Americans. One of the task force groups dealt with a Think Tank on Global Perstroika, which I was happy to co-chair along with a Soviet counterpart. The final report advocated the establishment of a Global Think Tank for an Interdependent Sustainable Future. The purpose of this project would be to support globally conscious, ecologically sensitive sustainable efforts within a cooperative transnational framework.

A transnational world order is beginning to emerge that will gradually take on responsibility for certain problems of the global commons through transnational structures and measures.

At the outset, representatives of five countries would be invited to participate: the United States, Soviet Union, China, India, and the United Kingdom. This would be primarily a non-governmental effort, although there could be close relationships to government. The representatives from the five countries would work together in a Council to develop policies for the think tank. There would be an annual meeting, to be held each year in a different Council member's country. Over time, other countries could be invited to join.

Initiatives would be organized for joint projects, including funding proposals to be submitted to foundations in the United States and elsewhere. The first three projects proposed at the Moscow Summit were sponsorship of a retreat to be held in the Soviet Union in Fall 1990, a faculty-student educational exchange program, and preparation of a book on "Global Perestroika" with representatives from the Council's five members contributing articles. It is our hope that this proposal for a global think tank finds favor here.

Each one of us who participates in conferences such as this one in Shanghai knows that it is easy to "talk" about the idea of global community. But it is difficult to "do" anything to make the talk real. A global Think Tank for an Interdependent Sustainable Future could be one modest action to utilize our collective experience and expertise and wisdom to contribute to the creation of a viable global community.

President's Council on Sustainable Development

PUBLIC LINKAGE, DIALOGUE, AND EDUCATION

Task Force Report

President's Council on Sustainable Development

In Abstract Given to Oberlin College Archives, 1997

During the administration of President Bill Clinton, I served on the Education Task Force of the President's Council on Sustainable Development participating in several national meetings, and submitting proposals. The Task Force report included a statement on our efforts in Wisconsin.

In 1983, the United Nations secretary general established a special new entity, The World Commission on Environment and Development. This was chaired by the Prime Minister of Norway, Gro Brundtland. Heavy pressure had been mounting on the UN to address the twin problems of the environment and the growing need for more rapid economic development to reduce the have/have-not gap in much of the world. In 1987, the Commission published its groundbreaking book, *Our Common Future*. This popularized the term "sustainable development." In June 1992, the UN sponsored a global conference held in Rio de Janeiro. Called the Earth Summit, it was attended by most governments and thousands of enthusiasts. A general blueprint was formulated to begin to implement sustainable development; it was called Agenda 21.

In June 1993, President Clinton established by Executive Order the President's Council on Sustainable Development. This Council was a partnership between government and businesses and nongovernmental groups. With 25 members, it was co-chaired by the president of the World Resources Institute and a top executive of the Dow Chemical Company. Six main task forces were formed to advise the president, one being on Public Linkage, Dialogue and Education. Its purpose: to foster dialogue with the public and to develop education activities. The task forces organized many meetings around the country and published their reports in 1997. Clinton extended the life of the Council's Public Linkage

Task Force through 1998. The final document published a paragraph on the work at High Wind and Plymouth Institute:

Plymouth, Wisconsin. The Plymouth Institute, which evolved from a 15-year-old community called High Wind, is a nonprofit consortium of environmental designers/builders, educators, artists, scientists, farmers, futurists, and entrepreneurs whose purpose is to define, demonstrate, and communicate values and practices of sustainable living. The 292 acres includes an organic farm, aquaculture system, solar homes, and a 70 acre ecovillage that is in the design phase. Also, cooperatively with several universities and school districts, it administers a comprehensive education and outreach program to local, national, and international communities. For example, Plymouth Institute/High Wind helped to organize Sustainable Wisconsin, a statewide initiative to build a public agenda for sustainable development. Founder and president of Plymouth Institute, Belden Paulson, believes that developing an environment ". . . where people live in honesty and harmony with one another and nature [allows them to] acknowledge and celebrate the divine interconnectedness of all life, and a commitment to holistic thinking and living."

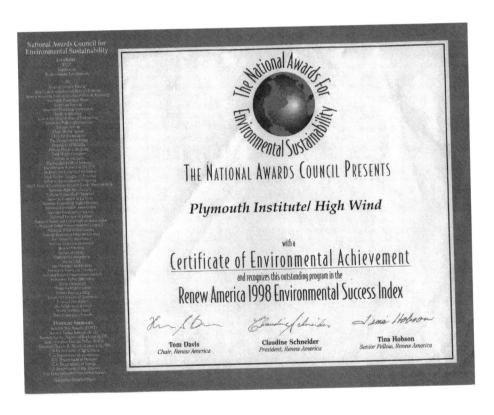

**Ten Suggestions for Development
of a National Sustainable Development Strategic Plan**

1. Encourage each college/university to offer a course/s in Sustainable Development.

2. Encourage each school district to offer an inservice course/s in Sustainable Development.

3. Encourage each state, city and local community to do Sustainable Development projects in their area, involving a multi-sector range of citizens and local leaders.

4. Utilize regional centers, citizen organizations and eco-communities already in place and committed to sustainable development to link together, collaborate and publicize their efforts.

Ten Suggestions for Development of a National Sustainable Development Strategic Plan

In Documents of the Educational Task Force of the President's Council on Sustainable Development, 1995

At one Task Force meeting, I submitted this piece.

Ten Suggestions for Development of a National Sustainable Development Strategic Plan

1. Encourage each college/university to offer a course/s in Sustainable Development.

2. Encourage each school district to offer an in-service course/s on Sustainable Development.

3. Encourage each state, city, and local community to do Sustainable Development projects in their area, involving a multi-sector range of citizens and local leaders.

4. Utilize regional centers, citizen organizations and eco-communities already in place and committed to sustainable development to link together, collaborate, and publicize their efforts.

5. Develop special programs for historically under-represented populations, including inner city, racial/ethnic, lower-income groupings. Keep in mind that these groups may suffer the most from environmental and sustainable deficiencies while knowing the least and having the fewest resources for solutions.

6. Encourage mass media to carry programs and publicize exciting initiatives regarding different facets of sustainable development.

7. Encourage clusters of think tank-type efforts to enlist creative thinkers to deepen comprehension of the meaning of sustainable development in all of its facets—environmental, economic, social, ethical/spiritual, etc.

8. Encourage linkages among local, state, regional, national, and international activities, ultimately to establish a clearinghouse for sustainable development.

9. Collaborate with various professional education organizations to design model, life-long curricula for sustainable development.

10. Explore linkages with counterparts in other countries, given that sustainable development must involve a comprehensive global strategy.

SUSTAINABLE WISCONSIN

Interim Steering Committee

Mayor Beverly Anderson
League of WI Municipalities

Juli Baker
Dept of Ag. Trade and Cons Prot

Lurton Blassingame
UW-Oshkosh

Tom Blewett
UW-Extension

Karen Demmerly
Student, UW-Stevens Point

Ilse Ehlert-Wagner
Waukesha Co Env Action League

April 24, 1995

TO: SUSTAINABLE WISCONSIN PARTICIPANTS
and
THOSE INTERESTED IN A SUSTAINABLE FUTURE
FROM: SUSTAINABLE WISCONSIN INTERIM STEERING COMMITTEE

On behalf of our committee and all who helped bring about the December 2, 1994 Consultation on Sustainable Wisconsin, we are pleased to present the enclosed materials. They reflect the efforts of the Consultation participants and our committee. We hope these materials provide a foundation upon which can be built a long-term initiative, bringing the people of Wisconsin together to plan a sustainable future for our economy and way of life.

A Communication to Sustainable Wisconsin Participants

In Sustainable Wisconsin, *April 1995*

Parallel to the UN and the President's Council initiatives, Wisconsin citizens began organizing sustainability-related action. A broad-based "Coalition for Survival" sponsored a citywide Town Meeting in fall 1991. It mustered hundreds of civic leaders, including elected officials. Several of us subsequently decided to create a statewide initiative. As co-chair with Barbara Markoff, I was impressed at the ease with which we attracted participants from all walks of life. We assembled a representative sample of participants for a Consultation held at Stevens Point, in the center of the state. A sustainable culture was interpreted not only as dealing with environment and economics but to build an all-round "healthy" community.

A statewide initiative has been set in motion to begin to formulate strategies and public policies for sustainable development in Wisconsin. Some 60 people convened at Stevens Point. They agreed to constitute themselves as SUSTAINABLE WISCONSIN and to establish an ongoing Steering Committee to take leadership in implementing an action agenda.

Here is the draft mission statement, as prepared by the Interim Committee:

Sustainable Wisconsin is an organization that represents diverse interests, including urban and rural regions, different cultures, businesses, environment and education.

Its mission is to help citizens of Wisconsin at both the state and local levels to formulate strategies and public policies for a sustainable economy and way of life.

In an opening presentation, our Consultation received a voice of strong support from George Meyer, head of the Wisconsin Department of Natural Resources, and endorsement and encouragement from Rolf Nordstrom of Minnesota's Environmental Quality Board. The draft of Minnesota's Strategic Plan for Sustainable Development, now being reviewed by the governor and legislature, is one of the most mature efforts of its kind in the country.

The assembled delegates at Stevens Point identified long-term trends that have influenced the direction of sustainability globally, in the United States and in Wisconsin. Over the last three decades, it was obvious that initial awareness/awakening have led to action initiatives. These are now culminating increasingly in globalization of the issues. On a huge sheet on the wall delegates made a "mind map" identifying at least a hundred issues to be considered as we construct a vision for Wisconsin's future.

The groups projected the following issues as related directly to Wisconsin:

- Tension between an increased pressure for legislation to protect the environment and pressure to decrease regulation due to denial of the impact of the problems;

- Increased grass roots organizations and citizen input;

- Increased environmental education;

- Unfavorable trends toward economic disparity and violence;

- Cycle of passing legislation but not implementing it.

The mind map helped to identify the most critical issues related to Sustainable Wisconsin. The term *sustainability* was broadened from earlier focus on the physical environment to its interrelationship to broader issues.

Key Issues Included:

a. *Deterioration of the social fabric*
Various subtopics under this heading included: Increasing cost of health care, people of color issues, gang and violence concerns, teen pregnancy, consumerism, economic disparity, violence, a sense of hopelessness about finding solutions, and the need to promote the values of life, family, and community.

b. *Education*
This topic included the need for environmental education, lifestyle changes, sharing of technology, funding, new models of schooling/learning, and in-depth exploration of what sustainable living really means for consumers, producers, and communities.

c. *Agriculture*
Issues associated with agriculture included loss of family farms, deterioration of rural communities, concerns with pesticides, and the need to promote local products.

d. *Natural resources management and biodiversity*
Subtopics included logging practices, industrial forestry, and habitat fragmentation. Environmental quality included water quality, wetland protection, and flood control.

e. *Urban sprawl*

Subtopics included strategic land use planning and transportation issues.

f. *Business and economic growth*

Subtopics included deterioration of urban areas, gaming and casino ventures, technology, environmental and economic incentives.

g. *Spiritual awareness and development*

Subtopics included need for tolerance of religious differences, and importance of spiritual/ethical concerns.

The day concluded with discussion of where Sustainable Wisconsin should go from here. There was a consensus that what had begun should continue and expand.

Time to Rethink How We See the World

COMMENTS ON KEN WILBER'S IDEAS—BELDEN PAULSON

SOME "BIG" QUESTIONS

I find Wilber's material quite mind-boggling as he seeks to construct his unified theory of evolution of consciousness. The questions are virtually endless, each leading to others. Here are a few.

1. Basic question: is there an "inner impulse" in the human condition toward "community" in its ultimate sense? A fundamental principle of holism is that isolated disparate parts unite into ever evolving more coherent and complex wholes. Yet there's an inherent conflict between the rich identity of the individual parts and their movement toward larger wholes, which in turn become new configurations of parts in an ever evolving spiral toward wholeness. Conceptually, a perfect balance of parts, working creatively in communion into wholes, is the essence of community. In the rare moments of our experience at High Wind when everything seemed to work perfectly, the parts/whole relationship truly was community. But historically, humanity seems to move in cycles; at one historical moment the focus is on the "parts" while at other times it's the "whole." (These periods may last for centuries). For example, in the period of ancient empires (e.g. Alexander, Rome), the "whole" dominated, followed by centuries of fragmentation in the "Dark Ages" which in turn was succeeded by the Holy Roman Empire, which sought to unite Christendom in

Comments on Ken Wilber's Ideas

September 1997

Several of us at the university and at Plymouth Institute/High Wind were finding trenchant insights in the writings of philosopher Ken Wilber. His many books were summarized in his *A Brief History of Everything*. A practicing Buddhist, with study in psychology and the physical and the social sciences, and immersed in both Eastern and Western religions, his fundamental exploration was the evolution of consciousness through history. This was evolution viewed not only biologically, but also as spirit in action—in effect, God at work.

We decided to pull together a number of thinking friends and colleagues for a weekend at High Wind to discuss Wilber. There was no agenda, no speakers. We explored three questions: 1) What do you think Wilber is saying? 2) What relevance (if any) does his thinking have for your own spiritual path? 3) What impact (if any) does this offer for your work? Here are some of my notes. See also the items on pages 354 and 357 depicting Wilber's four quadrants and stages of consciousness.

Some "Big" Questions

I find Wilber's material quite mind-boggling as he seeks to construct his unified theory of the evolution of consciousness. The questions are virtually endless, each leading to others. Here are a few:

1. **Basic question: Is there an "inner impulse" in the human condition toward "community" in its ultimate sense?** A fundamental principle of holism is that isolated, disparate parts unite into ever-evolving, more coherent and complex wholes. Yet there is an inherent conflict between the rich identity of the individual parts and their movement toward larger wholes, which in turn become new configurations of parts in an ever-evolving spiral toward wholeness. Conceptually a perfect balance of parts

working creatively in communion into wholes is the sense of community. In the rare moments in our experience at High Wind when everything seemed to work perfectly, the parts/whole relationship truly was community.

But historically, humanity seems to move in cycles; at one historical moment, the focus is on the "parts," while at other times it is the "whole." (These periods may last for centuries.) For example, in the period of ancient empires (e.g. Alexandria, Rome), the "whole" dominated, followed by centuries of fragmentation in the Dark Ages. This in turn was succeeded by the Holy Roman Empire, which sought to unite Christendom in Europe, but chaos again brought perpetual violence. The Thirty Years War, ending in 1648, ushered in the national state, bringing small warring factions into centralized political jurisdictions. Today the national state seems to be in transition: on one hand, there is a push toward some sort of global governance (especially in environmental and trade matters), but maybe more importantly today there is the move toward decentralization, ethnicity, tribalism, and individualism. Wilber argues that there is a process of evolution toward historical cycles of action/reaction.

2. **Basic question: How seriously should we take what is going on in one's mind/consciousness (left quadrant) when there may be little expression in one's behavior (right quadrant)?** Wilber's theory of evolution uses a "stages of development," with use of hierarchy ("holarchy") to identify one's own place in the spectrum of stages. (This could be an individual or a civilization.) If a person or civilization "moves up" the "ladder of consciousness" but is at a "lower level" in terms of behavior, this gets into the issue of theory and practice. (Wilber himself may be an example of this disparity.)

Wilber's framework is a brilliant intellectual construct, but there is little about a "strategy of implementation." In an article in *Shambhala* when he is asked about this, his main recommendation is contemplation/meditation. Many people experience an intellectual paradigm shift toward a more holistic view of the world, but how often does this translate into real commitment on the level of action in terms of how one commits talents, energies, and resources in real life? Likewise, culture/civilizations may appear more "advanced" in certain respects, but their materialism and destructiveness may compare unfavorably with more "primitive" counterparts.

3. **Basic question: How well does Wilber's methodology (which apparently comes out of a rigid daily regime of meditation, study, and writing and has resulted in brilliantly honed conclusions), fit the actual experience of real life?** By way of illustration, several articles in two issues of *Revision* (described as a journal of consciousness and transformation) raise all sorts of interesting criticisms. These "theme issues," devoted exclusively to Wilber's thinking, recognize his very significant contributions. One set of questions concerns how well Wilber has mastered all the fields of knowledge he uses. For the layman, the breadth of his transdisciplinary comprehension is breathtaking, but some specialists challenge his interpretations.

For example, three Western Buddhist scholars who have spent years with Buddhist cultures in Southeast Asia suggest that Buddhism's treatment of spiritual development has a circular and cyclical way of working, not in the linear "stages of growth" approach used by Wilber, which has its origin in European intellectual history (e.g. Hegel et al.). A scholar with long experience with indigenous cultures questions the validity of Wilber's "stages of development" model, which tends to exalt European-centered cultures when some more "primitive" peoples may have much to teach these more "advanced" societies. This touches again the theme of theory and practice. Another critic, with decades of clinical experience in psychedelic research with LSD and other psychoactive substances, questions how much Wilber really knows about transpersonal experience. although this is central to his ideas about the higher stages of spiritual development.

Spiritual Path

1. I find Wilber very useful in bringing together research and theories in a whole range of material to explain the human condition, both historically and for the present and future. After reading Wilber, most other titles seem superficial in contrast. Many of his concepts—such as Kosmos, flatland, holarchy, preconventional/conventional/post-conventional, the four quadrants, postmodernity, and the different fulcrum levels—provide for me an invaluable skeleton with which I can flesh out my own thinking. At the same time, while I am intellectually engrossed, I am not spiritually inspired. Maybe it is because in Wilber's framework the Ultimate Truth, the One Intelligence, the Big Mind, the fullness of the Kosmos is EMPTINESS.

    For me the idea of Emptiness is nebulous. I am drawn to sources like David Spangler, who talks about the energy that truly unites us with God—which represents the divine creative reality within us, and which we can never express because we are always unfolding it. For me, Wilber has some of the same "right quadrant" mental dimension that he discusses so much in his book: drawing the map but not exploring the quality of the mapmaker. I like David's meaning of The Christ (not as a Christian construct but in its fullness comparable to Wilber's Kosmos). He also uses the "sea of oneness," which in degrees we all share. His concept of "energy" (not petroleum) refers to the collective source into which we all tap and contribute to.

2. Having stated the above, I do find refreshing Wilber's forthright focus on hierarchy (holarchy) in his discussion of the evolution of consciousness. The idea of hierarchy has an ominous ring in our egalitarian culture, but it raises interesting issues. I will mention just two:

    a) Wilber recognizes that when a person reaches a higher stage than the "prevailing average" of the surrounding culture, he or she begins to appear a little "weird." One no longer "fits in." Does this lead to an identity crisis? Does it induce people to become "closet mystics"? Does it stimulate "playing games" that humorously touch only on the outer lining of the "real you"? Does it encourage people to narrow friendships to others "on your own wave length"?

    (b) Interrelated with (a), Does this lead to a "we-they" dichotomy, where one becomes judgmental, which can lead to alienation and conflict? Recently when those of us at Plymouth Institute designed a model for an ecological village that attempted to embrace values of a "post-conventional world," we were, in effect, shot down by the surrounding culture. In this context, does one retreat into a period of contemplation (seemingly Wilber's preference)? Do we seek to change others through education and/or political actions? Or do we simply recognize that the evolutionary process is slow and accept the price of inaction whatever the consequences? Probably all of the above.

Relevant questions as we explore our spiritual path.

The Work

1. As I reread Wilber, I pondered how far we could move in our public learning systems—i.e., public schools, universities—to explore the nature of consciousness as a basis for cultural transformation. To be on the cutting edge in discussing educational reform today, one focuses on "systemic change" and all the variables describing why learning does or doesn't take place. In Wilber's framework, most of this is right quadrant. Our learning systems seek to be value-free, heavy on science and technology and mapping "objective reality." Most of this effort is still "flatland."

   Some of our activity enters Wilber's Fulcrum five level, where learners critically examine existing conventions and begin to project possible alternative models and move from "sociocentric" to "worldcentric." However, if a major need facing our society and world is moral development—moving toward higher levels of spiritual development—is this an appropriate arena for public education, or does this get into domains outside of public systems (or are we getting into arenas of the Christian Right)?

2. I am working with a small planning group to design a model for a Global Learning Center. We are being urged by the Milwaukee Public Schools superintendent to "be radical, break out of the confines of existing rules and regulations to create something really new that works." The basic idea is to prepare a group of learners (100 to 200 students) to become world citizens. They would be able to function in the global marketplace, would contribute to building a sustainable world, and would combine technical and academic skills with personal and moral aptitudes to fulfill their own talents and contribute to the larger good.

   Wilber's books further convinced me that this learning experience should have a strong value orientation. As he pointed out in an article in *Yoga*, transformational change usually takes place on the "mental level, toward new systems," but global thinking and action in itself does not necessarily have anything to do with spiritual qualities. We face the intriguing question: What curriculum is needed to integrate the "left side" and "right side" quadrants for this Global Learning Center, and what kind of teachers are required to operate this learning enterprise?

   A note on succinct meanings of Wilber's terminology:
   - **Holarchy:** a pattern that unites separate and conflicting and isolated parts into a coherent unity or whole;

- **Kosmos:** the ultimate whole of reality, the entire universe of everything, physical and nonphysical;

- **Quadrants:** the interior and the exterior orientation of the individual and the collective. Every person or group falls in four parts or quadrants of developmental evolution. The two right-hand quadrants deal with the material objective world and are accessed through empirical observation. The two left-hand quadrants are subjective and deal with values and inner worlds—accessed through introspection and interpretation. The upper quadrants deal with individual realities, behavioral on the right hand, intentional (or how one thinks about something) on the left hand. The lower two quadrants deal with collective realities: social systems on the right hand, cultural or community systems on the left hand;

- **Fulcrums:** steps or stages in the ladder of evolution toward increased wholeness ;

- **Flatland:** state of a society that does not include the transpersonal or spiritual dimension;

- **Modernity**: descriptive of the rational, industrial, material world;

- **Post-modern**: transcends the material world, rejects that science can explain all realit;y

- **Pre-conventional**: human development before being socialized into any moral system;

- **Conventional**: when people learn and follow the values of mainstream society;

- **Post-conventional:** when people develop the capacity to reflect on and criticize the conventional.

THE TEN STAGES OF WILBER's EVOLUTION OF CONSCIOUSNESS

1. NEW BORN; sensation, perception

2. EMOTIONAL SELF; beginning of capacity to think , 1-3 years old

3. CONCEPTUAL SELF; begin to use symbols, concepts, language, 3-6 years

4 ROLE SELF; begin to understand rule-based tasks, socially accepted behavior, my ego not only one in universe, join group, nation, adopt conventions, begin around 6-7 years into adolescence, up to 14 years old. Most people never get beyond this mainstream culture level.

The Ten Stages of Wilber's Evolution of Consciousness

1997

Some of us have attempted to simplify and condense Wilber's ideas for practical use in our work and teaching. This meant summarizing fairly complex formulations conceptualized in his massive *Sex, Ecology and Spirituality* and other books, such as *A Brief History of Everything*.

These summaries include the following "Ten Stages" of development an individual might cycle through:

1. **New Born:** has sensations, perceptions

2. **Emotional Self:** beginning of capacity to think; one to three years old

3. **Conceptual Self:** begins to use symbols, concepts, language; three to six years

4. **Role Self:** begins to understand rule-based tasks, socially-accepted behavior; my ego not the only one in universe, joins group, nation, adopts conventions; begins around six or seven years into adolescence, up to14 years old. Most people never get beyond this mainstream culture level.

5. **Worldcentric Self, Mature Ego:** capacity for global awareness emerges, imagines different possible worlds, ability to criticize conventional culture; 11 to 15 years.

6. **Integrated Thinking:** Ability to integrate and synthesize mind-body, integrate all four quadrants—inner and exterior—awareness of interconnections also between human and natural worlds. This is rare and difficult to achieve, and few do. From this level, a person moves into higher levels of consciousness, the transpersonal.

7. **Psychic, Transpersonal**

8. **Subtle, Inner Light** (Levels 7-8 refer to Soul Development)

9. **Pure Spirit, Beyond Self** (levels 9-10 refer to Spirit)

10. **Non-Duality, "Isness"**

Every society has a certain *center of gravity*, we might say, around which the culture's ethics, norms, rules, and basic institutions are organized, and this center of gravity provides the basic cultural cohesion and social integration for that society

This cultural center of gravity acts like a magnet on individual development. If you are below the average level, it tends to pull you up. If you try to go above it, it tends to pull you down. The cultural center of gravity acts as a pacer of development—a magnet—pulling you up to the average expectable level of consciousness development. Beyond that, you're on your own, and lots of luck, because now the magnet will try to drag you down—in both cases, you're "outlawed."

from Wilbur's A Brief History of Everything

Building a Sustainable World: The Four Quadrants

In Wilber's discussion of a new world view, a change of consciousness and a change in institutions, he focuses on "the four quadrants." These are like maps of reality. They transcend all cultures: Eastern and Western, pre-modern and modern and post-modern, all religions and political ideologies. They look at the reality of individuals and society on their inner interior side and on the outer exterior side. More specifically as we examine the chart, on the right hand of the chart, we're dealing with empirically observed behavioral realities, while on the left side, we're focused on interior realities/experiences. The upper right and left quadrants focus on individuals, and the lower right and left quadrants focus on collective/societal realities.

Lisa and I have attempted to format Wilber's more complex maps in simple everyday terms with this diagram.

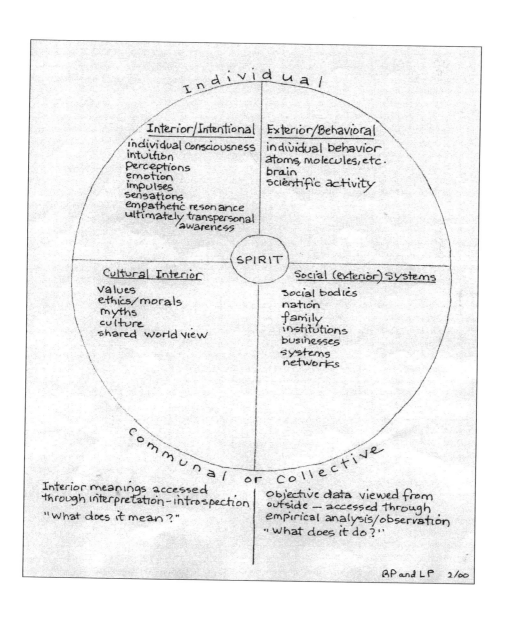

Individual

Interior/Intentional

individual consciousness
intuition
perceptions
emotion
impulses
sensations
empathetic resonance
ultimately transpersonal
awareness

Exterior/Behavioral

individual behavior
atoms, molecules, etc.
brain
scientific activity

SPIRIT

Cultural Interior

values
ethics/morals
myths
culture
shared world view

Social (exterior) Systems

social bodies
nation
family
institutions
businesses
systems
networks

Communal or Collective

Interior meanings accessed
through interpretation-introspection

"what does it mean?"

objective data viewed from
outside — accessed through
empirical analysis/observation

"what does it do?"

BP and LP 2/00

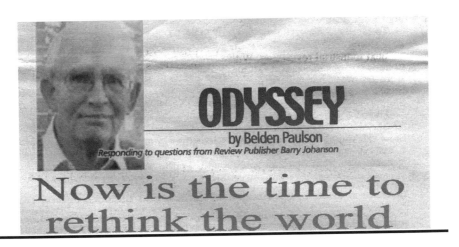

ODYSSEY
by Belden Paulson
Responding to questions from Review Publisher Barry Johanson

Now is the time to
rethink the world

Now Is the Time to Rethink the World

In The Review, *Plymouth, Wisconsin, September 25, 2012*

Is it possible to design a policy that attacks the federal deficit, provides jobs, and also confronts climate change and depletion of resources—all in one policy? Since they are interrelated, why not?

Tough issues. Seems we're all stuck in a kind of cultural vacuum. Our government is somewhat paralyzed, more or less incapable of making big decisions to solve problems. And not only government—it's all of us. Creating such a policy is a big job. It requires vision, and to mobilize the wisdom and will to make tough decisions dealing with complex realities. However, in the past when our country and each of us individually had to confront problems that momentarily seemed beyond us, we found solutions. Sometimes along with our own experience and intelligence, we also needed a dose of Factor X—the energy we harness from other dimensions, often referred to as Spirit.

Also, in addressing big problems such as the huge deficit, chronic joblessness, and ominous environmental concerns, we're probably not going to solve them separately one by one but need to attack them as a whole.

People of all stripes hunger for a vision of the future that goes beyond waffling and gridlock. They truly want to see an America that is sustainable. There is a fundamental urge to regain our "can do" spirit—our survival as a viable country and world leader is on the line. There are still partisans who believe that only they have the truth—there is no give and take. But most Americans know better.

All sides agree that we must drastically cut the deficit.

All sides emphatically agree that we must deal with joblessness.

Most of us, if not all, see the glaciers melting, temperatures rising, some resources running out. The perils of climate change and limited resources have to be confronted.

Where to begin? We need to think short run and long run. On the immediate scene, there's one policy that our political leaders of both parties are talking about: the Simpson-Bowles deficit blueprint.

We recall that in early 2011, the president established a bipartisan, 18-member debt panel co-chaired by ex-Republican senator Alan Simpson and former Democratic leader Erskine Bowles. Their final report in December 2011 promised to reduce $4 trillion of the deficit by 2020, and to cut popular programs of domestic spending and the military. It would also raise revenue by ending the Bush tax cuts for the wealthy, and other revenue measures including, possibly, a tax on carbon emissions. Other groups have refined the recommendations to win broad support. While there are critics everywhere, this is the closest we've come to "doable action."

This would be a terrific start, but why stop there? Let's use the momentum TO RETHINK HOW WE SEE THE WORLD—a big-picture, longer-run strategy to build a sustainable America. That means fulfilling today's needs without compromising the needs of future generations. We need a culture of sustainability, finding technologies that use fewer resources per unit of production. We need vehicles that deliver far more miles per gallon. We need to stimulate innovations in clean, emission-free power sources. Were we to put a price on carbon, businesses, in a massive way, would jump into risk-taking and new investments. We need not just to improve appliances and change light bulbs but begin to think in systems, for example, to design smart, sustainable cities—with energy-efficient buildings and factories, better use of infrastructure, land use with greenbelts and bike lanes and space for micro-wind turbines. Instead of subsidizing oil and coal, we need to inspire efficient clean technologies.

> We need a culture of sustainability, finding technologies that use fewer resources per unit of production.

A business colleague told me that a big bank with branches around the country was exploring ways to make every building energy efficient. Think of the savings possible for heat and air conditioning, the new kinds of jobs needed, not to mention eco-benefits.

Instead of Washington being a case study in dysfunction, it could become a launching pad for the next industrial revolution. With new designs promoting production efficiency, huge expenditures could be reduced across the board, with significant contributions to deficit reduction. Instead of a leadership vacuum in Wall Street focused on narrow thinking and greed, a new business culture of innovation would take over. The momentum that in recent years migrated to Europe and China would return home. This in turn would lead to a whole new arena of jobs. We know that in the old economy it was becoming evident that automation and globalization made it possible for America to produce all the goods and services required without its full labor force. Now an entirely different generation of jobs will be needed for an increasingly green environment.

As we begin to think what the sustainable culture would look like, we'll need to raise the existing low average conservation IQ. Obviously we're not just dealing with physical and economic and political problems; this will involve a shift in perception. We will face a great learning challenge, to which our educational institutions have hardly begun to respond. There are immense opportunities for R&D, and innovation in curriculum and teacher training. As we re-examine our lifestyle and everyday habits to reduce waste, control excess consumption, and choose eco-friendly products, think of the exciting challenges for the media and the arts as we cultivate new tastes and peer-group fashions.

> Obviously we're not just dealing with physical and economic and political problems; this will involve a shift in perception. We will face a great learning challenge, to which our educational institutions have hardly begun to respond.

There is the expectation that our corporate, capitalistic system would change. Currently it is based on short-term profit, concentrating wealth that maintains huge income disparities, with minimum loyalty to workers, or even the national welfare, or protecting the environment. The sustainability strategy can shift toward a more middle class-oriented capitalism. While the importance of profit and entrepreneurial innovation would remain, this model would respect the needs of workers who, after all, comprise most of the population. In America's earlier postwar years, the middle class was able to own a modest home, pay for health care and college, and retire with a manageable stipend. A sustainable economy would search for strategies that narrow the income gap and revitalize the middle class.

In conclusion, a sustainable America would significantly confront the deficit, joblessness, and ecological perils—worthy goals for 21st century America.

Joblessness: A Creative Response to One of America's Great, Long-term Challenges

Presented at World Future Society local chapter, May 15, 2013, published soon after in The Review.

As we evolve a more holistic transformative strategy, one of the big tests will be to explore solutions for joblessness that may require fundamental changes, in contrast to just dealing with the results of the latest recession. In 1983, when our university department organized a national conference on the future of work, the American and world economies had already experienced many "ups and downs." But over the years, decision-making brought back "normal" times. Even in 1983, the best thinking envisaged that some very big changes had to be considered. I explored this issue at the spring meeting of the World Future Society's Milwaukee chapter. The talk was published in the May 2013 edition of *The Review* in Plymouth, Wisconsin.

Our economy can now produce all the goods and services our society needs without its total labor force. Modern technology has brought untold benefits in improving our level of living and reducing much of the most arduous tedium of work. But as our country's wealth dramatically increases while the number of workers needed to make that wealth significantly decreases, three central questions arise:

- With a sizable percentage of the population without a full-time job to support themselves and a family, how will they cover the basic necessities of life?

- With increased numbers of people jobless, what will they do with their free time? Will they have the opportunity to utilize their talents?

- If the people who invest the capital (the stockholders) and those who are still employed (workers and executives) take all or most of the wealth they produce, how will this accentuate the already rising economic inequality in America? For example, the top 1 percent have more wealth than the bottom 90 percent.

Keep in mind these background details:

- According to recent US Bureau of Labor statistics (as of August 2012), 12.5 million people are unemployed; 2.6 million are the "forgotten unemployed" (unemployed for a year or more, some having given up any expectation of finding work); 8 million are under-employed (working part time). Total: 23.1 million. To be noted, among people ages 25-34, 26.6 percent are non-employed, the highest percentage in the industrial world.

- For companies to stay in business and compete globally, they must continually seek to increase their efficiency, adding automation devices that maximize productivity but require fewer workers.

- With technologies using computers and robots expected increasingly to take over the economy, we anticipate their use in many sectors. According to a recent issue of the *Future Policy Journal,* these sectors include: manufacturing (e.g. 3-D printers); health care (e.g., recent *Atlantic* issue on robots asking: Is your doctor becoming obsolete?); maintenance and domestic work (e.g., janitors, cleaners); professors (e.g., online courses); teachers (e.g., laptop computers); librarians (e.g., online book ordering); travel/rental car agencies (e.g., kiosks and online booking). The impact of these examples: more efficiency, fewer workers. This means that laptop computers, with some supervising teachers or technical assistants, can greatly reduce the need for classroom teachers. In some places I understand this is already happening and kids may actually learn better because they can progress at their own speed.

- Eminent social thinker Jeremy Rifkin in *The End of Work* concludes that this is only the beginning: World War II ended the 1930s depression and provided jobs; in the 1950s, the National Defense Highway Act, and in the 1960s, the Great Society poverty war provided jobs. For 40 postwar years, as people moved from manufacturing into services, new jobs opened up. Computers and robots are now ushering in a new and different era. Norbert Weiner, father of cybernetics, predicted that the long-term consequences of automation technology will bring "the greatest unemployment we've ever seen." Management consultant Peter Drucker foresaw capitalism facing an unprecedented new issue: the looming disappearance of labor as a factor of production. Rifkin poses this question: Will the ever-mounting profits of expanding wealth be used for societal benefit, or for enriching the corporate world and thereby increasing the have/have-not gap?

Not to be overlooked is the impact of this new technology on the black population that migrated to northern cities after World War II. They filled unskilled and semi-skilled jobs, but automation has wiped out many of their jobs. Respected sociologist Julius Wilson argues in *When Work Disappears* that the key factor in today's inner city pathology has been joblessness. Conservative writer Charles Murray observes in his *Coming Apart*: "Our nation is coming apart at the seams—not ethnic seams but the seams of class."

In 1983, we organized through the University of Wisconsin a national conference on "The Changing Role of Work." We assembled key leaders and thoughtful thinkers representing the best experience available—from business, unions, government, academia—to address the future of work, at that time with a less ominous future than today. Our two key-noters included path-breaking futurist Willis Harman. His seminal article in *The Futurist*, titled "The Coming Transformation," concluded that modern industrial society, using the kind of data described above about joblessness, is facing fundamental challenges that will require nothing short of historic transformative shifts.

The second keynoter was Richard Goodyear, vice president and legal counsel at Chrysler; the company had just received a government bailout to prevent bankruptcy. The company's CEO, Lee Iacocca, told us that we should invite Goodyear because he was responsible for the company's successful strategy. After the two talks, Goodyear whispered in my ear that Harman's transformation thesis was correct, but he'd never say it publicly.

We designed that conference around two tracks. Track One focused on the best ideas and practices for "what can be done here and now," assuming there is enlightened leadership that will focus on implementation. Track Two recognized that even the best of Track One will not be adequate. The long-run crisis of joblessness is more fundamental. It is related to dilemmas facing the industrial system itself, and some sort of transformation as proposed by Harman is required. This conference was 30 years ago. The challenges we face today are more stark and real.

> We designed that conference around two tracks. Track One focused on the best ideas and practices for "what can be done here and now," assuming there is enlightened leadership that will focus on implementation. Track Two recognized that even the best of Track One will not be adequate. The long-run crisis of joblessness is more fundamental. It is related to dilemmas facing the industrial system itself, and some sort of transformation as proposed by Harman is required.

Keeping in mind the data we know about joblessness, let us envisage examples of Track One and Track Two strategies to confront today's likely trends using ideas from Rivkin, Harman, Murray, and others.

A general Track One starting point is the need for an in-depth, bipartisan, national strategy that takes into account the short run and long run. The business community usually adds the great importance of reduced regulations and lower taxes to strengthen the economy and create jobs, although others note that much higher taxes in the postwar and Clinton years did not threaten near full employment.

Noteworthy **Track One ideas** include (in no particular order of importance):

- Critical importance of education and training; the unemployment rate of people age 25 and older with graduate and professional degrees is less than 4 percent, with BA degree less than 5 percent.
- More effort is needed to develop skills to match available jobs (there are 3 million unfilled jobs).
- Bring back jobs from overseas (tax policy is important).
- Create incentives for hiring different categories of the non-employed.
- Make investments in infrastructure-related jobs—also Depression-era WPA-type jobs.
- Reduce high corporate compensation to provide money for more hiring and experimentation for new strategies.
- Institute the 30-hour workweek and job sharing (used some places in Europe).
- Make a massive revitalization effort in inner cities and depressed rural areas to upgrade skills and cultural level.

The Track Two starting point recognizes that measures such as the above are valuable but insufficient. For example, Harman in his "Coming Transformation" article writes: "The United States and other industrial nations now face a series of dilemmas that may be insoluble except by a sweeping transformation of their societies." These are: the *growth dilemma* ("We need continued economic growth but we cannot live with the consequences."), the *control dilemma* ("We need to guide technological innovation but we shun centralized control."), the *distribution dilemma* ("The industrialized nations find it costly to share the earth's resources with less developed nations, but a failure to do so might prove even more costly."), and the *work-roles dilemma* ("Industrial society is increasingly unable to supply an adequate number of meaningful social roles.")

Noteworthy **Track Two ideas** and practices include:

- Guaranteed annual income as a matter of right to a minimal share in the production of society (no means test required). Proposed by economists Theobald and Heilbroner, and J. Robert Oppenheimer among others, but no action taken.

- Milton Friedman's "negative income tax." This is the same idea of guaranteed income. He unsuccessfully proposed this to presidents Nixon and Reagan, given that he preferred a direct cash payment instead of bureaucratic welfare for the poor.

- "Third sector support" that utilizes more fully the voluntary world. Rifkin proposes incentives and subsidies, including "social wages" and tax write-offs for voluntary work to utilize the vast pool of labor and talent for meeting community needs. Viewing a future where the market sector leaves vast joblessness, he asks: Will government use its resources "to finance additional police protection and build more jails to incarcerate a growing criminal class or finance alternative forms of work in the third sector?"

- Support for "learning and development." Harman in *Creative Work,* notes that when production and consumption are no longer the main focus of one's life, then the "learning society," which includes self and community improvement, takes on added importance.

- Business itself becomes an agent of transformation. Harman is convinced that people in business, not in government, are society's real drivers. He identified numerous business leaders to establish the World Business Academy to invest their creative energy in helping to move toward a viable future.

- An example of transformation in business that combines the corporate and social worlds is the Mondragon complex in Spain. Established in the 1950s, there are 102 cooperatives employing over 100,000 people; it is the seventh largest business in Spain, with annual revenue in the 6 billion euro range. Each cooperative donates 10 percent of its yearly profits to education and social projects, and 10 percent to a social entrepreneur pool for R&D. The highest paid workers earn no more than eight times the lowest paid workers, and despite the 20 percent unemployment and 50 percent among youth in Spain, Mondragon has no unemployment. This has happened through intelligent planning and voluntary reduction in work hours.

- Development of a sustainability policy that confronts the federal deficit, creates jobs, and focuses on ominous environmental perils. Two years ago, President Barack Obama established an 18-member bipartisan commission to figure out how to cut the deficit. Their recommendations included deficit reduction of 4 trillion dollars by 2020 and numerous other ideas to cut spending and raise revenue. The Obama administration has not acted on this. Today a comprehensive environment-sensitive sustainability strategy is feasible. It would create new industries to increase energy efficiency in America's buildings and manufacturing and would provide a massive array of new jobs. At the same time, costs incurred by government could be cut dramatically.

- Imaginative long-term thinking on our economic and cultural future is also needed. An example is found in Charles Eisenstein's *Sacred Economics,* where the role of money itself is considered. The theme here is that money seems to be destroying the efficacy of many of our human social systems and the Earth itself. The original purpose of money was to connect human gifts with human needs. Financiers have become masters of the universe, and new kinds of money are needed where gratitude and trust rather than money are what motivate peoples' actions.

Toward Learning to Build a Sustainable World

From symposium on "Energy, The Environment, and Sustainable Living," Oberlin College, May 28, 2000

In the life of the High Wind community, as well as in my latter university years and with other civic ventures, the four-quadrant context of problem-solving became for me more and more important. I framed my talk this way in a symposium at Oberlin College.

There is more and more evidence that we are using up the natural capital that sustains us. Hawkens and Lovins/Lovins conclude in their cutting-edge book *Natural Capitalism*: as human population moves toward doubling and the resources available per person drop by at least one-half to three-quarters, we must begin to design a new kind of industrial revolution. Most of this natural and living capital is not factored into the cost of production that has powered the tremendous growth that brought us the standard of living we enjoy today.

Obviously this is a physical and economic and political problem, but above all it involves a shift in perception. I am convinced that a change of consciousness will be the key factor in providing the basis for crossing the threshold of transformation toward a sustainable world. This shift in consciousness can be viewed from four vantage points that are all interrelated as one whole.

The first is SPIRITUAL, awakening and renewing our inner life, wrestling with our own spiritual connections. In essence, we are dealing with values, our deepest promptings, and motivations—a fundamental wisdom that will lead us to refashion our lives as ecological beings.

The second dimension is INTELLECTUAL, attaining the knowledge needed to build a sustainable world, which, in effect, is a paradigm shift leading to restructuring our institutions and living patterns. In turn, this will move us to reliance on renewable energy, sensitive land use, ecologically efficient transportation, population stabilization, and a conservation/recycling economy.

The third dimension is TECHNOLOGICAL, translating what we know into hands-on models of sustainable living. Such essentials as how we construct our buildings, how we produce our food and what we eat, how we dispose of waste, how we structure the systems of governance that regulate our lives—all honor an understanding of the interconnectedness and interdependence of all life.

The fourth dimension is COMMUNITY BUILDING, nurturing a sustainable culture that would include such values as cooperation, compassion, mutual empowerment, and long-term perspective, creating livable local communities within a global context.

What have we learned from our multiple experiences? Here is a sampling of thoughts:

- Most people today in America appear to be concerned about the environment. This is affirmed by public opinion polls. But when they come to realize that sustainable living is really a radical idea, which will probably mean upsetting the status quo and challenging some aspects of our mainstream culture, and that on a personal level it could mean significant changes in lifestyle, this interest may turn out to be mainly rhetorical. The key starting point is learning. The more one learns, the more one realizes that building a sustainable culture is not just for somebody else but is directly tied into one's own self-interest and the kind of world we will bequeath to our children and grandchildren.

> When they come to realize that sustainable living is really a radical idea, which will probably mean upsetting the status quo and challenging some aspects of our mainstream culture, and that on a personal level it could mean significant changes in lifestyle, this interest may turn out to be mainly rhetorical.

- Sustainability is a complex concept. The key is to find access points that are meaningful. For some people, the starting point is through direct observation. It is amazing how many people get turned on simply by experiencing our own solar home at High Wind, or by visiting the farm here where wonderful food is produced without chemicals. They start asking questions. For others, the access point is academic: reading and taking seminars and workshops. It is discussing the meaning of seminal ideas such as paradigm shifts and whole-systems thinking and the implications of these concepts for understanding sustainability. For others, it is an "inner knowing," an intuition pushing them "to do something," yet they are at a loss as to where to begin. All of these can be useful points of entry.

- Many people today are searching for "community." They want the satisfaction of belonging to something larger than themselves and to be with others who share the same values. But real community, even with its many benefits, has a price. One must be willing to give up some of the freedom of individual pursuits. It means sacrificing some privacy in order to serve the needs of the collective group—the larger whole. The experience of living in a fairly tight, small, working community, even for a relatively short time, is intense, and it is excellent preparation for sensing the meaning of creating a global sustainable community. It also magnifies areas of personal growth that are needed. It speeds up the journey to higher consciousness.

> Few political leaders seem willing to stick their necks out. One congressman friend of High Wind said he would like to support everything we stand for, but without a broad constituency behind him, he would be crucified politically.

- Public policies in a democratic society are unlikely to change until a broad constituency is created. Astute observers recognize that the 1990s were bullish economically but were a disaster ecologically. Most of the trends describing the health of the planet are negative. Few political leaders seem willing to stick their necks out. One congressman friend of High Wind said he would like to support everything we stand for, but without a broad constituency behind him, he would be crucified politically. The central challenge remains the same: to design a strategy for sustainability that launches a broad learning enterprise. As much as anything, this is what is needed in our political leadership.

Steps to Build a Sustainable Community and World

The first step is to see the world in a new way, and to commit to a paradigm shift. This is sensitivity to a sustainable culture based in whole system values—a new consciousness. This is likely to inspire acceptance of risk and willingness to take the consequences of that risk to challenge the status quo toward transformative efforts. The next logical steps are to develop concrete plans that translate values into policies, and then "just do it."

PARADIGM SHIFT
Shift values and practices toward a worldview that can fulfill today's needs without compromising the needs of future generations.

NEW CONSCIOUSNESS
Awaken and renew our inner life to nurture a culture with such values as compassion, cooperation, mutual empowerment, long-term perspective.

TRANSFORMATION
Fundamentally change institutions and lifestyles to protect and preserve natural capital while advancing the quality of life.

ENLIGHTENED ACTION
Design and implement a four-quadrant strategy that contributes to building sustainable community and world.

Sustainability: Postscript

Those of us familiar with Arnold Toynbee's classic *Study of History*, which details the collapse of ancient civilizations, are aware that inner decay as well as external pressure can be decisive. Although we cannot put our finger precisely on the fundamental cause(s) of the cluster of problems before us today, in our more intuitive moments, we sense that the boundaries of "business as usual" are obsolete. We need a new mindset to deal with escalating challenges. We need to take risks and prepare ourselves to give up certain amenities and habits. While we are convinced there are better solutions to some problems than what is out there, generally we are not yet prepared to consider paying the required price. Even though we may see no readily acceptable answers, some of us feel compelled to utilize whatever experience and creative energy we can muster to plunge in.

This is especially true when we're moving away from the "here-and-now," easier solutions to envisage fundamental shifts. It is these fundamental shifts that really could make a difference—that address "what *could be.*" This requires more exploration into the unknown, going beyond what we know and our existing comfort zones. If we're really seeking alternatives, we must rethink the world, develop new models, blast out of mainstream conventions. This will probably mean profound personal transformation along with challenging the vested interests and powers-that-be that are normally dedicated to preserving "what is." We recognize the huge inertias locked into the status quo, both in our personal lives and in prevailing institutional structures.

Recently I read a trenchant private report on an in-depth discussion held in 1985. It involved eight top administrators of major universities looking back on their struggles in the late sixties and early seventies, when their campuses erupted. There seemed to be three triggers for the campus turmoil: the Vietnam war and the draft, the emerging Civil Rights issue represented by black anger, and the seeming inability of the university (and societal institutions generally) to respond to the obsolescence of much of the surrounding culture. With surprising candor, the administrators concluded, "We were in over our heads." They admitted that too often they could not find creative ways to cope.

Is this part of the challenge we face today in attempting to build a sustainable world? Are we in over our heads?

We are definitely turned off by the *sustainababble* that Robert Engleman, president of the Worldwatch Institute, talks about in the Institute's new book *Is Sustainability Still Possible?* As he puts it, this "cacophonous profusion of uses of the word *sustainable* means anything from environmentally better to cool." So diminished is its value that we are lulled into "dreamy belief that all of us—and everything we do, everything we buy, everything we use—are now able to go on forever. . . ."

Scott Wicker, chief sustainability officer for the company UPS, talks about the business value of sustainability. UPS notes that "more than nine in ten business executives believe sustainability is of significant importance for their business." The statement says that "a sustainable supply chain minimizes business disruption and provides improved access to capital, which helps reduce risk." While the business world obviously has a very important contribution to make, caution is needed so that "sustainability" is not seen mainly as a strategy to sustain current practices.

The 1987 book *Our Common Future*, which came out of the UN study to deal with the two great global crises—environment and poverty—popularized the sustainability theme: to fulfill today's needs without compromising the needs of future generations. However, in emphasizing the importance of economic development for the poor by dramatically increasing production and consumption, the environment will then be open to exponential escalating threats.

In the university in the 1980s and early 1990s, I served on several commissions appointed by the top leadership to rethink its role of higher education in the future. These meetings brought together administrators and faculty and astute citizens from around Wisconsin and elsewhere. Although there were provocative task force reports focused on sustainability stimulated by two noted futurist keynoters, Mike Marien and Hazel Henderson, I'm not aware of significant results. Higher education recognizes intellectually that we live in a radically changing world, but this does not yet seem to apply to the institution itself. Now is the time for the institution to transform itself.

It would seem that the overwhelming challenge we face in making the next big leap toward building a sustainable world is the same kind of challenge that columnist Tom Friedman described in a recent *New York Times* piece dealing with American policy in the Arab world. He said that in Cold War days, American foreign policy focused on the exterior behavior of states. We overlooked their internal behavior because we needed them as allies. But today's policy now is linked much more to interior dimensions: governance and how people get along. In Cold War days, the tools, he wrote, were "guns, money and rhetoric." Today the need is to help facilitate internal change, so the people themselves have the will and capacity to take charge of their affairs to bring about peace and prosperity. While we can help, essentially it's up to them. He noted our limited capacity to direct change in places like Iraq, Libya, and Egypt.

Observe the parallel with our efforts today to change our unsustainable world into a sustainable one. This process depends in part on rigorous data on climate change and the interactions between the human and natural worlds, as being prepared by UN and think tank studies. We also need the technological advances in renewal energy and increasing energy efficiencies. These are valuable exterior tools. But like the foreign policy challenges, the critical priority least dealt with is the human dimension. Do we, the people, really want to move from a high-consumption culture into a lifestyle that uses less resources?

Are we ready to switch to smaller homes and cars, more pooling and sharing of tools and equipment, eating more locally grown food, restricting air travel, in general feeling satisfied with fewer things and less material stuff? Will business accept less growth that may mean lower compensation for staff and less profit for executives and shareholders? Are they willing to invest more to conserve resources and improve efficiency, and reorganize accounting practices for the real-world costs of natural resources and handling of waste and pollution? Will government be open to drastic reductions in expenses across the board, improved efficiency in policymaking, elimination of subsidies and pork?

One intriguing model as we project a more sustainable society is the four-quadrant strategy outlined by philosopher Ken Wilber and detailed earlier in this book. Wilber's approach gives full recognition to the importance of knowledge and technology, the central element in most mainstream treatments of sustainability. But it gives equal prominence to renewing our inner life and cultivating the values of individual and group consciousness, which can prepare us for refashioning our lives toward becoming ecological beings. Further, this model emphasizes the nurturing of a sustainable culture where we see ourselves not as self-serving individuals but as part of larger wholes—our local communities and the larger world.

During the years we offered seminars on sustainable futures, we always incorporated a student visit to the High Wind community. This was the highlight of the course for most participants because it represented a real-world strategy. The visit included a heavy dose of practical information with examples of technology about solar houses and the organic farm, but also a vibrant discussion of life in the community as detailed in Part III of this book.

The students learned that the future will require individual transformation and development of a conscious society—along with a clear understanding and acceptance of the impending crisis coming on rapidly in the areas of climate, depletion of resources, energy, inequality, joblessness.

The great challenge before us is to truly take to heart the principles expressed in the High Wind credo: To walk gently on the earth, To know the spirit within, To hear our fellow beings, To invoke the light of wisdom, and To build the future now.

References

This book is not an academic treatise. As the title indicates, it is *Notes from the Field*. Much of the material comes from project data, reports, and papers presented at professional meetings, notes related to courses, documents that may be used for policy-making. For people carrying out their work "in the field," description of what they are doing is found in these kinds of materials, although now and then books may also be published. I am the author of almost all of the items cited. A few of the major publications in which they appear are listed here:

"Citizens of No Country," *University of Chicago Magazine*, Feb. 1960.

"Development of Refugee Attitudes, Experiences of the Sardinia Project," *Research Group for European Migration Problems*, July/Sept. 1959.

"Genazzano: Little Moscow in South Italy," *Oberlin Alumni Magazine*, Jan. 1963.

"Revisiting Italy's Little Moscow," *World Politics Journal*, Fall 2001.

"The Obsolescent Village Reborn," *In Context*, Spring 1983.

"Difficulties and prospects for Community Development in Northeast Brazil," *Inter-American Economic Affairs*, Spring 1964.

Local Political Patterns in Northeast Brazil, A Community Case Study, Land Tenure Center, UW-Madison, 1964.

"Buddhist Asks: 'Not Peace Solution But Peace," *Milwaukee Journal*, April 1, 1971.

"Research, Training, and Action in Milwaukee's Inner Core: A Case Study about Process," *Adult Leadership*, April 1967.

"University Urban Extension in Milwaukee," *UWM Magazine*, Summer 1970.

A Reporting and Planning Model for Urban Community Development, UW-Extension,1976.

Olesen, Don, "Block Power," *Milwaukee Journal*, June 19, 1977.

"The Role of Citizen Elites in Effecting More Responsive Bureaucracies," *Urban Community Development Case Studies in Neighborhood Survival*, Community Development *Society*. Summer 1978.

"Status of Extension's Urban Programming," Special Urban Issue, *Journal of Extension*, Spring 1973.

Conroy, Bill, "A Revolution of Consciousness," *Crazy Shepherd*, Sept. 1985.

Davidson, Margaret, "Simply Solar," *Harrowsmith Country Life*, April 1995.

"Ecological Development—A vision that could become reality," *Sheboygan Press*, March 12, 2000.

"Community Dilemmas," *Communities*, Summer 1985.

"HighWind: A Retrospective," *Communities*, Winter 2009.

"Toward Global Sustainable Community—A View from Wisconsin," *Sustainable Global Communities in the Information Age*, Adamantime Press, 1997.

"Scenarios for Greater Milwaukee: Citizen Participation," *World Future Society Bulletin*, May-June 1983.

President's Council on Sustainable Development, *Public Linkage, Dialogue and Education Task Force Report*, Feb. 1997. (Report on Plymouth Institute.)

I have used various articles in this book published in *The Review*, an award-winning small-town newspaper based in Plymouth, Wisconsin, publisher Barry Johanson. Over several years beginning in 2009, I, along with Lisa, wrote 47 articles for *The Review*.

The High Wind community published a newsletter, *Windwatch*, editor Lisa Paulson 1980–2000. I authored a number of *Windwatch* articles used in this book.

I made frequent use of material from my memoir, *Odyssey of a Practical Visionary*, Thistlefield Books, 2009.

Several books and articles especially referenced:

Harman, Willis, *Global Mind Change*, Knowledge Systems, Indianapolis, IN,1988.

Harman, Willis, "The Coming Transformation," *The Futurist*, February and April, 1977.

Kuhn, Thomas, *The Structure of Scientific Revolutions*, University of Chicago Press, Chicago, 1962, 1970.

McLaughlin, Corinne, and Davidson, Gordon, *Builders of the Dawn*, Stillpoint, 1985

Rifkin, Jeremy, *The End of Work*, Tarcher Putnam,1995

Spangler, David, *Revelation: The Birth of a New Age*, Rainbow Bridge, 1976.

Somersan, Ayse, *Distinguished Service, University of Wisconsin Faculty and Staff Helping to Build Organizations in the State*, New Past Press, 1997.

Wilber, Ken, *A Brief History of Everything*, Shambhala Publications, Boston, MA, 1996.

World Commission on Environment and Development, *Our Common Future*, Oxford University Press, 1987.

Worldwatch Institute, *Is Sustainability Still Possible*, Island Press, Washington, DC, 2013.

Yamaguchi, Kaoru, (editor), *Sustainable Global Communities in the Information Age*, Adamantine Press1997

Made in the USA
Charleston, SC
31 January 2014